AUTOCAD
2000 3D
f/x and design

Brian Matthews

CORIOLIS

The Coriolis Group, LLC
14455 N. Hayden Road, Suite 220
Scottsdale, Arizona 85260

480/483-0192
FAX 480/483-0193
http://www.coriolis.com

Library of Congress Cataloging-In-Publication Data
Matthews, Brian, 1947-
    AutoCAD 2000 3D f/x and design / by Brian Matthews.
        p. cm
    Includes index.
    ISBN 1-57610-406-0
    1. Computer graphics. 2. AutoCAD. 3. Three-
dimensional display systems. I. Title.
T385.M37734 1999
604.2'0285'6693--dc21   99-42712
                                                CIP

Printed in the United States of America
10 9 8 7 6 5 4 3 2 1

President, CEO
Keith Weiskamp

Publisher
Steve Sayre

Acquisitions Editor
Mariann Hansen Barsolo

Marketing Specialist
Beth Kohler

Project Editor
Meredith Brittain

Technical Reviewer
Jon McFarland

Production Coordinator
Meg E. Turecek

Cover Design
Jody Winkler
additional art provided by Brandon Riza

Layout Design
April Nielsen

CD-ROM Developer
Robert Clarfield

 CORIOLIS

OTHER TITLES FOR THE CREATIVE PROFESSIONAL

3D Studio MAX R3 f/x and design
by Jon A. Bell

3D Studio MAX R3 In Depth
by Rob Polevoi

Adobe ImageStyler In Depth
by Daniel Gray

After Effects 4 In Depth
by R. Shamms Mortier

Bryce 4 f/x and design
by R. Shamms Mortier

Character Animation In Depth
by Doug Kelly

CorelDRAW 9 f/x and design
by Shane Hunt

Flash 3 Web Animation f/x and design
by Ken Milburn and Janine Warner

Illustrator 8 f/x and design
by Sherry London and T. Michael Clark

Photoshop 5 Filters f/x and design
by T. Michael Clark

Photoshop 5 In Depth
by David Xenakis and Sherry London

To my wife, Etta, and son, Edward:
Thank you for your help, patience,
and support while writing the book.

&

ABOUT THE AUTHOR

Brian Matthews (Raleigh, NC), a registered Autodesk author, is a professor in the Graphic Communications Program at North Carolina State University and a past director of the AutoCAD Training Center at Wake Technical Community College in Raleigh. He is also coauthor and tech editor for seven AutoCAD books, including *AutoCAD—A Concise Guide* and *AutoCAD 3D Companion*. In addition to teaching Graphic Communications and CADD at NCSU, he is currently undertaking research in distance education as applied to Graphic Communications. Brian was born in Bradford, West Yorkshire, England, and has been a citizen of the United States since 1986. He can be reached at **brian_matthews@ncsu.edu**.

Acknowledgments

It takes a lot of people and a lot of support to write a book, and I would like to thank the following people.

My wife, Etta, and son Edward, for their help, patience and support while writing the book—especially to Etta for her help in reviewing and editing my rough drafts.

The professional staff at Coriolis, including Meredith Brittain (project editor) for her persistence in keeping me on schedule and her eye for detail. Also, thanks to Mariann Barsolo (acquisitions editor) for her faith in my ability to undertake such a daunting task. Thanks also to the other members of the Coriolis team that worked on this book (you all know who you are), including Meg Turecek (production coordinator), April Nielsen (interior design and Color Studio layout), Jody Winkler (cover design), Beth Kohler (marketing specialist), and Robert Clarfield (CD-ROM developer).

A special thank you goes to Jon McFarland (tech editor) for his expertise and suggestions, and to Tiffany Taylor (copyeditor) for polishing the rough drafts into readable material.

My colleagues in the Graphic Communications Program at North Carolina State University, including Alice Scales, Eric Wiebe, Aaron Clark, and Ted Branoff, for feedback on my rough drafts and for their contributions to the book's artwork. Thanks also to my other colleagues in Technology Education—you are a great team to work with.

Bill Tryon, Autodesk Image Manager, for providing some of the images used in the book.

CONTENTS AT A GLANCE

PART I   **VIEWING AND WORKING WITH 3D DRAWINGS**

Chapter 1   3D Overview

Chapter 2   Standard 3D Views

Chapter 3   User Coordinate Systems

Chapter 4   Setting Up Perspective Views

PART II   **CREATING AND EDITING 3D MODELS**

Chapter 5   Geometirc Modeling

Chapter 6   Surface Modeling

Chapter 7   Solid Modeling

Chapter 8   Editing 3D Models

Chapter 9   3D Section Views

Chapter 10   Dimensioning And Geometrics

PART III   **RENDERING AND IMAGE PRESENTATION**

Chapter 11   Rendering 3D Models

Chapter 12   Image And Animation Files

TABLE OF CONTENTS

Introduction   xvii

PART I
VIEWING AND
WORKING WITH
3D DRAWINGS

Chapter 1
3D Overview   3
Using 3D Graphics In Different Fields   4
    Using 3D Graphics In Engineering   4
What's New In AutoCAD 2000 For 3D Modeling?   7
The World Of Three Dimensions   7
Important 3D Terminology   8
    Horizontal Plane Vs. Top View Or Plan View   8
    Frontal Plane Or Front View Vs. Elevation   9
    Profile Plane Or Right Side View Vs. Side Elevation   10
    Thickness Vs. Extrusion   10
    Local Vs. World Coordinate Systems   11
    Work Or Construction Plane Of The UCS   12
Representing Two Dimensions In 3D   12
    Types Of 3D Models   14
Creating 3D Models   16
    Creating A Solid Model   18
    Viewports   20
Drawing In 3D   21
    A Simple Solid Model   21
    Using And Understanding The UCS And Work Planes   24

Chapter 2
Standard 3D Views   33
Multiview Drawings And Standard 3D Views   34
Model Space Vs. Paper Space   36
    Model Space   36
    Characteristics Of Viewports In Model Space   38
    Characteristics Of Viewports In Paper Space   39
    Creating 2D Views From 3D Models For Multiview Drawings   41
    Using **VPORTS** With Layout Tabs   42
Alternate Views For Your 3D Models   46
    The **LAYOUT** Command   47
    Using Alternative Views Of A Model   48
    Using **SOLVIEW** To Set Up Orthographic Views   51
Paper Space Review   55

Chapter 3
User Coordinate Systems 57

Cartesian And Global Coordinate Systems   58
    World Coordinate System   59
    User Coordinate System   59
    The Right-Hand Rule   61
Construction Planes   62
    Using Construction Planes To Create Profiles   63
    Using Profiles To Create Your 3D Model   66
Review Of The User Coordinate System   71
    The UCS options   74
    Tips For Using Objects With The UCS   76
    The **UCSICON** Command   78
    Hiding Construction Lines In Paper Space   79
    Hiding Viewport Borders   79
Paper Space Scaling   79
    Printing Multiple Scales On The Same Drawing Sheet   80
    Realtime Scaling And Printing   83
Lining Up Drawings In Viewports   83

Chapter 4
Setting Up Perspective Views 87

3D Viewing   88
    Advantages Of 3D Viewing   88
    Parallel And Perspective Projection   89
    Creating A 3D Clamp   90
Dynamic Viewing   93
    Important Terms   93
    DVIEW And **DVIEWBLOCK**   94
DDVPOINT And The Viewpoint Presets Dialog Box   96
3D Views: Presets   97
UCS Per Viewport And 3D Orbit   99
The **CAMERA** Command   104

PART II
CREATING AND EDITING 3D MODELS

Chapter 5
Geometric Modeling 109

Types Of Geometric Models   110
The CAD Database   111
    3D Geometric Forms: Wireframe, Surface, And Solid Models   113
    Revolving A Closed Profile   114
    Software Rules: Integrity Gotchas   115

3D Wireframe From 2D Geometry   116

    Using **Thickness** To Create 3D Wireframes From 2D Geometry   117

Coordinate Systems   120

    Cylindrical Coordinates   120

    Spherical Coordinates   122

    Creating A Helix With 3D Coordinates   122

    Construction Or Work Planes   123

Primitives As Wireframes   124

    Using **REGION** To Change 2D Solids To 3D Wireframes   125

Chapter 6
Surface Modeling   **129**

Curves And Surfaces   130

    Types Of Curves And Surfaces   131

    Curve And Surface Parameters   133

    Bezier Curves And B-Splines   136

    True Spline Curves Vs. Polyline Spline Curves   137

3D Meshes And Geometric Generated Surfaces   141

    SOLID   141

    3D Mesh Surface Commands   143

Surface System Variables   156

Alternative 3D Mesh Applications   160

    Using **PFACE** (Polyface)   161

    Creating A Polyface Mesh   162

Chapter 7
Solid Modeling   **167**

Types Of Modelers   168

    Constructive Solid Geometry (CSG)   169

    Boundary Representation (B-Rep)   169

Solid Modeling: The Visualization Process   172

    Visualization Accuracy   173

Creating Solids   176

    BOUNDARY And **REGION** Commands   176

    A Look At Primitives   181

Creating A Simple Object   194

Parametric Design And Associativity   199

Chapter 8
Editing 3D Models   **203**

General Editing Hints For CAD Modeling   204

Associative Vs. Nonassociative Elements In A 3D Model   205

Associativity In A Surface Model   206

Associativity Of A Mesh   206

Associativity Of A 3D Face   207

Associativity In AutoCAD   208

Modifier Commands   208

   3DARRAY   209

   MIRROR3D   210

   ROTATE3D   211

   ALIGN   211

Changing Profiles In AutoCAD   212

   Creating A Swept Curve From A Profile   213

Spline Editing And Spline Variables   215

   Position   216

   Tension   216

   Bias   217

   Continuity   217

   SPLINEDIT   218

   Editing Smoothness For A Bezier, Quadratic, Or Cubic Mesh   218

Solids Editing   221

   SOLIDEDIT   221

   Face Editing   224

   Edge Editing   226

   Body Editing   227

General Editing Commands   228

   Boolean Operations   228

Analysis Of 3D Computer Models   234

   Uses for **MASSPROP**   235

Chapter 9
3D Section Views   239

Rules Of Section Views   240

Types Of Section Views   241

   Full Sections   242

   Half Sections   243

   Broken-Out Sections   244

   Revolved Sections   245

   Removed Sections   246

   Offset Sections   247

   Assembly Sections   248

   Auxiliary Sections   248

   Aligned Sections   249

   Phantom Or Ghost Sections   250

Creating Sections In AutoCAD   250

   SECTION   251

SLICE 252
SOLVIEW, **SOLDRAW**, And **SOLPROF** 254
Using **SOLVIEW** To Create Orthographic Views 257
Using **REVOLVE** To Create A Section View 262

Chapter 10
Dimensioning And Geometrics 265

Understanding Dimensioning And Geometrics 266
Size And Location Of Dimensions 267
Unidirectional And Aligned Dimension Basics 268
The Dimension Style Manager 268
ANSI Dimension Style Sheet 270
Dimension Commands 274
    Linear Dimensions 274
    Aligned Dimensions 276
    Radius Dimensions 277
    Diameter Dimensions 278
    Angular Dimensions 280
    Quick Dimensions 282
    Baseline Dimensions 283
    Continuing Dimensions 285
    Center-Mark And Center-Line Dimensions 286
    Ordinate Dimensions, Leader Lines, And Geometric Tolerancing 287
    DIMORDINATE Dimensions 287
    Quick Leaders 289
Geometric Dimensioning And Tolerancing 291
    Rules Of Geometric Tolerancing 295
Editing Dimensions 296
    Dimension Editing with **DIMEDIT** 297
    Dimension Text Editing With **DIMTEDIT** 299
    Dimension Text Editing with **DDEDIT** 299
Dimension Variables And **DIMOVERRIDE** 301
Associative Dimensions 302
The dim3d.lsp Program 305

PART III
RENDERING
AND IMAGE
PRESENTATION

Chapter 11
Rendering 3D Models 311

Rendering Considerations 312
Rendering Terms 313
The Render Commands 315
    HIDE, **SHADE**, And **RENDER** 315
The Render Dialog Box 322
Color And Lighting 326

Pigment Color Vs. Light Color   326

Understanding Lighting   330

Putting Lights In Your Model   335

Shadows, Fog, And Sunlight   336

Setting Up For An AutoCAD Rendering   339

Setting Up Scenes And Views   340

Attaching Materials To Your 3D Model   341

Attaching A Material By Object   341

Attaching A Material By Color   342

Using Layers To Attach A Material   344

Modifying A Material   345

2D Mapping Of A 3D Model   346

Bitmaps   346

Parametric Materials   347

Importing A 2D Material Into A 3D Model And Modifying It   347

Landscape Materials   348

LSNEW   348

LSLIB   348

LSEDIT   348

Quick Steps To Create And Place Landscape Objects   349

Chapter 12
Image And Animation Files   353

Images   354

Image Quality And File Types   354

Screen Resolution   358

Placing Images Into Presentation Documents   363

Importing And Exporting Images   365

Using The Image Manager   371

Creating Electronic Files For The Internet   374

Hyperlinks   378

Rendering Algorithms   380

Computer Animation Or Computer Simulation   383

Single Path Animation   384

Kinetic Animation   384

Key Framing   385

Creating Animations From Single Images   386

Calculating Animation Frames   387

Creating Scripts And Viewing Slide Files   388

Index   393

INTRODUCTION

It's a short jump—not a leap of faith—from two dimensions to three dimensions. This book provides you with a broad overview of how to move from 2D to 3D using AutoCAD 2000.

Throughout the book, each chapter will build upon your 3D knowledge base as it takes a broad look at both the practical and theoretical aspects of AutoCAD 2000 to help you work with 3D concepts. You'll learn that working in 3D is simply a matter of understanding and working within spatial conventions. AutoCAD is attuned to the 3D world, through its user coordinate system, construction planes, viewports, and the creation, editing, and manipulation of 3D primitives to form solid models.

Understanding how to visualize and fit multiple parts (primitives, profiles, and so on) together to form a true 3D model is essential in learning how to create 3D graphics. From beginning to end, you'll find this process explained via drawing practice paradigms and 3D construction techniques.

Practical Uses Of 3D Graphics

3D concepts aren't something to put off until a later date; they're used in every aspect of modern computer-aided design (CAD) work to form the basis of multiview engineering drawings—as 3D imaging tools, for kinematics and interference fit of parts, for 3D assemblies, in complex medical imaging, in flight technology, and much more.

A byproduct of automobile and aerospace technology, 3D graphics is becoming increasingly popular with designers and design teams, and is inherently simpler to use than when it first appeared in the 1960s. You'll find that today's work force uses 3D graphics for engineering assembly drawings, complex 3D animations, and NASA visualizations of spacecraft and space stations.

The use of 3D modeling allows you to create virtual mockups and prototypes prior to building the real thing. Doing so can save you time and money, especially when the prototypes indicate that parts don't fit or that they interfere with other parts.

3D graphics also allow practical design constraints. In the aerospace industry, for example, an airplane can include design constraints of aerodynamic safety, size, cost, weight, structural stress, and other functions such as speed, noise-to-weight ratio, and fuel economy. These factors can all be built into the 3D design graphics, which let you know if that extra coat of paint will be too heavy or cause too much friction over the skin of the aircraft to prevent takeoff.

Practical 3D examples include the 3D design of complex assemblies. For instance, the parts of the space station currently being assembled are all fully associative, which means that if you make a change to one part other components are automatically affected, because of its true 3D associativity. But designers don't work alone, and most assembly models are designed by a team rather than a single individual. That's where AutoCAD 2000 now comes into own with its new AutoCAD 2000 DesignCenter and its bidirectional associativity with reference drawings.

Another aspect of 3D is photorealism, which allows designers to show finished images of the product before it's been created. This, in turn, allows shortened product marketing time.

How To Use The Book

You don't have to be an AutoCAD expert to follow the techniques outlined in this book, but the book assumes you have a working knowledge of AutoCAD basics and that you have the desire to progress. From the front to back covers, you'll learn how to generate models in three dimensions.

In each of its three parts, this book provides thorough explanations and illustrations of 3D concepts, along with simple exercises that explain AutoCAD processes step by step. Because most people learn best by doing, to learn effective 3D modeling techniques, you should use the files on this book's companion CD-ROM to work through the exercises as they're presented. In addition, to help readers understand the AutoCAD processes, AutoCAD screen prompts and user input are often reproduced in the text. (Because a computer screen differs in size from the width of a page, you may see line wrap throughout the examples in the book that will not occur on your computer screen. Also, you'll notice that input by the reader is set in italics to differentiate it from the other text.)

By reading this book, you'll gain a complete understanding of the 3D interface of AutoCAD 2000. You'll learn how to set up and manage views in both paper space and model space. You'll gain experience with basic forms of 3D modeling—wireframe, surface, and solid—and you'll look at how to create multiview and pictorial engineering drawings from single 3D solid models. You'll create standard views in model space, place views in paper space, and set up and control viewports. You'll also join and edit multiple primitives to form 3D models, plus extrude and revolve spline paths to form solid objects. Further topics include how to create and use section views, intersections, and developments; how to place bitmap images into drawings; and how to send images over the Internet. Finally, you'll learn how to link images into a drawing and place images into presentation documents.

Here's a breakdown of what you'll find in each chapter.

Part I: Viewing And Working With 3D Drawings

Part I provides an overview of 3D terminology and graphics for engineers and technologists.

Chapter 1: 3D Overview

Chapter 1 reviews basic 3D modeling forms (wireframes, surfaces, and solids) and moves on to UCS coordinates and how local versus world coordinates are used in the overall picture of 3D geometry. You'll see how to create a 3D model by producing a simple profile drawing in 2D, converting it to 3D, and using the **UNION** Boolean operation to make a true 3D solid.

Chapter 2: Standard 3D Views

Chapter 2 will give you an understanding of 2D and 3D geometry so you can create multiview and pictorial engineering drawings. Topics covered include standard views in model space and how to place these views in paper space, as well as how to set up viewports with different commands, such as **VPORTS**, **MVIEW**, and **SOLVIEW**.

Chapter 3: User Coordinate Systems

Global and Cartesian coordinate systems, the right-hand rule, and working with construction planes are some of the principal tools of 3D modeling. In Chapter 3, you'll use these tools and UCS systems to learn how to create and extrude profiles. You'll also use Boolean operations to create a 3D solid.

Chapter 4: Setting Up Perspective Views

Chapter 4 covers parallel and perspective projection, with reference to 3D modeling and how orthographic projection is created from 3D models. You'll also read about **3DORBIT**, plus you'll set up and save different viewports.

Part II: Creating And Editing 3D Models

In Part II, you'll learn how wireframe, surface, and solid models are created, edited, and worked into solid object combinations.

Chapter 5: Geometric Modeling

Basics of 3D geometry open this chapter, which serves as an introduction to geometric modeling and wireframes. This chapter also covers revolving objects, 3D coordinates, and using 2D profiles to create 3D geometry.

Chapter 6: Surface Modeling

Curves, surfaces, and 3D meshes make up the bulk of this chapter, along with an in-depth look at how AutoCAD creates surfaces.

Chapter 7: Solid Modeling

Solid modeling topics include the use of primitives and how the CSG tree, B-REP, and Boolean operations are used in solid modeling. You'll also take a look at how to join and edit multiple primitives to form 3D models, as well as how to extrude and revolve objects along spline paths in order to form 3D solid objects. In addition, this chapter explains the importance of visualization as an aid to 3D construction techniques.

Chapter 8: Editing 3D Models

Because solid model editing is an important new feature of AutoCAD 2000, Chapter 8 takes an in-depth look at how to edit and revisit your work in order to make your 3D designs into more detailed solid models.

Chapter 9: 3D Section Views

Chapters 9 and 10 review 3D sections and 3D dimensioning. Chapter 9 provides an overview of 3D sections and introduces standards and techniques used to create all types of section views. The **SECTION**, **SLICE**, and **UCS** commands are reviewed, along with an in-depth discussion of the different forms of section views and how you can create different types of sections within AutoCAD.

Chapter 10: Dimensioning And Geometrics

The 3D dimensioning component of Chapter 10 involves setting up dimension styles. In addition to basic dimensioning, the chapter covers how to change the angle of dimensions and create dimensions in multiple types of drawings. To round out the chapter, you'll find an introduction to GD&T and associative dimensioning.

Part III: Rendering And Image Presentation

Part III covers rendering, animation, image presentation, RGB color basics, and how to make color choices for rendering an image file. These chapters also discuss how to use 3D digital images in 2D format and how to place AutoCAD images and walk-throughs into presentations.

Chapter 11: Rendering 3D Models

In addition to discussing rendering quality, rendering time, and rendering algorithms, this chapter covers RGB and HLS color, lights, scenes, and views. The chapter moves on to teach you how to add materials, textures, and bitmaps to your models. In addition, the chapter reviews 2D mapping of a 3D model and how to place landscape objects into a drawing.

Chapter 12: Image And Animation Files

Chapter 12 discusses incorporating bitmap images into drawings and sending images over the Internet, which you must know how to do in today's high-tech world. The chapter discusses file types and compression ratios, as well as AutoCAD's new image support and Image Manager and how to import and export images. The chapter looks at how an AutoCAD user can save, embed, and send images over the World Wide Web. It briefly mentions the use of the WHIP driver with Netscape and Microsoft Explorer.

The chapter also takes a look at animation, covering the different types of animations and the theory of how to set up paths, add cameras, and add sound and voice-overs to create realistic rendered walk-throughs. You'll also find tips for improving image quality, plus how to work with AutoCAD scripts and slides, in this chapter.

PART I

VIEWING AND WORKING WITH 3D DRAWINGS

3D OVERVIEW

1

3D graphics are becoming more popular
with designers, and now they're easier to work with
than when they first became popular in the 1960s.
With uses from simple engineering assembly
drawings to complex 3D animations and NASA
visualizations of spacecraft and space stations, 3D
concepts are here to stay.

Using 3D Graphics In Different Fields

Spawned by automobile and aerospace technology in the 1960s, 3D graphics are now being used in many different ways in many different fields—as imaging tools for kinematics, in complex medical technology and flight technology, and 3D design of complex assemblies, such as the MIR space station. You may also use 3D models to do virtual mock-ups and create virtual prototypes prior to building the real thing, which can save you time and money. 3D graphics also allow practical design constraints; in the aerospace industry, for example, you can design an airplane with design constraints of aerodynamic safety, size, cost, weight, structural stress, and other functions, such as speed, noise to weight ratio, fuel economy, and so forth. In such a case, 3D design graphics can let you know if that extra coat of paint will be too heavy or cause too much friction over the skin of the aircraft.

Most assembly models of today are not designed by a single individual but by a design team, which is where AutoCAD 2000 now comes into its own with its new AutoCAD Design Center. In this visual age, a further benefit of 3D design is photorealism, which allows designers to show finished product images before production, allowing a faster product marketing time.

Using 3D Graphics In Engineering

Design teams have always requested high-level 3D communication and integration to connect a product's 3D design phases with the analysis, production, and document-management phases. These higher levels of 3D communication improve product cycle time, enhance product design quality, and provide a higher level of intelligence behind the product design. AutoCAD 2000 aims to meet some of these design-team challenges.

AutoCAD 2000 includes a new ACIS 4 modeling engine that lets you create, edit, and visualize complex 3D models. You can also render and shade the models using a variety of modes such as Phong, Gouraud, wireframe, and flat shading. Intricate 3D models may be difficult for a customer to understand, however, so you may need to reduce the visual complexity of the 3D model. One option, especially for the AutoCAD operator, is to use 3D Orbit—a realtime rotating and zooming feature—along with its dynamic front and back clipping planes.

Three-dimensional computer-aided design (CAD) has been used as a graphic technology in engineering for many years. AutoCAD 2000 includes so many improvements that it's proving far superior to previous releases. With it, you can integrate full communication from the 2D design stage to the 3D design process, review, and production. In the past, designers drew multiview

2D orthographic paper drawings to represent 3D machine-made models. If a 3D part was required, the designer created a wireframe model. Now, as technology advances from CAD further into computer-integrated manufacturing (CIM), it's absolutely essential that you communicate three-dimensionally and generate a complete geometric representation of the 3D part to be manufactured.

3D parts are generated for the manufacturing process by creating a true solid or surface model. A true 3D model offers one unique advantage: Through the use and study of geometrics that lead to the creation of the model, you eliminate errors and ambiguities associated with a 2D representation of the 3D part. A true solid model also provides more information than a traditional wireframe model. You can use this information for stress or thermal analysis or throughput it as programming code to a numerically controlled (NC) milling or a shaping machine.

In multiview drawings, for example, a true solid model lets you create true Top, Front, Profile, and Hidden-Line-Removed views, plus true sections, slices, and shaded images. Figure 1.1 shows an example of a 3D pictorial of a combination wireframe and shaded image. (See the Color Studio in the middle of this book for a color version of this image.) You can also use the advantage of 3D geometric models to perform analysis testing and create design options for clients. In the graphic evolution of a mechanical part, you can use such analytic tools as interference checking, finite element analysis, or thermal image heat-transfer analysis. Alternately, in architecture, you can use sun shadowing to forecast how the orientation of a structure may be set to the advantage of the site, or you can create a simulated walkthrough of a design.

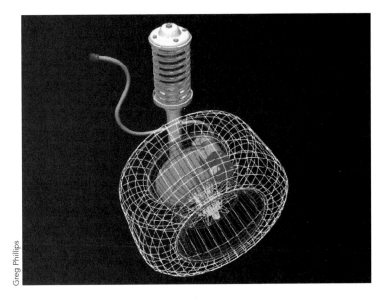

Greg Phillips

Figure 1.1
3D pictorial combination of a wireframe and shaded image.

But what's the future of 3D CAD as an emerging graphic technology in the engineering field? Well, the future of CAD is here—especially in manufacturing. In addition to the new 3D CAD design and analysis tools that let you create quality products, electronic document management (EDM) and product data management (PDM) tools make a paperless 3D environment possible. Thanks to these tools, a 3D model can go directly to rapid prototyping/tooling or an NC programming environment.

Engineers have started to integrate database and design management systems into the design process. The computerized solid model plays a central role as the communication medium throughout the manufacturing cycle. Using this integrated technology, you can automatically develop numerical control programs and process plans from the surface or solid model of an assembly part. By doing so, you can integrate multiple activities and improve the productivity of the manufacturing process, as illustrated in Figure 1.2.

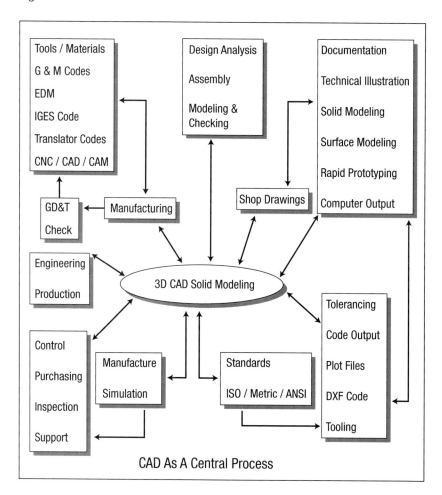

Figure 1.2
CAD is now an integrated element of the total manufacturing cycle.

What's New In AutoCAD 2000 For 3D Modeling?

AutoCAD 2000 includes a distinct set of new features that streamline communication and design all the way to production output. For example, you can use the new features to create document design drawings or customer desktop-publishing drawings for sub-part assemblies.

AutoCAD 2000 improves your ability to access, design, produce, and visualize drawings. The program also offers enhanced 3D User Coordinate System (UCS) viewing, 3D editing and shading, lineweight options, database connectivity, hatching and dimensioning options, and direct Web browser access. Other new features include:

- Multiple paper space layouts

- Nonrectangular viewports

- Viewport scaling

- Plotting features, such as ePlot (electronic plotting via email)

AutoCAD 2000 also includes:

- *Object Properties Manager (OPM)*—Used to edit and view objects within drawings.

- *Multiple Design Environment (MDE)*—A multitasking document interface you can use to drag and drop or cut and paste from multiple documents simultaneously.

- *AutoCAD DesignCenter (ADC)*—A must for ease of production. You can use it as a search tool and then copy parts of a drawing (such as blocks or layers) straight into the current drawing.

The World Of Three Dimensions

What do you need to know to create 3D drawings? You must be able to use certain 3D background tools and techniques, including 3D primitives, the UCS, viewports, and setting viewpoints to the viewports. The three main types of 3D model—wireframe, surface, and solid—play a major role in 3D graphics. As a bonus, later in the book you'll learn how to set up, render, save, and post your images onto the Web with AutoCAD DWF files.

Did you know that AutoCAD entities are expressed as X, Y, and Z coordinates? In past surveys, Autodesk has indicated that approximately 85 percent of AutoCAD operators know how to use only the X and the Y coordinates, because they use AutoCAD primarily to create 2D drawings. Don't be misled into thinking you're drawing in two dimensions as you enter X and Y coordinates with AutoCAD—you're really drawing in three dimensions, but the Z coordinate entity is set to the default of 0.

Important 3D Terminology

Before we move on to the rest of the book, it's important to define some 3D and AutoCAD terms that you must understand in order to work with 3D concepts. The various terms relating to 3D have different meanings depending upon their use.

Horizontal Plane Vs. Top View Or Plan View

An architect uses the term *plan*, whereas engineers commonly use the term *Horizontal plane* to indicate the Top view of a part. The term refers to the plan or Top view of the drawing from its initial viewpoint in 3D space. In this viewpoint, the X, Y, and Z axes are set to the following standard, called the *right-hand rule* (see Figure 1.3), where:

- *X*—A positive value pointing to the right on the screen
- *Y*—A positive value pointing up on the screen
- *Z*—A positive value pointing straight at the user in 3D space

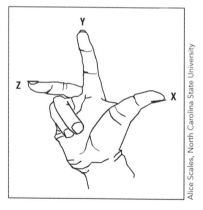

Alice Scales, North Carolina State University

Figure 1.3
The right-hand rule.

The UCS in the lower-left corner of your screen will display a W for World Coordinate System. This is the Horizontal plane—from this setting, you devise other planes. See Figure 1.4, which shows a UCS attached to a feature.

Every drawing contains more than one plane. Some of the possible planes are as follows:

- Horizontal plane
- Frontal plane
- Profile plane
- Oblique plane
- Inclined plane

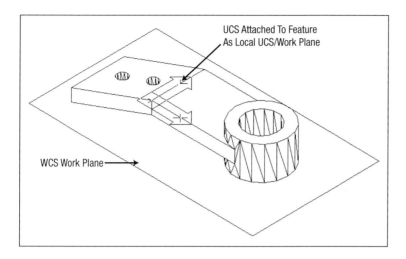

UCS Attached To Feature
As Local UCS/Work Plane

WCS Work Plane

Figure 1.4
A local coordinate system
attached to a feature of the
3D Model.

However, AutoCAD doesn't refer to any of these engineering terms as *planes*, but rather as *plan views*. The only reason an engineer might use the planes just listed would be to produce accurate dimensions, profiles, sections, and auxiliary views from the 3D model, in order to draw the model on a 2D blueprint sheet. Once you've created a 3D model, you can create any of these planes in a multiview drawing simply by using the viewpoint, the UCS, and/or **SOLVIEW** command to alter your view of the 3D model. In Chapter 4, you'll learn how to change your viewpoint to a precise angle or plane.

Frontal Plane Or Front View Vs. Elevation

An architect uses the term *front elevation*, whereas an engineer uses the term *Frontal plane* or *Front view*. The Frontal plane or Front view is equivalent to the architect's front elevation showing a full frontal view of the part to be created. Be aware, however, that this isn't what AutoCAD means by *elevation*. In AutoCAD, elevation is a height, not a view. It refers to a value of the Z coordinate, above or below the 0 datum. This value is useful, for example, when you need to work at a specific height above the zero datum of the UCS. Working in AutoCAD, elevation is relative to the current UCS. It isn't an architect's view—it's a coordinate in 3D space. Specifically, AutoCAD's **ELEVATION** command controls the Z coordinate value that's relative to the current UCS.

If you want to set the Front view of an object in AutoCAD, you don't use elevation. Instead, you set the UCS to X and then to 90. The result is a UCS set to the Front work plane.

Suppose you're an engineer and you set the elevation for a part you're creating to 45. Then, you begin drawing by entering your X and Y values. The datum of the Z height will automatically be preset to 45 for each point you draw. Setting the elevation to 45 doesn't mean you're giving the part a thickness of 45; doing so sets the part to a predetermined height of 45 above the 0 datum.

Let's look at another example. An architect might set the elevation of a floor height to 12'-0" and then draw the plan layout for the floor at that elevation. The drawing created is registered exactly 12'-0" above the previous floor height or the Datum plane. This elevation can be copied to the next level, and so on, all the way up to the roof.

Profile Plane Or Right Side View Vs. Side Elevation

An engineer uses the term *Profile plane* or *Right Side view*, whereas an architect uses the term *side elevation*. In a multiview drawing, the Profile plane is the same as a Right Side view. That's exactly where the view is located: on the right side of the Frontal plane, as you can see in Figure 1.5.

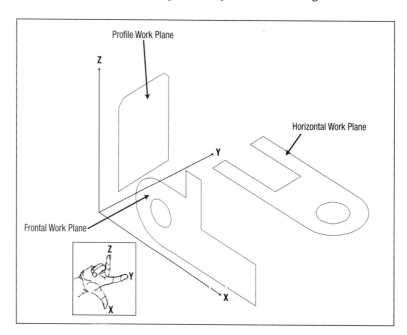

Figure 1.5
Horizontal, Frontal, and Profile planes.

Thickness Vs. Extrusion

Thickness and extrusion are similar. For example, set your view to SW Isometric and draw a rectangle. Pick the rectangle and then the Properties icon. In the resultant Properties dialog box, choose the Thickness option and notice it has zero thickness, and therefore no height. Change the zero thickness to 15 (or an arbitrary number) and close the dialog box. Because each line has thickness, the result is a box—even though the rectangle was drawn from the plan view with four lines.

You apply thickness by using the **PROPERTIES** command. Doing so gives a 2D drawing the appearance of a lookalike 3D wireframe drawing by providing Z height entities. Thickness works with single lines or polylines. The **PROPERTIES** command is used to control the thickness of a single object but the **THICKNESS** command affects all new entities globally. Remember, using the **PROPERTIES** command yields a drawing that *looks* like 3D, but is really a 2-1/2D wireframe drawing.

The **EXTRUSION** command is similar to the **THICKNESS** command, as you'll see in Figure 1.6, but you draw objects with closed polylines. The result is a 3D object that may be as complex or as simple as you wish. With extruded objects, you may use Boolean operations to combine or subtract the object from other 3D objects.

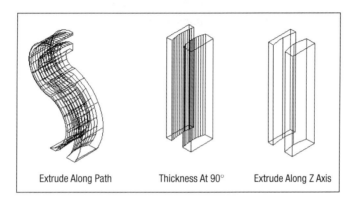

Extrude Along Path   Thickness At 90°   Extrude Along Z Axis

Figure 1.6
The **EXTRUSION** and **THICKNESS** commands are similar.

Local Vs. World Coordinate Systems

There are a number of coordinate systems: World Coordinate System, User Coordinate System, Entity Coordinate System (ECS), and Object Coordinate System (OCS). You have control over the WCS and UCS, and that's all. As we discussed earlier in this chapter, the WCS provides a base reference point you may return to at any time. See See Figure 1.7 for a look at a local UCS versus the WCS.

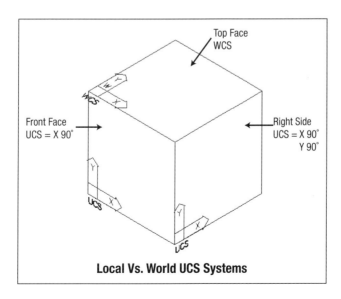

Local Vs. World UCS Systems

Figure 1.7
Local UCS versus World Coordinate System.

The term *User Coordinate System* refers to any number of coordinate systems that you create, not just a single coordinate system. You can create an unlimited number of UCS systems.

As Figure 1.8 shows, a W appears on the UCS icon when you're working in a WCS mode. You can also save and name each UCS you create.

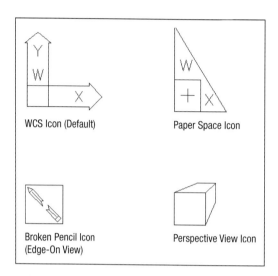

Figure 1.8
The different UCS icons.

You have no control over the ECS and OCS. They're strictly the coordinate system that was in effect at the time you created the object or entity. The ECS or OCS is saved with the object or entity in the AutoCAD database. You may restore the ECS or OCS as the current or local UCS at any time by choosing the object.

For example, open the ucs-entity.dwg file from the CD-ROM that accompanies this book. Type the command "UCS"; then, in your response, enter "e" for Entity or "o" for Object. (At the UCS prompt, you may also enter "n" for new and then "ob" for object.) Choose the entity you wish the UCS to refer back to. When the ECS or OCS is restored as the UCS, it's the same as any other UCS in effect at that time.

Work Or Construction Plane Of The UCS

The work or construction plane is a confusing concept in 3D. In AutoCAD, it's simply any UCS work plane you create in order to move about an object, as illustrated in Figure 1.9. Remember that the UCS is the right angle made by the direction of positive X, Y, and Z at any point in space.

Representing Two Dimensions In 3D

Three-dimensional manmade objects that you see and use every day are manufactured using outdated processes. The design process involves *ideation*: perfecting the idea using design-sketch iterations that are tested,

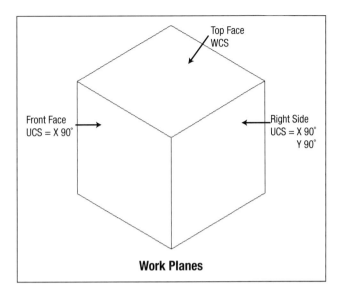

Work Planes

Figure 1.9
Top versus Front versus Right Side work planes.

described as 2D objects on flat, 2D paper, and then built to the designer's specifications. Until recently, this 2D work of describing the 3D part was done manually—designers used pencil and paper to create the working and pictorial drawings.

Because working drawings of 3D objects are prepared on flat, 2D paper, a standard method of 2D representation called *orthographic projection* is used to describe 3D objects. These working and assembly drawings are widely used in the engineering industry. See Figure 1.10. However, working and assembly drawings are limited in that they're 2D descriptions of a 3D object and must be interpreted as such by the engineer. Thus, the fundamental

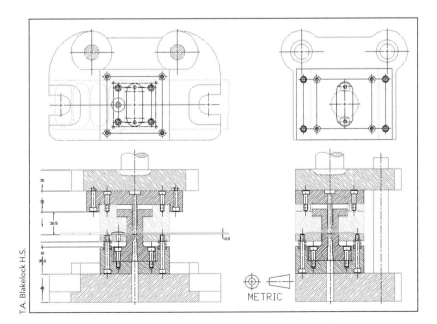

T.A. Blakelock H.S.

Figure 1.10
Typical assembly drawing of a 3D model.

difference between 2D drawings and 3D models lies in the description process—which is where computers enter the picture. You can now use computers from the initial 2D ideation process to the eventual testing and evaluation process of the 3D part. However, you create the 3D model in a variety of ways to suit your immediate and eventual goals.

Types Of 3D Models

AutoCAD uses three types of 3D model: wireframe, surface, and solid. A wireframe is simply a series of 2D lines, arcs, and/or circles given a third dimension (termed the Z height). The wireframe is useful as a visualization tool to view the 3D object you want to create. Often, in the CAD world, you may think of these as 2-1/2D models. It's as if you took a coat hanger and bent it into a 3D shape to represent your model. On the other hand, a surface model is a wireframe with a surface coating that allows you to visualize the object with slightly more understanding. Finally, a solid model is a true 3D model. You use a variety of 3D primitive shapes and extrusions to build up the model into the overall shape you want.

Wireframe Modeling

A wireframe is the most fundamental type of 3D model. It's a skeletal description of a 3D part, built up from a series of lines, points, and/or arcs. A wireframe model lets you examine the 3D edge characteristics of the part as they actually exist. You'll find no surfaces in a wireframe model. Because you see the part from all sides, a wireframe provides an enhanced visualization of a simple 3D part. It will help you generate standard views more easily, and it gives you a framework on which to place surfaces. See Figure 1.11. You can use wireframes for simple spatial relationship studies. Wireframe models are also used for prototyping—they reduce the need to create costly prototype parts, and they allow you to create perspective views of an object. A wireframe lets you use distance measurement to find the shortest distance in space between two edges.

Surface Modeling

A surface model is a thin 3D "shell" accurately formed in the shape of the part you're going to create. Surface models contain information about the profile edges of the object and the space between those edges. You can also retrieve points inside or outside the model. You create a surface model by combining 3D, topologically closed, curved, and flat surface elements to form a shell that encloses the part. See Figure 1.12. (Also, see the Color Studio in the middle of this book for a fully rendered image of the surface model shown in Figure 1.12.)

Comparing surface to wireframe models, you use surface models to provide more detailed information about the shell or surface of the part you're modeling. For example, you might use a surface model to remove hidden

USING SCULPTED SURFACES

Some CAD systems use a more general representation called a *sculpted surface*. Sculpted surfaces are created by one of a family of surface commands that generate parametric surface patches of Coons, Ferguson, or Bezier techniques. You can use a sculpted surface to create a transition between adjacent surface edges. Typical surface types include surfaces of extrusion, surfaces of revolution, ruled surfaces, tabulated cylinders, planes, and swept and lofted surfaces.

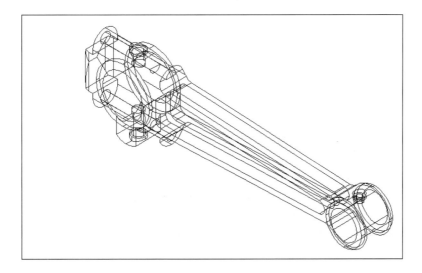

Figure 1.11
One type of wireframe model.

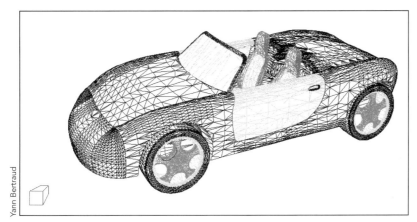

Yann Bertraud

Figure 1.12
Hidden surface model.

lines within a presentation drawing. Or, you might use a surface model as an information database for numeric illustration of the surfaces of a spatial solid model. With a shaded model, you can use a surface model to create a faceted model for a shaded rendering.

Solid Models

Solid modeling differs from wireframe and surface modeling in two ways: The information is more complete, and constructing the model is more straightforward. Often, a solid model maintains two principal types of descriptive data: topology data and geometric data.

With some CAD systems, as you create a solid model, the system maintains the model's boundary representation, as well as a record of the primitive shapes and operations used to create it. In AutoCAD, however, if you use the **MASSPROP** command, you can generate data from the solid model and then use it to produce accurate information about the characteristics of the model. **MASSPROP** generates specific data such as mass, volume, weight, surface area, and intersections between two or more surfaces.

A solid model is also more capable of being rendered and having material and texture mapping applied to the model for photorealistic renderings. See Figure 1.13. (Also, see the Color Studio in the middle of this book for a color version of this image.)

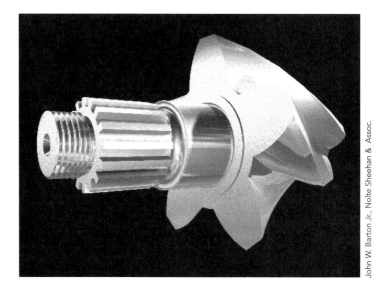

John W. Barton Jr., Nolte Sheehan & Assoc.

Figure 1.13
Rendered solid model.

Comparing solid models to surface and wireframe models, solid models generate the most information about a part. They also contain enough data to support downstream applications. Wireframe and surface models are more error-prone than solid models. For instance, wireframe models often have dangling edges, and surface models may be missing closures.

Creating 3D Models

Once you've created a 2D drawing, you can convert the 2D entities of the drawing to what emulates 3D entities with very little extra work. You do so by using the **DDMODIFY** (or **PROPERTIES**) command (and its **Thickness** suboption to change the entity's thickness [Z dimension]. Now, let's look at background 3D tools and produce some simple 3D drawings.

First, create an object and give it thickness by following these steps:

1. Change your viewpoint to SE Isometric view (choose View|3D Views|SW Isometric). Set the UCS to X 90°.

2. Using the **POLYLINE** command, create a profile with the dimensions shown in Figure 1.14 (remembering to close the last entity). Or, open the 2d-profile.dwg file from this book's companion CD-ROM, as seen in Figure 1.14. The UCS is preset, ready for you to change the profile to a thickness of 15mm.

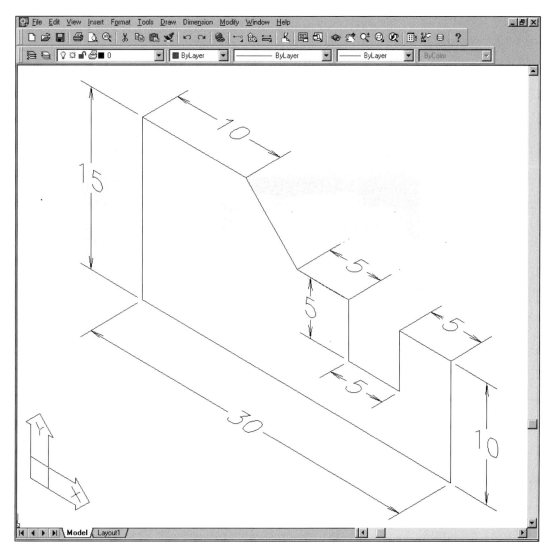

Figure 1.14

Create the outline of the 2D profile shape.

3. Pick the object, and then use the **DDMODIFY** or **PROPERTIES** command to give the object 15mm thickness, as described earlier.

4. Use the **LIST** command to check the information about the object you created.

The generated list will indicate that the object you just created has thickness—but it isn't a 3D solid. Thickness adds entities to your drawing in 3D space as Z height. Thus, the entities make the drawing *appear* to be three-dimensional. Remember, all AutoCAD entities are expressed as X, Y, and Z coordinates. The result of using the **DDMODIFY** command is a wireframe drawing that looks like it's 3D. But it isn't a true 3D drawing: It's a 2D drawing with thickness (what was referred to back in the dark ages as a two-and-a-half dimensional drawing). To sum up, changing an entity's

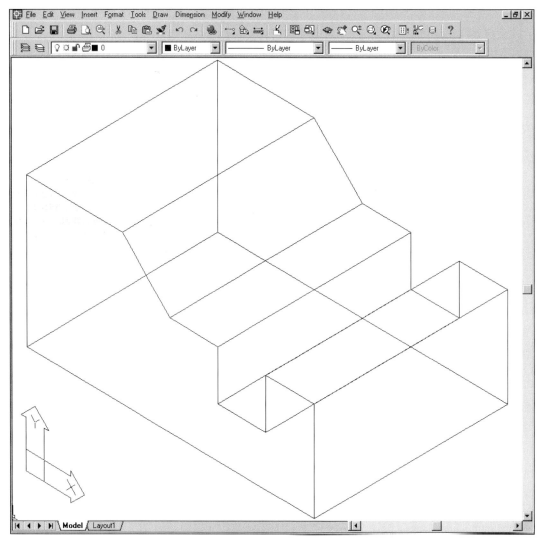

Figure 1.15
One effect of using the **PROPERTIES** command to change 2D to 3D entities.

thickness yields a drawing that looks 3D but is really a 2-1/2D wireframe drawing. See Figure 1.15. So, what produces a true 3D drawing? Let's review that question.

Creating A Solid Model

There are numerous ways to create a solid model with AutoCAD 2000.

Extruding A 2D Object

One way is to extrude a 2D object in a lineal Z direction. This is particularly useful for rectilinear parts. To use this method, you create a closed polyline formed to the profile or shape you want (as seen in Figure 1.14); then, extrude the closed polyline in the Z direction. As mentioned earlier, using **DDMODIFY** or **PROPERTIES** to alter thickness doesn't result in a true 3D solid. Instead, if you create a profile using a closed polyline and use the **EXTRUDE** command, you can extrude or sweep the existing entities along

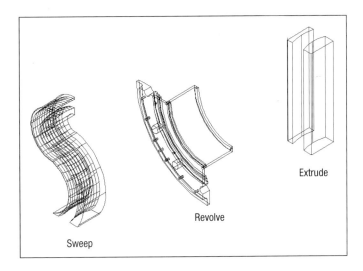

Figure 1.16
Examples of profile shapes using **EXTRUDE** and **REVOLVE** commands. (Using the **Path** suboption with **EXTRUDE** produces a sweep.)

a path. Doing so adds Z height to the polyline entities of the profiles, as you can see in Figure 1.16.

Revolving An Object About A Cylindrical Axis

You can also create a cylindrical type of solid model by revolving an object about an axis. Again, it uses a polyline as a profile shape, which you revolve about a central axis. You may create fully revolved cylindrical parts or, alternatively, you can create partially revolved parts in 30, 45, 60, 90, 180, or 270 degree increment angles of your choice (as you can see in the center part of Figure 1.16).

Using The Basic Primitives

A third technique for creating a solid model uses some of the basic primitive shapes shown in Figure 1.17. Most solid-modeling software programs use primitives—basic shapes created for you. These primitives include Box, Sphere, Cylinder, Cone, Wedge, and Torus. To create a true solid model, you combine basic shapes into composite solids by using the Boolean operations **Union**, **Subtract**, and **Intersect** to either combine objects or cut them away from one another. Then, you use the **CHAMFER** and **FILLET**

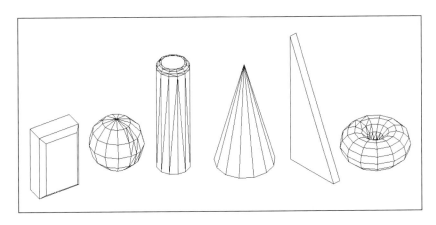

Figure 1.17
Basic primitive shapes.

commands to edit the edges of your 3D model. In later chapters, we'll review, use, and edit these basic shapes in great depth. But for now, understand that most solid modelers have a set of primitives that let you create composite solids, along with a set of Boolean or other operation tools that let you modify the built-up primitives.

Viewports

To begin drawing three-dimensionally, you need to view or visualize your model from different angles. You may do this by setting up multiple 2D viewports and then drawing in two dimensions as you move around the Horizontal, Frontal, or Profile plane of each 2D view or plane of the 3D drawing. Figure 1.18 illustrates this technique. This may be a new way of visualizing for you, but the technique can be enjoyable to learn and use. Alternately, you can create a 3D solid in one viewport in model space and then use the **SOLVIEW** command to set up Horizontal, Frontal, and Profile work planes for each 2D view or plane of your 3D multiview drawing in paper space. You'll find **SOLVIEW** extremely useful, and I'll discuss it in depth in later chapters.

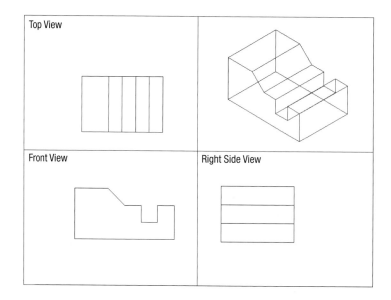

Figure 1.18
Using 2D viewports to view a 3D drawing, showing Horizontal, Frontal, and Profile planes (also known as Front, Top, and Right Side views).

Working in 3D, you'll soon learn that by using viewports and the UCS, you can view your drawing from many angles. Also, as you work with viewports, you can draw on one side of a 3D drawing at a time. This is the key to 3D drawing—often, you don't need to actually draw in three dimensions. You can simply draw in two dimensions on each part of the drawing or work plane, or within a 2D viewport. Nevertheless, for the sake of practice, let's produce a simple solid 3D drawing. In this chapter, you'll create the part shown in Figure 1.19.

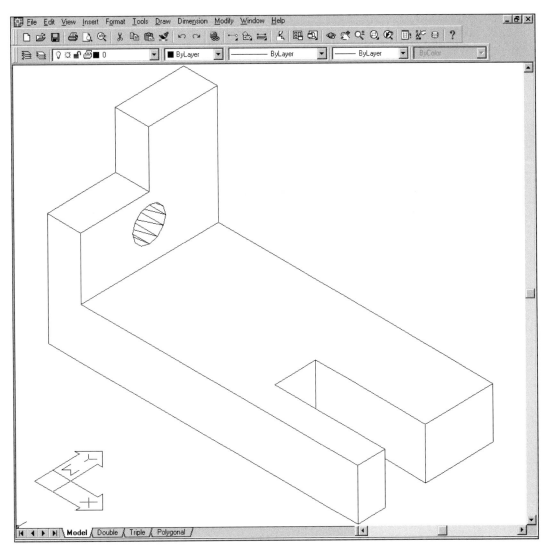

Figure 1.19
The completed corner plate.

Drawing In 3D

Begin by setting up your drawing. See Figure 1.20. You can either use the 3D-graphics prototype drawing (startfile.dwg) on the CD-ROM that accompanies this book or open a new AutoCAD 2000 drawing. If you are starting a new drawing, choose Metric and then choose the following settings for your drawing:

1. Set the Limits to 0,0 in the lower left corner and Upper Right to 220,120.

2. Set the Grid to 5 and the Snap to 5.

3. Choose Zoom|All.

A Simple Solid Model

For this exercise, you'll create a solid model of a corner plate. You'll use the **POLYLINE** command to create some profiles; then, you'll edit the profiles

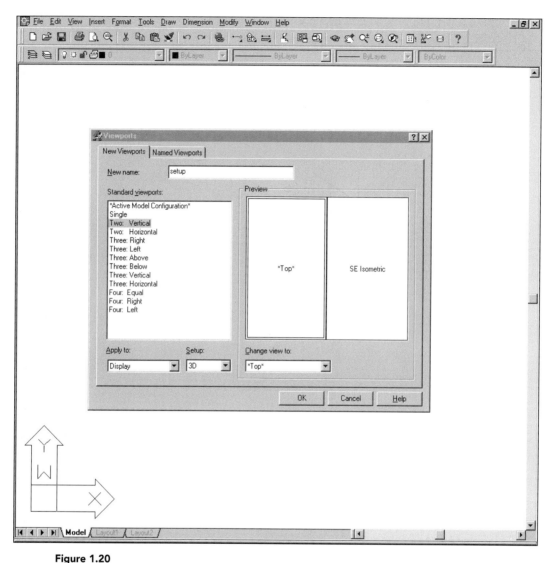

Figure 1.20

Setting up the screen viewports for the first 3D drawing.

and extrude them. Next, you'll move about the UCS, create holes, and subtract the holes through a Boolean operation. In Chapter 2, you'll further work up the drawing and capture the Top, Front, Right Side, and Pictorial views from the solid model.

To begin, load the file startfile.dwg from the CD-ROM that accompanies this book and save the file as corner-plate. Figure 1.21 shows the dimensions of the keyplate part you'll create. Now, follow these steps:

1. From the View pull-down menu, choose Viewports.

2. Pick 2 Viewports.

3. Set the left viewport to Plan (Top view) and the right viewport to SE Isometric view. (Notice that the UCS is currently set to the World Coordinate System [a "W" appears in the UCS icon].)

Note: The startfile.dwg file on the CD-ROM is set to Step 3 in the adjacent list with the two viewport settings. The corner-plate.dwg file, also on the CD-ROM, is complete with profiles and UCS settings ready for you to use the **EXTRUDE** command.

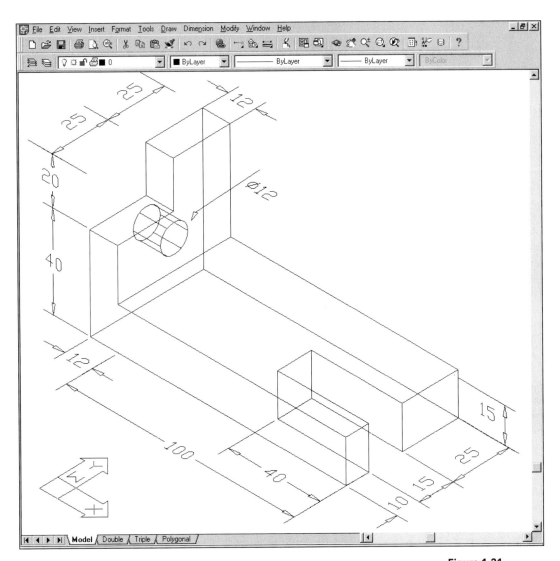

Figure 1.21

The complete corner-plate model with dimensions.

4. Referring to Figure 1.21 for the dimensions of the object, use the **PLINE** command to draw an outline of the 2D plan profile as follows:

```
Command: pline
Specify start point: 0,0
Current line-width is 0.0000
Specify next point or [Arc/Close/Halfwidth/Length/Undo/
   Width]: @100<0
Specify next point or [Arc/Close/Halfwidth/Length/Undo/
   Width]: @10<90
Specify next point or [Arc/Close/Halfwidth/Length/Undo/
   Width]: @40<180
Specify next point or [Arc/Close/Halfwidth/Length/Undo/
   Width]: @15<90
Specify next point or [Arc/Close/Halfwidth/Length/Undo/
   Width]: @40<0
Specify next point or [Arc/Close/Halfwidth/Length/Undo/
   Width]: @25<90
```

```
Specify next point or [Arc/Close/Halfwidth/Length/Undo/
    Width]: @100<180
Specify next point or [Arc/Close/Halfwidth/Length/Undo/
    Width]: c
```

Refer to Figure 1.22 for the completed outline in the World Coordinate System.

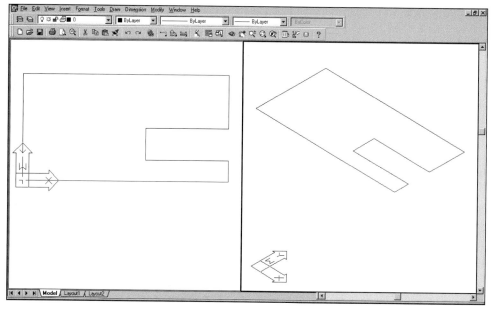

Figure 1.22

The completed outline in the World Coordinate System.

5. Activate the **EXTRUDE** command, pick the object, and extrude the profile through its Z height by 18mm, and choose zero as the angle of taper for extrusion, as shown in Figure 1.23.

6. Use the **LIST** command to check the object; notice that it's now listed as a 3D solid.

Now, let's look at how to use the UCS to move around drawings and how to set up a simple 3D work plane.

Using And Understanding The UCS And Work Planes

This time, using the same part you just created, you'll make another profile and employ the UCS to move about the drawing work plane. But what is a UCS?

A User Coordinate System, or UCS, is actually an infinitely large series of planes that fill out in all three directions. Yet you require simply a flat work plane. It lets you move about an object and create object entities in work planes other than the normal plan mode of the World Coordinate System (WCS). The WCS is simply a CAD reference tool. It's a starting point—a base you can reference and return to as you change work planes around

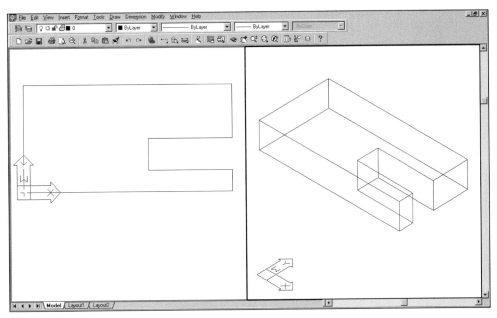

Figure 1.23
The extruded 3D solid.

your 3D part. The UCS icon arrow will indicate that you're in the World Coordinate System by displaying a W. If you create a coordinate system other than the WCS, it's called a User Coordinate System. You may create as many UCSs as you wish, but there is only one WCS.

An example will help explain this coordinate system. NASA and Russian astronauts working on the MIR space station often looked as if they were upside down. But, due to the astronauts' depth of perception and orientation from earth, and because of zero gravity, the space station didn't seem upside down to them. The space station was the astronauts' reference or work plane, and they worked around it. It's the same with 3D objects in AutoCAD—you use a flat plane or work plane as a reference point. In order to draw on different work planes, you use a UCS to work around the object you create.

In the outer-space example, the words *up* and *down* have no absolute meaning for astronauts. These terms are relative. Likewise, *up* and *down* have no absolute meaning in AutoCAD. However, you need a precise way to describe object entities. Normally, when you refer to *up* and *down* in 3D, you're referring to a positive Z coordinate. Thus, the UCS is a way of referencing yourself to the object you create, because it has X, Y, and Z coordinates.

You know that the X, Y, and Z axes are always at 90 degrees relative to each other. Look at the extreme lower-left corner of your AutoCAD window, where all the lines intersect at 0,0,0. Movement to the right is in the positive X direction. Movement toward the top of the screenis in the positive Y direction. To the left of the screen lies negative X, and below the grid on your screen lies negative Y. But where is the Z entity? Let's look at the UCS icon you normally see on your screen, as shown in Figure 1.24. You'll see the UCS icon sitting at the point of origin where the lines intersect.

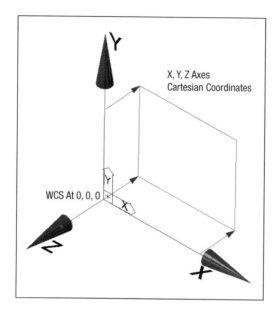

Figure 1.24

The X, Y, and Z coordinates are 90 degrees from each other.

The X part of the arrow points in the positive X direction, and the Y part of the arrow points in the positive Y direction. If you look directly at X and Y, the positive Z is coming straight at you, and negative Z is going away from you.

Now, let's use the UCS to draw in a different work plane about the part you created earlier, shown in Figure 1.25. Be sure you're in the drawing editor. You'll create a second rectangular profile using **POLYLINE** and then use the **EXTRUDE** command to extrude the profile through its Z entity 12 millimeters. Refer back to Figure 1.21 for the model's dimensions. Follow these steps:

1. Change the UCS to a work plane about the side view:

```
Command: ucs
Current ucs name: *WORLD*
Enter an option [New/Move/orthoGraphic/Prev/Restore/Save/
   Del/Apply/?/World] <World>: x
Specify rotation angle about X axis <90>: 90
```

Notice how the UCS has rotated itself into a vertical position—it rotated about the X axis.

You're now in the Front work plane. It's a good idea to save the UCS work planes you create (especially in a start file or template file):

2. Save the Front work plane as follows:

```
Command: ucs
Current ucs name: *NO NAME*
Enter an option [New/Move/orthoGraphic/Prev/Restore/Save/
   Del/Apply/?/World] <World>: s
Enter name to save current UCS or [?]: front
```

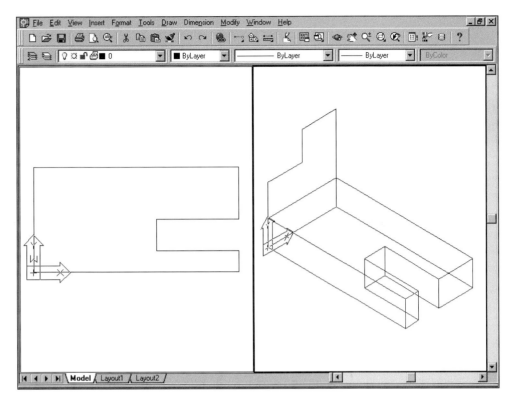

3. Move the Front work plane about the Y axis and resave it:

```
Command: ucs
Current ucs name: front
Enter an option [New/Move/orthoGraphic/Prev/Restore/Save/
  Del/Apply/?/World] <World>: y
Specify rotation angle about Y axis <90>: 90
```

Notice how the UCS has rotated about the Y axis. You're now in the Side work plane. (The UCS should look like the right viewport of Figure 1.25.)

4. Save the Side work plane as follows:

```
Command: ucs
Current ucs name: *NO NAME*
Enter an option [New/Move/orthoGraphic/Prev/Restore/Save/
  Del/Apply/?/World] <World>: s
Enter name to save current UCS or [?]: side
```

5. Use the **PLINE** command to draw in this Vertical work plane:

```
Command: pline
Specify start point: 0,0
Current line-width is 0.0000
```

Figure 1.25
The completed polyline in the Side work plane.

```
Specify next point or [Arc/Close/Halfwidth/Length/Undo/
   Width]: @50<0
Specify next point or [Arc/Close/Halfwidth/Length/Undo/
   Width]: @60<90
Specify next point or [Arc/Close/Halfwidth/Length/Undo/
   Width]: @25<180
Specify next point or [Arc/Close/Halfwidth/Length/Undo/
   Width]: @20<-90
Specify next point or [Arc/Close/Halfwidth/Length/Undo/
   Width]: @25<180
Specify next point or [Arc/Close/Halfwidth/Length/Undo/
   Width]: c
```

6. Use the **EXTRUDE** command to extrude the profile back –12 milli-meters and choose the angle of zero, as shown in Figure 1.26.

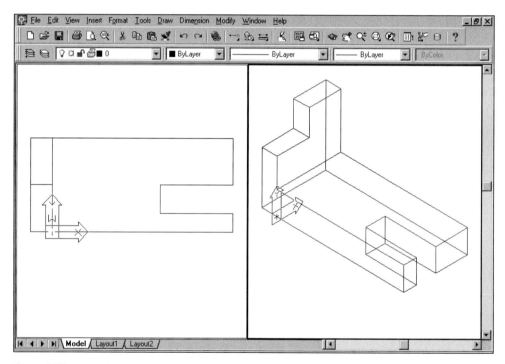

Figure 1.26

Preparing to join the two extruded parts.

7. Set the UCS back to the World Coordinate System:

```
Command: ucs
Current ucs name: side
Enter an option [New/Move/orthoGraphic/Prev/Restore/Save/
   Del/Apply/?/World] <World>: <Press Enter>
```

8. Use the **UNION** command to join the two solids, as shown in Figure 1.26. (This command appears in the Modify menu, under the Solids Editing item.)

9. Use the **HIDE** command (located in the View menu) to see the result.

10. Use the **LIST** command on the solid to see that you've created a true solid from two simple polylines.

11. Use the **REGEN** command to return to your 3D wireframe.

Now, let's create a circle on the Side work plane of the model. Be careful—if you try to draw the circle without first setting the UCS, the circle will be on the Horizontal plane, as shown in Figure 1.27. (Try it and see.)

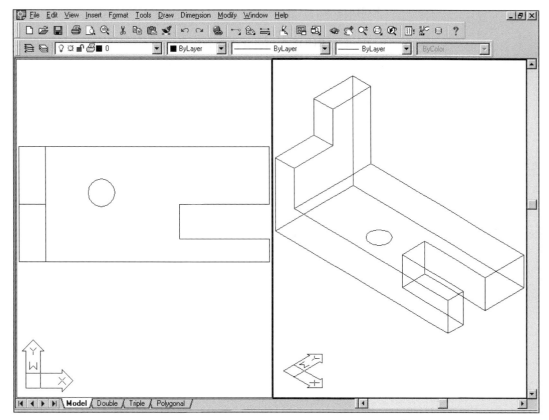

Figure 1.27
Circle in the wrong work plane.

How do you draw on the Side work plane? Look at Figure 1.28 and follow these steps:

1. Change the UCS to a work plane about the Side view:

   ```
   Command: ucs
   Current ucs name: side
   Enter an option [New/Move/orthoGraphic/Prev/Restore/Save/
     Del/Apply/?/World] <World>: r
   Enter name of UCS to restore or [?]: side
   ```

   Notice how the UCS has rotated into a vertical position. You're now in the Side work plane.

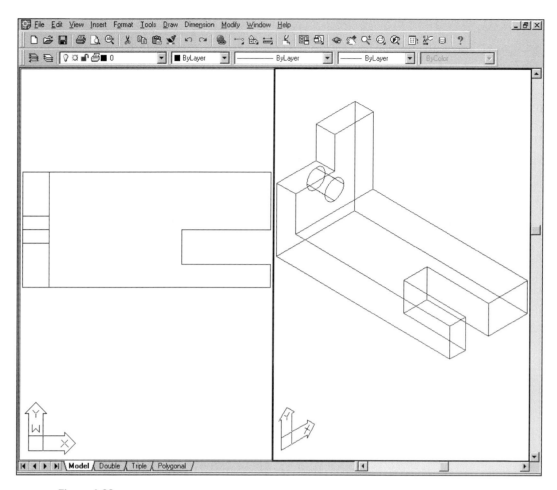

Figure 1.28
The plate with the extruded circle at 25,30.

2. Draw the circle:

```
Command: circle
Response: Specify center point for circle or [3P/2P/Ttr (tan
   tan radius)]: 25,30
Response: Specify radius of circle or [Diameter]: 6
```

3. Use the **EXTRUDE** command to extrude the circle –24 millimeters, as shown in Figure 1.28.

4. Use the **SUBTRACT** command (located in the Modify menu under the Solids Editing item). This command is in two parts: Choose the object(s) you wish to keep, press Enter, and then choose the object(s) you wish to remove.

5. Use the **LIST** command on the solid to see that you've created a true solid from two simple polylines and a circle.

6. Use the **REGEN** command to return to your 3D wireframe.

Moving On

This first chapter has provided you with a flavor of some of the tools and techniques you can use to generate basic 3D drawings in AutoCAD. The User Coordinate System is the key to working successfully in 3D AutoCAD—a mistake in the UCS can cause errors in your drawing. Now, we'll go step by step into each of the 3D AutoCAD tools. In the next chapter, you'll work extensively with 3D views, multiview drawings, and paper space. So, let's take that next step and work with more 3D drawings.

STANDARD
3D VIEWS
2

This chapter will help you understand how to develop 2D views from 3D models and how to communicate in three dimensions.

Multiview Drawings And Standard 3D Views

As you'll see in this chapter, you can communicate, present ideas, and create effective presentations through orthographic projection. You can also use standard orthographic projection to quickly transfer 3D ideas and sketches onto two-dimensional paper. You do so by using the Model and the Layout tabs of the AutoCAD drawing editor, which in turn allow you access to both model and paper space. Through knowing how to use these two spaces, you can create effective presentations for your target audience. How to move from model space to paper space is an important aspect to understand when working in 3D.

Computers today are used in the initial 2D sketching (ideation) process to the eventual testing (analysis) and evaluation (prototyping) process of the 3D part. However, as engineers prepare working and assembly drawings of three-dimensional objects on flat, two-dimensional paper, they use a standard method of 2D representation called *orthographic projection* to describe 3D objects. Gaspard Monge, a French professor, developed a systematic approach to the description of engineering drawings. He was the inventor of multiple views and orthographic projection through his *La Géométrie Descriptive*, which was published in 1795. His engineering students at the French Polytechnic School used his orthographic projection methods as a description method for laying out working drawings and parts. Today, these methods are widely used for laying out working drawings in the construction, architecture, and engineering industries. However, working, detail, and assembly drawings are limited—they're 2D descriptions of 3D objects or parts. They must be interpreted as such through precise descriptions, tolerances, and dimensional communication by the architect, engineer, or technician creating the drawings. Thus, standard methods are required for communicating ideas onto two-dimensional paper.

Toward this end, the American National Standards Institute (ANSI) describes a series of common codes and standards used with third-angle projection in the USA. Standards set by the International Standards Organization (ISO) are used for creating international metric drawings. Other examples of drawing standards exist, such as the British Standard for first-angle projection, used in the UK. In addition, each company has its own internal drawing standards. These standards help engineers describe drawings in industry-standard ways, so that all engineers and designers can read any drawings created to these precise communication specifications. If your company does work for an overseas contractor, you must conform to its definitions of projection.

Nevertheless, one fundamental difference exists between a 2D drawing and its 3D model: the description and creation process. The computer has come a long way as a production tool for use in this process. Designers may create computer-generated 3D models in a variety of ways to suit their immediate and eventual goals. The immediate goal may be a rough prototype of a part, or it may be the final creation of a detailed part. You use this initial 3D model to create 2D views. As you can see in Figures 2.1 and 2.2, the 2D views are placed to depict the 3D part.

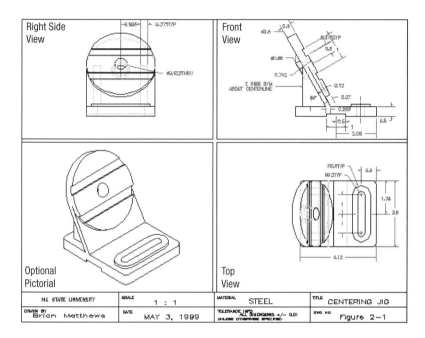

Figure 2.1
First-angle projection view (Europe).

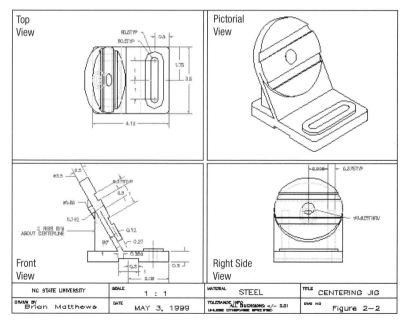

Figure 2.2
Third-angle projection view (USA).

Model Space Vs. Paper Space

AutoCAD has two distinct spaces: model space and paper space (via the Layout tab). In past AutoCAD releases, you drew at full size in the units of your choice. Then, you'd try to plot the drawing to scale using oversize text and text-related objects (such as dimensions) to fit the sheet borders. The process was confusing—and it wasted paper, because you had to remember to leave a margin for the pinch wheels if you were using a pen plotter. The Layout tab for paper space corrects these difficulties. Just remember, the purpose of model space is to create 3D drawings. The purpose of paper space is to set up a 2D print space. Don't try to draw 3D drawings in paper space—it's only good for plotting at scale.

Of course, in model space you still create your drawing in real-world units and at true full-size scale. But you now choose the Layout tab and switch into paper space when you're ready to plot. Then, you simply set your paper space drawing limits to match the sheet size on which you want to plot. You use the **VPORTS** command to restore the viewports you created in model space into paper space, and then you scale the model in the model space viewports with the **ZOOM-XP** option. Finally, you plot your drawing.

Principally, paper space is where you plot or print drawings and where you lay out views of orthographic drawings and pictorials prior to printing. If you look in the lower-left corner of an AutoCAD 2000 drawing, you'll notice three drawing tabs labeled Model, Layout1, and Layout2. Paper space offers a valuable feature: It lets you create different scales on the same sheet. It doesn't matter whether your drawing is 3D or 2D. In addition, you set your drawing limits in paper space to the actual size of the drawing area on your paper for your specific plotter. Doing so lets you plot at 1:1 true scale. (Chapter 3 discusses setting up and using scales in more depth.) See the "Characteristics Of Viewports In Paper Space" section later in this chapter for the benefits of using viewports in model space versus the Layout tab space.

Finally, if you're modeling solid 3D engineering models, you have the option of using the **SOLVIEW** command to create Top, Front, and Side views. For example, you can set the scale to 1 for full-size or .5 for half-full-size. You'll use **SOLVIEW** later in this chapter—first, let's clear up some terminology.

Model Space

Model space is a drawing space in which you can construct drawings in either 2D or 3D. You build your 2D geometry or your 3D model in model space before you enter Layout or paper space. Older AutoCAD releases used only model space. In the ACAD.DWT prototype template drawing supplied with AutoCAD, model space is the default. To distinguish it from paper space, Model and Layout tabs appear in the lower-left corner of your screen.

As you create your drawing geometry in model space, you also have the flexibility to create viewports by entering "vports" at the command line or choosing Viewports|New Viewports to open the Viewports dialog box. You can also choose the Display Viewports Dialog icon. If you need to create, alter, or reset viewport configurations, use the Change View To drop-down list when the viewport is active. Finally, to save your options, click on the OK button of the Named Viewports dialog box to save the tiled viewport configuration. You can then use the saved configuration in paper space by restoring it. Notice that viewports themselves are entities in every sense of the word. You can move them, resize them by using the **GRIPS** or **SCALE** command, or copy or erase them.

You draw all your 3D entities on the Model tab (model space) with X, Y, and Z coordinates. While you're still in model space, notice the shape of the UCS icon in the lower-left corner of the drawing editor. X, Y, and W appear on it; you'll reference them in the next chapter. You use the Layout1 and Layout2 areas to set up drawings for 2D printing or plotting. (In prior releases, these Layout tabs were termed paper space—let's keep to the same terminology here.) Within Layout1 and Layout2, you use the New Layout, Layout From Template, Page Setup, and Display Viewports Dialog commands from the Layouts toolbar to place standard drawing title templates or drawing titles you've created. Once again, notice the shape of the UCS icon in the lower-left corner of the drawing editor. It's a different triangular shape, and only X and W appear on it (again, you'll come back to this topic in the next chapter.)

VPORTS

The **VPORTS** command lets you construct different viewports. In paper space, you organize multiple views of your 3D model and add annotations for plotting. Paper space is primarily two dimensional, and you should set its limits to the dimensions of the border on the sheet on which you want to plot. To move into paper space, click on one of the Layout tabs in the lower-left corner of your screen.

When you first enter paper space, no viewports are visible. You must use the **VPORTS** or **MVIEW** command to create new viewports or restore existing viewport configurations (saved while in model space). As you switch to your drawing geometry in model space and then return via the Layout tab to paper space, your viewports are displayed in the same placement and size that you left them.

PSPACE And PS

PSPACE and **PS** are switch commands that take you back to paper space from model space. When you click on a Layout tab, you access paper space. Within paper space, you can also choose to go into either model space (via the **MS** alias) to work on the drawing or to stay in paper space. This 2D space allows you to plot or print your drawing at a scale of your choice.

MSPACE And MS

The **MSPACE** and **MS** switch commands allow you to move from paper space into the model space area of the viewport. Doing so allows you to work on the 3D model in your drawing.

Characteristics Of Viewports In Model Space

The following are the characteristics of tiled (model space) viewports (see Figure 2.3) versus nontiled viewports:

- In model space, you construct 3D models and 2D drawings at full scale, with dimensions.

- Use the **VPORTS** command to create viewports and viewport settings, which you can save for later use.

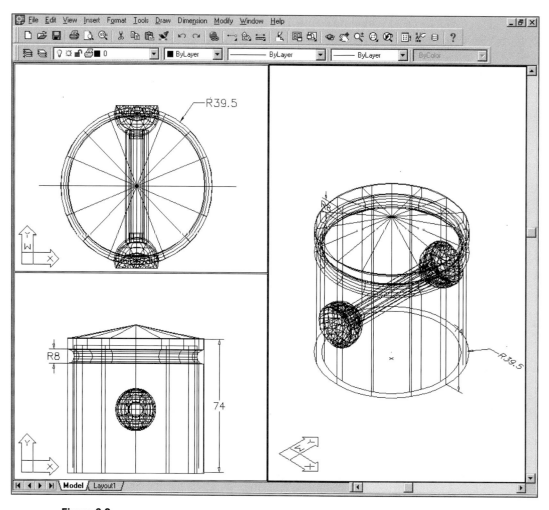

Figure 2.3

Viewports in model space.

- Viewports are tiled. They can't overlap and are always adjacent to one another.

- One viewport at a time is active. Your cursor crosshairs appear only in the active viewport (although moving the cursor arrow to a different viewport allows you to pick that viewport and make it active).

- You can plot only the active viewport. The UCS icon appears in each viewport if the icon is set to On.

- You're in model space only. You zoom and pan within the active viewport.

- The number of viewports is limited by your operating system (the system variable **MAXACTVP** limits the value to a number from 2 to 64).

Characteristics Of Viewports In Paper Space

To enter paper space, you click on the Layout tab and then click on the Display Viewports Dialog button or choose New Viewports from the View menu. Here are some characteristics of paper space viewports (see Figure 2.4):

- The word *Paper* replaces *Model* in the status bar, and the triangular Paper Space icon appears (if it's set to ON).

- You create or restore viewports with the **SOLVIEW**, **MVIEW**, or **VPORTS** command.

- Each viewport contains a view of your object in model space. For example, you can set different viewports to get Top, Front, Right, and Pictorial views.

- Viewport shapes aren't limited. For example, you can create circular, rectangular, trapezoidal, or polygonal viewports.

- The UCS viewpoint and scale magnification may be different in each viewport.

- Viewport borders are entities. You can erase, move, scale, and stretch the viewports.

- You can place viewports onto layers. For example, to achieve professional plotting results, you might create a layer named Vports and assign it a color. Then, using the **CHANGE** command, you could place the borders of all your viewports onto that layer. Just prior to plotting, you'd freeze the layer.

- You can zoom and pan around Layout or paper space, resulting in some viewports being partially or fully off screen.

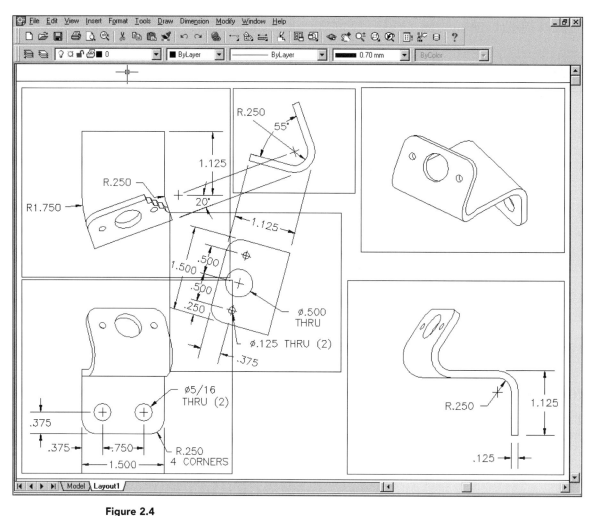

Figure 2.4
Viewports in paper space.

- Viewports aren't tiled—you can overlap them, separate them, or arrange them in multiple ways to suit the drawing.

- Views in paper space can be saved and restored with the **VIEW** command.

- You can switch back and forth between model space and Layout (paper space) with the **MS** (or **MSPACE**) and **PS** (or **PSPACE**) commands.

- Each viewport resides on the layer on which it was created. The viewport border adopts its color from its layer, but the border linetype is always continuous.

- You place notes for the drawing's revision history, border, parts list, title block, and so on in paper space.

- The **VPORTS**, **PSPACE**, **MSPACE**, and **VPLAYER** commands are active. (The **PLAN**, **VPOINT**, and **DVIEW** commands are disabled until you activate the **MS** command.)

- You may plot all your viewports at once.

- The default number of viewports that may be active on screen in Auto-CAD 2000 is 64. This setting is limited by the system variable **MAXACTVP**.

- Your cursor crosshairs extend across the entire graphics screen, independent of each of your viewports.

- You can turn viewports on and off with the **MVIEW** command. By default, they're on when you create them. Turning some viewports off will speed regeneration time.

- When you print and need to hide a 3D pictorial, use the **MVIEW** command. It has a **hideplot** subroutine that lets you pick the border of the viewport you want to hide. (It removes hidden lines in a viewport as you plot from paper space.)

- Different layers may be frozen and thawed from viewport to viewport with the Layer Properties Manager dialog box. (Doing so lets you view hidden lines or dimensions within specific views.)

Creating 2D Views From 3D Models For Multiview Drawings

Figure 2.5 shows the six main orthographic projection views: Top, Left, Right, Front, Rear, and Bottom. Usually, you create Top, Front, and Right views of an object—the result is called *third-angle projection*. In computer modeling, you create 3D models in what is called model space. Once you've created your 3D model, you can easily use the **VPORTS** or **MVIEW** command to create 2D multiview, assembly, and standard drawings of Top, Front, and Side views of your model in the Layout or paper space. Through orthographic projection, the process simply comes down to locating where you want to place each of the views onto the layout sheet in paper space.

The advantage of using orthographic projection views (known in AutoCAD as viewports) is that you may rotate your User Coordinate System (UCS) parallel to the Front, Top, or Side view to work with the object along a fixed orthographic construction plane. Doing so helps you create and adjust your 3D geometry. Plus, having three orthographic projection views and one Pictorial view will help you visualize where the object is in 3D space. The main AutoCAD commands you use to create and use viewports are **VPORTS**, **MVIEW**, **SOLVIEW**, and **MVSETUP**. You can also save and restore viewports.

Before you move into using viewports, let's review a few details. The viewports you create in model space are *tiled*, which means they're static and can't overlap each other. However, they have multiple setting options that

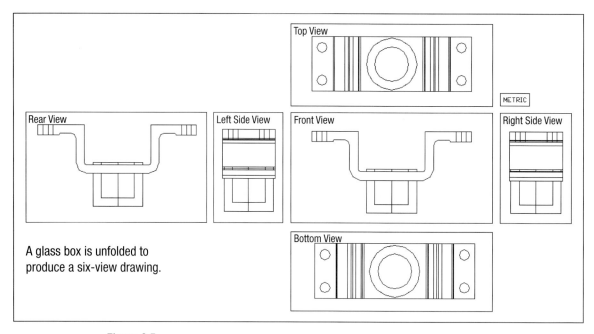

Top View

METRIC

Rear View   Left Side View   Front View   Right Side View

A glass box is unfolded to
produce a six-view drawing.

Bottom View

Figure 2.5

Six main orthographic
projection views.

let you set up different views of the same model. For example, you can easily create first- and third-angle views of a 3D part. You may also save the viewport settings and then transfer those settings into the Layout or paper space area. On the other hand, Layout or paper space viewports float and may overlap each other, as illustrated in Figures 2.4 and 2.6. You can restore into this space your previous viewport settings. In addition, you can place the borders of the viewports onto a layer, which lets you hide them prior to plotting. You'll find more in-depth explanations of viewport characteristics later in this chapter. But for now, let's look at using the **VPORTS** command to set up single and multiple viewports.

Using **VPORTS** With Layout Tabs

Let's see how AutoCAD 2000 can make you more productive. After you create 3D models, the **VPORTS** command lets you place and create instant orthographic views. Using **VPORTS**, you can orient viewports in both the model space and the paper space areas. But remember, you can create and save viewports only in model space.

Let's see how to use the **VPORTS** command within the Layout1 tab space to create and restore multiple viewports. Specifically, you'll create Top, Front, and Right orthographic projection views and an SE Isometric view as a pictorial.

First, you'll open a drawing into a single viewport. Then, you'll set up multiple viewports and restore the settings in paper space. Nevertheless, as you open 3d-model.dwg from the CD-ROM in your drawing editor, notice that it's a 3D drawing of a simple part. Choose the Layout1 tab, and a Page

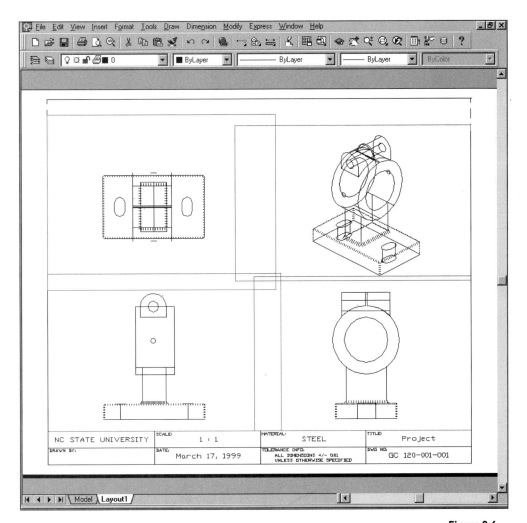

NC STATE UNIVERSITY | SCALE: 1 : 1 | MATERIAL: STEEL | TITLED Project
DRAWN BY: | DATE: March 17, 1999 | TOLERANCE INFO: ALL DIMENSIONS +/- 0.01 UNLESS OTHERWISE SPECIFIED | DWG NO: GC 120-001-001

Figure 2.6

Overlapping orthographic and pictorial viewports.

Setup dialog box will open. Click on OK to accept the default settings. The paper space viewport is allowing the user to see into and create/edit in model space but not moving or copying the model into paper space. You can move back and forth between the Model and Layout1 tabs easily. You can also plot your drawing from paper space. For now, close the drawing without saving it.

Again, open 3d-model.dwg from the CD-ROM in your drawing editor. To create, set up, save, and restore multiple viewport settings, choose the Display Viewports Dialog icon or type "vports" at the command prompt to access the Viewports dialog box, shown in Figure 2.7. You should notice a few standard settings before moving on. The Viewports dialog box lets you set the views of your 3D drawing to Top, Front, Right, SE Isometric, and other options. Notice, however, that as you enter the dialog box, the Standard Viewports list is set to *Active Model Configuration*. The Preview window is set to *Current*, and the Setup value is 2D.

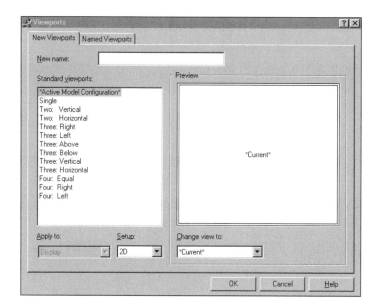

Figure 2.7
The standard Viewports dialog box in model space.

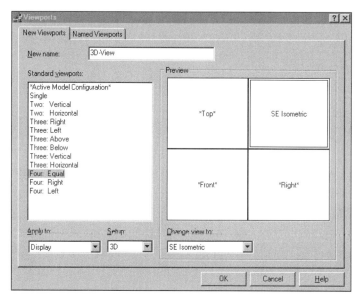

Figure 2.8
The modified Viewports dialog box settings for 3D views in model space.

Now, let's see how easy it is to set up the drawing for your 3D views. Refer to Figure 2.8 as you follow these steps:

1. In the New Name box, enter the name "3D-view". Naming each viewport setting is important, because you can use the setting later when you access either Layout tab and move into paper space.

2. In the Standard Viewports list, choose Four: Equal. Notice that you now have four previews of *Current* in the Preview window.

3. In the Setup: box, choose 3D. Notice that your four previews instantly change in the Preview window.

4. Click on OK to save your viewport settings. You now have four instant views: Top, Front, Right, and SE Isometric. But remember, you're still working only in model space.

What extra steps do you have to perform to set up the Layout tabs space? Let's look at that process:

1. Choose a Layout1 tab, and a Page Setup dialog box will open. At upper-left is a named label box that is currently named Layout1. Change the label to 3D-plot and click on OK.

2. A single viewport of the 3D model will appear on screen. Use the **ERASE** command and erase the viewport by picking its border. (You're going to set up four viewports similar to those you just created in model space.)

3. Choose the Display Viewports Dialog icon or type "vports" at the command line to access the Viewports dialog box. Two tabs appear at upper left: New Viewports and Named Viewports. Choose the Named Viewports tab and activate the saved 3D-view option by clicking on it.

4. Click on the New Viewports tab and choose the Four: Equal option.

5. In the Viewport Spacing field, set the spacing to 0.10.

6. Make sure the Setup value is still set to 3D-Plot. Click on OK.

7. The command prompt will now indicate **Specify first corner or [Fit] <Fit>:** Enter the coordinates "0,0". At the **Specify opposite corner:** command prompt, enter the coordinates "10.6,8".

You're now ready to plot all the viewports at one time. But you still must correctly scale the viewports in order to plot at 1:1 (full scale) in the Plot dialog box. Here's how you do it:

1. Using the **MS** alias or **MSPACE** command, access the Top, Front, and Right Side viewports in turn.

These commands actually access the model space of the Layout1 tab. The **MS** command lets you enter each viewport independently and work on the 3D model. In addition, if you use the **ZOOM** command while the **MSPACE** command is active, you can scale the model. (Zoom simply changes the perception of the model but it does not true scale it—that is, enlarge or reduce it, like the Scale command. It simply corrects the perception of the image.) You'll see this technique in more depth in the next chapter.

2. In each viewport, enter "zoom", press Enter, and then enter "1/25XP" to set a 1:25 metric scale.

Figure 2.9
The completed drawing in
paper space.

3. Use the **PS** or **PSPACE** command to return to the Layout space. Now, you're ready to plot at 1:1 scale in the Plot dialog box. Figure 2.9 shows the completed drawing in paper space.

From this exercise, you've learned that you can easily set up multiple viewport configurations in model space. You can then transfer those configurations to paper space in order to plot the multiple viewports. But before moving further into the subject, let's look at the differences between model space and paper space.

Alternate Views For Your 3D Models

This section will show you how to create and work with different types of viewports. Specifically, you'll look at viewport sizing, placement, and shape. When you worked with past AutoCAD releases, you had to create a whole library of prototype files. The prototype drawings were useful, but you had to change to a new prototype every time the output size of your drawing media changed. This was especially true if you were changing or alternating the viewport positions or configuring in 2D paper space. In essence, you needed a different prototype drawing for any new difference in paper space. Now, due to the enhancements of AutoCAD 2000 and new command options, you can use the **VPORTS** New Viewports options to build alternate ways to view drawings, rather than creating multiple template or prototype libraries. The next chapter will provide a more in-depth look at methods for setting up alternate views for 3D drawings. For now, let's look at some viewport basics.

The **LAYOUT** Command

The **LAYOUT** command lets you copy, delete, create, rename, save, or set any type or style of layout sheet you may need in paper space. Your objective in the following exercise is to create three layout sheets with multiple viewport configurations. If you need to, you can also use this drawing as a prototype or template file to assist with future multiple configurations. Follow these steps:

1. Start a new drawing and name it vport-restore.dwg. Choose English Units. Make sure you're in model space. At the command prompt, respond to the prompts as follows:

   ```
   Command: layout
   Enter layout option [Copy/Delete/New/Template/Rename/SAveas/
     Set/?] <set>: r
   Enter layout to rename: <Layout1> <Press Enter>
   Enter new layout name: 3D-view
   Layout "Layout1"renamed to "3D-view"
   ```

2. Press Enter or the spacebar to return the **LAYOUT** command. Or, type "layout" at the keyboard or click the right button on the mouse and choose the new AutoCAD 2000 Repeat feature from the floating menu. Continue to respond to these prompts:

   ```
   Command: layout
   Enter layout option [Copy/Delete/New/Template/Rename/SAveas/
     Set/?] <set>: r
   Enter layout to rename <3D-view>: layout2
   Enter new layout name: Triple
   Layout "layout2" renamed to "Triple"
   ```

3. Press Enter to return the **LAYOUT** command, or press the right button of the mouse and use the new AutoCAD 2000 Repeat feature. Continue as follows:

   ```
   Command: layout
   Enter layout option [Copy/Delete/New/Template/Rename/SAveas/
     Set/?] <set>: n
   Enter new Layout name <Layout1>: Polygonal
   ```

You've now created three layout sheets for paper space. Again, make sure you're in model space. Don't go into the 3D, Triple, or Polygonal layout sheet—you need to create the saved viewports first. To do so, continue as follows:

4. Press the Display Viewports Dialog button to access the Viewports dialog box.

5.   In the New Name box, enter the name "3D-view". (Remember, naming the viewport setting is important, because you'll use it later as you access a Layout tab and move into paper space.)

6.   In the Standard Viewports list, choose Single. Notice that you have a preview of *Current* in the Preview window.

7.   In the Setup box, choose 3D. Then, choose SW Isometric from the Change View To drop-down list and you will see your view change in the Preview window.

8.   Click on OK to save your viewport settings.

Now, you need to reopen the Viewports dialog box to enter another viewport's setting:

9.   At the command prompt, enter "vports" to open the Viewports dialog box.

10.   In the New Name box, enter the name "Triple".

11.   In the Standard Viewports list, choose Three: Right.

12.   In the Setup box, choose 3D. Your preview will change to a Top, Front, and SE Isometric view in the Preview window.

13.   Click on OK to save your viewport settings.

You now have two sets of saved views. But instead of creating the next view with **VPORTS**, you'll create the Polygonal view directly with the **MVIEW** command. Before you continue, **SAVE** the drawing file as "vport-restore.dwg".

If you haven't created vport-restore.dwg and have simply read through this section, you may open the file from the CD-ROM. Now, let's move into paper space and restore the saved viewports.

Using Alternative Views Of A Model

In 3D graphics, to explain a model in more depth you often need to see views of the model other than just orthographic views. These alternate views include section views, assembly views, enlarged detail views, isometric and auxiliary views, and possibly an odd perspective view for desktop publishing or Web work. You've already reviewed viewport characteristics and learned how to use the Viewports dialog box to create and save multiple viewports. Another command, **MVIEW**, also lets you configure and orient viewports. You can use **MVIEW** to set up single, multiple, or polygonal-style viewports. Let's review how to create alternate view styles.

In model space, you have the ability to create tiled viewports in essentially any formation you want. The only model space limitation is that the viewports remain tied to each other. But are there any other ways to produce viewport configurations within model space and then transfer them to paper space? Or, can you use alternate methods to create views in paper space alone? The simple answer to both these questions is yes, and the answer comes by using **MVIEW** along with **VPORTS**.

Using **MVIEW** To Restore Multiviews Into Viewports

When you first activate **MVIEW**, the command has a number of options: **ON**, **OFF**, **Fit**, **Hideplot**, **Lock**, **Object**, **Polygonal**, **Restore**, **2**, **3**, or **4**. Your initial concern in this exercise will be to use the **Restore**, **Object**, and **Polygonal** options, but you'll quickly learn to use the remaining options once you have some viewports on screen. Remember, you can't invoke the **MVIEW** command while you're in model space—AutoCAD will indicate that the command isn't allowed in the Model tab.

The procedure for restoring viewports is simple. You pick the 3D-view tab and enter the **MVIEW** command. Enter "R" for restore, and enter a restored viewport name. If a Page-Setup dialog box pops up, click on OK; then, erase the viewport the dialog box made by picking its border. Let's try it. Enter the following responses at the command prompt:

```
Command: mview
Specify corner of viewport or [ON/OFF/Fit/Hideplot/Lock/Object/
  Polygonal/Restore/2/3/4] <Fit>: r
Enter viewport configuration name or [?] <*Active>: 3D-view
Specify first corner or [Fit] <Fit>: f <or press Enter>
```

Press Enter to return the **MVIEW** command, or press the right button of the mouse and use the new AutoCAD 2000 Repeat feature from the resultant floating menu. Choose the Triple Layout tab in your drawing screen. Erase the viewport if one appears. Continue as follows:

```
Command: mview
Specify corner of viewport or [ON/OFF/Fit/Hideplot/Lock/Object/
  Polygonal/Restore/2/3/4] <Fit>: r
Enter viewport configuration name or [?] <3D-view>: Triple
Specify first corner or [Fit] <Fit>: f
```

Remember that even though these viewports look similar to model space viewports, and even though they're currently tiled, the triple viewports you created are independent viewports that you can resize, erase, copy, move, place on layers, and so on. You've now set up two versions of paper space and two viewports.

To finish the exercise (and in order to see some new AutoCAD 2000 features), let's create a couple of polygonal feature objects and then use them as viewports. In this case, AutoCAD is referring to a polygonal shape as any shape or feature—it doesn't mean just the **POLYGONAL** command. Choose the Polygonal Layout tab in your drawing screen. Again erase the viewport if one appears. Respond to the command prompts as follows:

```
Command: ellipse
Specify axis endpoint of ellipse or [Arc/Center]: 1.5,4.5
Specify other endpoint of axis: 5,0
Specify distance to other axis or [Rotation]: r
Specify rotation around major axis: 290
```

Now, create a polygonal object for use as a viewport:

```
Command: polygon
Enter number of sides <4>: 8
Specify center of polygon or [Edge]:  <Pick the center of the
  circle at 3.5,6>
Enter an option [Inscribed in circle/Circumscribed about circle]
  <I>: c
Specify radius of circle: 2
```

Next, you'll reactivate the **MVIEW** command with the new **Polygonal** feature. When you do, **MVIEW** will move into polyline-creation mode and then let you create an object of a desired shape. Specifically, you'll use the **Polygonal** feature first to draw a line; next, you'll transfer to an arc mode; and then you'll use the **Close** option to end the command. See Figure 2.10 for the completed exercise. Respond to the command prompts as follows:

```
Command: mview
Specify corner of viewport or
[ON/OFF/Fit/Hideplot/Lock/Object/Polygonal/Restore/2/3/4]
  <Fit>: p
Specify start point: 10,6
Specify next point or [Arc/Close/Length/Undo]: 7.75,7.75
Specify next point or [Arc/Close/Length/Undo]: 5.5,4.5
Specify next point or [Arc/Close/Length/Undo]: a
Enter an arc boundary option
[Angle/CEnter/CLose/Direction/Line/Radius/Second pt/Undo/Endpoint
  of arc]
<Endpoint>: 10,2.75
Enter an arc boundary option
[Angle/CEnter/CLose/Direction/Line/Radius/Second pt/Undo/Endpoint
  of arc]
<Endpoint>: cl
```

You just created three unusually shaped viewports: an ellipse, an octagon, and a polygon. You need to use one last subset of the **MVIEW** command to activate the ellipse and octagon:

```
Command: mview
[ON/OFF/Fit/Hideplot/Lock/Object/Polygonal/Restore/2/3/4]
  <Fit>: o
```

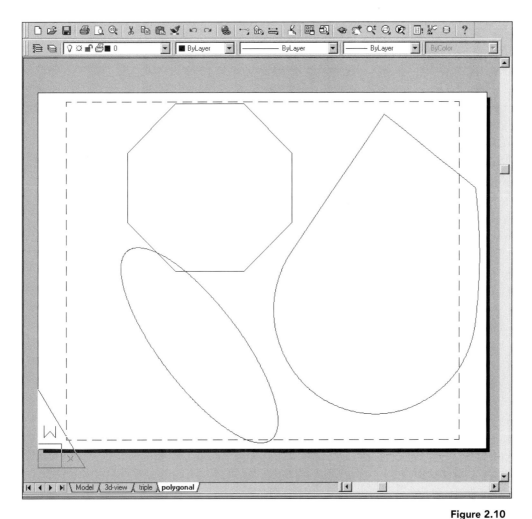

Figure 2.10
The completed polygonal viewports.

```
Select object to clip viewport: <In turn, choose both the ellipse
object and the octagon object. Doing so activates the shapes into
viewports.>
```

To complete the exercise, let's use **INSERT**—a newly refined AutoCAD 2000 command that lets you insert drawings into drawings. At this point, you should have either created the Vport-restore.dwg or opened up vport-restore.dwg from the CD-ROM. Check to ensure you are in the Model tab. Then, either enter the **INSERT** command or choose Block from the Insert menu to open the Insert dialog box shown in Figure 2.11. But first, use the **MS** command to access model space of one of your viewports.

In the dialog box, choose Browse and bring in the piston.dwg file from the CD-ROM. Check to ensure that your settings are the same as those shown in Figure 2.11.

Using **SOLVIEW** To Set Up Orthographic Views

The **SOLVIEW** command provides another method for setting up orthographic views. **SOLVIEW** is superior to some of the other options because it

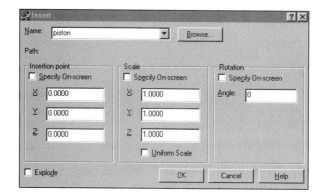

Figure 2.11
The Insert dialog box.

sets up layers according to your named views. After you've created a 3D model, **SOLVIEW** will help you develop alternative orthographic views of it. To implement **SOLVIEW**, work in a multistep process:

1. Choose the Page Setup command from the File menu to open the Page Setup dialog box, shown in Figure 2.12.

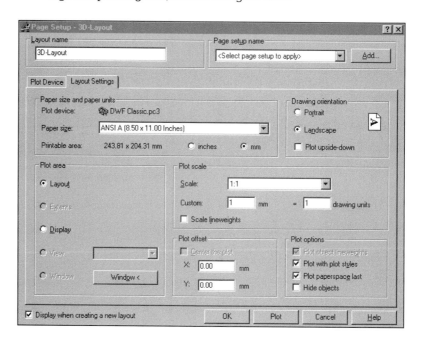

Figure 2.12
The Page Setup dialog box.

2. In the upper-left corner of the Layout Settings tab, enter the new layout name "3D-Layout". (Make sure you are not in the Model tab or the box will be grayed out.)

3. For this example, set the Scale to 1:2. Click on OK.

You'll see the name at the bottom of your sheet is now set to 3D-Layout. Continue as follows:

4. Choose the Draw|Solids|Setup|View menu item to access the **SOLVIEW** command (or enter "solview" at the command prompt).

As you use **SOLVIEW**, you'll place location points on your drawing sheet for each view you create. The best way to do this is by presetting the grid and snap. Next, you'll provide a scale (1 for full size, .5 for half-full size, and so on). In turn, you'll provide a name for each of the views (such as Top, Front, or Side). You do this because the **SOLVIEW** command is automatically creating layers for you. You'll select a surface parallel to the orthographic view and repeat the **SOLVIEW** command for the Front and Side views. (Remember to leave room for dimensions.) If you have complicated parts, you may also place isometric, trimetric, section, or auxilliary views with the **SOLVIEW** command. Then, you'll use **VPOINT** to change the view. Finally, you can set lineweight at the plot pen parameters or use the new Lineweight option of the object's properties through the **DDMODIFY** or **PROPERTIES** command.

You use orthographic projection views in a number of ways to depict your object or part. So, let's look at how to create and set up standard views as multiview drawings. Later, you'll examine assembly views and nonrectangular viewports. For this next part of the exercise, refer to Figure 2.13.

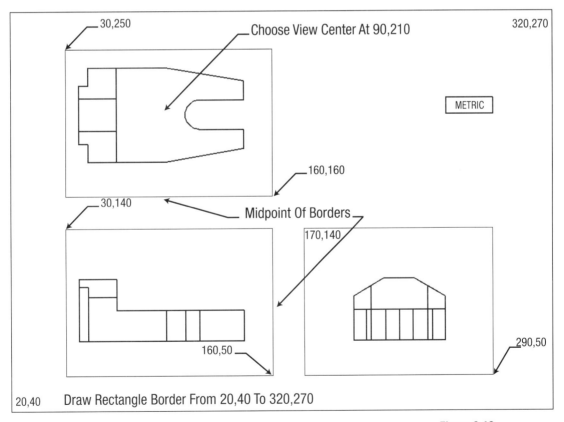

Figure 2.13

Viewport placing for the **SOLVIEW** command.

From the CD-ROM, open the keyplate.dwg file. Your objective is to create Top, Front, and Side views, with a pictorial view as a bonus to aid your final presentation drawing. See Figure 2.14. First you may want to choose the

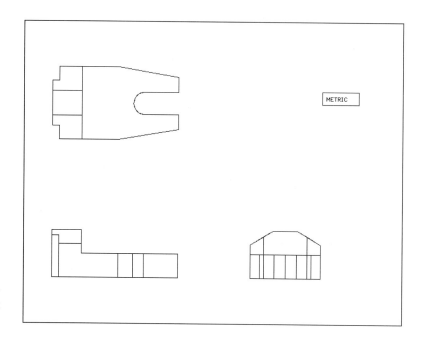

Figure 2.14
Completed viewport placement
for the **SOLVIEW** command.

Layout1 tab, then set your Grid to 10. Now, enter the following values at the command prompt:

```
Command: solview
Enter an option [Ucs/Ortho/Auxiliary/Section]: u
Enter an option [Named/World/?/Current] <Current>: <Press Enter>
Enter view scale <1>:1
Specify view center: <Choose a location on screen>
Specify view center <specify viewport>: <Press Enter>
Specify first corner of viewport: <Choose a location on screen>
Specify opposite corner of viewport: <Choose a location on
    screen>
Enter view name: top
UCSVIEW = 1  UCS will be saved with view
Enter an option [Ucs/Ortho/Auxiliary/Section]: o
Specify side of viewport to project: <Choose the midpoint of the
    border>
Specify view center: <Choose a location on screen>
Specify view center <specify viewport>: <Press Enter>
Specify first corner of viewport: <Choose a location on screen>
Specify opposite corner of viewport: <Choose a location on
    screen>
Enter view name: front
UCSVIEW = 1  UCS will be saved with view
Enter an option [Ucs/Ortho/Auxiliary/Section]: o
Specify side of viewport to project: <Choose the midpoint of the
    border>
Specify view center: <Choose a location on screen>
Specify view center <specify viewport>: <Press Enter>
Specify first corner of viewport: <Choose a location on screen>
Specify opposite corner of viewport: <Choose a location on
    screen>
```

```
Enter view name: side
UCSVIEW = 1  UCS will be saved with view
Enter an option [Ucs/Ortho/Auxiliary/Section]: <Press Enter>
Remember to turn off or Freeze your VPORTS layer.
```

Finally, for a more professional-looking drawing, choose the Layer icon and freeze the VPORTS layer. You should now have the completed drawing on screen as seen in Figure 2.14. The **SOLVIEW** command is one you may use to place orthographic views of a solid model, in many configurations. Later in the book, you'll look at the **SOLVIEW**, **SOLDRAW**, and **SOLPROF** commands.

Paper Space Review

To complete the chapter, let's quickly review some points of interest. Throughout this chapter, you created a number of settings and configurations. As you did so, you learned that a number of configurations readily lend themselves to being set up ahead of time. You can place the bulk of the settings you've worked on in this chapter in a template file (or a series of template files) and choose them as you need them. For example, you can set up your paper space, layout, viewport, and UCS settings in a template with some of the configurations outlined earlier. That way, you can begin a new drawing that uses these configurations.

You'll use viewports primarily to aid your 3D modeling. However, here are some additional review comments for paper space:

- You must remember to set up paper space limits and a paper space title block, depending on the size of the output paper you're going to use.

- Consider any standard text that you'll place next to the viewports. (This text isn't limited to the title block.)

- Consider the viewpoint angle that you want for each viewport. Should it be one of several orthographic or isometric views? Will it be a plan view? And should any of the viewports remove hidden lines when they're plotted?

- Determine the number of viewports, their size, their spacing, and where you want to place them in paper space. Remember that you can create viewports with the **MVIEW** command. Set them on a layer called **VPORTS**.

- Think about the visibility of layers within each viewport. You may need hidden, phantom, or center lines to describe salient parts to ANSI standards.

Moving On

In this chapter, you learned how to develop 2D views from 3D models and how to communicate in three dimensions. You were introduced to paper space and model space, along with simplified orthographic projection. These features let you quickly communicate 3D ideas and sketches onto two-dimensional paper.

In the next chapter, you'll examine the UCS in depth and look at creating standard scale settings for your 3D drawings. You'll also learn how to set up 3D construction and 3D work planes. In addition, you'll learn about the new **3DORBIT** command and the new feature that gives you true what-you-see-is-what-you-get (WYSIWYG) line-weight settings within a drawing.

USER
COORDINATE
SYSTEMS

*In this chapter, you'll discover the importance
of User Coordinate Systems and X-Y-Z
construction planes for 3D work.*

Cartesian And Global Coordinate Systems

The new AutoCAD 2000 commands we'll introduce in this chapter will help you learn how User Coordinate Systems (UCSs) affect drawing in 3D. You'll become familiar with construction planes and work planes, and you'll learn how UCSs help you draw in different 3D planes as you move about the drawing. In work planes, you'll find the right-hand rule to be one of the simplest 3D rules you'll ever have to learn. Once you've completed your model, you use ZOOM with the center magnification feature to scale your image to a true scale in paper space before sending it to the printer.

Most CAD systems use the Cartesian coordinate system along with three 2D coordinate methods of data entry: Absolute, Relative, and Polar. (We'll briefly review the 3D coordinate systems of data entry [Spherical and Cylindrical] in Chapter 5, along with wireframe 3D modeling.) René Descartes (1596-1650), a French mathematician and philosopher, invented the Cartesian coordinate system, the most common system in use today. He laid the foundation for analytical geometry by linking geometry and algebra into curve equations and linear descriptions. His Cartesian coordinate system represents geometric entities through algebraic and numerical expressions, so that a straight line can be represented by a linear equation—for example, $ax + by + c = 0$. The Cartesian coordinate system is still in use today, representing both 2D and 3D points and lines in space. All the 2D or 3D geometric data of your drawing entities are stored in relationship to a coordinate system, along with the drawing's orientation to the coordinate system—through the right-hand rule.

You use 3D Cartesian coordinates to create the various component parts of your drawing. The system uses three mutually perpendicular axes—X, Y, and Z—that intersect at an origin point. These X, Y, and Z axes extend from the origin in both a negative and a positive direction, as you can see in Figure 3.1.

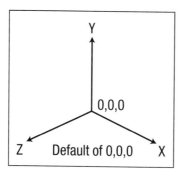

Figure 3.1
The Cartesian coordinate system.

In 3D modeling systems, a default or global coordinate system defines the 0,0,0 point about which you start to draw in 3D and to which you can always return as a point of reference. AutoCAD places the global point—or *World Coordinate System (WCS)*—at 0,0,0 as its standard default coordinate system, to distinguish it from other UCS or local coordinate systems as established by the user. The global WCS is permanent, and we use it as a start point to create both a 2D and a 3D drawing.

Yet as we create individual component parts of a 3D drawing, we still need the flexibility to move around the drawing for specific tasks. This is achieved by using a local coordinate system. In AutoCAD, this local coordinate system is termed the *User Coordinate System (UCS)*. The UCS may also be set or created relative to an object or relative to the global or WCS. The number of UCSs within a drawing is unlimited, but the drawing will have only one WCS—it's the global default. Some of the many proprietary CAD systems on the market include an *Object Coordinate System (OCS)* or an *Entity Coordinate System (ECS)*. These systems aren't local or global, but are merely attached to the object about which they were made. They can't be set or changed by the user—they're defined by the entity.

World Coordinate System

The World Coordinate System of AutoCAD is the standard or default UCS. This basic WCS system is adequate for most users creating 2D drawings—they just want to draw using X and Y coordinates and keep to a simple plan view or Top work plane. You can recognize the WCS by the UCS icon in the lower-left corner of your screen, which displays an X, Y, and W to indicate it's in WCS default mode. AutoCAD always adopts the WCS at the start of a new drawing, assuming you haven't replaced it with a different UCS in your template start file. Here's a hint: Always try to keep the origin in the lower-left corner of the 3D model you create at 0,0,0. Doing so maintains positive points and positive lengths in your 3D model's geometry, which is important because older NC (numerically controlled) machines don't interpret negative coordinates or negative lengths.

User Coordinate System

Drawing in 3D requires you to move around your drawing in 3D space to access different drawing planes or construction planes—for example, the Top, Front, and Profile planes. When you move the UCS origin point away from the default WCS of 0,0,0 into 3D space or any 2D space, both the icon and the name will change. The icon is now called the UCS icon as opposed to the WCS icon. All UCSs are coordinate systems established by the user. However, 3D solid models often require you to establish one or more UCSs with new 0,0,0 origins. The purpose of these new origins is to set up different planes and/or axes that point in different directions. AutoCAD doesn't limit the number of UCS systems in a drawing, so you may set up as many UCS systems as you need.

Realize that once you've defined a new UCS, all the coordinates you enter and all the coordinates displayed are based on this UCS. However, you may override a UCS and enter WCS drawing coordinates if you precede your data entries with an asterisk. For example, if you were in a UCS and you entered "*100,140,80" or "@*50<60<30", AutoCAD would interpret these values as WCS coordinates and treat them as such within the drawing. (The asterisk acts as an override control.)

Here are a few other points to remember about using a UCS:

- You may use the asterisk as a switch between the WCS and UCS at any time during the drawing process.

- The UCS is independent of the current viewpoint, although the viewpoint can automatically be tied into the current UCS.

- Even though you may have multiple viewports activated, you may have only one UCS active at a time.

- Because the UCS and the viewpoint don't necessarily coincide, you'll want to pay close attention to the UCS icon's appearance to help you see the current orientation of the three axes. See Figure 3.2 for some examples.

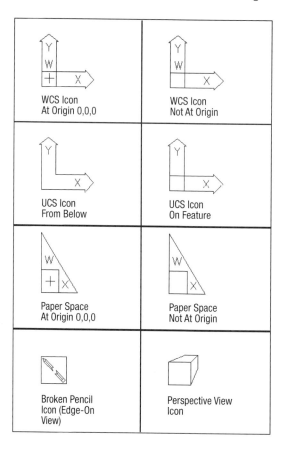

Figure 3.2
The various UCS icons.

- When you save a drawing, the current UCS is saved with it and automatically becomes the initial coordinate system when you open that drawing the next time.

- Remember to keep the UCS origin in the lower-left corner of the 3D model you create at 0,0,0. Doing so maintains positive points and positive lengths in your 3D model's geometry, which is important because older numerically controlled (NC) machines don't interpret negative coordinates or negative lengths.

The Right-Hand Rule

In AutoCAD and most other CAD systems, all the 2D or 3D geometric data of your drawing entities is stored in relationship to a coordinate system, along with the drawing's orientation to the coordinate system through the right-hand rule. The right-hand rule is simply an orientation mnemonic to help you visualize where the X, Y, and Z axes are oriented in 3D space. (The majority of CAD systems use the right-hand rule for their coordinate system, with a few using the left-hand rule.) According to the right-hand rule, the X, Y, and Z axes are always oriented in relation to each other as illustrated in Figure 3.3. When your right hand is positioned with your thumb symbolizing the positive X axis and the first finger representing the positive Y axis, the positive Z axis points in the direction of the second finger.

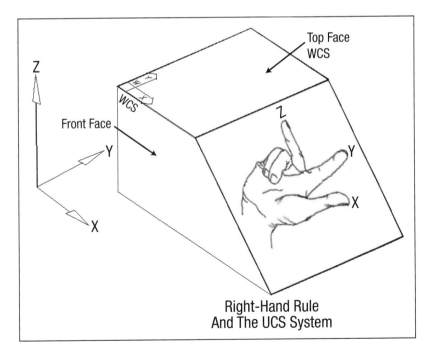

Right-Hand Rule
And The UCS System

Figure 3.3
Right-hand rule to show X, Y, and Z on the right hand.

In addition, working with 3D requires that you rotate objects frequently about a given axis. This rotation follows a variable of the right-hand rule. The variable is such that when the thumb of your right hand points along the positive direction of a given axis, as you see in Figure 3.4, then positive rotation about that axis follows the direction of your curled fingers.

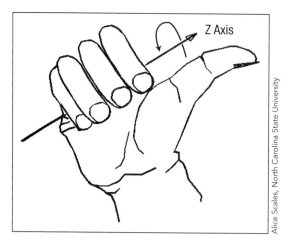

Figure 3.4
Using the right-hand rule for rotation.

So how does this right-hand rule apply to orthographic projection? To answer this question, you need to think back to the multiview drawings in Chapter 2, and how and why you placed them. If you remember, the Top view shows width and depth, the Front view shows width and height, and the Side view shows depth and height. Each of these multiview situations shows only two out of three coordinates, because in any view you're looking straight down on only one of the three planes (the Horizontal plane, the Front plane, or the Profile plane).

Construction Planes

Even though a construction plane may exist in the permanent WCS, generally, a *construction plane* is any X-Y plane of a temporary or auxiliary coordinate system, such as AutoCAD's UCS. A construction plane, or *work plane*, lets you work on an entity that can't be edited in its own plane or the global coordinate system. Many construction planes may be defined in model space, but only one is active at any given moment.

You may wonder why we need different coordinate systems or construction planes and why we can't have a simple, static global system. The reason is that complex 3D geometry is difficult and sometimes impossible to construct if you have only a single X-Y construction plane attached to a basic global or WCS. By working with the flexible UCS, AutoCAD provides you the versatility to place your X-Y construction planes anywhere in space and orient them at any angle. This adaptability lets you place multiple entities into a complex configuration using simple X-Y distances in the new X-Y plane. Let's work through a sample 3D problem that uses all three planes (see Figure 3.5).

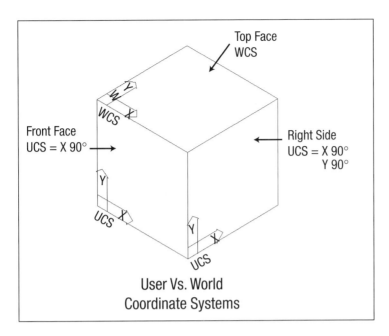

User Vs. World
Coordinate Systems

Figure 3.5
Construction planes (work planes)
in model space.

Using Construction Planes To Create Profiles

From the CD-ROM, open the work-plane.dwg drawing. This drawing is in metric. (You'll find that it's equivalent to the 3D setup drawing you created in the last chapter with a single 3D viewport.) Within the drawing file is a cube; *Top*, *Front*, and *Side* are written on the cube's faces to help you visualize as you create your profiles. (You'll freeze the layer Cube, the layer where the entities exist, later.) The objective of the exercise is to create a series of work planes and 3D profiles in the Top, Front, and Side view planes. To achieve this, you'll work with the UCSs as construction planes for these views and then extrude the 3D profiles into a solid model.

First, because you're in the WCS, you can use it for the Top view and Top construction plane. You need to create the Front UCS and the Side UCS construction planes. Make your Front construction plane by rotating the UCS about the X axis 90 degrees. Respond to the UCS commands as follows:

```
Command: ucs
Current UCS name: *WORLD*
Enter an option [New/Move/orthoGraphic/Prev/Restore/Save/Del/
  Apply/?/World] <World>: n
Specify origin of new UCS or [ZAxis/3point/OBject/Face/View/
  X/Y/Z] <0,0,0>: x
Specify rotation angle about X axis <90>: 90 <or press Enter>
```

At this point, notice that your UCS rotated itself into a vertical position and the *W* disappeared, indicating the UCS is no longer in WCS mode. (This may be difficult to see because it sits adjacent to the left side UCS drawn on the cube, but the point to notice is that the UCS did rotate itself into the vertical position.) You'll now save this UCS as *Front*, and the name will appear in the new AutoCAD 2000 UCS dialog box. You activate this new AutoCAD 2000 command with **UCSMAN**, short for *UCS manager*. So let's save your UCS to Front first and then we'll look at **UCSMAN**:

```
Command: ucs
Current UCS name: *NO NAME*
Enter an option [New/Move/orthoGraphic/Prev/Restore/Save/Del/
  Apply/?/World] <World>:s
Enter name to save current UCS or [?]: front
```

Repeat the UCS command to create the Side construction plane, and you'll be ready to draw. You need to rotate the UCS again by 90 degrees in the Y direction and then save the setting. Let's perform both steps at once this time:

```
Command: ucs
Current ucs name: front (indicates you're currently set to front)
Enter an option [New/Move/orthoGraphic/Prev/Restore/Save/Del/
  Apply/?/World] <World>: n
Specify origin of new UCS or [ZAxis/3point/Object/Face/View/
  X/Y/Z] <0,0,0>: y
Specify rotation angle about Y axis <90>: 90

Command: ucs
Current UCS name: *NO NAME*
Enter an option [New/Move/orthoGraphic/Prev/Restore/Save/Del/
  Apply/?/World] <World>: s
Enter name to save current UCS or [?]: side
```

Choose Named UCS from the Tools menu to activate the UCS dialog box. Or, at the keyboard, use the new AutoCAD 2000 command **UCSMAN**. In Figure 3.6, the names *Side* and *Front* appear in the Named UCSs page of the dialog box. Your three construction planes are World, Front, and Side.

To recap, the Top plane is in the World Coordinate System. The Front and Side planes are named accordingly. Referring to Figure 3.6, pick the World

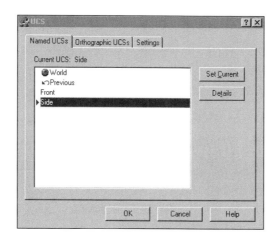

Figure 3.6
The new AutoCAD 2000 UCS dialog box.

name option and click on Set Current. Then, click on OK. Now, you're ready to draw your 3D profiles and extrude them into a 3D solid.

At this point, you'll begin working in the different construction planes you just created. Figure 3.7 shows the dimensions for the completed 3D model. You'll break it down into three profiles for the Top, Front, and Side construction planes. You'll then extrude and solidify them simultaneously with one of the AutoCAD 2000 solids-editing commands. Remember that this drawing is in METRIC; you can create it in several easy steps. You'll see a general outline of the steps listed first, which gives you the overall picture; then, you can work through the specific commands at your own pace.

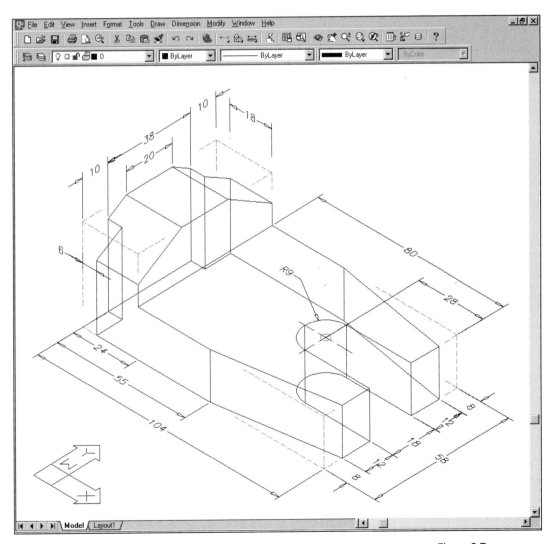

Figure 3.7
Dimensioned pictorial of the 3D model.

1. Freeze the Cube layer before you start the drawing.

2. Set the UCS to World and to the Top work plane. Set the current layer to Top and create the Top profile.

3. Set the layer to Front. Restore the UCS to the Front work plane and create the Front profile.

4. Set the layer to Side. Restore the UCS to the Side work plane and create the Side profile.

5. Reset the UCS to World.

6. From the Modify menu choose Solids Editing and the **INTERSECT** command. Pick all three components you just created. Wait for the results, change the color of your model to an AutoCAD Color Index of 140, and then shade the model.

If you only need practice at using the **EXTRUDE** command and want to use the quick steps just listed, the work-profile.dwg drawing is available on the CD-ROM. It contains all the profiles, ready to extrude, along with the UCS settings and the layers required. Otherwise, read the following sections for more detailed instructions on how to create a simple 3D model.

Using Profiles To Create Your 3D Model

Referring back to the six steps just listed, let's examine the detailed sequence of commands you'll go through to create the simple 3D model. First, check to make sure you've frozen the Cube layer. Next, be sure the Top layer is current and you're in World (WCS) mode. Refer to Figure 3.8 for the absolute coordinates.

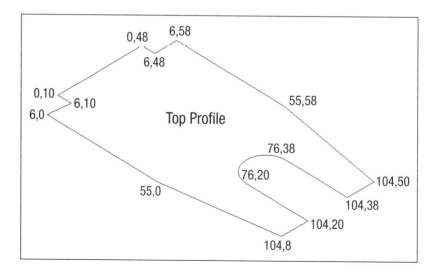

Figure 3.8
Creating the Top profile.

Creating The Top Profile

Use the **POLYLINE** command to create the first profile as follows:

```
Command: pline
Specify start point: 6,0
Current line-width is 0.0000
Specify next point or [Arc/Close/Halfwidth/Length/Undo/Width]: 6,10
Specify next point or [Arc/Close/Halfwidth/Length/Undo/Width]:
  0,10
Specify next point or [Arc/Close/Halfwidth/Length/Undo/Width]:
  0,48
Specify next point or [Arc/Close/Halfwidth/Length/Undo/Width]:
  6,48
Specify next point or [Arc/Close/Halfwidth/Length/Undo/Width]:
  6,58
Specify next point or [Arc/Close/Halfwidth/Length/Undo/Width]:
  55,58
Specify next point or [Arc/Close/Halfwidth/Length/Undo/Width]:
  104,50
Specify next point or [Arc/Close/Halfwidth/Length/Undo/Width]:
  104,38
Specify next point or [Arc/Close/Halfwidth/Length/Undo/Width]:
  76,38
Specify next point or [Arc/Close/Halfwidth/Length/Undo/Width]: a
  (for arc)
[Angle/CEnter/CLose/Direction/Halfwidth/Line/Radius/Second pt/
  Undo/Width]: 76,20
[Angle/CEnter/CLose/Direction/Halfwidth/Line/Radius/Second pt/
  Undo/Width]: l (for line)
Specify next point or [Arc/Close/Halfwidth/Length/Undo/Width]:
  104,20
Specify next point or [Arc/Close/Halfwidth/Length/Undo/Width]:
  104,8
Specify next point or [Arc/Close/Halfwidth/Length/Undo/Width]:
  55,0
Specify next point or [Arc/Close/Halfwidth/Length/Undo/Width]:
  6,0
Specify next point or [Arc/Close/Halfwidth/Length/Undo/Width]: c
  (for close)
```

The first profile is now complete. You may want to freeze the layer, but before you do set the current layer to Front. Refer to Figure 3.9 for the absolute coordinates and restore the UCS to the Front work plane.

Creating The Front Profile

Create the Front profile as follows:

```
Command: pline
Specify start point: 0,0
Current line-width is 0.0000
Specify next point or [Arc/Close/Halfwidth/Length/Undo/Width]:
  104,0
```

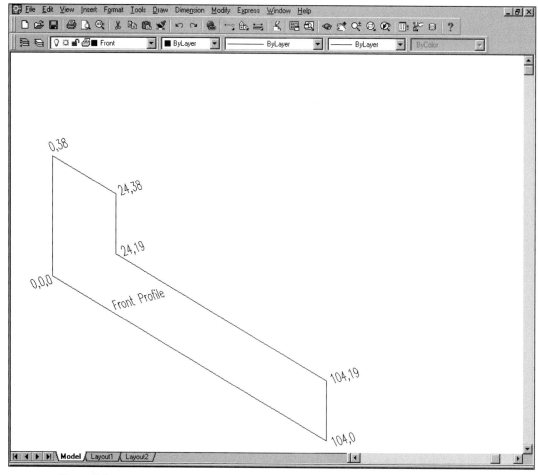

Figure 3.9

Creating the Front profile.

```
Specify next point or [Arc/Close/Halfwidth/Length/Undo/Width]:
  104,19
Specify next point or [Arc/Close/Halfwidth/Length/Undo/Width]:
  24,19
Specify next point or [Arc/Close/Halfwidth/Length/Undo/Width]:
  24,38
Specify next point or [Arc/Close/Halfwidth/Length/Undo/Width]:
  0,38
Specify next point or [Arc/Close/Halfwidth/Length/Undo/Width]: c
  (for close)
```

The second profile is now complete. Again, you may want to freeze the layer, but before you do, set the layer to Side.

Creating The Side Profile

Referring to Figure 3.10, restore the UCS to the Side work plane and create the Side profile as follows:

```
Command: pline
Specify start point: 0,0
```

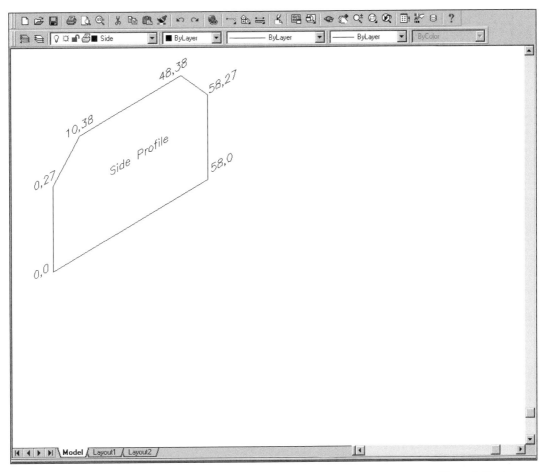

Figure 3.10
Creating the Side profile.

```
Current line-width is 0.0000
Specify next point or [Arc/Close/Halfwidth/Length/Undo/Width]:
  58,0
Specify next point or [Arc/Close/Halfwidth/Length/Undo/Width]:
  58,27
Specify next point or [Arc/Close/Halfwidth/Length/Undo/Width]:
  48,38
Specify next point or [Arc/Close/Halfwidth/Length/Undo/Width]:
  10,38
Specify next point or [Arc/Close/Halfwidth/Length/Undo/Width]:
  0,27
Specify next point or [Arc/Close/Halfwidth/Length/Undo/Width]: c
  (for close)
```

The third profile is complete. You need to thaw the Top and Front layers, and then set the current layer to 0. Restore the UCS to the World (WCS) mode. Refer to Figure 3.11 to see the three profiles.

Extruding The Profiles

Now you need to extrude each of the profiles in turn. At the keyboard, use the **UCSMAN** command to activate the UCS dialog box. Choose World, click

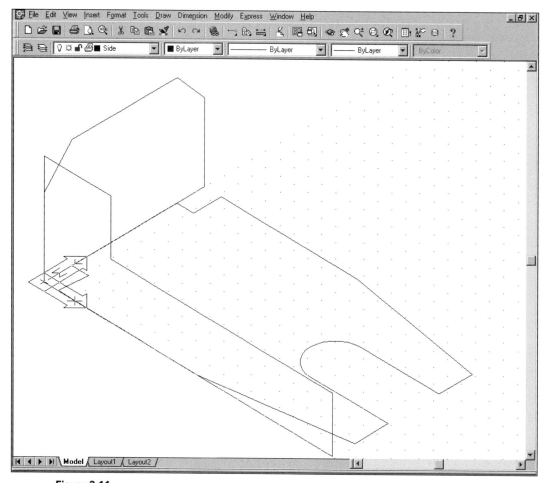

Figure 3.11

The complete profiles before solids extrusion.

on Set Current, and then click on OK. Doing so restores the Top work plane. Now, follow these steps:

1. Choose the Extrude option from the Draw|Solids menu. Extrude the Top profile up 38mm, using 0 taper to the extrusion.

2. Activate the **UCSMAN** command and restore the Front UCS work plane.

3. Choose the Extrude option from the Draw menu. Extrude the Front profile away from you -58mm. (That's minus 58, because Z points away from you.) Use 0 taper to the extrusion.

4. Activate the **UCSMAN** command and restore the Side UCS work plane.

5. Choose the Extrude option from the Draw menu. Extrude the Side profile 104mm, using 0 taper to the extrusion. Figure 3.12 shows the three extruded profiles prior to using the **INTERSECT** command.

6. Reset your UCS back to the World system; then, from the Modify menu, choose Solids Editing and the Intersect option. Pick the three

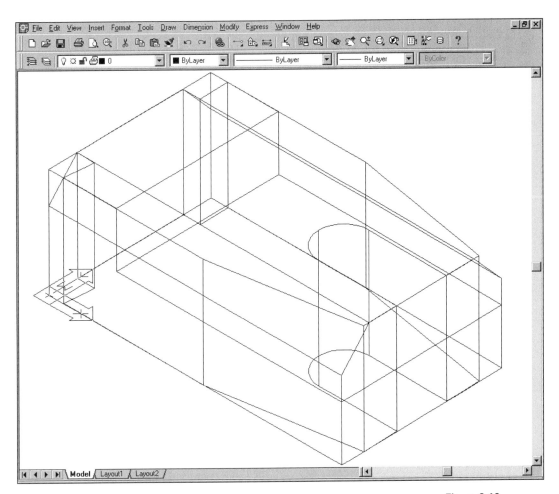

Figure 3.12
The complete profiles before using **INTERSECT**.

components you just created and then press Enter. Wait for the results. (You may want to change the color of model, perhaps to number 9 or 140.) Shade the model, then use the **SHADEMODE** command with its 2D option to return to your wireframe. Figure 3.13 shows the completed model.

So, what did you learn from this exercise? You found that creating different 2D work planes allows you to draw and extrude multiple 2D profiles into 3D solids quickly. And with those profiles, you can use the **INTERSECT** command to create a fast 3D working model. You can use this technique to improve your efficiency as you create rough 3D working models.

Review Of The User Coordinate System

The **UCS** command creates, saves, or restores a User Coordinate System. Let's review some of the many options of the **UCS** command. The Tools menu contains four UCS options: Named UCS, Orthographic UCS, Move

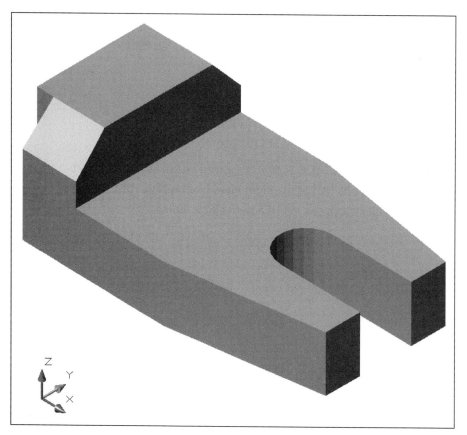

Figure 3.13
The completed model.

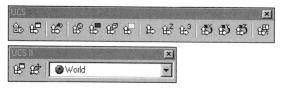

Figure 3.14
The UCS toolbars.

UCS, and New UCS. You may also access these options from the UCS and UCS-II toolbars, shown in Figure 3.14.

The UCS options are as follows:

- *Named UCS*—Provides functions to manage the use of named UCSs. The icon, found under the expanded UCS button on the main toolbar or the Tools menu (as Named UCS...) opens the UCS dialog box, which you accessed earlier by keying in the **UCSMAN** command. You cannot program the Named UCSs in the UCS dialog box directly; you have to key in the **UCS** command and set your UCSs from the command line prompt. Then, use the dialog box to access the different UCS values. Note the six predefined orthographic values found under the Orthographic UCS tab, built in to get you started: Top, Bottom, Front, Back, Left, and Right. It's also important to note that in the UCS dialog box, the UCS Settings tab offers you the option to Update View To Plan When UCS Is Changed. This option sets the UCSFOLLOW variable to 1 or 0. If you place a checkmark in the box, AutoCAD will automatically establish the plan view each time you change to a new UCS.

- *Orthographic UCS*—These options let you access six predefined built-in values: Top, Bottom, Front, Back, Left, and Right. These values were created about the WCS, so the Top view is the same as the current view. Bottom sets the UCS to the Bottom view, Left sets the UCS to the Left view, Right sets the UCS to the Right view, Front sets the UCS to the Front view, and Back sets the UCS to the Back view.

- *Move UCS*—This option lets you move the origin of the UCS icon to a new X, Y, or Z location on your drawing.

- *New UCS*—As shown in Figure 3.15, this option lets you set your UCS to World, Object, Face, or View, in addition to the Plus Origin, Z axis Vector, 3 Point, and X, Y, and Z filters you used earlier. (The next section describes the UCS setting options in more detail.)

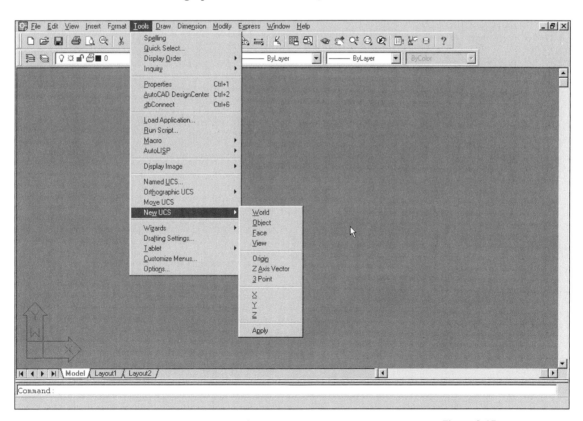

Figure 3.15
The New UCS submenu.

The UCS options

Let's examine the various options you can use to set the UCS. Begin by choosing the UCS icon located in the Standard toolbar or enter "UCS" at the command prompt. Notice the options provided:

```
Command: ucs
Enter an option [New/Move/orthoGraphic/Prev/Restore/Save/Del/
  Apply/?/World] <World>: n
```

If you enter "N", you have further options:

```
Specify origin of new UCS or [ZAxis/3point/OBject/Face/View/
  X/Y/Z] <0,0,0>:
```

Let's first look at the new UCS options (see Figure 3.16) and then come back to the remainder. Entering "N" leads to this subset of additional options (beyond the default options, which I'll discuss next):

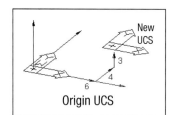

Figure 3.16
Origin UCS.

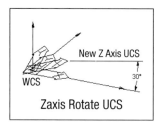

Figure 3.17
Zaxis rotate UCS.

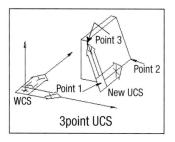

Figure 3.18
3point UCS.

- *New Origin*—You may pick or enter coordinates for the origin of a new UCS. In turn, this option moves the coordinate system to a new origin away from the location of your current system. The X, Y, and Z axes still point in the same directions as your current system. See Figure 3.16.

- *Zaxis*—The Z axis vector allows you to enter new coordinates for the origin of a new UCS (which is different from the origin of your current system) followed by a point through which the positive Z axis will pass. (Hint: This option is extremely useful if you need to quickly designate a new Z direction in order to extrude an object, but you don't mind which direction your X and Y axes point.) See Figure 3.17.

- *3point*—This option lets you enter three points to determine a new UCS: the origin point, a point on the positive X axis, and a point on the positive Y half of the X-Y plane. Once the X and Y axes are determined, the Z axis is determined by the right-hand rule. (Hint: This option is extremely useful if you need to set a new coordinate system to an object feature of your 3D model. To connect precisely to an object feature, don't forget to use your Object Snap [OSNAP] modes.) See Figure 3.18.

- *Object*—Using an object in your drawing as a feature (such as a solid, an arc, or a circle) is a useful method of defining a new UCS. Remember, the positive Z axis will be oriented toward the same direction as when the object was created. See the next section for tips on using objects with the UCS.) See Figure 3.19.

- *Face*—This new feature lets you set the face of your 3D model as a UCS. It prompts you to select the face of your solid object—you can specify any face to which you need to move. Then the feature prompts you to enter an option (such as Next/Xflip/Yflip) or press Enter to accept the chosen face. See Figure 3.20.

- *View*—Using this option, you can adopt the current viewing direction as the direction of the negative Z axis (the origin remains unchanged). Basically, it orients the UCS to be coplanar with your computer screen, so you're looking directly at the UCS as you look at your monitor. (Hint: The View option is handy when you want to plot a drawing from a particular viewpoint, it will allow you to place text in the drawing so that the text will appear straight on when plotted.) See Figure 3.21.

- *X/Y/Z*—The X Axis Rotate, Y Axis Rotate, and Z Axis Rotate filters let you rotate X, Y, or Z by any angle, either by entering an angle from the keyboard or by picking two points. You used this feature in one of the earlier exercises. The filter rotates the new coordinate system around the specified axis. (The origin remains unchanged.) Remember, the right-hand rule determines the direction of rotation. See Figure 3.22.

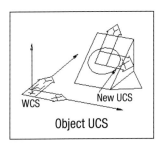

Figure 3.19
Object UCS.

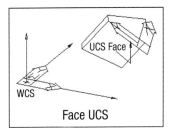

Figure 3.20
Face UCS.

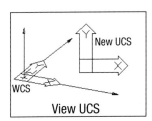

Figure 3.21
View UCS.

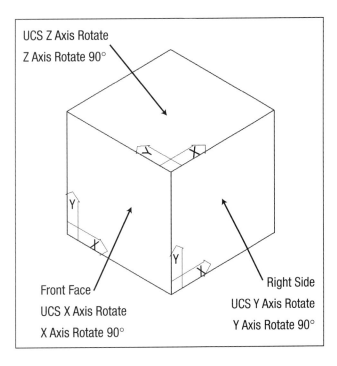

Figure 3.22
X/Y/Z axis rotate options.

If you don't press N, you get to choose from these default options:

- *Move*—This option lets you move your UCS to another location.

- *OrthoGraphic*—This option switches your UCS into orthographic mode.

- *Prev*—The Previous option lets you return to the previous coordinate system. AutoCAD will remember your 10 previous coordinate systems, regardless of whether you saved them (that is, whether they're named or unnamed).

- *Restore*—Restore is a subcommand that allows you to restore a named UCS. Using the Restore option is faster than setting a new UCS each time.

- *Save*—The Save feature lets you save a UCS to a name of your choice. You should get into the habit of saving and naming your UCSs.

- *Del*—The Del option allows you to delete a named UCS.

- *Apply*—The Apply option lets you choose a viewport to which you can apply the current UCS. The default is current.

- *?*—When you forget the named coordinate systems you've created, the ? option will help you remember them.

- *World*—This option resets AutoCAD to the WCS from the current coordinate system.

Tips For Using Objects With The UCS

The Object Coordinate System (OCS) lets you use an object to determine a new coordinate system. It's a quick yet useful method of defining a new UCS by simply attaching it to one of the objects in your drawing. One point to note is that the positive Z axis of the object is oriented in the same direction as when the object was first created. This orientation, in turn, forces the X-Y axis to be parallel to the X-Y plane that was in use when the object was first created; however, the direction of the X and Y axes may differ. AutoCAD lets you use several types of objects, including: 2D polyline, arc, circle, dimension, face inserted block or attribute, line, point, and solid. Figure 3.23 illustrates some of these object types.

The object coordinate system has specific ways in which the starting point, the new UCS origin, and the X axis and Y axis are reattached to a chosen object. If ever you decide to use the object coordinate system, here are the ways to use OCSs with these object types:

- *2D polyline*—The starting point of the 2D polyline becomes your new origin, and the positive X axis runs through the polyline's next vertex.

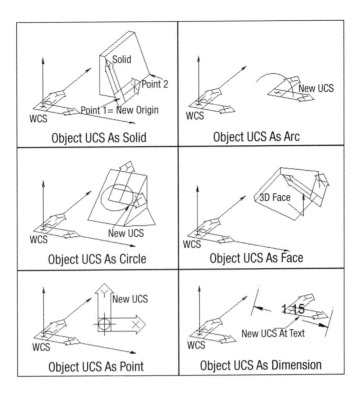

Figure 3.23
Using objects with the UCS.

- *3D face*—The first point of the **3D Face** command becomes your new origin, the positive X axis runs through the second point, and the fourth point lies on the positive half of the X-Y plane. (Note: Remember, the **3DFACE** command works in a butterfly method exactly like the **2DSOLID** command by using pickpoints **1, 2, 4,** then **3**—not in a standard clockwise direction as pickpoints **1, 2, 3, 4.** See Figure 3.24. The only difference between the **3DFACE** and **2DSOLID** commands is that **3DFACE** allows different Z coordinates.)

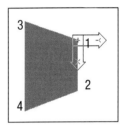

Figure 3.24
The **3DFACE** command.

- *Arc*—The center of an arc becomes your new origin, and the positive X axis runs through the end of the arc that's visually nearest the pick point.

- *Circle*—The center of a circle becomes your new origin, and the X axis runs through the pick point.

- *Dimension*—The middle point of the dimension text becomes your new origin, and the positive X axis runs the same direction as the positive X axis in effect when the dimension was drawn.

- *Inserted item (for example, a block, text, attribute tag, or attribute value)*—The insertion point becomes the new origin, and its rotation angle is 0 of the new UCS.

- *Line*—The end point of a line nearest to the pick point becomes your new origin, and the positive X axis usually runs through the other end of the line.

- *Point*—The central location of a point (the insertion point) becomes its new origin, and AutoCAD determines the rest.

- *Solid*—The first point of a solid becomes the new origin, and the positive X axis runs through its second point.

The **UCSICON** Command

The **UCSICON** command lets you control the display of the UCS icon. Once you understand the UCS icon, you'll find that it gives you valuable information about your current coordinate system. When you set the UCS icon, the command affects the current viewport.

AutoCAD uses a number of basic icon symbols, both in model space and paper space, to indicate what's happening with the current UCS; refer back to Figure 3.2 to review the basic UCS icon symbol shapes. For example, when your current UCS is in the WCS, you'll see a *W* in the Y part of the UCS icon. Alternately, when your UCS icon is at the origin of your current coordinate system, you'll see a plus sign (+) in the UCS icon. When your current viewpoint is looking at your 3D model from underneath (where it originates from a negative Z location), the square box in the corner of your UCS icon is absent.

If you enter "UCSICON" at the command prompt, you have a number of choices: ON, OFF, All, Noorigin, and Origin. The default is ON.

You may turn the UCS icon on or off in your current viewport. The All option is used as an exception to allow you to change all your viewports to the same setting simultaneously—it simply copies the current X, Y, and Z settings of your UCS icon to all your other viewports. When you use the Origin option, AutoCAD toggles on and/or off the location of your icon from the origin of your current coordinate system. For example, it changes the location of the UCS icon from the origin point to the lower-left corner of the chosen viewport.

In addition to the default icon, your UCS icon can appear as a broken pencil in a box or as a cube, as you saw in Figure 3.2. For example, when your direction of view is parallel to the X-Y work plane of the current UCS, the icon appears as a broken pencil in a box. (Hint: When this UCS icon occurs, you can always change your UCS view direction.) When you're in a perspective view, the UCS icon will appear as a cube. Finally, AutoCAD indicates that you're in paper space by displaying the triangular icon shown in Figure 3.2. These alternate symbols operate the same way as the standard UCS.

Hiding Construction Lines In Paper Space

When you place a 3D pictorial into a multiview drawing in paper space, you're often required to hide lines in order to provide more realism in your 3D model. If you were simply drawing in model space and you needed to hide lines, you'd simply check the Hide Lines box in the Print dialog box. This isn't the case with paper space: You have to use the **MVIEW** command.

For this example, assume that you have four viewports in paper space, that you're creating multiview drawings in third-angle projection, and that you want to hide lines in the upper-right pictorial viewport. Also, assume that at print time you don't want to hide lines in the remaining three viewports.

As long as you choose the Layout1 tab, it doesn't matter if you're in model space or paper space. The **MVIEW** command will switch you to the correct space from model space or paper space and then back to where you started. To hide lines in paper space, first make sure that the Hide Lines checkbox in your Print dialog box is *not* checked. If it is, AutoCAD may want to hide the lines in all your viewports—not just the one you select. Now, respond to the command prompts as follows:

```
Command: mview
[ON/OFF/Fit/Hideplot/Lock/Object/Polygonal/Restore/2/3/4]
  <Fit>: h
Hidden line removal for plotting [ON/OFF]: on
Select objects: <Pick the border of the upper-right viewport and
  press Enter>
```

The viewport you select with the **HIDEPLOT** option of **MVIEW** hides your 3D model lines when you next print.

Hiding Viewport Borders

Professional multiview drawings don't show viewport borders. They're clean, neat, crisp drawings. Still, you may ask how you can hide your paper space borders and keep the viewports without erasing any part of your drawing, as shown in Figure 3.25.

The answer lies in the fact that when paper space viewports are created, they're entities. If you place these entities onto layers—such as a **VPORTS** layer—then just before you print, you can simply freeze the layer. Freezing the layer doesn't affect what's in the viewports, but it changes the visibility of the borders for the viewports.

Paper Space Scaling

How often have you plotted a drawing and found it was the wrong scale? Or brought a model space drawing into paper space and printed it, only to find that it wasn't to scale? *Zoom scaling* is a feature of paper space that allows you to create different scales in different viewports on the same sheet.

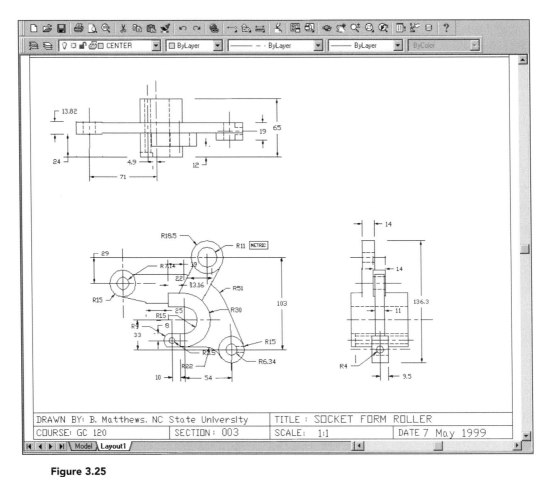

Figure 3.25

Typical drawing of Top, Front, and Right Side views in paper space without borders and without a pictorial view.

It's one of the most valuable features of paper space, and it doesn't matter if you're drawing in 2D or 3D—the zoom feature and technique work equally well for both 2D and 3D drawings. Here's how to use the **XP** option of the **ZOOM** command in paper space.

First, note that the model's physical size doesn't change in any way. (A size change occurs with the **SCALE** command.) The **ZOOM** command uses **XP** at the end of the **ZOOM** factor to view the scale of the image in the active viewport by the ratio you entered. For example, if you had a large drawing of a machined part on screen and you entered "ZOOM 2xp", the drawing in the viewport would be set to a scale twice that of full size in paper space. Thus, what has changed is the **ZOOM**ed view of your entity in relation to the paper space units. As a result, you have a correctly scaled picture of exactly what your final print will look like.

Printing Multiple Scales On The Same Drawing Sheet

A particularly attractive feature of paper space is that in addition to producing multiple drawings on the same sheet, you can also set drawing scales. By using **ZOOM *n*XP** (where ***n*** is the scale variable), you can also set different scales to each of those multiple drawings on that same sheet. To scale a single mechanical drawing, for example, you might need it set to 1=10. Thus, your **ZOOM *n*XP** factor would be set to 1/10xp within the viewport. Using a 1=100 scale factor, the **ZOOM** would be set to 1/100xp. Or, using a 1=1.25 scale factor, you'd set the **ZOOM** to 1/1.25xp, and so on. Let's see how it's done, first for mechanical scales and then for architectural scales.

Mechanical Example

This particular mechanical example uses metric scales, but the principle is the same whatever type of scale you're using. Open the metric-scale.dwg drawing from the CD-ROM. The drawing includes a pre-inserted file that's zoomed to incorrect multiple configurations in its three viewports. The trick is to use the **ZOOM Center** feature in each of the viewports, thereby zooming and centering the image of your model about the same center coordinate you've chosen. Follow these steps:

1. Choose the Layout1 tab to enter paper space. Then, use the **MS** command to enter model space and pick the upper-left viewport. Within this viewport, do a **ZOOM Center** set to 0,0,0, and then a **ZOOM** magnification of 1/20xp.

2. Repeat the procedure for the lower-left viewport. First do a **ZOOM Center** set to 0,0,0, and then a **ZOOM** magnification of 1/20xp. You now have two viewports scaled correctly to a 1=20 scale factor.

3. Pick the far-right viewport. Again, set **ZOOM Center** to 0,0,0, and then do a **ZOOM** magnification of 1/10xp. Use the **PS** command to get back to paper space.

4. Remember to use the **MVIEW** command and use the **Hideplot** subcommand on the pictorial viewport. Also turn off the **VPORTS** layer.

5. You're now ready to print the drawing. When you do so, remember to be in paper space and to set the Print dialog box to print at the Extents, at a 1=1 scale factor, and to mm.

Architectural Example

Here's another example: Open the arch-scale.dwg drawing from the CD-ROM. Again, this example has six pre-inserted files, some of which are zoomed to a wrong scale. The example will use three architectural scales: 1/4"=1', 1/2"=1', and 1"=1'. The drawing limits in paper space are set from 0,0 to 34,22. The limits then let you plot at a scale of 1=1 from paper space, which is the true size of a 34×22 sheet of paper, as shown in Figure 3.26.

On the sheet is a plan view of a large architectural area, which you'll set to 1/4"=1'. You'll set a detail to 1/2"=1' and an enlarged detail to 1"=1'.

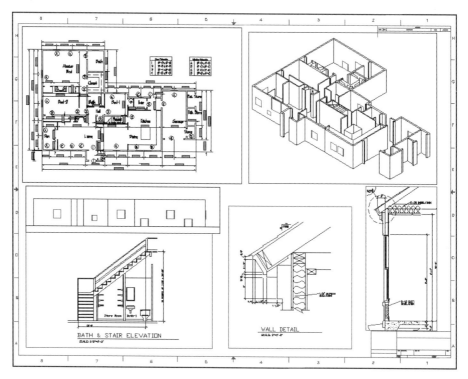

Figure 3.26

Architectural drawing with multiple drawing scales.

(The remaining views are correct.) Let's take the plan view first, because this view will be plotted at 1/4"=1'. Check to ensure you are in the Layout1 tab, and then use the **MS** command and pick the upper-left viewport. Next, you'll use the **ZOOM Center** option with a magnification of 1/48xp. (Note: In each of the viewports you are going to work with in this example, the UCS Origin was set to a specific 0,0,0 location at the center of each drawing to speed up the exercise.) You may wonder how you calculate architectural scales. And, how do you change 1/4"=1' into 1/48xp, to use with the **ZOOM** command? To answer this question, you calculate the 1/48xp as 4 times 12 equals 48 (that is, 12 inches to a foot and 4 quarters within an inch). If you calculate the 1/2"=1' scale, you'll need to set the scale to 1/24xp. Follow these steps:

1. Choose the Layout1 tab to enter paper space. Use the **MS** command to change to model space and then pick the upper-left viewport. Within this viewport, first do a **ZOOM Center** set to 0,0,0, and then a **ZOOM** magnification of 1/48xp. This command will scale the plan view to the correct scale for plotting.

2. Repeat the procedure for the lower-left viewport. First do a **ZOOM Center** at 0,0,0, and then a **ZOOM** magnification of 1/24xp. You now have two viewports scaled correctly to a plot scale factor.

3. Pick the lower far right viewport. Again, set it to a **ZOOM Center** of 0,0,0, and then a **ZOOM** magnification of 1/16xp. Use the **PS** command to get back to paper space. Note: The lower middle viewport is preset to 1/3xp.

4. Remember to use the **MVIEW** command and use the **Hideplot** subcommand on the pictorial viewport and on the front elevation viewport. Then turn off the **VPORTS** layer.

5. Finally, you're ready to plot the drawing. When you do so, remember to be in paper space and to set the Plot dialog box to print at the Extents, at a 1=1 scale, factor, and the Printable Area to inches.

Realtime Scaling And Printing

Here are some hints to keep in mind when you're using the *n*XP feature of **ZOOM**, before you start to print or plot your drawings:

- For a professional-looking drawing, don't plot the borders of the viewport: Turn off or freeze the **VPORTS** layer. Remember, viewport borders are entities, and they can be placed on layers. If you use the **SOLVIEW** command for multiview drawings, your viewports are created on the **VPORTS** layer. When you turn the **VPORTS** layer off, your viewport borders disappear.

- Don't forget to revert to paper space before you print. You do so in order to print the entire paper space. If you're in model space and in a viewport when you print, AutoCAD will only print one view.

- Once you've used the **ZOOM** *n*XP feature, try not to **ZOOM** again in that viewport. Instead, use the **PAN** command to move about. If it's imperative to use **ZOOM**, then simply reapply the **ZOOM** *n*XP feature again before you print.

- Changing the size of the viewport can also affect the size of the model image. If you need to change the size of the viewport itself, remember to reapply the **ZOOM** *n*XP feature in that viewport.

Lining Up Drawings In Viewports

Here are more hints to keep in mind when you're working with viewports and before you start to print or plot your drawings. If you have drawings within viewports that are misarranged and they're in first-angle or third-angle projection, the views of your drawings may also be misaligned. Good drawing practice is for the Top, Front, and Side views to be aligned both vertically and horizontally. The easiest way to do this is to use the standard

Viewport dialog box to create and save views. Then, use **ZOOM Center** with a **ZOOM** *n***XP** magnification in each of the viewports that have to be aligned.

You just used the **ZOOM Center** along with the **ZOOM** *n***XP** magnification feature in the previous examples. Notice that this feature also centrally locates the images within the viewports, placing them in mid-position within each viewport as you use the command. This option lets you easily line up the models in your drawings.

Another option is to use the paper space grid to snap and size your viewports equally. If your viewports aren't equal size, simply pick on the edge of the viewport border and use the grips to manipulate it into position and size.

Some CAD operators set up a series of horizontal and vertical lines as a grid, and then snap their viewports to this grid. Doing so allows you to line up your viewports visually.

Another technique uses the **MVSETUP** command. In past AutoCAD releases, it was a bonus command, used for setting up drawing limits and drawing-sheet sizes. But one of its little-used functions aligns object entities within adjacent paper space viewports. This book's companion CD-ROM contains a drawing labeled piston-file.dwg. See Figure 3.27, which may be used for the **MVSETUP** exercise. Here's how to use **MVSETUP**:

1. Check to ensure you're in paper space and your multiple viewports are zoomed to the correct **ZOOM** *n***XP** scale (the piston-file.dwg is zoomed to the correct scale).

2. Set your OSNAP to endpoint, and then at the command prompt enter "mvsetup":

   ```
   Command: mvsetup
   ```

3. At the command prompt, enter "a" for Align:

   ```
   Enter an option [Align/Create/Scale viewports/Options/Title
     block/Undo]: a
   ```

4. From the list of suboptions that appears next, you need to choose between h for horizontal or v for vertical alignment. For the piston-file.dwg, choose v:

   ```
   Enter an option [Angled/Horizontal/Vertical alignment/Rotate
     view/Undo]: v
   ```

5. Choose a basepoint with OSNAP set to Endpoint; then, move to the next viewport and again use OSNAP set to Endpoint to pick a second

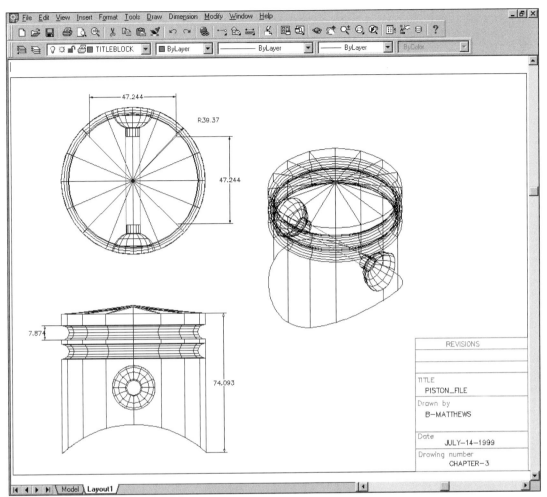

Figure 3.27
Aligned drawings in paper space viewports.

point. This second point should line up with the first basepoint of your object. In piston-file.dwg, choose the upper viewport first, with the center of the piston as your basepoint; then, pick the lower viewport and pick the top middle apex of the piston. The alignment should then be correct. See Figure 3.27.

Moving On

This chapter has taken the mystery out of the use and applications of User Coordinate Systems and provided you with examples of the many ways you can put UCSs to use. UCSs are essential components of the world of 3D, allowing you to work in different 2D construction planes within 3D space. The UCS tool is often underused or misunderstood in AutoCAD—learn it, and it will serve you well and increase your productivity.

In the next chapter, you'll review 3D views and 3D Orbit, which allows true 3D rotation of your model.

SETTING UP PERSPECTIVE 4 VIEWS

One of the final steps in 3D modeling is to generate images from 3D views. This chapter discusses the 3D viewing commands you use to create alternate 3D views.

3D Viewing

Dynamic viewing (**DVIEW**), 3D viewpoint (**DDVPOINT**), **UCS**, and **3DORBIT** are the main commands you use to set up perspective views. These commands allow you to set up 3D views from any point in model space, yet your models are still shown in wireframe view.

Once you construct your 3D model, AutoCAD lets you view it from multiple vantage points. Even though you can view your 3D model from any point in 3D model space, AutoCAD really uses only two types of views: parallel projection and perspective. Every selected view may be seen in either parallel projection or perspective projection. Parallel projection views represent the traditional drafting views; orthographic and isometrics are types of parallel projection views. Alternately, perspective views simulate real human vision or perspective, such as the type of view a camera produces. In the Color Studio in the middle of this book, you'll find examples of parallel and perspective views, including fully rendered views of assembly drawings.

3D viewing includes a variety of options designed for looking at 3D models. By now, you've realized that for 2D drawings the regular **ZOOM** and **PAN** commands are adequate. But 3D viewing or dynamic viewing of 3D models demands much more skill and expertise, along with a wider variety of 3D viewing commands (such as **DVIEW**, **DDVPOINT**, **UCS**, and **3DORBIT**). Yet, just what are the advantages of dynamic viewing?

Advantages Of 3D Viewing

When you're viewing a 3D model, it's helpful to be able to see the model from all sides and all angles. This wide array of views allows you to, for example:

- Visually interference-check the fit of parts in an assembly.

- Reference-check before sending models for rapid prototyping and design verification.

- Set the view of your 3D model to either a parallel projection view or a perspective view.

- Clip planes—that is, see inside the 3D model by clipping entities near or away from the observer through front and back clipping planes. (Both **DVIEW** and **3DORBIT** have this option.) *Clipping* is simply hiding designated front or back edges to make the view appear cropped (clipped), letting you see part of the model in detail.

- Change the 3D view of your 3D model dynamically—that is, change it visually on screen as you select a view.

The **DVIEW**, **DDVPOINT**, and **3DORBIT** commands let you work with these features and more.

Parallel And Perspective Projection

Engineering drawings use parallel projection as a standard. The theoretical viewpoint of parallel projection is an infinite distance from the model you're viewing, so the projection lines from the model to the projection plane are always parallel (hence the term *parallel projection*).

Every view you select in an engineering drawing can be seen in either a parallel projection or a perspective projection. With parallel projection, it doesn't matter if your 3D model is a long distance from the viewer or close to the viewer, because the model appears the same size on the projection plane. The projection plane can be a sheet of paper or, in this case, a display screen.

A typical engineering drawing shows how to manufacture a certain component, part, or assembly, so it's important to have precise alignment and dimensioning as standard features of such drawings. Parallel projection helps make these features standard in a CAD drawing. Standard drawing practice includes creating the drawing to national standards, and the American National Standards Institute (ANSI) defines codes and standards for the different types of engineering drawings. Working drawings, for example, include assembly drawings that show how parts fit and are assembled, along with part drawings that show how the parts are manufactured, a parts list that includes all the parts in the assembly, and specifications that show or list details for manufacture and assembly. Figure 4.1 shows an example of an aligned dimensional drawing.

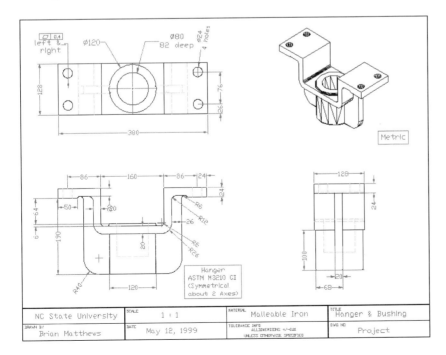

Figure 4.1

Engineering working drawing.

Filippo Brunelleschi (1377-1446), the architect of the great dome of Florence, was one of the first to rediscover the lineal perpective views that had been known to the Greeks and Romans but had been lost over the centuries. Lineal perspective views often show models differently on the projection plane than do parallel projections, mainly because the projection points of a perpective view converge at a theoretical viewpoint. The projection points are a specific distance from the model being viewed (not at infinity). For example, if the real location and the theoretical location are different, distortions can and do occur. One such distortion, which we'll discuss in the "Dynamic Viewing" section later in this chapter, occurs when the **DVIEW** command uses the **Zoom** option and the focal length of the camera is set too short.

Nevertheless, in perspective views, a model that's quite a distance away from you will appear smaller on the projection plane than one that's nearer. In addition, edges that would truly be parallel on the actual model appear to meet at a distant vanishing point in perpective views. Thus, perpective-view projection makes models appear the way they do in the real world—especially if the real viewer's location is close to the theoretical viewpoint at which the projection was first made. Figure 4.2 shows some sample perspective views.

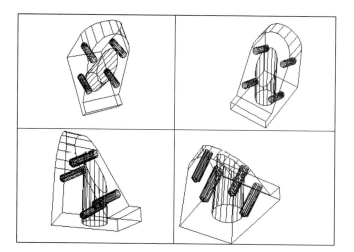

Figure 4.2
Perspective views of a model.

Creating A 3D Clamp

Before we talk more about the specifics of 3D viewing, we need a sample drawing to work with. You can work through the steps that follow, or you can access the completed clamp.dwg on the CD-ROM.

Start a new metric drawing and save it as clamp.dwg. Set up three new viewports using the **VPORTS** command. In the Viewports dialog box, choose New Viewports and set the new viewports by choosing Three: Right. In the Setup box, set the viewports as 3D and enter the label "3D-clamp" in the

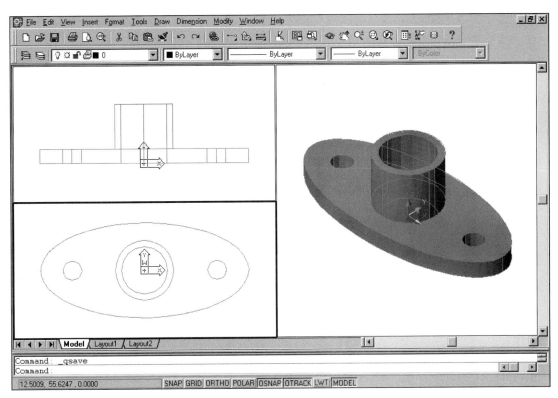

Figure 4.3
The completed clamp.

New Name box. Click on OK to accept the settings. You should have three views: Top, Front, and SE Isometric. Figure 4.3 shows the completed clamp.

Now, follow these steps:

1. From the Draw menu, choose Ellipse|Center, specify the center as 0,0,0, and set the endpoint of the axis to 90,0 and the other axis to @40<90, as follows:

```
Command: ellipse
Specify axis endpoint of ellipse or [Arc/Center]: C
Specify center of ellipse: 0,0,0
Specify endpoint of axis: 90,0
Specify the distance to other axis or [Rotation]: @40<90
```

2. From the Draw menu, choose Solids|Cylinder. Set the center point for the base at 0,0,0 and specify a radius of 25mm and a height of 50mm:

```
Command: cylinder
Specify center point for base of cylinder or [Elliptical]
  <0,0,0>: 0,0,0
Specify radius for base of cylinder or [Diameter]: 25
Specify height of cylinder or [Center of other end]: 50
```

3. Repeat the **CYLINDER** command, setting the start point at 0,0,0 and specifying a radius of 20mm and a height of 50mm:

```
Command: cylinder
Specify center point for base of cylinder or [Elliptical]
   <0,0,0>: 0,0,0
Specify radius for base of cylinder or [Diameter]: 20
Specify height of cylinder or [Center of other end]: 50
```

4. Repeat the **CYLINDER** command, setting the start point at -62.5,0 and specifying a radius of 8mm with a height of 12mm:

```
Command: cylinder
Specify center point for base of cylinder or [Elliptical]
   <0,0,0>: -62.5,0
Specify radius for base of cylinder or [Diameter]: 8
Specify height of cylinder or [Center of other end]: 12
```

5. Repeat the **CYLINDER** command, setting the start point at 62.5,0 and specifying a radius of 8mm with a height of 12mm:

```
Command: cylinder
Specify center point for base of cylinder or [Elliptical]
   <0,0,0>: 62.5,0
Specify radius for base of cylinder or [Diameter]: 8
Specify height of cylinder or [Center of other end]: 12
```

6. You now have four cylinders and one ellipse. Extrude the ellipse up 12mm:

```
Command: extrude
Select objects: <Select the ellipse you created>
Specify height of extrusion or [Path]: 12
Specify angle of taper for extrusion <0>: 0
```

7. Union the large cylinder to the ellipse and then subtract the remaining cylinders to complete the 3D model part:

```
Command: union
Select objects: <Select the ellipse you created>
Select objects: <Select the large cylinder and press Enter>

Command: subtract
Select solids and regions to subtract from ..
Select objects: <Select the ellipse you created and press
   Enter>
Select objects: <Select the remaining three cylinders and
   press Enter> (i.e., inner and two small cylinders)
```

8. Use the **CHANGE** command and change the color of the completed 3D solid to color 8 (gray).

You may want to zoom the viewports so that they resemble Figure 4.3. To do so, within each viewport, use Zoom Extents. Then, use the **ZOOM** command at the keyboard, and at the prompt type in ".9x" and press Enter. Alternatively, if you wish to practice restoring viewports in the Layout1 tab, use the **MVIEW** command and restore (to fit) the 3D-clamp views you saved at the beginning of the exercise. You may also wish to **ZOOM Center** the upper- and lower-left viewports to 1/50xp. Set the right pictorial to a **ZOOM Center** of 1/30xp. You'll access this completed clamp drawing for the remainder of the chapter.

Dynamic Viewing

Before you move on to the discussion of dynamic viewing, this section defines some terms and commands you'll be using.

Important Terms

For a full understanding of dynamic viewing, you need to be familiar with the following terms:

- *Camera*—The 3D viewer or viewpoint. The **CAMERA** command allows you to change camera and target locations. See the "UCS Per Viewport and 3D Orbit" section later in this chapter for uses of the camera.

- *Clipping*—Removing items or parts of an item from the display. Items closer to the camera than the front clipping plane won't be seen. Items farther from the camera than the back clipping plane won't be displayed. Clipping planes are always perpendicular to the line of sight. See the "UCS Per Viewport and 3D Orbit" section later in this chapter for uses of clipping.

- *Distance*—For both front and back clipping planes, measured along the line of sight with the zero distance located at the target. Distances can often be entered with the keyboard, mouse, or slider bar. Positive distances are measured toward the camera; negative distances are measured away from the camera.

- *Field of vision*—The angle, from the camera, within which objects are visible.

- *Lens focal length*—Controls the field of vision. A short focal length gives a wide field of vision and, if too short, produces a distorted image. A long focal length gives a narrow field of vision and, if too long, produces a perspective image that's difficult to distinguish from a parallel projection.

- *Line of sight*—The vector from the camera to the target.

- *Target*—The exact point at which the camera aims.

DVIEW And DVIEWBLOCK

Now that some of the key dynamic viewing terms have been defined, you're ready to learn about a couple of the dynamic viewing commands. **DVIEW** is an AutoCAD 2000 keyboard command that dynamically sets your 3D model to a view of your choice. You can use this command only in model space. Either create the clamp.dwg using the steps just outlined or open the clamp.dwg from the CD-ROM. Activate the pictorial viewport and then enter "dview" at the command prompt. Respond to the prompts as follows:

```
Command: dview
Select objects or <use DVIEWBLOCK>: <Pick the clamp and press
   Enter>
Enter option
[CAmera/TArget/Distance/POints/PAn/Zoom/TWist/CLip/Hide/Off/
   Undo]: tw
Specify view twist angle <0.00>: <twist the viewpoint to your
   model with your mouse pointer>
```

Enter "dview" at the command prompt. (Remember, the command is disabled if you're in paper space.) Instantly, you're prompted to select objects or use the new AutoCAD 2000 **DVIEWBLOCK** feature (which uses the outline of a house). At the Select Objects prompt, you indicate the preview objects AutoCAD will drag as you move about the screen. (Hint: Select only a few choice objects, because the objects you select are dragged as a preview image when you change views. If you select too many objects, you'll slow the process of dragging and updating the image.) After you choose the desired view, AutoCAD redisplays the full model in a new view.

If you press Enter instead of selecting objects, a dynamic viewing block will appear, as illustrated in Figure 4.4. The **DVIEWBLOCK** is a 3D model created to help you rotate your 3D model in real time and thus indicate how you want the view to look. (Hint: This command is so flexible that it allows you to create your own **DVIEWBLOCK** block in a 1×1×1-unit area. You just need to remember to set its origin at the lower-left corner.)

Figure 4.4
The new AutoCAD 2000 **DVIEWBLOCK** feature.

If you enter **DVIEW** at the command line, you'll see the main options of the **DVIEW** command: CAmera/TArget/Distance/POints/PAn/Zoom/TWist/CLip/Hide/Off/Undo. Several of the listed **DVIEW** suboptions—distance, zoom, and clip (front and back)—use slider bars that appear on screen to indicate a choice of angle, distance, or zoom magnification. When you move the mouse, the preview objects change and a diamond slider bar appears to indicate the amount of change. After selecting your preview objects, you can enter any of the following options:

- *CA (Camera)*—Using realtime orbiting lets you rotate the camera or viewpoint around the target. You can toggle or you can enter an angle up or down from the current XY construction plane, using the keyboard.

- *TA (Target)*—Using realtime orbiting lets you rotate the target point you're looking at around the camera (like turning your head). You can toggle or you can enter an angle using the keyboard.

- *D (Distance)*—Changes the distance from your model. (Distance makes no sense in parallel projection, so the theoretical viewpoint is at infinity.) This option automatically turns on perspective view. You can enter distance at the keyboard or slider bar. (Hint: If you want to view more or less of the model without turning on perspective, use the **DVIEW Zoom** feature.)

- *PO (Points)*—Lets you enter X,Y,Z coordinates, first for the target and then for the camera. If you're in a perspective view when you select this option, you'll be returned to parallel projection until you've selected your coordinates.

- *PA (Pan)*—Lets you pan the display in any direction. You can specify a displacement distance using the keyboard or mouse.

- *Z (Zoom)*—Using the slider bar lets you zoom in/out or increase/decrease your field of vision. This option is similar to the **ZOOM** command. However, if you're in a perspective viewport, the feature lets you change the focal length of your camera lens. The default focal length when you enter perspective is 50mm, which gives a view similar to that of a 35mm camera with a 50mm lens. (Hint: Don't use a short focal length, because it gives you a wide view with a lot of distortion, like the 200mm fish-eye lens distortion on a regular camera. Alternately, with a long focal length, you get a narrow view similar to a telephoto lens.)

- *TW (Twist)*—Lets you rotate your view about a line of sight from the camera to the target. You may enter a twist angle at the keyboard or use the mouse.

- *CL (Clip)*—Using the slider bar lets you clip the model. Enter "f" to set the distance of the front clipping plane ("e" sets it at the camera "eye") or to turn it on or off. The default position for the front clipping plane is at the camera "eye." Front clipping is always on when you're in perspective. Enter "b" to set the distance of the back clipping plane or to turn it on or off.

- *H (Hide)*—Lets you remove hidden lines in the selected objects.

- *OFF (Off)*—Turns off perspective. To turn it back on, use **D (Distance)**.

- *U (Undo)*—Undoes the previous **DVIEW** operation. You can undo as often as necessary while you remain in the **DVIEW** command.

After using one of these options, you'll be returned to the **DVIEW** prompt. To exit **DVIEW**, press Enter; AutoCAD will regenerate the drawing to your chosen setting.

DDVPOINT And The Viewpoint Presets Dialog Box

The Viewpoint Presets dialog box lets you set up a 3D parallel projection view. At the keyboard, type "ddvpoint" or choose 3D Views from the View menu, and then select Viewpoint Presets to open the Viewpoint Presets dialog box, shown in Figure 4.5. The purpose of the Viewpoint Presets dialog box is either to let you set up a working view in order to start work on your 3D model or to set it up in order to check your complete 3D model from a specific viewpoint in 3D space.

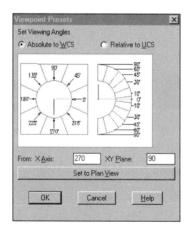

Figure 4.5
The Viewpoint Presets
dialog box.

In the Viewpoint Presets dialog box, you select a first viewing angle relative to the X axis and a second viewing angle relative to the the XY plane of the World Coordinate System (WCS). You can do so by clicking your pointing device on the sample images and moving the sample pointers or by entering values directly for the X axis and the XY plane in the boxes provided:

- The viewing angle relative to the X axis is defined through 360 degrees around the 3D model.

- The viewing angle relative to the XY plane is defined as any angle above or below 90 degrees from the horizontal.

You may also click on Set To Plan View to set your drawing relative to the current User Coordinate System (UCS). Click on OK to accept and retain the settings you made.

Referring back to Figure 4.5, whichever radio button at the top of the dialog box (Absolute To WCS or Relative To UCS) is selected determines whether the two angles you specify will be measured from the WCS (absolute Cartesian coordinates) or from the current UCS (relative Cartesian coordinates). See Chapter 3 to review the differences between WCS and UCS.

Again referring to Figure 4.5, you'll see two charts that indicate viewing angles. The left chart represents your angle in the horizontal XY viewing plane from the X axis. At the center of the chart is the coordinate origin point 0,0,0; the black moveable pointer is an indicator line that points toward your viewing location. The other chart represents the XY angle, which you may set to above or below the horizontal ground plane. You can pick in the wedge areas and choose one of the standard angles, or you can pick within the empty area near the moveable pointer to specify an angle. Alternately, type an angle in the X Axis or XY Plane field.

You create standard isometric views when you set the From: X Axis to 45, 135, 225, or 315 degrees and set the XY Plane to 35.3 degrees. The standard isometric view settings are:

- *SW Isometric*—225 degrees

- *SE Isometric*—315 degrees

- *NE Isometric*—45 degrees

- *NW Isometric*—135 degrees

Remember, you can also set these angles to relative coordinates instead of absolute coordinates by selecting the Relative To UCS radio button. A standard plan view occurs any time you set your elevation above the XY plane to 90 degrees. (Hint: A shortcut for specifying the plan view is to click on the Set To Plan View button.)

3D Views: Presets

Choosing 3D Views from the View menu displays the cascading menu shown in Figure 4.6, complete with preset options for standard orthographic and isometric views. The menu lists Viewpoint Presets, VPOINT, Plan View, Top, Bottom, Left, Right, Front, Back, SW Isometric, SE Isometric, NE Isometric, and NW Isometric. (As explained in the previous section, the Viewpoint Presets options opens the Viewpoint Presets dialog box.)

The **VPOINT** command is a vector-mode command; you enter it from the keyboard as vector coordinates to generate a selected view. The prompt asks you to specify a vector coordinate viewpoint or a direction of rotation, or to press Enter to display the compass and tripod:

```
Command: vpoint
Specify a view point or [Rotate] <display compass and tripod>:
  <Press Enter>
```

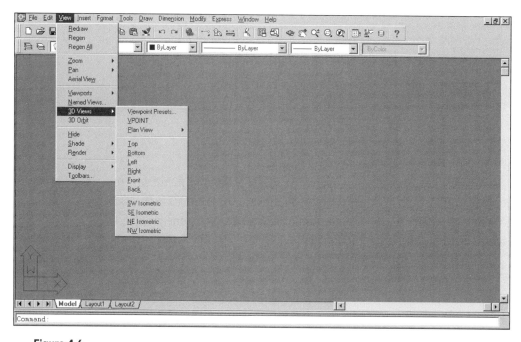

Figure 4.6

The 3D Views cascading menu, showing view presets.

Choosing the default option (by pressing Enter) activates the **VPOINT** tripod (vector mode) that allows you to set the viewpoint using the compass and axis tripod, as illustrated in Figure 4.7.

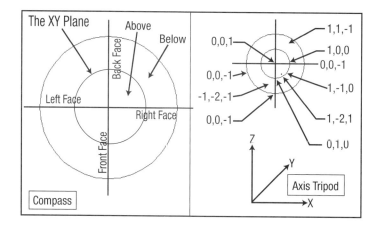

Figure 4.7

Setting the viewpoint with the compass and axis tripod.

To use the compass, place yourself at the North Pole above the surface of the globe and look to the center of the globe. The compass can be thought of as a flattened globe. The center is the North Pole, the outer circle is the South Pole, and the inner circle is the equator. As you move your mouse pointer around the compass, the compass tripod shows the relative positions of the positive X, Y, and Z axes. Select your viewpoint by locating the appropriate point on the compass. The vector from that point to the center of the (round) globe defines your line of sight.

Choose the **Vector** option to activate the **VPOINT** vector mode and specify the viewpoint with X,Y,Z coordinates. When prompted, enter the X, Y, and Z coordinates, separated by commas. The line of sight is a vector from the entered coordinates to the origin 0,0,0. The distance from the coordinates isn't important—only the direction. Thus, a viewpoint location of .5,1,1 is the same as 1,-2,2 or 5,-10,10. A view similar to the standard isometric views is created when you specify a vector that has X and Y coordinates of 1 or -1 and a Z coordinate of 1.

The vector settings available on the 3D Views cascading menu are Top (0,0,1), Bottom (0,0,-1), Left (-1,0,0), Right (1,0,0), Front (0,-1,0), Back (0,1,0), SW Isometric (-1,-1,1), SE Isometric (1,-1,1), NE Isometric (1,1,1), and NW Isometric (-1,1,1). To use these preset views, simply pick the appropriate viewport you want the setting to be in and then choose the predefined setting. The **ZOOM** and **PAN** commands work as usual, no matter what viewpoint you select.

Choose the **Rotate** option of the **VPOINT** command to activate the vector rotation mode. The **Rotate** option is the same as the visual charts in the Viewpoint Presets dialog box (Figure 4.4), which you use to set the X axis and the XY plane. (The angle preset for the X axis is defined as any viewing angle relative to the X axis rotating through 360 degrees around the 3D model, and the viewing angle relative to the XY plane is defined as any angle above or below 90 degrees from the horizontal.) Work with the **Rotate** option as follows:

```
Command: vpoint
Specify a view point or [Rotate] <display compass and tripod>: r
Enter angle in XY plane from X axis <270>: <Enter an angle>
Enter angle from XY plane <90>: <Enter an angle>
```

If you choose Plan View from the 3D Views cascading menu, you'll see three more options:

- *Current UCS*—A plan view of the current UCS.

- *World UCS*—A plan view of the World Coordinate System.

- *Named UCS*—A named view of a previously saved UCS. You're prompted to enter the name of the desired UCS.

UCS Per Viewport And 3D Orbit

The remainder of this chapter looks at two more AutoCAD 2000 features: UCS Per Viewport and 3D Orbit. From the CD-ROM, open the 3d-orbit.dwg drawing. Before you start working with the drawing, activate the new Auto-CAD 2000 3D Orbit toolbar. Place the toolbar in the upper center of your

screen, but not attached to the top edge—let it float, as shown in Figure 4.8. Notice that the 3D Orbit toolbar has the following buttons: 3D Pan, 3D Zoom, 3D Orbit, 3D Continuous Orbit, 3D Swivel, 3D Adjust Distance, 3D Adjust Clip Planes, Front Clip On/Off, and Back Clip On/Off. If you activate the command and right-click with your mouse you'll see more options, including Pan, Zoom, Orbit, Projection (Parallel and Perspective), Shading Modes, Visual Aids (Compass, Grid, and UCS Icon), Reset View, and the preset standard views.

To use the new feature that gives you a UCS per viewport, access the Viewports dialog box. To do so, choose Viewports from the View menu and then select Named Viewports. Click on the New Viewports tab and enter "3D_Orbit" in the New Name field. In the Standard Viewports section, select Four: Equal and choose 3D from the Setup list. In the Preview area, check to be sure the settings are as the same as those shown in Figure 4.9: upper left Top, lower left Front, lower right Right, and upper right SE Isometric. Finally, click on OK to save the settings. Immediately, you'll have four views of the 3d-orbit.dwg drawing on screen. (Hint: If you wish, you can now use the **MVIEW** command and restore the viewport settings of the four UCS views into paper space.) But for this part of the exercise, let's stay in model space and look at the **3DORBIT** command.

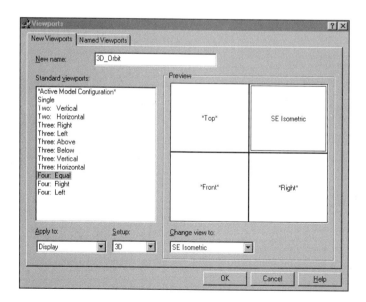

Notice that all the UCS views you created gave you a plan view of your 3D model (a view from the top looking directly down onto your model). This is the new UCS Per Viewport feature, which allows you to work on your model in true views. It sets up each viewport to the UCS you've chosen—Top, Front, Side, Isometric, and so on—and then automatically forces the UCS to go to the UCS View option you set. You need to make the upper-right Isometric view active by picking in the viewport and then look at it using **3DORBIT**.

3DORBIT works only in model space, not in paper space. This command allows you true 3D rotation and clipping (both front and back planes). So if you need to view the underneath of an object or have a projection view other than Isometric (such as perspective), this is the command to use. It also allows shading and zooming in addition to clipping. From the toolbar or the View menu, choose 3D Orbit. Immediately, a circle will surround your 3D model, with four smaller circles attached to its quadrants. The circular orbiting planes are set up as visual guidelines; they're called *arcballs*.

When the **3DORBIT** command is active, the target of your view is static and the camera location (your point of view) moves about the target. The center of the arcball—not the center of the object you're viewing—is the target point. (An alternative is to use the **3DCORBIT** option, which allows continuous orbit without any of the visual guidelines. In **3DCORBIT**, if you move your cursor into the arcball, it will change to a circle divided into four quadrants by smaller circles, and the view moves freely. If you move the cursor back outside the arcball, you revert to a circular pointing device.)

Pick anywhere on the model—say, the lower-left quadrant—and use your mouse to rotate the model with true 3D rotation. Because you are in a **Shademode**, the UCS icon is a colored icon: the X axis is red, the Y axis is green, and the Z axis is blue. You'll see that as you move your mouse to rotate the model, the icon follows you, which is indicative of your start point in 3D space.

Activate the **3DORBIT** command and from your 3D Orbit toolbar, pick the down arrow (in the naming box), and you'll see the standard views listed. You may choose any of the listed views, and the model will instantly switch to that view. For example, pick the 3D Adjust Clip Planes button. The Adjust Clipping Planes viewport will appear, containing a view of the model with a line running through the Z axis of the Top plane. You can visually move this clipping plane line to the front or back of your model. Try moving it a small distance away from you so it isn't on the center line. Notice that as you move the line, your model in the SE Isometric viewport starts to hide some of its line geometry—it's showing you the clipping plane in realtime view. When you have the clipping plane where you want it, choose the Create Slice icon and close the Adjust Clipping Planes viewport. Another useful feature is the 3D Adjust Distance button, which allows you to use the realtime **ZOOM** feature. Simply move the mouse to **ZOOM** the model in or out.

3D Orbit shading modes provide you with multiple options:

- *Wireframe*—Shows your 3D model in a 3D view, with lines and curves representing the boundaries of your model. Any material applied to the flat geometry is visible, whereas material applied to solid objects isn't visible. See Figure 4.10.

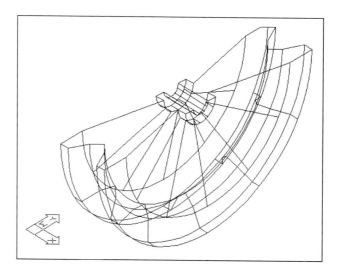

Figure 4.10
Wireframe 3D uses lines and curves to show your 3D model.

- *Hidden*—Shows your 3D model in a 3D view. The back faces of the 3D model are hidden. See Figure 4.11.

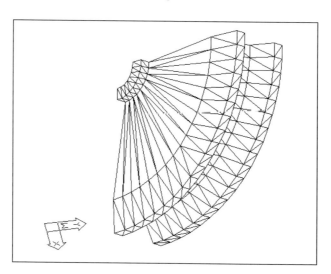

Figure 4.11
Hidden hides the back faces and uses a hidden wireframe view.

- *Flat Shaded*—The faceted polygonal faces of your 3D model are shaded, which provides the model with a less smooth and flatter appearance. See Figure 4.12.

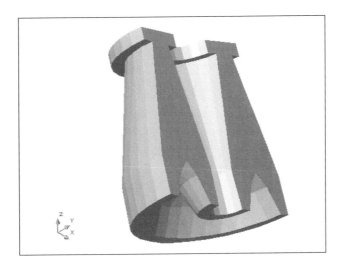

Figure 4.12
Flat Shaded shades in 3D and gives a faceted look.

- *Gouraud Shaded*—Provides a smoother, more realistic appearance. Besides shading your 3D model, it also smooths the edges between faceted polygon faces. See Figure 4.13.

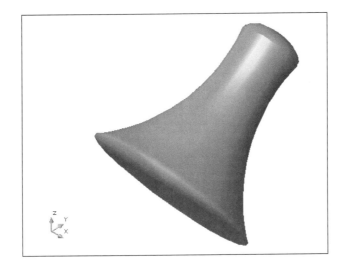

Figure 4.13
Gouraud Shaded smooths edges for realism.

- *Flat Shaded, Edges On*—A combination of the Flat Shaded and Wireframe options, with the 3D model flat shaded in wireframe mode. See Figure 4.14.

- *Gouraud Shaded, Edges On*—A combination of the Gouraud Shaded and Wireframe options, with the 3D model Gouraud shaded in wireframe mode. See Figure 4.15.

After you exit the **3DORBIT** command, shading is still applied to your 3D model. You need to use **SHADEMODE** to revert to your original shading prior to using **3DORBIT**.

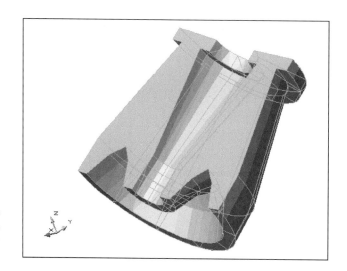

Figure 4.14
Flat Shaded, Edges On shades
with a flat basic algorithm and
also shows the wireframe.

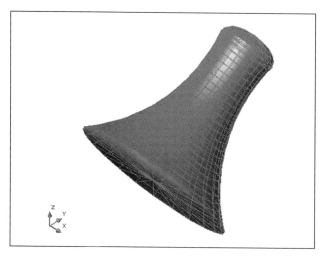

Figure 4.15
Gouraud Shaded, Edges On
shades with a Gouraud algorithm
and also shows the wireframe.

To exit 3D Orbit, press Enter or Esc, or right-click and choose Exit from the
resulting shortcut menu.

The CAMERA Command

Some of the commands we just reviewed use a camera. Prior to entering the
3D View commands, you can preset a camera's position and target. The
CAMERA command lets you change the point from which you view the
objects in 3D space and the point that you aim at in 3D space. The point
about which you view your 3D model is the camera location, and the point
at which you aim your view is the target location.

For example, when you use the **3DORBIT** command, the default target
location is the center of your 3D view—which in this instance isn't the center of your model. If you use the **CAMERA** command before you start 3D
Orbit, you can change the camera and target view location points for the
3DORBIT command prior to entering the 3D Orbit.

If you've just opened the 3d-orbit.dwg file, the **CAMERA** prompts are as follows:

```
Command: camera
Specify new camera position <181.4667,-180.7714,258.4872>:
  210,149,0
Specify new camera target <-25.4418,26.1370,51.5788>: <Press
  Enter>
```

You can follow these quick steps to change the camera and target locations:

1. On the command line, enter "camera" and the prompt "Specify new camera position:" is returned.

2. Use the pointing device, or enter an X,Y,Z coordinate, to set the camera location, or press Enter to accept the coordinates.

3. The next prompt of "Specify new camera target:" is returned. Use the pointing device, or enter an X,Y,Z coordinate, to set the target location, or press Enter to accept the coordinates.

Moving On

This chapter has taken some of the mystery out of the use and applications of 3D viewing. It has also provided you with examples of the 3D View commands for AutoCAD 2000, an essential component to modeling in 3D. In the next few chapters, we'll begin an in-depth look at the true 3D world of wireframe, surface, and solid modeling.

PART II

CREATING AND EDITING 3D MODELS

GEOMETRIC MODELING 5

Geometric modeling means constructing, editing,
and representing physical objects as computer data.
To a large extent, a CAD system is a computer
program that does geometric modeling. This
chapter discusses how you can use AutoCAD 2000
to generate 3D wireframe models.

Types Of Geometric Models

The three fundamental types of geometric models are wireframe, surface, and solid. This chapter discusses geometric and wireframe models in particular and how they relate to surface and solid models. Modern 3D CAD modeling software allows 2D geometric projections to be created automatically for higher productivity, as opposed to early CAD systems, which started with 2D wireframe geometry and produced each view as a separate 2D image. However, you'll see that wireframe modeling in AutoCAD is different from surface or solid modeling, because it can also produce ambiguity in your model. So whatever the purpose of your 3D modeling is—whether it's to produce prototype 3D wireframe models or wireframe pictorial displays instead of 2D orthographic projection views—this chapter will provide you with an overview of 3D geometric forms.

The past few chapters have looked at the way a 2D drawing represents the visual aspects of an object from a specific viewpoint in space (that is, front, Top, Right Side, and Pictorial views). Now, let's move on and review CAD from a 3D, in-depth viewpoint. A wireframe or a surface model, for example, contains a description of the object's appearance from any viewpoint in 3D space. This is all well and good, but what benefit does a solid model have over a wireframe or surface model?

Besides containing a description of the object's appearance from any viewpoint in 3D space, a solid model also contains the object's description plus further information about the object's shape and possibly the material of which it's made. The solid model, for example, can include details of an object's centroid, mass properties, moment of inertia, volume, radius of gyration, and center of gravity. In addition, the element data of a 3D model may be exported to a numerically controlled (NC) toolpath or to Finite Element Analysis software to let you use the 3D model in more depth.

Here are some specific advantages offered by various AutoCAD commands and other features as you work with 3D models:

- *3DORBIT*—Look at your 3D model from any viewpoint in 3D space.

- *SECTION*—Create section views of solids.

- *SOLVIEW*—Create 2D views such as orthographic, auxiliary, and sectional views of 3D objects or parts.

- *INTERFERE*—Check for interference and for 3D solids that occupy the same space.

- *HIDE or MVIEW* with **Hideplot**—Remove hidden lines.

- *SHADE, SHADEMODE, or RENDER*—Do realistic shading.

- *Finite Element Modeling software*—Perform engineering (FEA) analysis.

- *Export Data dialog box*—Export the model to create animation from the file images you export. You may use programs such as Adobe or Paint Shop Pro to blend your individual images into animations, or you may use AutoCAD's script function along with a series of slide files.

- *DXF and ANSI files*—Allow you to extract data, such as data for manufacturing.

How did the 3D wireframe revolution occur? Even though 3D modeling was spawned by the automobile and aerospace technology of the 1960s, it was still a mainframe tool and required lots of computing power—that is, until the Sketchpad idea was born, an idea that provided a wedge to open up new fields of computing.

In 1962, an MIT doctoral candidate named Ivan Sutherland revolutionized CAD by creating a Sketchpad that allowed the user to interact graphically with the computer. He came up with the Sketchpad idea through the use of a light pen and a visual display. Thus, basic CAD systems that began life as a Sketchpad and took root in the 1960s started with 2D orthographic geometry, in which each view was created as a separate 2D image. Then, in the 1970s, 3D wireframe and surface modelers improved this 2D geometry. In turn, engineers and engineering designers thought the new solid modelers of the 1980s would provide in-depth design solutions. But the modelers were difficult and unfriendly to use, because their Boolean operations were cumbersome for the engineers to grasp. However, since the 1980s, solid modeling has become more user friendly and interactive. It's slowly becoming the standard tool of total design choice through electronic document management (EDM). It's to this end that AutoCAD 2000 has pushed the envelope again and promises to be a unique Year 2000 production and design tool.

The CAD Database

In today's electronic world, where EDM can play a major part in the overall design process, the 3D CAD database, in addition to providing both 3D solid model information, is also used for 2D drawings and blueprints. Also, it's often used as the base for manufacturing and production runs. So in modern terms, CAD generations form a hierarchy that parallels the level of design. Early CAD systems were developed to model and manipulate the lower levels of a design (i.e., 2D drawing). Modern CAD systems extend to higher levels of design—that is, a top-down approach in which you build a 3D model first and then create 2D drawings, as illustrated in Figure 5.1.

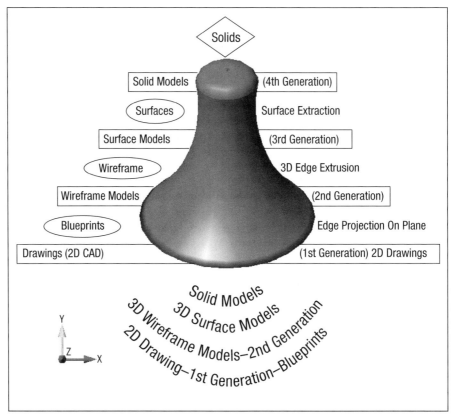

Figure 5.1

The top-down approach of design hierarchy.

How is CAD geometry generated, what elements does it use, and how are these elements defined to generate this database? The database that allows us to create CAD geometry can be defined as elements made from straight lines, curves, or spline curves (see Figure 5.2).

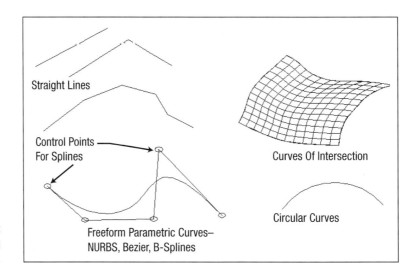

Figure 5.2

Straight line and curvilinear entities.

Overall, your 3D AutoCAD geometry may be created from

- Straight lines (parallel or nonparallel geometry lines)

- Circular curves or conics (circles and arcs)

- Spline curves (polylines or polyarcs)

At this point you're aware that elements are used to generate your geometry database, but how do 3D model types differ? As previously mentioned, you can create wireframe, surface, and solid models, and each of these 3D models has specific uses for geometric forms. But what type of geometric element creates which type of 3D model, and how does the software check for integrity in the model?

3D Geometric Forms: Wireframe, Surface, And Solid Models

AutoCAD provides certain 3D wireframe objects, such as 3D polylines (which can have only a Continuous linetype) and splines. Built into the surface and solid modelers are geometric wireframe elements or primitives. The surface modeler includes 3D objects such as Box3d, Pyramid, Wedge, Dome, and so on. The solid modeler includes Box, Sphere, Cylinder, Cone, Wedge, and Torus; both sets of primitives provide a wireframe display, but both the surface modeler and the solid modeler use a different modeling technique because of their required computing power. The primitives provide more description than simple vertices and edges as required for a wireframe, but you can also use them for shading or rendering.

Wireframe

A 3D wireframe model is a skeletal description of a 3D object, and due to this skeletal simplicity, it's fast and economical within the CAD database. A 3D wireframe display, on the other hand, is how the image of your model looks on screen—it's a natural progression of your 2D projections. It's important for you to understand that AutoCAD uses both the 3D-wireframe model and the 3D-wireframe display. However, a basic wireframe model has no surfaces and involves two types of elements: *edges* and *vertices* (or *node points*), where the edge of each object represents the model. The node points (junctions or corners) are located in 3D space and represent the lines connecting each vertex point. The resulting skeletal model is composed of points, lines, and arc curvilinear elements that describe the edges of the 3D object or model.

Surface

A surface model is more sophisticated than a 3D wireframe. The surface model uses wireframe geometry and algebraic equations to define an area between the edges of the model, thus producing a surface. Surface modelers use many forms of algebraic equation; AutoCAD uses a general polygonal mesh that's planar, which lets you create approximate curved surfaces. Within AutoCAD, you may choose to change to Bezier, cubic, or quadratic equations as your choice of surface model. (See Chapter 8 for details.) You may also use a surface model for NC programming.

Solid

From the space enclosed by the surfaces, a solid model forms a closed volume. Using AutoCAD, you may create primitive, composite, extruded, and/ or revolved solids. As previously indicated, in some solid modelers a solid model will contain information about the object's shape and the matter from which it's made (steel, for example). It will also provide element data (such as mass property, moment of inertia, volume, and center of gravity). Like a surface model's data, this element data may also be exported to NC toolpath or Finite Element Analysis software to allow greater use of the 3D model.

You'll find solid modeling the easiest type of 3D modeler to use. With the AutoCAD solid modeler, you can make 3D objects by creating basic 3D shapes: boxes, cones, cylinders, spheres, wedges, and torii (donuts). You can then combine these shapes to create more complex solids by joining or subtracting them or finding their intersecting (overlapping) volume. You can also create solids by sweeping a 2D object along a path or revolving it about an axis, as shown in Figure 5.3. If you use Mechanical Desktop, you can also define solids parametrically and maintain associativity between 3D models and the 2D views you generate from them.

Revolving A Closed Profile

One way to create a wireframe is to revolve a profile in a circular motion. From the CD-ROM, open the revolve-2.dwg drawing, shown in Figure 5.3. Notice that the drawing includes a closed profile, created in the World Co-ordinate System (WCS), and that we're in the Side work plane. From the Solids section of the Draw menu, choose Revolve. Pick the closed polyline as the object (remember, only closed polylines can be revolved), then pick the axis end points A and B, and enter "180" for the number of degrees of revolution:

```
Command: revolve
Current wire frame density: ISOLINES=4
Select objects: <Pick the closed profile>
Select objects: <Press Enter>
Specify start point for axis of revolution or define axis by
  [Object/X (axis)/Y (axis)]: <Choose point A>
Specify endpoint of axis: <Choose point B>
Specify angle of revolution <360>: 180
```

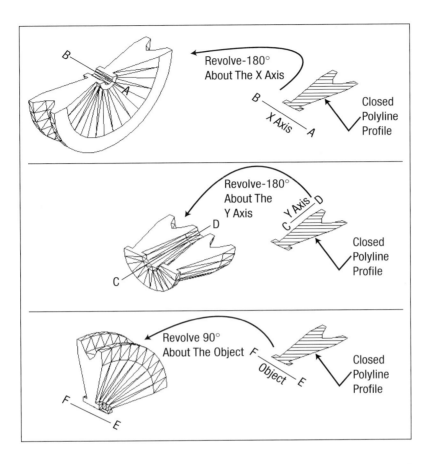

Figure 5.3
Revolving a closed profile.

Revolving the simple profile into a 3D wireframe produces some universal questions. When you look at a 3D wireframe model, how do you determine which is the bottom or the top? How do you define the front or the back of the 3D wireframe object? How does the AutoCAD software maintain integrity within the database and check the validity of the model? Let's take a look.

Software Rules: Integrity Gotchas

To maintain integrity within the database and the validity of the model, AutoCAD has to check certain rules as it creates your model. In addition to checking face normals, the software checks the geometry of your model, as follows:

- Every edge in your model may connect to only two adjacent vertices.

- Every vertex is associated with at least three edges to place it.

- Within the model, every vertex must have a coordinate locator to place it.

- To form a closed loop within every face, every face should contain at least three edges.

You don't see software checking your geometry; algorithms built into the software look for certain rules to maintain integrity. Euler operations, for example, is one method used to check elements. You'll find a more in-depth explanation of Euler operations in Chapter 7.

Ambiguity Gotchas

Sometimes it's hard to visualize which is the front or the back of an object, or which is the bottom versus the top. A number of factors can produce ambiguity in an electronic model. The UCS provides us with a way of distinguishing up from down. In Figure 5.4, which shows the Necker Cube, notice that it's hard to figure out which face is front and which face is back. Figure 5.5 shows that the same edge and vertex list can be used to describe different models that are equal in size. The same list can describe different objects, depending upon how they're interpreted.

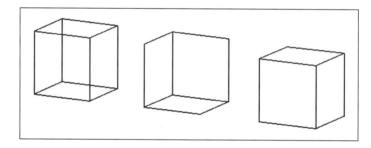

Figure 5.4
With the Necker Cube, it's hard to define the front and back faces.

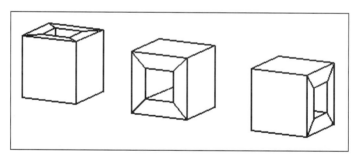

Figure 5.5
The same edge and vertex list describes different objects, depending upon how they're interpreted.

3D Wireframe From 2D Geometry

One of the easiest ways to create a wireframe model is to create a 2D profile and then use the **CHANGE** command with the **Thickness** option to give it depth. Remember that this isn't a true 3D model—it's 2-1/2D.

An alternative to using **Thickness** is to create a profile and then use the **EXTRUDE** command, which gives you a 3D solid model. Remember the basic rule for 2D profiles extruded into a solid: Any profile you create must be closed. The exception is in wireframe and/or surface modeling. In addition, as shown in Figure 5.6, you can use **REVOLVE** to create circular geometry.

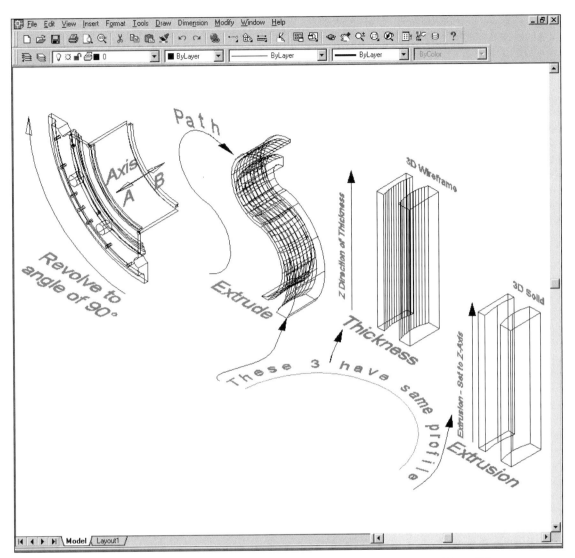

Figure 5.6
You may use **Thickness**,
EXTRUDE, or **REVOLVE** on
a 2D profile.

Using **Thickness** To Create 3D Wireframes From 2D Geometry

The objective in this next exercise is to create a simple profile with a polyline, and then use **Thickness** to give the illusion of depth. You'll place a circle into the 2-1/2D drawing and also give it thickness. See Figure 5.7 for the complete profile, wire-1.dwg, which can be found on the CD-ROM.

Start a new drawing and use English units. Name the drawing wire-1 and set your 3D View to SE Isometric. Rotate the UCS about the X axis 90° as your Front work plane (you may wish to set your Grid and Snap to .25):

```
Command: ucs
Current ucs name: *WORLD*
Enter an option [New/Move/orthoGraphic/Prev/Restore/Save/Del/
  Apply/?/World]
```

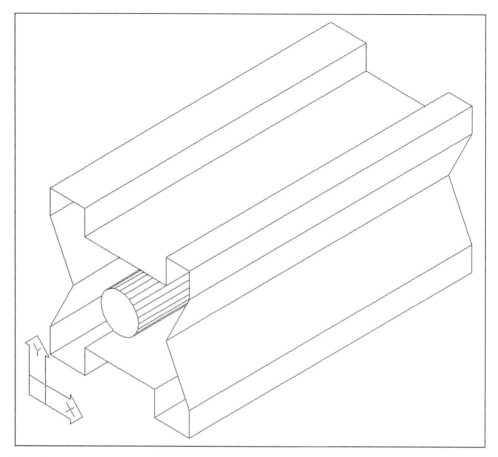

Figure 5.7

Use **Thickness** in the wire-1.dwg profile to create a 3D wireframe.

```
<World>: x
Specify rotation angle about X axis <90>: 90
```

Now, zoom into an area of your screen from -1.5,-1.5 to 5.5,5.5:

```
Command: zoom
Specify corner of window, enter a scale factor (nX or nXP), or
  [All/Center/Dynamic/Extents/Previous/Scale/Window]
  <real time>: -1.5,-1.5
Specify opposite corner: 5.5,5.5
```

You can give depth to the drawing, especially if you preset the **Thickness** beforehand. You can also use the Properties dialog box from the Standard Toolbar and set the **Thickness** after you've completed the profile.

For the purpose of this exercise, it's best to wait until you've completed the profile and then use one of the alternate options for setting **Thickness**. However, if you choose to, you can set **Thickness** at this time. To do so, choose Thickness from the Format menu and set it to –3.

Next, using the **PLINE** command, enter the following points:

```
Command: pline
Specify start point: 0,0
Current line-width is 0.0000
Specify next point or [Arc/Close/Halfwidth/Length/Undo/Width]:
  0,.25
Specify next point or [Arc/Close/Halfwidth/Length/Undo/Width]:
  .25,.75
Specify next point or [Arc/Close/Halfwidth/Length/Undo/Width]:
  0,1.25
Specify next point or [Arc/Close/Halfwidth/Length/Undo/Width]:
  0,1.5
Specify next point or [Arc/Close/Halfwidth/Length/Undo/Width]:
  .375,1.5
Specify next point or [Arc/Close/Halfwidth/Length/Undo/Width]:
  .375,1.25
Specify next point or [Arc/Close/Halfwidth/Length/Undo/Width]:
  1.125,1.25
Specify next point or [Arc/Close/Halfwidth/Length/Undo/Width]:
  1.125,1.50
Specify next point or [Arc/Close/Halfwidth/Length/Undo/Width]:
  1.5,1.5
Specify next point or [Arc/Close/Halfwidth/Length/Undo/Width]:
  1.5,1.25
Specify next point or [Arc/Close/Halfwidth/Length/Undo/Width]:
  1.25,.75
Specify next point or [Arc/Close/Halfwidth/Length/Undo/Width]:
  1.5,.25
Specify next point or [Arc/Close/Halfwidth/Length/Undo/Width]:
  1.5,0
Specify next point or [Arc/Close/Halfwidth/Length/Undo/Width]:
  1.125,0
Specify next point or [Arc/Close/Halfwidth/Length/Undo/Width]:
  1.125,.25
Specify next point or [Arc/Close/Halfwidth/Length/Undo/Width]:
  .375,.25
Specify next point or [Arc/Close/Halfwidth/Length/Undo/Width]:
  .375,0
Specify next point or [Arc/Close/Halfwidth/Length/Undo/Width]: c
```

Enter "c" to close the polyline back to the 0,0,0 startpoint.

Now, create a circle at the coordinate of 0.75,0.75,0 with a radius of 0.2.

If you waited to set the **Thickness**, you now have a number of options or commands to choose from. You can use the **CHANGE** or **CHPROP** command-line option, or you can open the Properties dialog box from the Standard Toolbar, or use the **DDMODIFY** or **CH** commands.

For this example, at the command prompt, enter "CHPROP" (short for "change properties") and pick the objects you just created. Then, at the command prompt, set the **Thickness** to –3, and you've quickly produced a simple wireframe object. Here's the final step to set the **Thickness** of the closed profile into a 3D wireframe.

```
Command: chprop
Select objects: Specify opposite corner: <Pick the closed
  polyline>
Select objects: <Press Enter>
Enter property to change [Color/LAyer/LType/ltScale/LWeight/
  Thickness]: t
Specify new thickness <0.0000>: -3
Enter property to change [Color/LAyer/LType/ltScale/LWeight/
  Thickness]: <Press Enter>
```

Your complete model should be similar to Figure 5.7 (wire-1.dwg is also on the CD-ROM).

You've looked at simple coordinates for entering AutoCAD data; now, let's move on and review some of the other methods of entering 3D coordinate data, along with an example of creating a Helix in AutoCAD using Cylindrical Coordinates.

Coordinate Systems

As we discussed in Chapter 3, the global coordinate system of every AutoCAD 3D model is initially set to a default system, the World Coordinate System (WCS). In addition, you can use a local coordinate system called the User Coordinate System (UCS). There's no limit to the number of UCSs within a drawing, but there will be only one WCS.

Five coordinate systems are in use today: absolute, relative, polar, spherical, and cylindrical. The absolute, relative, and polar systems use 3D Cartesian coordinates to create the various component parts of your drawing. Cartesian coordinates (discussed in Chapter 3), which are the most common method of coordinate system in use today, use three mutually perpendicular axes—X, Y, and Z—that intersect at an origin point, as illustrated in Figure 5.8. The spherical and cylindrical methods of coordinate entry are for 3D use. They don't create cylinders and spherical objects—they're simply extensions of 3D coordinate systems. Let's briefly review them, and then move on to creating 3D wireframe drawings.

Cylindrical Coordinates

Absolute 3D cylindrical coordinates are specified as two distances and one angle:

- Radial distance (r1) from the drawing origin's point on the XY plane

- Angle (a1) subtended by the XY axis and the radial distance vector

- The projected Z height distance (d1) from the polar coordinate perpendicular to the XY plane

For example, 25<30,35 defines a point 25 units from the UCS origin point, 30 degrees from the X axis in the XY plane, and 35 units as a Z value, as

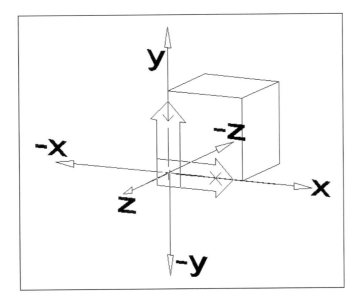

Figure 5.8

X, Y, and Z axes extend from the origin in both negative and positive directions.

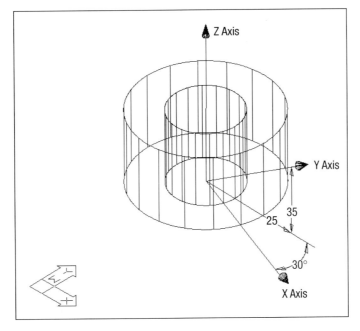

Figure 5.9

Cylindrical coordinates: two distances and one angle.

illustrated in Figure 5.9. You'll note that this method is similar to the 2D-entry method of 2D polar coordinates—it just requires an extra distance for the Z coordinate.

You enter relative cylindrical coordinates by placing the @ symbol in front of the coordinates. The @ symbol indicates that you're working from the last known point (that is, the relative coordinate). For example, the relative cylindrical coordinate @24<30,25 indicates a location point 24 units in the XY plane from the last point entered (not from the absolute origin point), at an angle of 30 degrees from the positive X direction. In turn, the line extends 25 units to a Z coordinate.

Spherical Coordinates

3D spherical coordinates are specified as one distance and two angles:

- Vector (r1) of the radial distance from the point of origin to a specified point

- Angle (a1) between X axis and projection of radial distance vector on the XY plane

- Angle (a2) between XY plane and radial distance vector

For example, 25<30<60 defines a point 25 units from the UCS origin in the XY plane, 30 degrees from the X axis in the XY plane, and 60 degrees up from the XY plane, as shown in Figure 5.10.

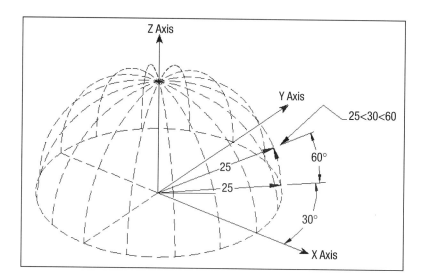

Figure 5.10
Spherical coordinates: one distance and two angles.

Creating A Helix With 3D Coordinates

Using 3D-coordinate entry is quite simple, if you think about how it works. Let's take cylindrical coordinates as an example. In this case, the center point of your 3D coordinates is the center of a circle—you'll enter your coordinates in a circular pattern.

You know from past experience that when you enter standard 2D polar coordinates, you use a distance and an angle. If you want to move to the right (or East), you enter 0 degrees. Vertical or upward is 90 degrees, to the left is 180 degrees, and downward is 270 degrees.

Cylindrical coordinates are simply an extension of this method, except you also enter a third coordinate that specifies Z height.

For the next exercise, it's important to set the work plane correctly before you create the drawing, and also to know whether you need to produce the drawing about a Horizontal or Vertical plane. In this instance, you'll create the drawing in a Vertical plane from the WCS and use relative cylindrical coordinates.

Start a new drawing, use metric units, and name it helix-1.dwg. (This drawing is also available on the CD-ROM.) Set your 3D viewpoint to SE Isometric and activate the **3DPOLY** command (choose 3D Polyline from the Draw menu). For this exercise, your UCS is set to the default WCS, so your work plane looks down on the helix. Notice the use of relative cylindrical coordinates with the @ function or symbol added to each of the coordinate entries:

```
Command: 3dpoly
Specify start point of polyline: 0,0,0
Specify endpoint of line or [Undo]: @100<0,10
Specify endpoint of line or [Undo]: @100<90,10
Specify endpoint of line or [Close/Undo]: @100<180,10
Specify endpoint of line or [Close/Undo]: @100<270,10
Specify endpoint of line or [Close/Undo]: @100<0,10
Specify endpoint of line or [Close/Undo]: @100<90,10
Specify endpoint of line or [Close/Undo]: @100<180,10
Specify endpoint of line or [Close/Undo]: @100<270,10
Specify endpoint of line or [Close/Undo]: @100<0,10
Specify endpoint of line or [Close/Undo]: @100<90,0
Specify endpoint of line or [Close/Undo]: @100<180,10
Specify endpoint of line or [Close/Undo]: @100<270,10
Specify endpoint of line or [Close/Undo]: <Press Enter
  to complete the command>
```

Notice the pattern of the 3D coordinate entry method—all you changed each time was the angle about which you rotated your coordinates. Thus, your 3D coordinates rotated in a circular pattern. Save the drawing for later use in the Surfaces chapter. If you wish to, you can now use the **PEDIT** command and **SPLINE** the helix. (See the "Bezier Curves and B-Splines" section of Chapter 6.) Figure 5.11 illustrates the basic Helix without splining on the left and the Helix with splining on the right.

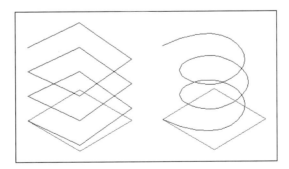

Figure 5.11
The completed Helix using cylindrical coordinates (shown without splining on the left and with splining on the right).

Construction Or Work Planes

Just to recap, in addition to the WCS construction plane, a construction plane may be any XY plane of a temporary or an auxiliary coordinate system. Remember that construction or work planes are simply references that can't be translated or rotated about their own or the global coordinate system. You may have multiple construction planes defined in model space, but only one may be active at any given moment.

Now that we've reviewed coordinates, let's move on to look at primitives, produce another practical example, and look at how to use regions to change 2D solids to 3D wireframes.

Primitives As Wireframes

As mentioned in the opening of the chapter, the surface modeler in Auto-CAD is different from the solid modeler, because AutoCAD uses a hybrid modeling database. With most hybrid modelers, the strategy is to support a high-level constructive solid geometry (CSG) tree hierarchy (for solid models) that may then be intentionally translated into a lower-level Non-Uniform Rational B-Spline (NURBS) surface or boundary-representation (B-Rep) model. If you look at the Draw menu and notice both the Solids commands and the Surfaces > 3D Surfaces (3D Objects), you'll see that each has a set of built-in primitives. Remember, *primitives* are simply objects AutoCAD defines for you as Box, Wedge, Cone, Sphere, and so on; you just supply the insertion point and size dimensions as you create them (see Figure 5.12). Yet these primitives aren't all the same type of entity. You use one set of primitives for surface modeling and the other set for solid modeling. Each has a different function and each uses a different algorithm or modeling engine, such as the ACIS 4, which provides you with a set of primitives that you can use for solid modeling. These primitives can also be converted to a wireframe for your 3D models.

Figure 5.12
A set of primitives.

However, a surface primitive is created as a polygonal meshed surface as opposed to a solid entity. Nonetheless, because each type of primitive modeler uses a different method to construct and edit 3D models, you shouldn't mix surface models with solid models. AutoCAD is forgiving and provides a small amount of conversion between model types, such as solids to surfaces and surfaces to wireframe. Just realize that you can't convert wireframe models to surface models or surface models to solid models.

Be careful as the **EXPLODE** command breaks down a primitive, but AutoCAD has no command to convert a wireframe back to a 3D primitive. You can, for example, explode surface primitives down to 3D faces. You can also explode a solid primitive down to a region; then, in turn, if you explode the region, you simply get lines in 3D space. Nevertheless, you can use primitives to create models composed of multiple 3D object entities, such as spheres, cylinders, boxes, cones, toruses, and so on. You'll find this technique especially useful when you need to create simple polygonal shapes and then explode them. Another option is to use the **REGION** command to create a wireframe. Simply create a profile with lines, arc, circles, and so on, use the **REGION** command to form a 2D solid, and then extrude the region into an object. Alternatively, create a closed polyline and change its **Thickness**.

Using **REGION** To Change 2D Solids To 3D Wireframes

The objective in this exercise is to create a different type of wireframe. You'll create a profile from lines, place a few circles to represent holes, and then use the **BOUNDARY** command to form the profile into a 2D solid. Finally, you'll subtract the holes from the profile and extrude it to give it depth, thus making it a 3D wireframe.

For this example, start a new drawing and set it to metric units; name the drawing wire-2.dwg (also available on the CD-ROM). Now, follow these steps:

1. Set your 3D Viewpoint to SE Isometric and set the UCS to X - 90 as your Front work plane:

```
Command: ucs
Current ucs name: *WORLD*
Enter an option [New/Move/orthoGraphic/Prev/Restore/Save/
  Del/Apply/?/World] <World>: X
Specify rotation angle about X axis <90>: 90
```

You should now be in the Front work plane. (If you wish, you may save the UCS to Front.)

2. Zoom into an area of your screen from -10,-20 to 50,50:

```
Command: zoom
Specify corner of window, enter a scale factor (nX or nXP),
  or [All/Center/Dynamic/Extents/Previous/Scale/Window]
  <real time>: -10,-20
Specify opposite corner: 50,50
```

3. Create the profile lines using the **LINE** command:

```
Command: line
Specify first point: 0,0
Specify next point or [Undo]: 30,0
Specify next point or [Undo]: 30,10
Specify next point or [Close/Undo]: 25,10
Specify next point or [Close/Undo]: 25,5
Specify next point or [Close/Undo]: 20,5
Specify next point or [Close/Undo]: 20,10
Specify next point or [Close/Undo]: 15,10
Specify next point or [Close/Undo]: 10,15
Specify next point or [Close/Undo]: 0,15
Specify next point or [Close/Undo]: c
```

4. Place two circles as holes in the Front work plane of the part. (Your UCS should still be set to the Front work plane.) Create a circle at 7.5,10 with a radius of 1.5; then, create a second circle at 7.5,2.5, again with a radius of 1.5.

In the Front work plane, you now have a series of lines and circles that you need to solidify and subtract from each other. To create this part into a region, look at the lower section of the Draw menu and notice the Boundary and Region options. These two commands can also be used with solid and surface modeling, but you'll use them here to create a wireframe. Boundary uses *ray casting* (a technique which sends out rays in all directions on your current work plane to locate the boundary) to create a region or polyline boundary of the resultant ray casting shape.

From the Draw menu, choose Boundary to activate the Boundary Creation dialog box, shown in Figure 5.13. (You'll find the dialog box similar to the Advanced tab of the Boundary Hatch dialog box, because it can create the region or boundary formed by Boundary Hatch dialog box and then lets you keep the resultant shape without hatching it.) The boundary you create can be either a region or a polyline. The trick is to use the **BOUNDARY** or **BPOLY** command to make a region the exact outline shape of the front face of your model; you can then use it either to mesh the region as a surface or to extrude the region as a solid. Now, let's look at the details.

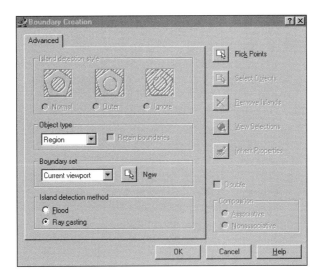

Figure 5.13
The Boundary Creation
dialog box.

Within the Boundary Creation dialog box, notice the drop-down arrow buttons for Object Type and Boundary Set, plus the Flood and Ray Casting radio buttons. Also notice the New and Pick Points buttons.

You need to set the Object Type to Region and ensure the Boundary Set is at Current Viewport. Pick the Ray Casting radio button (either Flood or Ray Casting will work in this case) and then click on the Pick Points button to revert to your drawing. Pick any internal point within the 2D profile you just created, and notice that doing so highlights the outside of the profile. Before you press Enter, you also need to pick an internal point in each circle to create a complete regional boundary set—press Enter only when everything is highlighted. The command prompt will indicate that **BOUNDARY** created three regions. If you use the **LIST** command and pick the main object you created, AutoCAD should indicate that the object is a region, with an area of 337.5000.

You may use the region to mesh a surface or extrude it into a solid. In this case, you'll work with **EXTRUDE**, but first you need to remove the two cutout holes from the region using the **SUBTRACT** command. From the Modify menu, choose Subtract from the Solids Editing section. At the Select Objects prompt, choose the large region you created, press Enter, and then choose both of the circles and press Enter. This process creates a thin 2D solid surface on which the two circles appear as holes cut into the surface. Use the **LIST** command again on the object; the area should now be 323.3628. Thus, you've subtracted the circles from the region as two holes, and the result is a thin 2D solid surface.

The final task is to use **EXTRUDE** to extrude the part a distance of –20 with 0 taper You'll find the **EXTRUDE** command in the Solids section of the Draw menu. Your 3D wireframe is now complete, as shown in Figure 5.14.

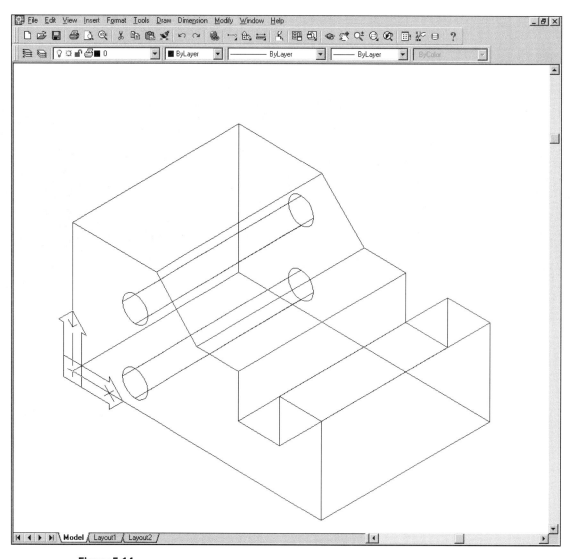

Figure 5.14
The completed
wire-2.dwg drawing.

Moving On

In this chapter, we've looked at 3D wireframe and 3D geometric modeling: constructing, editing, and representing physical objects as X,Y,Z computer data, even if you start your coordinates as 2D data or profiles.

If you just require a 3D wireframe, the wireframe, surface, and solid model types are interchangeable to a small extent, but it's best not to mix the three. Primitive modeling for 3D wireframes is feasible, but it's quite rare to create a 3D drawing from just simple primitives.

As you'll see in the next chapter, the surface modeler in AutoCAD is different from the solid modeler, due to AutoCAD's use of a hybrid modeling database.

SURFACE
MODELING

6

Surface modeling in AutoCAD 2000 is an exciting method of creating 3D components. This chapter explains some of the theory of surface modeling, along with practical working examples of surface and edge creation commands.

Curves And Surfaces

All 3D surface models have both curves and surfaces. This chapter guides you through different curve and surface modeling techniques and editing principles, from basic splines to polygonal meshes. On the way, you'll look at Bezier and B-spline curves, and how to change a standard mesh into either a quadratic, cubic, or Bezier surface. In addition, if you refer to the color section of this book, you'll see many examples of 3D rendered surfaces and 3D solid models in both opaque and transparent form.

As opposed to a wireframe, which is mainly defined by its edge geometry, a surface model consists of both edge curves and surfaces. Unlike Mechanical Desktop, which creates true curved surfaces, the surface modeler in AutoCAD 2000 defines its faceted surfaces as an approximate polygonal mesh. It does so simply because the faces of the mesh are planar; hence, the resultant mesh only approximates a curved surface. With this understanding (that faceted surfaces in AutoCAD 2000 are not true curved surfaces, but meshes), this chapter will take you step by step through surface modeling and will review the AutoCAD commands you use to create surface models.

Boat, automobile, and airplane manufacturers and industrial designers are the principal users of curves and surface modeling tools. An automobile, for example, is initially derived from artistic sketches—it progresses from design review and design iterations to fulfill aesthetics, aerodynamics, fuel economy, safety, speed, and handling; then, it's converted to 3D geometry. Alternately, an airplane is formed about arbitrary curved shapes and a constrained physical design that's aerodynamically shaped. The aerodynamic skin is attached to this physical design by design constraints and design iterations. Design constraints for an airplane include aerodynamic safety, size, cost, weight, structural stress, and other functions, such as speed, noise-to-weight ratio, fuel economy, and so forth. In addition, the surface modeling tools in use today make numerically controlled (NC) machining possible, and they include sophisticated rendering tools for photorealism. Photorealism allows designers to show finished images of a product before it has been created, which in turn allows shortened product marketing time. Let's examine how AutoCAD creates surface models.

What do you use to model the surface of a product or design, and what are the different types of surfaces? To create simple surfaces, you may use a geometric modeler; for more complex surfaces, you can use a parametric modeler that lets you create freeform curves.

Three common representations allow you to form surfaces:

- Constructive or polygon mesh surfaces

- Freeform or parametric surfaces

- Derivative surfaces

Constructive surfaces consist of revolved, tabulated, and ruled surfaces that use splines or curves for input. AutoCAD is a Non-Uniform Rational B-Spline (NURBS) modeler and uses polygon meshing to create 3D mesh surfaces. *Freeform surfaces* consist of meshes, B-splines, patch, swept, and lofted surfaces, which again use splines or curves for input parameters. *Derivative surfaces* are created from existing surfaces and include fillets between two surfaces, two curves, or a surface and a curve (see Chapter 8 for more information about fillets). These are the main types of surfaces you'll use, and this chapter looks at them in depth. The next section reviews the different kinds of curves and surfaces used in both 3D surface modeling and solid modeling.

Types Of Curves And Surfaces

Several types of curves and surfaces are used in 3D modeling. Curves, for example, consist of straight lines, conic sections, and freeform parametric curves and intersection curves. Surfaces, on the other hand, consist of planes, freeform parametric surfaces, quadratic surfaces, blended or derived surfaces, and superquadrics.

Why does a 3D modeler have to use both curves and surfaces? Reflect on a boat design as an example and think about the ribs and the complex shape. Your boat design would have a start point and an endpoint, and if you took cross-sections at points equidistant along the length of the boat, each cross-section would be different. In effect, each cross-section is a rib, and you draw each of the different rib shapes using curve geometry. You could, for example, draw a sequence of straight lines around a rib from point to point, then spline the straight lines into a series of smooth curves. At this juncture, you'd have a series of smooth curve shapes and the start and ending point of the boat, but no surface. In other words, you'd have the framework built, and you'd now need to add a skin.

One way to place the skin or surface over the framework is to *loft* between the ribs. And with some 3D modeling software, as long as you have more than three ribs, you may *loft* (or, alternately, blend) the series of cross-sectional curves into a smooth surface, as shown in Figure 6.1. Alternately, you can create blended surfaces from freeform surfaces that were originally separated. Take an airplane wing, for example, which is a complex shape. You'd need to create cross-sections at intervals along the wing, and then loft the separated freeform sections to form an aerodynamic shape or surface.

So, why does a surface modeler use both curves and surfaces? You need different types of curves to create the complex framework, plus different types of surfaces to place a skin over the complex curves.

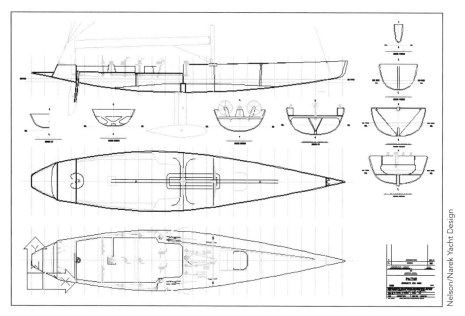

Nelson/Narek Yacht Design

Figure 6.1

Cross-sectional curves formed into a smoothed surface ready for lofting.

Curve Types

Surface modeling uses these types of curves:

- Straight lines

- Conic sections, including parabolas, circles, ellipses, and hyperbolas

- Freeform parametric curves, including NURBS, Bezier curves, and B-splines

- Curves of intersection

Figure 6.2 shows these different curves. In addition, splines are useful to create irregular-shaped curves and also for drawing arbitrary curved shapes about a constrained physical design.

For example, automobile designers use many types of complex curves that have to flow into a smooth shape with an irregular surface skin placed over the complex curves. (You can find an example of such an automobile design in this book's color section.) To create this complex or freeform curve design, the designer could use splines. Splines, originally used by loftsmen, were flexible pieces of wood or metal used by ship, aircraft, and automobile designers to draw smooth curves. The splines had *ducks* (weights or control points) attached to them, which were used to pull the splines in various directions. In AutoCAD, these ducks are control, order, or vertex points. A cubic spline has an order of 4, for example—the higher the order of a spline, the more control points it will have. AutoCAD provides the option to use different types of curves, such as Bezier curves and B-splines. (These are explained in more detail in the section "Curve And Surface Parameters" later in this chapter.)

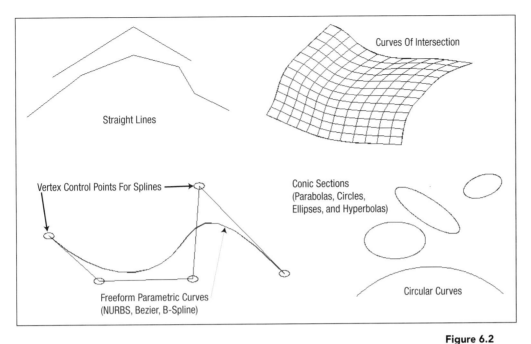

Figure 6.2

Types of curves.

Surface Types

You've seen that surface modeling consists of curves and surfaces and that you can create different curve shapes and then place a surface skin over the curves to form a blended surface. But what are the different types of surfaces? They're as follows:

- Planes (meshes)

- Freeform, including parametric surfaces

- Quadric surfaces, consisting of types of conic sections that include Torii, (ellipsoid) sphere, cylinder, cone, and dome

- Blended surfaces from freeform surfaces that were originally separated

Unlike Mechanical Desktop, you'll find that AutoCAD is limited as a surface modeler; Figure 6.3 shows a variety of surface types.

Curve And Surface Parameters

You may use straight polylines between vertices to create curves by using polylines and then splining. This sounds like an ambiguous statement, but you'll see how this method may create different curves to surfaces. Remember that one of the methods used to form surfaces is to generate a freeform or parametric surface by using splines or curves. Without a set of connecting splines or curves, you have no means to create freeform surfaces (which in turn consist of meshes, B-splines, patch, swept, and/or lofted surfaces). Each of these options uses splines or curves for input parameters—that is, the curves are the boundaries of the mesh surface. Nevertheless, AutoCAD has two versions of a spline curve, and these are controlled in specific ways, which are discussed next.

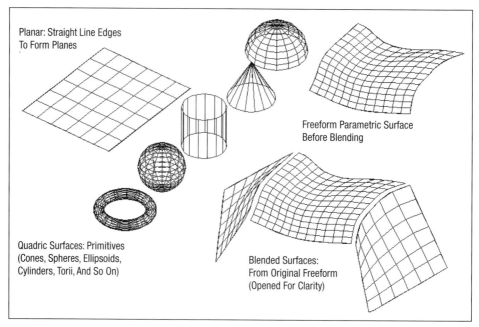

Figure 6.3

Types of surfaces.

As you'll see by looking at the Draw menu, which shows Polyline and 3D Polyline, there are two types of polyline: 2D and 3D. Also notice the **Spline** option, which we'll revisit later in the chapter. To understand the different versions of spline curves, let's work through a simple exercise that compares two freeform curves: a polyline and a true spline (Non-Uniform Rational B-Spline), shown in Figure 6.4. Using different colors, you'll create the two curve types over each other as a comparison. In the first part of the exercise, you'll draw a series of straight lines using the **POLYLINE** command as listed in the coordinates below. In the second half of the exercise, which you'll find in the section "True Spline Curves Vs. Polyline Spline Curves," you'll draw a true spline. This comparison will show you the differences between the two different types of curves in AutoCAD.

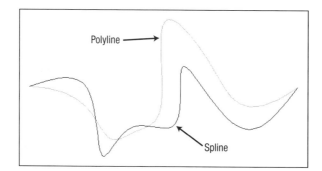

Figure 6.4

A polyline and a spline drawn at the same vertices to show two different AutoCAD curves.

The following list of coordinates is in metric units, so open a new drawing and specify metric units. Create two layers: Cubic, using the color green; and NURBS, using the color blue. Set the current layer to CUBIC, and then use the **PLINE** command and enter the following list of coordinates:

```
Command: pline
Specify start point: 40,190
Specify next point or [Arc/Close/Halfwidth/Length/Undo/Width]:
   100,190
Specify next point or [Arc/Close/Halfwidth/Length/Undo/Width]:
   120,120
Specify next point or [Arc/Close/Halfwidth/Length/Undo/Width]:
   150,150
Specify next point or [Arc/Close/Halfwidth/Length/Undo/Width]:
   190,150
Specify next point or [Arc/Close/Halfwidth/Length/Undo/Width]:
   200,240
Specify next point or [Arc/Close/Halfwidth/Length/Undo/Width]:
   240,210
Specify next point or [Arc/Close/Halfwidth/Length/Undo/Width]:
   260,150
Specify next point or [Arc/Close/Halfwidth/Length/Undo/Width]:
   320,190
```

Press Enter to complete the command. You now have an unusual set of straight connected lines on screen. At the keyboard, enter the **PEDIT** command and pick the polyline you just created. While you're still in **PEDIT**, enter "s" (for spline) to see the straight lines turn into a series of smoothed (splined) curves. Press Enter to complete the command. You now have an *interpolated spline* curve, or cubic spline curve. (In mathematics, it's the lowest order of polynomial that can define a nonplanar curve.)

Next, pick the splined curve polyline with your mouse. *Grips* (small blue square boxes) will appear at each of the vertices, and the original line will change to a ghosted line. (Grips appear at the vertex node points, before the polyline was splined.) Notice that each vertex point (apart from the first and last vertex) isn't touching the splined curve. While you still have the blue grips on screen, pick any one of the vertex points: It will turn red. (It's now called a *hot grip*.) Then, while holding the hot grip, slowly start to move your mouse pointer away from the adjacent vertices (but don't pick a point—just move the pointer). Notice that a rubber-band line appears, showing you the resultant shape of moving the vertex point away from the splined entity. Move the line and pick any point on screen, and then repeat the process. Remember, the previous section mentioned that splines had ducks (weights or control points) attached to them. In this instance, the ducks are similar to the hot grips that let you interpolate the spline curve vertex points. In general CAD terms, they're termed *control points*, because they're outside the curve. These control points thus *weight* your curve.

However, this interpolated spline is a mathematical method to allow you to generate points on a curve, and you can use a number of different types: Bezier, B-spline, and so on. AutoCAD provides a number of options to which you can change splines and surface meshes, including quadratic, cubic, and Bezier curves.

Bezier Curves And B-Splines

During the 1960s, Pierre Bezier of Renault cars developed a system of curves that combined features of interpolation and approximation to polynomials. The interpolating polynomials pass through a static set of control point coordinates (termed *through points*), such as when you use a true spline in AutoCAD; see the upper portion of Figure 6.5. The approximate polynomials pass adjacent to the control points (termed *weighted control points*), such as when you create a splined AutoCAD polyline (see the lower portion of Figure 6.5). (You use **PEDIT**, for example, to provide a smooth fit as a splined object.)

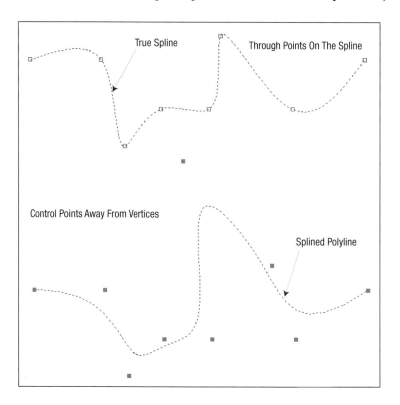

Figure 6.5
The differences between through points and control points in AutoCAD.

What has Pierre Bezier got to do with AutoCAD? That's a good question, because if you're going to use polylines, you're going to use **PEDIT**. Then, you have to interpolate spline curves from cubic spline curves into an alternative form of smoothness—such as Bezier curves, B-splines, or quadratic B-splines. But why use Bezier curves, or any other form of curve?

You need to remember that a spline in AutoCAD fits a smooth curve to a sequence of points within a specified limit. AutoCAD's surface modeler uses NURBS mathematics, which stores and defines a class of curve and surface data. For example, in a Bezier curve the first and last control points define the exact ending points of the curve, and the intermediate points influence the path or shape of the curve. In addition, the first two and last two control points define lines tangential to the starting and ending points of the curve.

Sounds confusing, doesn't it? That's just what Pierre Bezier thought, and he looked for an easier method of creating less complex freeform curves. He wanted something that was easy and would let him shape and control freeform curves on the Renault cars he designed. Thus, Bezier curves give good control (points) to give a blended curve. With a Bezier curve, for example, if you moved a control point, the curve changed in the immediate vicinity of the control points. But if this change was too constrained, and you needed more local curve control, you'd use a B-spline or NURBS curve.

Thus, a B-spline is a special case of the Bezier curve. (It's an approximation, and it gives more control when you need to edit the curves.) B-spline curves employ an arbitrary number of control points. Nonetheless, you use B-splines for more precise local control over the curve. Thus, when you move a B-spline control point, only the curve defined by the new point and the vertices adjacent to it are altered. The resultant curve changes only in the immediate vicinity of the control points—the whole curve doesn't change, as in a Bezier curve. Hence, in AutoCAD you'd use B-splines or a true NURBS spline for better curve and surface control.

True Spline Curves Vs. Polyline Spline Curves

A true spline in AutoCAD fits a smooth curve to a sequence of through points within a specified limit. The surface modeler in AutoCAD uses NURBS mathematics, which stores and defines a class of curve and surface data. Freeform parametric curves include Bezier curves, B-splines, and NURBS. Thus, using the **Spline** option from the Draw menu allows you to create true NURBS curves using through points (as opposed to editing a polyline with the **Spline** option to give you an approximate spline), where the polyline curve is defined or *weighted* through control points. In AutoCAD, spline curves are used to create extruded and/or revolved surfaces.

Now, let's continue our earlier exercise, which compares two freeform curves: a polyline and a true NURBS spline. If necessary, refer back to the "Curve And Surface Parameters" section for the steps to create the polyline. After you've created the polyline, set your layer to the NURBS layer and use the **SPLINE** command with the same coordinate list. (Use zero for the Start and End tangents.) In this instance, notice that the curved line has through points attached at each of the coordinate points. Using the **PEDIT** command, choose the polyline and spline it. Notice that the control points on the polyline are away from the curved line. Try using your grips on both the polyline and spline.

What are the advantages of using a spline curve as opposed to a polyline and then splining the polyline? If you did the exercise above, the simple answer is curve control. Remember, true spline curves use through points, which are created by interpolating the spline through a set of points that lie on the desired path of the curve. This method creates curved boundaries far more accurately than polylines for both 2D drafting and 3D modeling.

A further advantage is that by using grips or the **SPLINEDIT** command, you can edit or alter your true splines without losing integrity in the database. Your database integrity is lost if you use **PEDIT** and smooth a polyline. Let's look at a few of the options and system variables that spline curve editing will allow for curve control:

- *Polyline with spline curve*—Polylines, polysplines, and true splines define complex curves, contours, and boundaries. In the example shown in Figure 6.6, each vertex is a control point, and you can use grips to move each vertex point. You use **PEDIT** to create a splined polyline, which is simply a B-spline. The spline passes through the first and last control points as shown. Three system variables are used for control: **SPLINETYPE**, **SPLINESEGS**, and **SPLFRAME**.

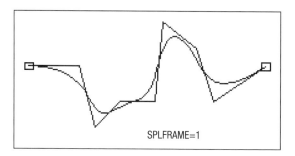

Figure 6.6
Polyline with spline curve.

- *Quadratic B-spline curve*—This Bezier curve passes through the first and last control points. The curve uses the remaining vertex control points to form a blended curve. To create the quadratic B-spline (Bezier curve), set the **SPLINETYPE** to 5, as shown in Figure 6.7.

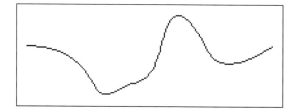

Figure 6.7
Quadratic B-spline curve.

- *Cubic B-spline curve*—Less precise than a Bezier curve. The system variable **SPLINESEGS** sets the weight of control points to form a tighter curve or looser curve. The system variable **SPLINETYPE** set to 6 forms a cubic B-spline, as shown in Figure 6.8.

- *Curve-fit spline curve*—Less precise than the cubic curve. The system variable **SPLINESEGS** sets the coarseness or weight of the control

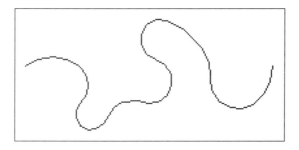

Figure 6.8
Cubic B-spline curve.

points to form a tighter or looser blended curve. Another variable (a subset of the **SPLINEDIT** command)—Splinedit|Refine|Elevate—may be used, which usually requires an integer between 4 and 26. If you enter a value greater than the current value, the number of control points will increase uniformly across the spline for more localized control. Try drawing a spline; then, set the **SPLINEDIT** command's **ELEVATE** variable to 9 and see the instant result. See Figure 6.9.

Figure 6.9
Curve-fit spline curve.

- *True **SPLINE** curve*—Using AutoCAD's true **SPLINE** command results in a curve that is more precise than the Bezier curve. **SPLINEDIT** sets the weight of a vertex control point to allow a tighter or looser curve. The higher the weight value, the nearer the spline is pulled to the control point. **SPLINEDIT** also lets you add control points directly onto the spline curve. See Figure 6.10.

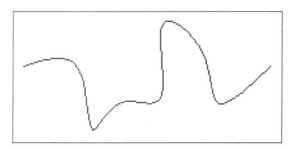

Figure 6.10
True **SPLINE** curve.

Each of the examples shown in Figures 6.6 through 6.10 indicate just one curve object. You'll see that each of the examples appears quite different, but realize that they were all drawn using the same coordinate points—it's merely the different variable settings that create the different types of spline curves. Working with just one curve object at a time allows you to have more control. The next step is placing a surface; you need to reflect upon a few simple rules as you close geometric elements prior to placing a surface. Modeling for closure rules refer to geometric progression, which specifically refer to points on curves, curves on surfaces, and so on.

Rules Of Geometric Progression: "Modeling For Closure"

The rules of geometric progression refer to points on curves, curves on surfaces, and surfaces on solids. Geometric elements follow a logical progression that, when constructed correctly, will help ensure closure of your model. *Modeling for closure* and error checking begin with X,Y,Z coordinate points and progress to a closed solid volume. Ensuring model closure begins with proper creation and manipulation of your points (X,Y,Z coordinates) and curves (lines, arcs, polylines, and so on). Here are some hints, as illustrated in Figure 6.11:

- *Points on curves*—The point is a basic geometric element that's the basis of all geometric curves. Remember that during wireframe and surface operations, internal controls for model integrity and closure in solid models aren't automatically applied. Thus, to ensure correct closure of your surface model, you should begin with the correct creation of your node points (corners) and your curves (polylines or splines).

- *Curves on surfaces*—As points (X,Y,Z coordinates) are the defining elements for curves, curves are in turn the defining elements for surfaces. Always generate curves from existing surfaces.

- *Curve modification*—Be aware how local curve modification may affect associated surface geometry. Some CAD operators indicate it's better to try to use simple curves (lines and arcs) instead of splines.

- *Closed area*—Surfaces must form a closed area to define a surface and should always share curve boundaries when they meet.

- *Connecting edges*—Connecting edges should share existing boundaries and should have equal lengths per side. Any connecting points need to be coincident to connecting edges.

At this point, we've looked at, generated, compared, and edited curves. Because we've exhausted the possibilities of manipulating curves, let's move on to 3D meshes and geometric generated surfaces, and the AutoCAD commands associated with them.

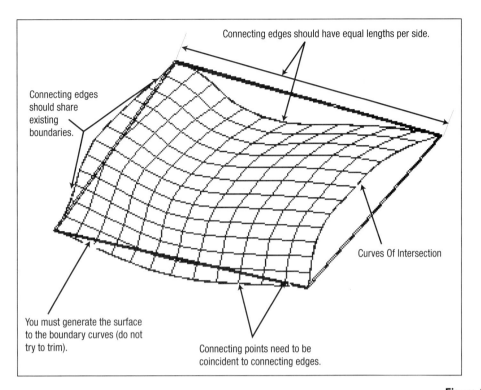

Connecting edges should have equal lengths per side.

Connecting edges should share existing boundaries.

Curves Of Intersection

You must generate the surface to the boundary curves (do not try to trim).

Connecting points need to be coincident to connecting edges.

Figure 6.11
Modeling for closure.

3D Meshes And Geometric Generated Surfaces

As we saw earlier, three common representations allow you to form surfaces:

- Constructive or polygon mesh surfaces

- Freeform or parametric surfaces

- Derivative surfaces

AutoCAD is a NURBS modeler and uses polygon meshing to create 3D mesh surfaces. It lets you create surface meshes, splines, extrusions, and revolutions of surfaces. The polygonal modeler lets you create geometric-generated surfaces through the **RULESURF**, **TABSURF**, **REVSURF**, and **EDGESURF** commands. Obviously, when you use these commands, you need to understand the purpose and requirement of each type of mesh and then select the correct one for the job. The following sections review the different polygonal surface modeling options and look at possible uses for each. (For more information on editing meshes, see Chapter 8.)

SOLID

One of the simplest surface commands for placing a surface on an entity is **SOLID**. You create a 3D wireframe first and then use the **SOLID** command to attach a surface to your 3D wireframe, working around each surface of the part until it's complete. The only problem with this command is that it's tedious to work with, especially if you have a lot of faces. It's also limited in what it can do. It doesn't work well with curves, for example, but it works well for individual plane faces. Open the wire.dwg drawing from the CD-ROM, and attach surfaces to each of the part's faces using the **SOLID** command. Remember that you must set the (UCS) to the face you are working on, set your (OSNAP) tools to endpoint, and then use the **SOLID** command. See Figure 6.12 for a finished comparison of two entities—one using **SOLID** with the **HIDE** command on a wireframe drawing, and one without.

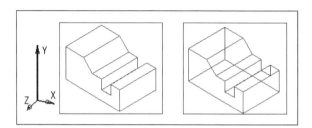

Figure 6.12

The image on the left shows the result when the **SOLID** and **HIDE** commands are used; the image on the right shows the result when they are not used.

Remember, the **SOLID** command works in a butterfly fashion: upper left to upper right, and then lower left to lower right, or similar. See Figure 6.13 for an illustration of the incorrect versus the correct butterfly pick method.

Figure 6.13

The incorrect butterfly pick method is shown on the left; the correct method is shown on the right.

For the correct order of pick points for wire.dwg, use the pick points as shown in Figure 6.14. Remember that you must set the UCS to the face you are working on (in the case of Figure 6.14, the UCS should be set to the Front face), then use the **SOLID** command; otherwise, you'll be drawing a solid surface on the wrong plane or face of your 3D model.

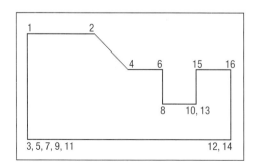

Figure 6.14

The correct order of pick points for wire.dwg.

In addition, two variables work with the **SOLID** command, **FILL** and **FILLMODE**. The system variable **FILLMODE** stores the **FILL** setting, which is either ON or OFF. **FILLMODE** indicates if lines, polylines, and so on are filled in:

- 1 = default (objects are filled)

- 0 = Objects are not filled

3D Mesh Surface Commands

As you choose Surfaces from the Draw menu, you'll notice these options and commands: 2D Solid, 3D Face, 3D Surfaces, Edge, 3D Mesh, Revolved Surface, Tabulated Surface, Ruled Surface, and Edge Surface; alternately, you may choose the Surfaces toolbar with its set of icons. As you'll see in the illustrations on the next several pages (Figures 6.15 to 6.28), with AutoCAD, you can use meshes to approximate different kinds of 3D surface shapes or surface primitives. You define a mesh using a series of 3D surface elements that can curve in any direction in space. Each of the mesh's surface elements has four sides, four vertices (corners), and up to four edges in common with adjoining surface elements. But the mesh can't have thickness.

Both the **3DMESH** and **PFACE** AutoCAD commands allow you to create a freeform polygonal mesh, as illustrated in Figure 6.15, whereas the **REVSURF**, **TABSURF**, **RULESURF**, and **EDGESURF** commands create regular surfaces. They allow you to create a large number of surface elements automatically as you select certain objects to define the mesh. If you look at Figure 6.15, you'll see that **EDGESURF** was used to create the two mesh surfaces, also known as *Coons surfaces*. (In the early 1960s, MIT researcher Steve Coons developed a method of interpolating surfaces bounded by four curves, which he termed the Coons patch.)

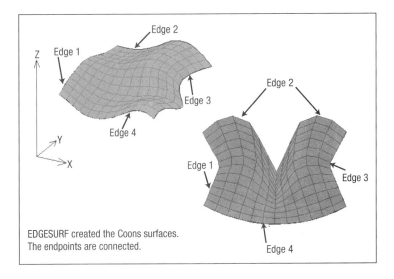

Figure 6.15
3D mesh surfaces.

The **3DMESH** command, although designed mainly for use in AutoLISP programming, allows you to define an irregular mesh by entering the location of every vertex point, one by one. (See the discussion of **PFACE** and **3DMESH** later in this chapter.) The ways to control density of resolution are described in the "Surface System Variables" section; they include **SURFTAB1** and **SURFTAB2**. In the "Alternative Applications" section, you'll find the **3DMESH**, **PFACE**, and **3DFACE** polygonal mesh surface modelers for use with AutoLISP applications, which let you create multiple faces simultaneously. There are other ways to create meshes; one of the main methods is to use surface primitives. AutoCAD has a number of built-in primitives, but be aware that surface primitives and solid primitives are not the same. They each use a different modeling kernel.

3D Surface Primitives

If you choose 3D Surfaces from the Draw|Surfaces menu, the submenu provides a variety of standard geometric shapes constructed from meshes. They're also available on the Surfaces toolbar. Figure 6.16 shows the 3D Objects dialog box and a typical list of nine standard 3D Surface objects: Box3d, Pyramid, Wedge, Dome, Sphere, Cone, Torus, Dish, and Mesh. At the end of the chapter, two further commands are discussed: **PFACE** and **PEDIT**. Also at the end of the chapter is a list of surface system variables. A further surface option is the **EDGE** command. This is merely an on/off toggle for edges of faces, which you'll review next.

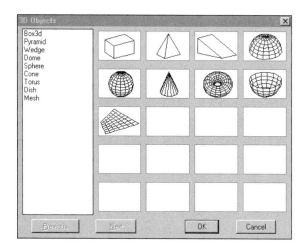

Figure 6.16
The 3D Objects dialog box.

EDGE Command

The **EDGE** command lets you toggle the visibility and invisibility of edges. To use the **EDGE** command, create a 3D wireframe using the **3DFACE** command, and then use **EDGE** by simply picking which edges should be invisible. (See **3DFACE** and **PFACE** at the end of this chapter.) You might want to use the **EDGE** command with the 3dmesh-1.dwg (from this book's companion CD-ROM) on some of the faces just to see how it works. Remember to explode the 3D mesh (only once) into 3D faces; otherwise, it won't function. Then, pick any arbitrary face to hide. Do *not* save the file.

3DMESH Command

The **3DMESH** command lets you create an open mesh, one vertex at a time, as shown in Figure 6.17, which is a 4×6 mesh. Understand that in order to determine the size of a 3D mesh, you count the number of node or vertex points—that is, M multiplied by N (the size of a 3D mesh is not the number of faces). (For more on editing meshes, see Chapter 8.)

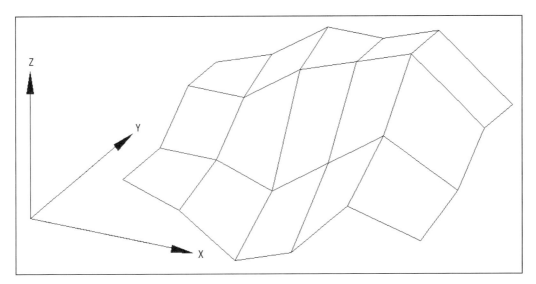

Figure 6.17
3DMESH allows you to create meshes based on vertex locations.

At the **3DMESH** prompt, enter the number of vertices in the M direction and then the number of vertices in the N direction. (Remember, AutoCAD 2000 defines the location of each vertex in the 3D mesh through M and N— that is, the row and column indices of the vertex.) Both M and N require an integer from 2 to 256.

In turn, AutoCAD prompts for the X,Y,Z vertex location (coordinate) of each vertex point. The M and N positions identify each vertex point, which in turn prompts for Vertex numbers (0,0), Vertex (0,1), Vertex (1,0), Vertex (1,1) and so on. The **3DMESH** command prompts for the vertex points in the N direction and then proceeds to the M vertex points. As you locate the last Vertex point, AutoCAD creates the 3D mesh.

3DMESH produces an open mesh, which you may close in one or both directions by using the **PEDIT** command. **PEDIT** joins the first to the last vertex in either the M or N direction. Three system variables control accuracy of the 3D mesh: **SURFU** for the M direction, **SURFV** for the N direction, and **SURFTYPE** for the type of surface (for a quadratic B-spline surface, set **SURFTYPE** to 5; for a cubic B-spline surface, set **SURFTYPE** to 6; for a Bezier surface, set **SURFTYPE** to 8). Then, use the **Smooth** option of **PEDIT**.

The mesh in Figure 6.17 shows the relationship between the order of the vertices, especially as they appear in the prompts of the **3DMESH** command, with the M and N directions.

Let's work through an exercise that creates a 3×4 polygonal mesh, as you can see in Figure 6.18. Remember that to determine the size of a 3D mesh, you count the number of node or vertex points (the size is not the number of faces). So in this case, you'll have 3×4=12 vertex location points. Start a new drawing in English units and name it 3dmesh-1.dwg. (This drawing is also available on the CD-ROM.) Set the 3D Viewpoint to an SE Isometric view. Activate the **3DMESH** command and follow the prompts as follows:

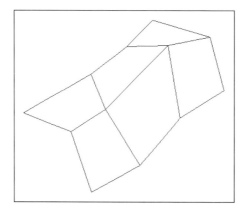

Figure 6.18
3DMESH used to create a 3D surface.

```
Command: 3dmesh
Enter size of mesh in M direction: 3
Enter size of mesh in N direction: 4
Specify location for vertex (0, 0): .5,-.5,-.5
Specify location for vertex (0, 1): 1,3.1,0
Specify location for vertex (0, 2): .5,5.5,-.5
Specify location for vertex (0, 3): .5,7,.25
Specify location for vertex (1, 0): 3,.5,0
Specify location for vertex (1, 1): 3,2.5,0
Specify location for vertex (1, 2): 2.5,6.5,1
Specify location for vertex (1, 3): 3,8.5,.5
Specify location for vertex (2, 0): 6,-.5,-.5
Specify location for vertex (2, 1): 6.5,2,0
Specify location for vertex (2, 2): 5.5,5,0
Specify location for vertex (2, 3): 5.5,7.5,0
```

Now, set the surface type. When you've completed entering the 3D mesh vertex location points, you need to know how the system variables affect the resultant mesh. Realize that all you have so far is an arbitrary 3D mesh with 12 specific vertex location points. (These 3D points could also have been set by a 3D coordinate pick device or measuring machine.) As I discussed earlier, three system variables control accuracy of the 3D mesh: **SURFU** for the M direction, **SURFV** for the N direction, and **SURFTYPE** for the type of surface. Set the **SURFU** variable to 24 and the **SURFV** variable to 18. Set the **SURFTYPE** variable to 5 (the default is 6). Now, use the **Smooth** option of **PEDIT**, and notice how the surface changed and smoothed out to an 18×24 mesh face. See Figure 6.19. What you've produced is a quadratic B-spline surface instead of the rough arbitrary 3D mesh surface your initial pick points started with. (Try setting **SURFTYPE** back to 6 and then to 8. Use **PEDIT** again and notice the difference in quality and coarseness of the surface.)

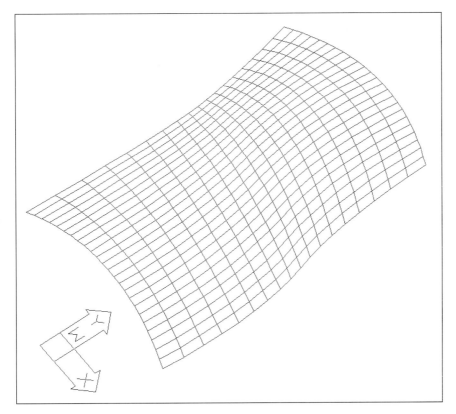

Figure 6.19
The smoothed 3D mesh set to a quadratic B-Spline surface.

REVSURF Command

The **REVSURF** command creates a surface-of-revolution mesh from a path curve and an axis of revolution. This process converts a 2D profile into a 3D mesh object: You create your 3D object by revolving a 2D profile about a central axis to sweep out a surface. (Think of it as the central axis of a cylindrical object.) **SURFTAB1** determines the faces placed about the rotation axis. You control the **SURFTAB1** (M mesh size) using an integer from 3 to 1,024. Remember that M mesh is the vertical face. **SURFTAB2** controls the N mesh size (N is horizontal) and determines how many faces are used to simulate the curves created by arcs or circles in the path curve. Let's work through an example.

In this exercise, you'll open the revsurf.dwg file from the CD-ROM and use it to create revolved surfaces. You'll need to reset your **SURFTAB1** and **SURFTAB2** values to 24. To use **REVSURF**, follow these steps:

Note: The direction of the axis of revolution runs from the end nearest its pick point to the opposite end. In turn, this direction and the right-hand rule determine the direction of rotation for the two angles.

1. Create your path curve. The easiest way to do this is to use an open polyline and then **SPLINE** it. Alternately, create the path curve using a line, circle, arc, or other type of line. Note that the polylines are premade for you in revsurf.dwg on this book's companion CD-ROM. You'll see the polyline paths as red in the upper left and blue in the lower right of the drawing.

2. Using a normal line, create a single axis of revolution. Your axis of revolution is usually a line or an open polyline (in which case only the endpoints are important). Your path curve doesn't need to lie in the same plane as the axis of revolution. See Figure 6.20.

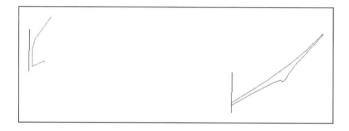

Figure 6.20
The created profile and axis of revolution for two surfaces of revsurf.dwg.

3. Activate the **REVSURF** command by choosing Revolved Surface from the Draw menu or the Surfaces toolbar. (Hint: Before using **REVSURF**, set the layer to the color you wish the object to be colored.)

4. At the prompt, select your path curve first (the generatrix)—that is, pick the red or blue polyline of the revsurf.dwg. Then, select the axis of revolution; enter the start angle and then the included angle. In revsurf.dwg, press Enter to both these prompts to accept the defaults. The rotated images appear in Figure 6.21.

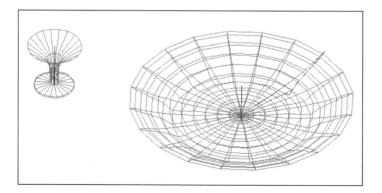

Figure 6.21
The result of rotating the profiles around the axes.

5. Remember to set the view to NE Isometric (this is preset in revsurf.dwg). Shade or render the resultant surface models, which should resemble those in Figure 6.22.

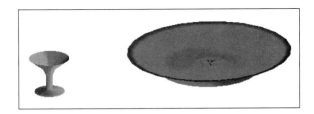

Figure 6.22
The finished rendered forms.

TABSURF Command

The **TABSURF** command creates a surface extrusion as a tabulated surface mesh from a path curve and a direction vector. The command is similar to **REVSURF**, except that it creates a straight ruled surface instead of a revolved surface. It's a special case of the ruled surface generated by a straight line as it moves parallel to itself along a curve. **SURFTAB1** controls the number of intervals along the path curve; the default value is 6. The mesh is generated in the direction of the nearest endpoint.

As an exercise, we'll open the tabsurf.dwg drawing from the CD-ROM and use it to create surface extrusions as shown in Figure 6.23. You'll need to reset your **TABSURF1** value to 20 or higher. Follow these steps:

(SURFTAB 1)

1. Activate the **TABSURF** command by choosing Tabulated Surface from the Draw menu or the Surfaces toolbar.

2. At the prompt, select first the path curve and then the direction vector.

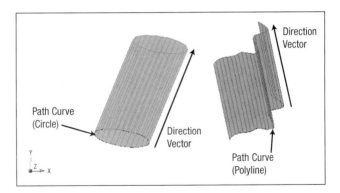

Figure 6.23
TABSURF creates a profile surface mesh model from a path curve and a direction vector.

The path curve, which can be a line, circle, arc, or polyline, is normally called the *generatrix*. The direction vector line (normally called the *directrix*) determines two components: the direction and the distance the path curve will move as it travels along the profile shape to create the surface.

In a tabulated surface mesh, the M mesh is 2, and it increases in the direction of the direction vector. The N mesh increases in the direction of the path curve, and it's determined by the **SURFTAB1** system variable.

For example, if you preset **SURFTAB1** to 20 and use a line, arc, circle, or spline-fit polyline as a path line, you'll have 20 equally spaced vertices in the N mesh direction. Or, if you set **SURFTAB1** to 20 and your path curve is a 2D polyline that has both line and arc segments, vertices will occur at the ends of each line segment, and each arc segment will be divided into 20 equally spaced vertices. (See the section "Surface System Variables" for more information about **SURFTAB1** and **SURFTAB2**.)

RULESURF Command

The **RULESURF** command creates a polygonal mesh between two entities. The entities may be arcs, circles, lines, points, 2D polylines, 3D polylines, or splines. The rule when using **RULESURF** is that either both entities must be open (created with lines or arcs, for example) or both entities must be closed (created with circles or planes). Note that only one entity in your selection may be a point to create a cone-shaped object.

The **RULESURF** command creates an M and an N mesh. The default value of the **SURFTAB1** variable is 6, and it's used to alter the number of facets generated. The 0,0,0 vertex is located at the beginning of the entity you select first. The M direction will increase from the first entity (your point, line, arc, circle, or 2D polyline, etc.) to the second object, and it's always set to 2. The N direction increases from the beginning to the end of the first entity if it's an open entity and is determined by the system variable **SURFTAB1**. (See "Surface System Variables," later in the chapter.)

You can also use **RULESURF** as a connector of different profiles. For example, in a new drawing, set the 3D Viewpoint to an SE Isometric view, and also set the UCS to a Front view (X to 90). Create two alternate profiles (such as a circle and a square) at different locations on screen. Set **SURFTAB1** to 12 and then connect the profiles using **RULESURF**.

You can open the rulesurf.dwg drawing from the CD-ROM and use it to create meshed surfaces as shown in Figure 6.24. Or create the simple lines as seen in Figure 6.24 and then use the **RULESURF** command. Note that the square boxes on the object lines denote your pick points. In the lower portion of Figure 6.24, you can see that choosing opposite pick points can cause a butterfly effect to your ruled surface.

Sometimes as you use **RULESURF** with a closed entity, you need to know where the N direction will be located in order to construct the entity. In such a case, it's simply a matter of knowing where the N direction starts and ends. Here are some hints and examples:

- *Circle and polyline*—When you use a circle and a polyline, you may get unusual results with **RULESURF** if you pick incorrectly. The ruled surface may cross over itself. One way to correct the problem is to reconstruct the polyline in reverse order. As an alternative, you can

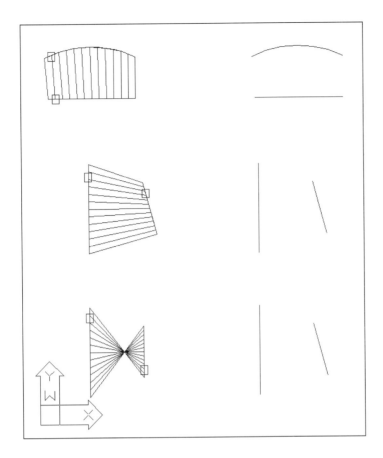

Figure 6.24
RULESURF creates polygonal surface meshes.

use two polyarcs instead of the circle, or re-create the circle in the same location but on a mirrored construction plane.

- *Closed polyline*—If your entity is a closed polyline, the N direction will start at the last vertex point of the polyline.

- *Circle and tilted construction plane*—If your entity is a circle, the N direction starts at the circle's zero-angle point. If you use **RULESURF** between the two circles, the edge lines joining the vertices usually won't cross each other as long as the construction plane for one circle is parallel to the construction plane of the other circle. However, if the second circle is drawn on a construction plane that's tilted or rotated in relation to the first construction plane, the edge lines may cross each other or give an hourglass or butterfly effect. Try to pick each circle parallel to each other and in the same plane.

Now, let's work through an exercise that uses **RULESURF** to place a surface on a 3D spiral. You'll copy one line of the spiral up 25mm and then use **RULESURF** to connect the two edges as surfaces, as in a true spiral. (Figure 6.25 shows the completed polygon surface mesh of a spiral.) Start

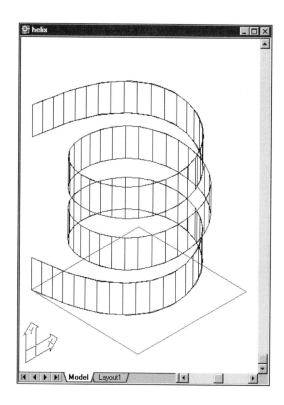

Figure 6.25

The completed polygon mesh surface of the spiral.

a new metric drawing and name it spiral.dwg. (This drawing is also available on the CD-ROM.) Set the 3D Viewpoint to SE Isometric and keep the UCS at World coordinates. Now, follow these steps:

1. Choose 3D Polyline from the Draw menu and then respond to the command prompts as follows:

```
Command: 3dpoly
Specify start point of polyline: 0,0,0
Specify endpoint of line or [Undo]: @100,0,10
Specify endpoint of line or [Undo]: @0,100,10
Specify endpoint of line or [Undo]: @-100,0,10
Specify endpoint of line or [Undo]: @0,-100,10
Specify endpoint of line or [Undo]: @100,0,10
Specify endpoint of line or [Undo]: @0,100,10
Specify endpoint of line or [Undo]: @-100,0,10
Specify endpoint of line or [Undo]: @0,-100,10
Specify endpoint of line or [Undo]: @100,0,10
Specify endpoint of line or [Undo]: @0,100,10
Specify endpoint of line or [Undo]: @-100,0,10
Specify endpoint of line or [Undo]: @0,-100,10
Specify endpoint of line or [Undo]: <Press Enter to complete
   the command>
```

2. Now that you've created the spiral , you need to reset the UCS, to X 90:

```
Command: ucs
Current ucs name: *WORLD*
Enter an option [New/Move/orthoGraphic/Prev/Restore/Save/
  Del/Apply/?/World] <World>: x
Specify rotation angle about X axis <90>: 90
```

3. Use the **COPY** command to copy the spiral up 25mm from 0,0,0 to @0,25:

```
Command: copy
Select objects: <Pick the spiral you created>
Specify base point or displacement, or [Multiple]: 0,0,0
Specify second point of displacement or <use first point as
  displacement>: @0,25
```

4. Set the system variable **SURFTAB1** to a value of 96:

```
Command: surftab1
Enter new value for SURFTAB1 <6>: 96
```

5. Use the **RULESURF** command to create the surface between the two spiral elements:

```
Command: rulesurf
Current wire frame density: SURFTAB1=96
Select first defining curve: <Pick the lower curve>
Select second defining curve: <Pick the upper curve>
```

Your spiral is now complete.

EDGESURF Command

The **EDGESURF** command uses four adjoining sides as boundary definitions to create a freeform mesh. It's a Coons surface mesh with four connected edges. (The endpoint of each side should connect with the start point of the next side and so on to form a closed loop.) Remember that you'll connect this to other patches to form the overall surface of your 3D model; you don't make one patch in a vacuum. Anyway, don't think you can create a polyline with four sides and then close it, because doing so won't work: The mesh must have four separate edges. You can create any of the four sides as a combination of arcs, lines, polyarcs, and/or polylines. Remember that as you start the **EDGESURF** command and when you pick the first edge, it's the first edge pick point that determines the M direction. It's also good practice to choose the same beginning point for each of the four sides or the end of each side, respectively. For example, don't choose the end of one edge and then the beginning of the next, or the final mesh will cross and look strange. (You can set different types of smoothed surfaces in AutoCAD to be Quadratic, Cubic, or Bezier. Use the **DDMODIFY** or **PROPERTIES** command to set the surface type. See Chapter 8.)

Let's work through an exercise that creates four true spline lines, each connected by their vertex points. Then, we'll use the **EDGESURF** command to create a Coons surface patch. Start a new drawing using English units and name it edgesurf.dwg. (This drawing is also available on the CD-ROM.) Choose Spline from the Draw menu and follow the prompts below (see Figure 6.26 for the pick points):

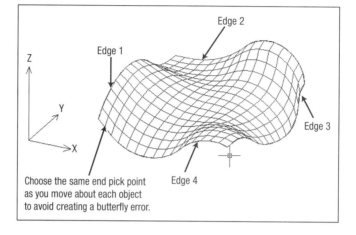

Figure 6.26
Using **EDGESURF** to create a freeform mesh between four objects. The endpoints must connect.

1. Create the first curve (where the text below reads <*Press Enter*><*Press Enter*>; make sure you press Enter twice and then enter 0 degrees for the start and end points of the line):

```
Command: spline
Specify first point or [Object] : 1.1,3.5,0
Specify next point : 1.4,4.1,0
Specify next point or [Close/Fit tolerance] <start tangent>:
   1.8,4.4,0.3
Specify next point or [Close/Fit tolerance] <start tangent>:
   2.0,4.3,0
Specify next point or [Close/Fit tolerance] <start tangent>:
   2.3,4.5,0 <Press Enter> <Press Enter>
Enter start tangent: 0
Enter end tangent: 0
```

2. Create the second curve:

```
Command: spline
Specify first point or [Object]: 2.3,4.5,0 <or use your
   OSNAP to the endpoint of the last curve>
Specify next point: 2.8,4.4,0.3
Specify next point or [Close/Fit tolerance] <start tangent>:
   3.3,4.5,-0.3
Specify next point or [Close/Fit tolerance] <start tangent>:
   3.5,4.7,0
Specify next point or [Close/Fit tolerance] <start tangent>:
   4.0,4.6,0.2
```

```
Specify next point or [Close/Fit tolerance] <start tangent>:
  4.3,4.3,0
Specify next point or [Close/Fit tolerance] <start tangent>:
  4.4,4.1,0 <Press Enter> <Press Enter>
Enter start tangent: 0
Enter end tangent: 0
```

3. Create the third curve:

```
Command: spline
Specify first point or [Object]: 4.4,4.1,0 <or use your
  OSNAP to the endpoint of the last curve>
Specify next point: 3.7,3.9,0.3
Specify next point or [Close/Fit tolerance] <start tangent>:
  3.7,3.5,0
Specify next point or [Close/Fit tolerance] <start tangent>:
  3.9,3.2,-0.3
Specify next point or [Close/Fit tolerance] <start tangent>:
  3.5,3.2,0
Specify next point or [Close/Fit tolerance] <start tangent>:
  3.3,3.2,0
Specify next point or [Close/Fit tolerance] <start tangent>:
  3.1,3.0,0 <Press Enter> <Press Enter>
Enter start tangent: 0
Enter end tangent: 0
```

4. Create the fourth curve:

```
Specify first point or [Object]: 3.1,3.0,0 <or use your
  OSNAP to the Endpoint of the last curve>
Specify next point: 2.9,3.2,0
Specify next point or [Close/Fit tolerance] <start tangent>:
  2.6,3.2,-0.3
Specify next point or [Close/Fit tolerance] <start tangent>:
  2.3,3.05,0
Specify next point or [Close/Fit tolerance] <start tangent>:
  1.8,3.0,0.3
Specify next point or [Close/Fit tolerance] <start tangent>:
  1.5,3.1,0
Specify next point or [Close/Fit tolerance] <start tangent>:
  1.2,3.4,-0.3
Specify next point or [Close/Fit tolerance] <start tangent>:
  1.1,3.5,0 <Press Enter> <Press Enter>
Enter start tangent: 0
Enter end tangent: 0
```

5. Set the value of **SURFTAB1** to 20:

```
Command: surftab1
New value for SURFTAB1 <6>: 20
```

6. Set the value of **SURFTAB2** to 20:

```
Command: surftab2
New value for SURFTAB2 <6>: 20
```

7. Perform the **EDGESURF** command to create a mesh:

```
Command: edgesurf
Current wire frame density: SURFTAB1=20 SURFTAB2=20
Select object 1 for surface edge: <Pick edge 1>
Select object 2 for surface edge: <Pick edge 2>
Select object 3 for surface edge: <Pick edge 3>
Select object 4 for surface edge: <Pick edge 4>
```

Surface System Variables

You can use a number of system variables to set different system settings for surfaces. These variables are explained in more depth in Chapter 8. Here are some hints and examples of the more important surface system variables:

- *SURFTAB1*—Controls the number of surface elements in the M direction of a mesh and determines the faces placed about the rotation axis. You control **SURFTAB1** (M mesh size) using an integer from 3 to 1,024. Remember that M mesh is the vertical face.

- *SURFTAB2*—Controls the number of surface elements in the N direction of a mesh. The system variable determines how many faces are used to simulate curves created by arcs or circles in the path curve. (Remember that M and N indicate the row and column indices of the surface elements.)

- *SPLFRAME*—An on/off (0 or 1) switch that controls the splined smoothed surface or frame. When the system variable **SPLFRAME** equals 0, the smoothed spline is displayed. When **SPLFRAME** is non-zero (that is, 1), the smoothed spline and the defining spline are displayed. The default value of the variable is 1. See Figure 6.27.

- *SPLINETYPE*—Controls the type of curve to be generated by the **Spline** option of the **PEDIT** command. The variable's default value is 6, which produces a cubic B-spline. A setting of 5 produces a quadratic B-spline.

- *SPLINESEGS*—An integer value from –32,768 to 32,767. The default value is 8. For a smoother generated curve and less-specified segments, set **SPLINESEGS** to a negative value. Doing so forces AutoCAD to generate segments with the absolute value of the setting, and in turn applies a fit-type curve to the segments, yielding a smoother curve.

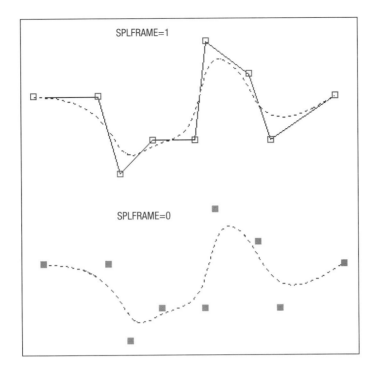

Figure 6.27
You can use **SPLFRAME** to show both the creating and the splined geometry. When the **SPLFRAME** variable is set to 1, the profile and spline are shown; when it is set to 0, only the spline is shown.

- *SURFTYPE*—Controls the level of smoothness to create a quadratic, cubic, or Bezier surface. Open the mesh-sysvar.dwg from this book's companion CD-ROM. It has four edges ready to accept a freeform mesh. Use the **EDGESURF** command to mesh the object; then, set the system variables to adjust to the three surface smoothness types. The smoothness settings for the three surface types are as follows:

  - *Quadratic*—**SURFTYPE** equals 5. The minimum mesh for a quadratic surface is 3x3. Use the **EDGESURF** command at its default setting on the mesh-sysvar.dwg; then, set the variables **SURFU** to 12, **SURFV** to 8, and **SURFTYPE** to 5. Use **PEDIT** to pick the drawing and enter the suboption "s" for smooth surface. The mesh will change to the new settings. See Figure 6.28.

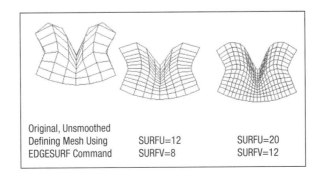

Original, Unsmoothed
Defining Mesh Using
EDGESURF Command

SURFU=12
SURFV=8

SURFU=20
SURFV=12

Figure 6.28
Controlling the level of smoothness to create a quadratic B-spline surface (**SURFTYPE**=5).

- *Cubic*—**SURFTYPE** equals 6. The minimum mesh for a cubic B-spline is 4x4. After opening the mesh-sysvar.dwg, use the **EDGESURF** command at a default setting; then, set the variables **SURFU** to 20, **SURFV** to 12, and **SURFTYPE** to 6. Use **PEDIT** to pick the drawing and enter the suboption "s" for smooth surface. The mesh will change to the new variables. See Figure 6.29.

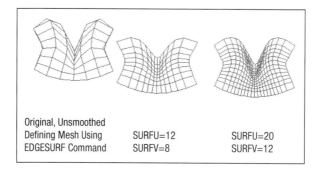

Figure 6.29
Controlling the level of smoothness to create a cubic B-spline surface (**SURFTYPE**=6).

Original, Unsmoothed Defining Mesh Using EDGESURF Command   SURFU=12 SURFV=8   SURFU=20 SURFV=12

- *Bezier*—**SURFTYPE** equals 8; the Bezier surface type is possible only when both M and N are less than 12. After using the **EDGESURF** command at its default setting on the mesh-sysvar.dwg, set the variables **SURFU** to 12, **SURFV** to 8, and **SURFTYPE** to 8. Use **PEDIT** to pick the drawing and enter the sub-option "s" for smooth surface. Reset the variables **SURFU** to 20, **SURFV** to 12, and use **PEDIT** with its smooth surface option. See Figure 6.30.

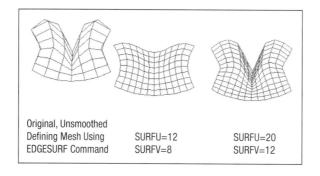

Figure 6.30
Controlling the level of smoothness to create a Bezier surface (**SURFTYPE**=8).

Original, Unsmoothed Defining Mesh Using EDGESURF Command   SURFU=12 SURFV=8   SURFU=20 SURFV=12

Adjusting Surface Smoothness

Here are some more hints and system variable examples for adjusting surface smoothness. (For practice adjusting smoothness, bezier.dwg is available on the CD-ROM.) These items are explained in more depth in Chapter 8:

- *Smooth Mesh*—You can smooth a mesh by editing it with the **PEDIT** command and selecting the s option. The level of smoothness is determined by system variable **SURFTYPE**, whereas the number of vertices is determined by system variables **SURFU** and **SURFV**.

- *Quadratic surface*—The system variable setting **SURFTYPE** controls the level of smoothness. A setting of 5 produces a quadratic B-spline surface that has a low level of smoothness.

- *Cubic surface*—The variable **SURFTYPE** controls the level of smoothness. A setting of 6 produces a cubic B-spline surface with a medium level of smoothness.

- *Bezier surface*—The variable setting **SURFTYPE** controls the level of smoothness. A setting of 8 produces a Bezier surface with a high level of smoothness, as illustrated in Figure 6.30. Notice that smoothness and conformity are inversely related—the smoother the surface, the less it conforms to the defining mesh.

- *SURFU*—Used with **PEDIT** to control the number of M elements in a smoothed surface. System variables **SURFU** and **SURFV** control the number of elements in the smoothed surface. **SURFU** controls the number of elements in the M direction of the mesh, **SURFV** in the N direction. High values in **SURFU** and **SURFV** produce a fine, smoothed mesh, but they also take longer to regenerate on the screen.

- *SURFV*—Used with **PEDIT** to control the number of N elements in a smoothed surface. Don't confuse **SURFU** and **SURFV** with **SURFTAB1** and **SURFTAB2**, which control the number of vertices in the original (unsmoothed) mesh. **SURFU** and **SUFRV** apply only to smoothed surfaces.

- *TABSURF and RULESURF commands*—**SURFTAB1** determines the number of surface elements in the N direction. (M is always 2 for these types of meshes.) Note that the smallest possible value for either the **SURFTAB1** or **SURFTAB2** variable is 2.

- *REVSURF and EDGESURF commands*—**SURFTAB1** determines the number of surface elements in the M direction, whereas **SURFTAB2** determines the number in the N direction. You enter **SURFTAB1** and **SURFTAB2** at the command line.

- *PEDIT*—Allows you to edit polylines and three-dimensional polygon meshes. Choose Polyline from the Modify menu or the Edit Polyline icon from the Modify II toolbar. You can smooth a mesh by editing it with the **PEDIT** command and selecting the s option. The level of smoothness is determined by system variable **SURFTYPE**, whereas the number of vertices is determined by system variables **SURFU** and **SURFV**.

> **Note:** When a mesh is closed in a given direction, the number of surface elements and the number of vertices in that direction are equal. When a mesh is open in a given direction, the number of vertices is one more than the number of surface elements.

- *SPLINEDIT*—Lets you edit splined lines. [Fit Data/Close/Move vertex/ Refine/rEverse/Undo/eXit] are the subcommand options. Your splines may be closed or open (that is, the endpoints of the splines may be connected or not connected). When you choose a closed spline, the **Close** option will internally adjust to **Open** and provide you with a choice of opening it. If the spline you pick has no fit data, you'll find the **Fit Data** option unavailable. *Fit data* consists of all the tangents associated with splines created by the **SPLINE** command, plus all the fit points and the fit tolerance.

- *SPLINEDIT* *(fit points and splined lines)*—The fit points of splines are shown in your choice of grip color when you select a spline created with the **SPLINE** command.

- *SPLINEDIT* *(control points and polylines)*—The control points of polylines are shown in your choice of grip color when you select a spline created with **PLINE** (polyline). **SPLINEDIT** automatically converts splined polylines to spline objects. You'll automatically convert a splined polyline even if you select it and exit **SPLINEDIT**.

- *SPLINEDIT* *(fit data)*—Your spline may lose its fit data if you:

  - Refine your spline curve in any form.

  - Fit the spline curve to a tolerance and then move its control vertices.

  - Use the **Purge** option when editing the spline curves on your model.

  - Fit the spline curve to a tolerance and then open or close the spline curve.

Alternative 3D Mesh Applications

3DMESH, **PFACE**, and **3DFACE** are polygonal mesh surfaces designed for AutoLISP applications where multiple faces are created at a time. Both the **3DMESH** and **PFACE** commands allow you to create a freeform polygonal mesh surface. (For more about mesh editing options, see Chapter 8.) Here's an overview of these commands:

- *3DMESH*—Used to create a freeform surface. You simply determine the spacing between rows and columns, and the **3DMESH** command makes combined multiple 3D faces about an object's surface, where Rows equals M and Columns equals N.

GENERALIZATIONS ABOUT MESHES

A mesh is said to be open or closed in the M and/or N direction. It's open in a given direction if the last surface elements in that direction are separate from the first ones; it's closed if the last surface elements are joined to the first.

You can edit a mesh as a unit with the usual editing commands. Also, if you use the **LIST** command on a mesh, the mesh is listed as a polyline, and you can use the **PEDIT** command to move individual vertices and fit a smooth surface to the mesh.

When you explode a mesh, the elements become individual 3D faces. When you use the **HIDE** command, the surface elements of the mesh hide other objects and other mesh surfaces behind them.

(3DMESH)

- *PFACE*—Similar to **3DFACE** in that it creates a polygon mesh, and you create the mesh vertex by vertex, but you also assign the vertices to the created faces of the mesh. **PFACE** also lets you create surfaces with invisible internal divisions, so you can create a mesh of any topology. **PFACE** is unlike other meshes, which let you specify any number of vertices and 3D faces. Thus, it helps you avoid creating unrelated 3D faces with the same vertices.

- *3DFACE*—Creates a solid surface as a single mesh entity. (Don't confuse the solid surface with solid modeling.) With **3DFACE**, you may apply Z coordinates for the X, Y, and Z corner points to form a section of a surface plane in 3D space. Use **3DFACE** to create a flat or curved surface by locating the surface boundary or edges; do *not* use it to create curved surfaces.

Using **PFACE** (Polyface)

PFACE is similar to the **3DMESH** command, because it creates irregular surface polyface meshes and each polyface mesh is created vertex by vertex. For example, if you were to create a complex mesh vertex point by vertex point, the task would be rather tedious. This is why **3DFACE** and **PFACE** were intended to be used with AutoLISP or other programs.

Nonetheless, a polyface mesh is different than a 3D mesh in a few ways:

- *Edges and vertices*—At the outset, a 3D mesh is made up of three or four vertices and three or four edges. In contrast to this, a polyface mesh may have many edges and vertices assigned to one face.

- *Editing*—Using grips, you can edit a polyface mesh—at least, you can move the vertex points. (In past AutoCAD releases, a polyface mesh couldn't be edited.) You edit a 3D mesh with the **PEDIT** command. Your polyface mesh can be scaled or moved, but it can't be internally edited. (See Chapter 8.)

- *Exploding*—If you explode a polyface mesh, it will break it down into a number of 3D faces whose "internal" edges are invisible. The edges of the 3D faces may be made invisible by picking with the **EDGE** command.

Creating A Polyface Mesh

The basic steps when using the **PFACE** command are as follows:

1. Locate each vertex point.

2. Define each face and assign as many vertices as needed to create the face.

3. At the prompt for Vertex1, Vertex2, and so on, locate each vertex using **OSNAP Endpoint**.

4. Enter the vertex numbers that correspond to each location. Press Enter when you've finished locating the vertices.

5. You'll be prompted for each of the vertices assigned to Face1, and so on. Enter them by vertex number and then press Enter when you've finished. You're then prompted for Face2; assign the vertices and press Enter when you're done.

6. You can make an invisible edge by placing a minus sign in front of the vertex number. Then, the edge between that vertex and the next vertex is invisible. If you place a minus sign in front of the last vertex assigned to a face, the edge between the last and the first vertex will be invisible.

7. You can assign a color or layer to each face independent of the current layer and color. To do so, enter "layer" or "color" when prompted for the first vertex of any face; then, enter the layer or color at the prompt.

8. You'll be asked again for the first and subsequent vertices for that face.

Figure 6.31 depicts one type of Polyface mesh created with both 2D and 3D coordinate values.

Let's work through an exercise that creates a polyface mesh object using **PFACE**. Figure 6.32 illustrates the completed simple polyface you'll create as viewed from an SE Isometric view. Start a new metric drawing and name it pface-1.dwg. Set your 3D Viewpoint to SE Isometric and keep your UCS at World coordinates. Now, follow these steps:

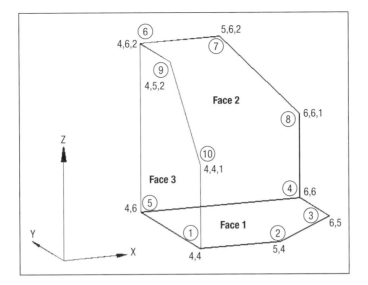

Figure 6.31
PFACE can be used with X, Y, and Z values.

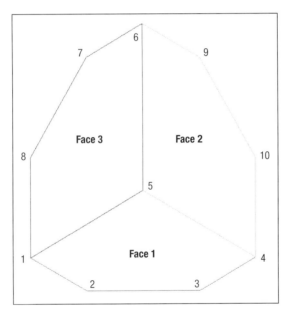

Figure 6.32
The completed rendered **PFACE** mesh.

1. Zoom into a window of the drawing from 530,330 up to 330,1030.

    The prompts are as follows:

    ```
    Command: zoom
    Specify corner of window, enter a scale factor (nX or nXP),
      or [All/Center/Dynamic/Extents/Previous/Scale/Window]
      <real time>: w
    Specify first corner: 530,330
    Specify opposite corner: 330,1030
    ```

2. Activate the **PFACE** command and respond to the prompts as follows:

```
Command: pface
Specify location for vertex 1: 450,450
Specify location for vertex 2 or <define faces>: 550,450
Specify location for vertex 3 or <define faces>: 650,550
Specify location for vertex 4 or <define faces>: 650,650
Specify location for vertex 5 or <define faces>: 450,650
Specify location for vertex 6 or <define faces>: 450,650,250
Specify location for vertex 7 or <define faces>: 550,650,250
Specify location for vertex 8 or <define faces>: 650,650,150
Specify location for vertex 9 or <define faces>: 450,550,250
Specify location for vertex 10 or <define faces>: 450,450,150
Specify location for vertex 11 or <define faces>: <Press
  Enter>
Face 1, vertex 1: Enter a vertex number or [Color/Layer]: c
Enter a color number or standard color name <BYLAYER>: red
Face 1, vertex 1: Enter a vertex number or [Color/Layer]: 1
Face 1, vertex 2: Enter a vertex number or [Color/Layer]
  <next face>: 2
Face 1, vertex 3: Enter a vertex number or [Color/Layer]
  <next face>: 3
Face 1, vertex 4: Enter a vertex number or [Color/Layer]
  <next face>: 4
Face 1, vertex 5: Enter a vertex number or [Color/Layer]
  <next face>: 5
Face 1, vertex 6: Enter a vertex number or [Color/Layer]
  <next face>: <Press Enter>
Face 2, vertex 1: Enter a vertex number or [Color/Layer]: c
Enter a color number or standard color name <1 (red)>: green
Face 2, vertex 1: Enter a vertex number or [Color/Layer]: 4
Face 2, vertex 2: Enter a vertex number or [Color/Layer]
  <next face>: 5
Face 2, vertex 3: Enter a vertex number or [Color/Layer]
  <next face>: 6
Face 2, vertex 4: Enter a vertex number or [Color/Layer]
  <next face>: 7
Face 2, vertex 5: Enter a vertex number or [Color/Layer]
  <next face>: 8
Face 2, vertex 6: Enter a vertex number or [Color/Layer]
  <next face>: <Press Enter>
Face 3, vertex 1: Enter a vertex number or [Color/Layer]: c
Enter a color number or standard color name <3 (green)>:
  blue
Face 3, vertex 1: Enter a vertex number or [Color/Layer]: 1
Face 3, vertex 2: Enter a vertex number or [Color/Layer]
  <next face>: 5
Face 3, vertex 3: Enter a vertex number or [Color/Layer]
  <next face>: 6
Face 3, vertex 4: Enter a vertex number or [Color/Layer]
  <next face>: 9
Face 3, vertex 5: Enter a vertex number or [Color/Layer]
  <next face>: 10
```

```
Face 3, vertex 6: Enter a vertex number or [Color/Layer]
  <next face>: <Press Enter>
Face 4, vertex 1: Enter a vertex number or [Color/Layer]:
  <Press Enter>
```

Moving On

As you've seen in this chapter, surface modeling can be a complex subject. Having learned about 3D surface modeling, you're now ready for solid modeling. The next chapter introduces you to AutoCAD 2000's ACIS Solid Modeler.

7 SOLID MODELING

*Solid modeling is an exciting method of creating 3D
components, and the more you use it, the easier it
becomes. This chapter explains some of the theory
of solid modeling, along with practical working
examples of how to use various primitive and
Boolean commands.*

Types Of Modelers

A solid geometric model includes not just the vertex and edge data of a wireframe model, but also the surface data (topology) and the internal volume for a true 3D model. It also provides a better way to construct and store 3D geometry. The benefits of solid modeling are the comprehensiveness of the model, its efficacy, and its accuracy, as well as more complete design creation methods. In addition, solid modeling supports automation via computer interpretation and reasoning about 3D shapes. In other words, it provides some of the foundation for computer geometric reasoning, which is necessary for "smarter" engineering systems.

The two prevalent types of modelers are constructive solid geometry (CSG) and boundary representation (B-REP). Most 3D modeling software uses both CSG and B-REP as a hybrid system. AutoCAD 2000, for example, uses a hybrid combination of CSG and B-REP. (It also uses Non-Uniform Rational B-Splines [NURBS] for surface modeling generation.)

CSG applies Boolean logic to volumes to determine the inside and outside faces of the 3D model. To create a complex 3D model, the CSG object is not made as a single object—it is created by combining, removing or associating simple objects called *primitives* into a single object or model. In order to formulate this loose combination of primitives into a true 3D model, you use the Boolean set operations:

- *Union (+ or ∪)*—Adds parts together

- *Subtract or difference (–)*—Removes parts or features

- *Intersection (* or ∩)*—Intersects overlapping volumes into a single feature

A B-REP model stores a complete description of all the surfaces bounding the object, including the inside and outside faces. A typical B-REP model stores the object's geometry in a large and complex database structure. The geometry includes surface equations, curve equations and points, and topology of faces, edges, and vertices. To recap, AutoCAD uses a hybrid modeling system (CSG and B-Rep for solids and NURBS for surfaces), and it also uses Boolean operations to let you work with the solid primitives you create. Let's move on and expand upon these modeling kernels.

If you look at AutoCAD's Modify menu, you'll see the Solids Editing option with the subcommands **UNION**, **SUBTRACT**, and **INTERSECT**. You use these Boolean commands to combine simple primitives and simple extruded shapes into more complex 3D models. Thus, Boolean commands let you create composite solids or composite regions. You'll find more about Boolean operation commands in Chapter 8.

Constructive Solid Geometry (CSG)

The ACIS 4 solid modeling engine in AutoCAD is its main 3D modeling engine. It's produced by Spatial Technology, Inc. to provide a 3D solid model file format. AutoCAD reads the model stored in the ACIS file format and constructs a 3D object, 3D solid, or region within your AutoCAD drawing.

You use simple polygonal primitives to create CSG solid models composed of multiple 3D object entities. AutoCAD's solid model primitive commands include **BOX**, **SPHERE**, **CYLINDER**, **CONE**, **WEDGE**, **TORUS**, and so on. Advanced 3D techniques such as **EXTRUDE** and **REVOLVE**, along with the Boolean operations **UNION**, **SUBTRACT**, and **INTERSECT**, allow you to define complex portions of a solid model. As you'll see from the illustration in Figure 7.1, you combine primitives via the Boolean operations of **UNION**, **SUBTRACT**, and **INTERSECT**.

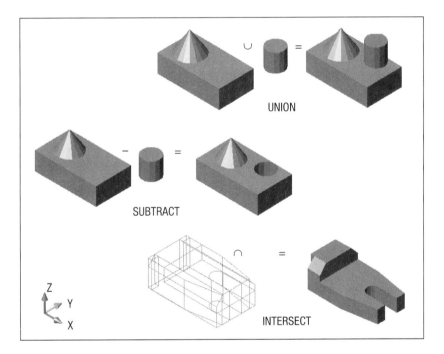

UNION

SUBTRACT

INTERSECT

Figure 7.1
A CSG model is a procedure for constructing 3D solid models.

As you can see in Figure 7.2, AutoCAD stores CSG objects using a tree database structure. Leaf nodes represent primitives, and branch nodes represent Boolean operations. As you can see in the simple solid model in the upper-right corner of the figure, the cone has been added to the box primitive, and the cylinder primitive has been subtracted to form a through hole. Each subtree represents a legitimate solid—that is, primitive in this example.

Boundary Representation (B-Rep)

As you can see in Figure 7.3, a B-Rep solid model is composed of surface elements. Do not be confused by thinking of it as a surface modeler, because it's not; it's simply the B-Rep way of solid model representation. With

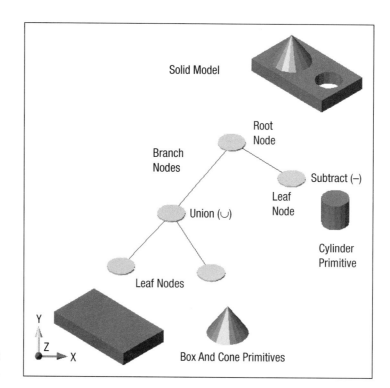

Figure 7.2
CSG tree database.

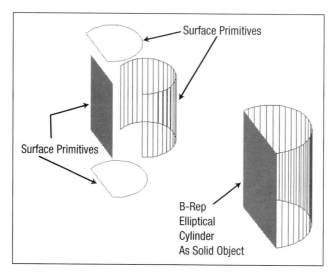

Figure 7.3
B-Rep surface model composed
of four surface elements (three
planar, one cylindrical).

B-Rep, the AutoCAD database stores a list of your model's vertices and how each vertex connects to form edges and airtight boundaries. Thus, B-Rep stores the boundaries of your solid object in your CAD database. In turn, the surfaces between the edges are calculated mathematically (through Euler's formula) as they form the surface between the points, lines, and curves that define the edges of your model. B-Rep modeling differs from traditional, conventional modeling, although you still use Boolean logic to union, subtract, and intersect volumes.

Although a nonsolid CAD system may represent surfaces, a B-Rep must also guarantee that the surfaces form a complete partition of space. As you can see in Figure 7.3, four surface elements comprise the solid model (a section of an elliptical cylinder); three elements are planar and one element is cylindrical. Each of the surface elements is assembled to form an "airtight" boundary that enclose the 3D space being used by the model. Thus, the B-Rep model stores a complete description of all of the four surfaces bounding the object. A typical B-Rep stores the geometry of the object in a large, complex database. As mentioned earlier, AutoCAD uses a hybrid modeler (CSG and B-Rep); the strategy is to support a high-level CSG tree hierarchy that may then be intentionally translated into a lower-level B-Rep model.

Euler's Formula

In 1730, Leonhard Euler (1707–83) became a professor of physics to the Academy of Sciences at St. Petersburg. The founder of pure mathematics, he was born in Basel, Switzerland. As a physicist and mathematician, he made many important contributions to mechanics, calculus, number theory, geometry, and problem-solving methods in observational astronomy. Today, we use his formula to check faces and edges in geometric elements.

The faces used in B-Rep systems are alignable—that is, they have an inside face and an outside face. This information is encoded by numbering the edges in a sequence, such that the right-hand rule defines a vector (a directional indicator) that points outward from the object. The stored database within the drawing allows the model to be shaded or rendered at a faster rate, by only rendering the outside faces—that is, the faces that will be seen. So when you enter the **RENDER** command and see the **Discard Back Faces** option, this is what it's looking for—the *face normals* to determine which side of the face to render. Remember, face normals are determined by the way in which a face is drawn in a right-hand rule coordinate system (as in AutoCAD). Yet how do you determine which surface is facing out and which surface is facing in? The answer to that question is, if you draw each face counterclockwise, the face normals will point outward; if you draw the faces clockwise, the face normals will point inward.

Moving on to Euler's formula, B-Rep is correct if its elements are connected accurately—in other words each edge should be connected to two nodes (vertices) and to two faces. You can see this principle in Figure 7.4, which shows the corner of a cube (that is, a three-sided pyramid). To describe Euler's formula, it uses the equation $V - E + F = 2$, where V is the number of vertices, E is the number of edges, and F is the number of faces. In Figure 7.4, there are four vertices or node points, six edges that connect the nodes, and four faces. So all the components are thus interconnected through the formula.

Now that you understand some of the background theory, let's look further at what you need to do to visualize how you work in three dimensions and

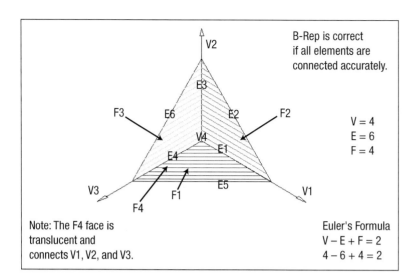

B-Rep is correct if all elements are connected accurately.

V = 4
E = 6
F = 4

Note: The F4 face is translucent and connects V1, V2, and V3.

Euler's Formula
$V - E + F = 2$
$4 - 6 + 4 = 2$

Figure 7.4
Euler's formula is used to check elements.

simplify your modeling process. Often, you can simplify a complex 3D component by either sketching out the steps or by using a storyboard technique. Visualizing how to put a 3D model together is extremely useful, because often the process will help you work through some of the sophisticated modeling steps or creation process. Thus, if you think the modeling steps through at the beginning, it often helps your productivity in the long run (especially if you avoid having to go back and redraw the whole part, just because you forgot something at the outset).

Solid Modeling: The Visualization Process

Visualization is the process of transferring thoughts and ideas from the ideation process onto 2D sketch paper and subsequently into a 3D CAD model. Traditionally, the engineer, designer, or architect would visualize a design in 3D and then sketch or draw the ideas and design intent in 2D. Often, a part may be so complex that the designer will also sketch the actual modeling procedures and processes in order to model the 3D part in CAD more efficiently.

Figure 7.5 shows such a visualization. (A color version of this figure appears in the Color Studio in the middle of the book.) For the example shown in Figure 7.5, you'd visualize the steps as follows:

1. Create the first profile in the World UCS and extrude up 19mm.

2. Create the second profile in the Side UCS and extrude away –24mm (as Z points at you).

3. Union the two extrusions.

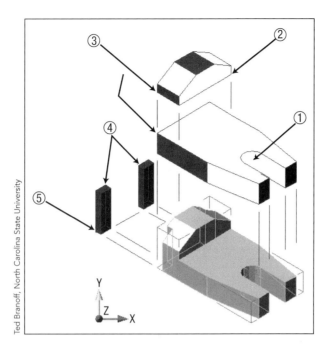

Ted Branoff, North Carolina State University

Figure 7.5
Visualization is a great tool for working with 3D geometry.

4. Create two solid boxes as primitives (that is, create one box, then copy it 47mm).

5. Subtract the two boxes from the main solid.

Visualization means that if you're the designer, you can focus directly on the development and refinement of your 3D model. In addition, by using a 3D solid modeler, you can produce standard 2D view drawings for production of the 3D model. AutoCAD does this automated task through the **SOLVIEW** and **SOLDRAW** commands, which allow you to produce easily any type of view, including primary and secondary auxiliary views and section views.

This visualization procedure is a great tool for emerging 3D geometrists, who need to visualize the steps, procedures, and processes of how they think they will create the 3D part. For example, Figure 7.5 illustrates how they can visualize and sketch the primitives, regions, and Boolean operations they will use to model the part. Figure 7.6 shows an alternative process. (A color version of this figure is included in the Color Studio in the middle of the book.) Much energy, therefore, is unconsciously devoted to the process of visualizing and translating 3D ideas into a format suitable for production, which is a vital component of design. Later in the chapter, you'll work with an example from its start as a visualization (Figure 7.24) to its finish as a shaded model.

Visualization Accuracy

During the creation of your 3D solid model, visualization accuracy may come into question (not to be confused with the visualization process just

Brad Stuart, Autodesk, Inc.

Figure 7.6
Visualization is used as a tool for solid modeling. The designer can visualize from an ink sketch to a 3D isometric wireframe to the finished product.

discussed.) This issue doesn't reflect on the measurement accuracy of the model, but rather on its visual correctness. Visualization accuracy is important in CAD work; often, as 3D solid modeling primitives are created in a drawing, they show basic tesselation lines in the initial wireframe view. *Tessellation lines* are short lines used to help you visualize a curved surface. For example, the more tessellation lines you use in your drawing, the smoother the appearance of your model will be.

In AutoCAD, planar shapes (faceted representations) are used to represent curves to cones, cylinders, spheres, and torii. A few variables to the solid modeling commands allow you visualization control for accuracy and visualization adjustment:

- *ISOLINES*—Upgrades the visual qualities of the tesselation lines

- *FACETRES*—Upgrades shading qualities

- *VIEWRES*—Upgrades circles and curves in general

Unlike other releases, in Release 2000 you can control the variables of the modeling commands after you place your primitives. The **ISOLINES** system variable is a visual control to the number of solid curve lines of your primitives. See Figure 7.7. Remember, I'm talking about visual accuracy—not measurement accuracy.

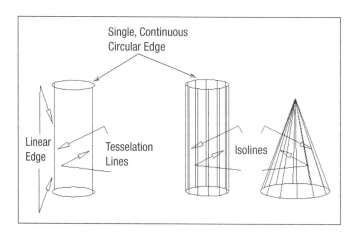

Figure 7.7
ISOLINES controls the number of tesselation lines in a primitive.

ISOLINES

The **ISOLINES** variable controls the number of tessellation lines used to visualize curved portions of a primitive to a wireframe/solid model. See Figure 7.7. The initial default value is 4, with valid integer values from 0 to 2047. Take a cylinder and a cone, as examples; in these instances, never set the **ISOLINES** variable to 0. The 3D wireframe of the cylinder would revert back to two circles, as two planar surfaces, one at the top, the other at the bottom of the original cylinder. The cone would revert to a point and a circle.

For example, start a new drawing in either English or Metric units, and set your 3D View to SE Isometric. Draw both a 3D cone and a 3D cylinder of any height and any depth. Zoom to the drawing extents and notice the low number of tesselation lines. Use the **HIDE** command and now notice the difference in visualization from the wireframe lines to the hidden view lines. Upgrade the **ISOLINES** variable from 4 to 20 as follows:

```
Command: isolines
Enter new value for ISOLINES <4>: 20
```

Then, use the **REGEN** command to regenerate the tesselation line database. Notice the change in the wireframe lines. Try the **HIDE** command again and note that nothing changed in the hidden view. Now, let's look at **FACETRES** and what it achieves as a visual variable. (Keep your example drawing on screen.)

FACETRES

The **FACETRES** system variable adjusts the smoothness of shaded or hidden-line objects. Values are from 0.01 to 10, and the initial default value is 0.5.

From the previous example, which you still have on screen, you'll have noticed that the **ISOLINES** variable controls the curves of your 3D wireframe model. Your hidden lines are controlled by **FACETRES**; it's currently set to 0.5. Upgrade the hidden lines as follows:

```
Command: facetres
Enter new value for FACETRES <0.5000>: 10
```

Then, use the **REGEN** command to see the visual difference.

VIEWRES

The **VIEWRES** command adjusts the smoothness of circular objects. Values are from 1 to 20000, and the initial default value is 100.

For example, in the same view as your two solid primitives on screen, draw a circle of any size and zoom in tightly three or four times into the edge of the circle. Notice that the nearer you zoom in to the circle, the more it appears as a polygonal representation. You overcome this representation by upgrading the **VIEWRES** command. So, zoom back out until you see your primitives located on screen; then, set your two primitives back to the original settings (that is, set **ISOLINES** to 4). Also, set your **VIEWRES** command to 1 and notice how all your models become polygonal shapes in plan. Now, upgrade the **ISOLINES** variable to about 48 and then set the **VIEWRES** variable to 20000 as follows:

```
Command: viewres
Do you want fast zooms? <Y>
Enter circle zoom percent (1-20000) <1>: 20000
```

If you need to, use **REGEN** to regenerate the view. You'll find the visualization accuracy of your model is improved, if not near perfect. Remember, I'm talking about visual accuracy—not measurement accuracy.

Creating Solids

AutoCAD allows you to create solid primitives and surface primitives. It's important not to confuse solid model commands with 3D mesh/surface object commands, which are similar. You can, for example, use the **BOX**, **SPHERE**, **CYLINDER**, **CONE**, **WEDGE**, and **TORUS** commands to create solid primitives. You can also use the 3D Objects dialog box with its surface primitive option to create surface models with a similar appearance, but the 3D Objects dialog box doesn't produce solid model primitives. This chapter will refer only to solid primitives. Hint: Use the **LIST** command on the object if you're unsure of its origin. **LIST** identifies a solid object as a 3D solid, and a surface object as a type of mesh and polyline. (You'll find all these commands on the Solids toolbar. Or choose Solids from the Tools menu to display the list of Solids commands.)

BOUNDARY And REGION Commands

A *region* is a 2D enclosed area created from a closed shape called a *loop*. A *loop* is a curve or a sequence of connected curves that defines an area on a plane with a boundary that doesn't intersect itself. Loops can be combinations of lines, polylines, circles, arcs, ellipses, elliptical arcs, splines, 3D faces, traces, and solids. The objects that make up the loops must either be closed or form closed areas by sharing endpoints with other objects. The objects must also be coplanar (on the same plane).

Here are some important points about regions:

• A region is a closed 2D area treated as a single AutoCAD entity.

• A region has an area associated with it in addition to its edge information.

• A region is a 2D solid with no height.

• Regions make geometric constructions easier; they're useful for determining cross-sectional properties, such as area or moment of inertia.

- Regions convert closed polylines, splines, or a selection of objects, forming a closed area into a single solid region.

- Areas made up of intersecting lines or overlapping objects won't form regions.

- Areas must either consist of closed objects, such as closed splines and polylines, or the selection of objects must match end-vertex to end-vertex to form the closed area.

- The **SUBTRACT** command will remove one region from another region.

- The **UNION** command will join one region with another.

Using the **BOUNDARY** or **REGION** command, you can convert a closed polyline, a spline, or an assortment of entities that form a closed area into a single solid region. You'll find these commands located in the Draw menu. (The **REGION** command is also located on the Draw toolbar.) The **BOUNDARY** command activates the Boundary Creation dialog box. If you choose Region as the Object Type and select Ray Casting, you can then click on the Pick Points button to pick the internal boundaries of your objects. Each closed area is then converted into a separate region.

A *boundary* can be composed of arcs, blocks, circles, ellipses, lines, 2D polylines, splines, and even paper space viewports. Every boundary component you create should at a minimum be partially within your current view.

When you model with regions, you're using the concept of Boolean operations to develop geometry. The AutoCAD solid modeler can perform volumetric (3D) and planar (2D) Boolean operations, whereas the region modeling module of AutoCAD performs only 2D Boolean operations.

Regions can be used in many ways to create 3D models. Let's look at three of the alternative uses for regions.

- In this example, your objective is to find the area and other properties of the drawing. You'll create the profile of template.dwg, then find the area of the drawing by using **SUBTRACT** to subtract the cutouts (inner circular slots) from the main outline. See Figure 7.8 for the dimensions. To get you started, here's a brief outline of the procedures. Open a new file using metric units and name it template.dwg. (If you prefer, you can find template.dwg on this book's companion CD-ROM; it's ready for you to use the **REGION** command, then extrude its depth.) Start at 0,0,0 with the center of your first circle, working outwards. Create the end arcs at 60 degrees (as shown in Figure 7.8) and trim to the circles. Next, use the **REGION** command to produce the main circle and the two inner

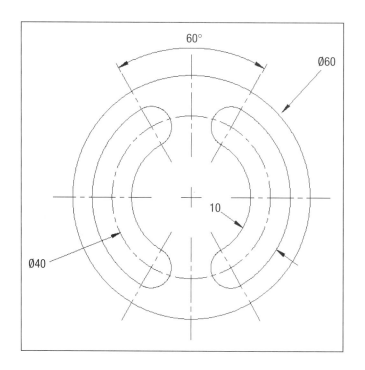

Figure 7.8
Create the template.dwg profile and use **REGION** to find the area.

circular slots as regions. (Remember to use the **SUBTRACT** Boolean command to remove the two circular slots from the main circle.) Then, to quickly find the overall area, use the **LIST** command—you should have an overall area answer of 1832.5957. Finally, you can use **EXTRUDE** to give the model a depth of 12mm, and use the **MASSPROP** command to secure more information about the part.

• In this simple example, create the profile of the outline.dwg; then, use **BOUNDARY** with the **Ray Casting** option and select any internal point. Use **EXTRUDE** to create a solid 10mm thick. See Figure 7.9, which shows the dimensioned part. Here's how to get started. Open a new metric drawing and name it outline.dwg (or use the outline.dwg

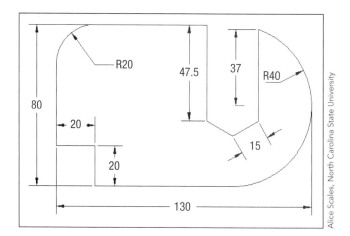

Figure 7.9
Create outline.dwg and use **REGION** to combine the arcs and lines.

on the CD-ROM). Next, using lines and arcs, create the drawing starting at 0,0,0 in the lower-left corner. Use the **REGION** command to combine the single entities into a region; then, use the **EXTRUDE** command to give the model a 10mm depth.

* Another practical use for regions is that you can use them as you draw in different UCS work planes of your drawing. In this example, using region profiles, you can use the **EXTRUDE** command to extrude a region. Start a new drawing, label it isolines.dwg, and use English units. Or, you can find isolines.dwg on the companion CD-ROM; it's preset to the Front work plane and ready for you to use **REGION** and **EXTRUDE**. (You'll also find three fixed node points in 3D space, for the three cylinder hole locations shown in Figure 7.10.) First, set your UCS to the Front work plane (that is, revolve the UCS through X about 90 degrees) and create the front profile using the **LINE** command. See Figure 7.10 for dimensions. While you're still in the Front UCS, use the **REGION** command to combine the lines into a region; then, use **EX-TRUDE** to extrude the Z component –2 units (minus 2—away from you). Remember to set the UCS to the correct work plane before you create the through holes. The two .5 holes are on the Top work plane, and the .375 hole is on the Side work plane. Once you've created the hole cylinders, use the **SUBTRACT** command to remove the holes from the extruded part.

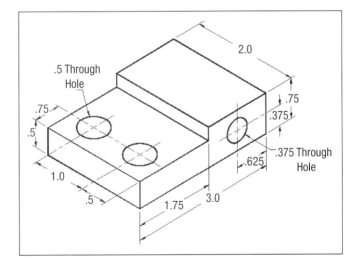

Figure 7.10
Set the UCS to the Front work plane and create the profile; then, use **REGION**.

REGION Exercise

Here's another example of using **REGION**, but in more detail. The objective of this exercise is to use the Boundary Creation dialog box to create region objects and to simplify the construction of the cross-section of a simple gear.

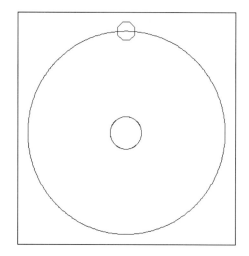

Figure 7.11

Create a circle and a polygon at the quadrant of the circle.

The illustration in Figure 7.11 is typical of a simple gear mesh or cog that you might find on any engineering part. The outline of the exercise is as follows:

1. Start a new metric drawing and name it gear-1.dwg. (You can find this file on the book's companion CD-ROM.) Don't change the view. Draw a circle with a diameter of 125mm on your screen:

```
Command: circle
Specify center point for circle or [3P/2P/Ttr (tan tan
  radius)]: 0,0
Specify radius of circle or [Diameter]: d
Specify diameter of circle: 125

Command: circle
Specify center point for circle or [3P/2P/Ttr (tan tan
  radius)]: 0,0
Specify radius of circle or [Diameter]: 10
```

2. You need to begin constructing the gear teeth. Start by constructing one polygon as a single gear tooth. Place the center of the eight-sided polygon at the upper QUADrant of the main circle:

```
Command: polygon
Enter number of sides <4>: 8
Specify center of polygon or [Edge]: quad
Enter an option [Inscribed in circle/Circumscribed about
  circle] <I>: i
Specify radius of circle: 6
```

3. To create the remainder of the gear teeth, use the **ARRAY** command with the **Polar** option to array 20 inscribed polygons around the

larger circle. Use the center of the large circle (0,0) as the center point
of the array:

```
Command: array
Select objects: <Pick the polygon just created>
Enter the type of array [Rectangular/Polar] <R>: p
Specify center point of array: 0,0
Enter the number of items in the array: 20
Specify the angle to fill (+=ccw, -=cw) <360>: <Press Enter>
Rotate arrayed objects? [Yes/No] <Y>: <Press Enter>
```

Your polygon layout should look like the one shown in Figure 7.12.

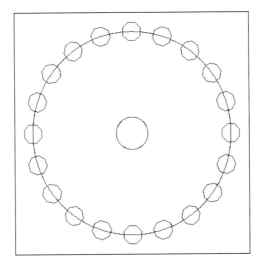

Figure 7.12
Array the polygon around the
center of the circle.

At this point, you may need to do a ZOOM – ALL, to ensure that the entire
circle is in the viewport, or the **REGION** command will not work properly.

Using the Boundary Creation dialog box with the Region and Flood options,
you can make all the objects into a region and then, by the use of the **SUB-
TRACT** command, instantly subtract the polygons from the circle. The region
modeler is more efficient than using the **TRIM** command, because it removes
all the small polygons from the large circle to create the gear or chain cog in
one operation. (If you're using Release 2000, choose Subtract from the Solids
Editing section of the Modify menu to perform the Boolean subtraction of
the polygons from the large circle.) Now, change your 3D View to SE Isometric and extrude the example up 20mm. Change the color to number 254 and
then shade it. The finished result will be similar to Figure 7.13.

A Look At Primitives

Activate the Solids toolbar or choose Solids from the Draw menu, as shown
in Figure 7.14. You'll see a number of options for creating solid model primitives. Note that for this list of primitives, as mentioned earlier, **ISOLINES**

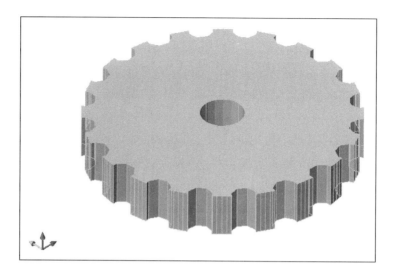

Figure 7.13
The finished shaded gear.

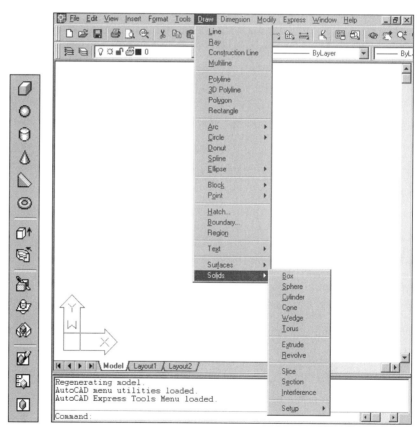

Figure 7.14
Options for creating solid
model primitives are available
from the Solids toolbar and the
Draw menu.

controls the number of tessellation lines used to visualize curved portions of your wireframe or solid model; its initial default value is 4. (Remember that once you create your solid primitive, you can now stretch it or change its size. Using Release 2000, you use **SOLIDEDIT** to edit the face, edges, and body of your solid primitives. See the "Solids Editing" section in Chapter 8.)

Here's a basic description of each solid primitive command:

- *BOX*—Constructs a 3D solid box.

- *SPHERE*—Constructs a 3D solid sphere.

- *CYLINDER*—Constructs a 3D solid cylinder.

- *CONE*—Constructs a 3D solid cone.

- *WEDGE*—Constructs a 3D solid with a sloped face tapering along the X axis.

- *TORUS*—Constructs a donut-shaped solid.

- *EXTRUDE*—Constructs unique solid primitives by extruding existing 2D objects.

- *REVOLVE*—Constructs a solid by revolving a 2D object about an axis.

- *SLICE*—Slices a set of solids with a plane.

- *SECTION*—Uses the intersection of a plane and solids to create a region.

- *INTERFERENCE*—Constructs a composite 3D solid from the common volume of two or more solids.

- *Setup*—Offers three suboptions: Drawing, View, and Profile. You use the setup options once you've created the 3D solid and you need to lay out the drawing in paper space before printing. (We'll explore the Drawing, View, and Profile setup options in Chapter 9.)

Let's look at each of these options in more detail.

BOX

The **BOX** command (equivalent to choosing Draw|Solids|Box) constructs a 3D solid box. With this command, you can create slabs and cubes of any size.

Start a new drawing with English or metric units. Set your 3D View to SE Isometric and activate the **BOX** command. (You may need to zoom in to the 0,0,0 section of the screen.) The command line prompts you to either locate one corner of the box on screen or enter "c" for the center of your box. You then have three choices, as follows:

- Pick a second point for the diagonal corner of the base of the box and then enter a height to the top of the box (see Figure 7.15 for the completed example):

```
Command: box
Specify corner of box or [CEnter] <0,0,0>: <Press Enter>
Specify corner or [Cube/Length]: 10,4,6
```

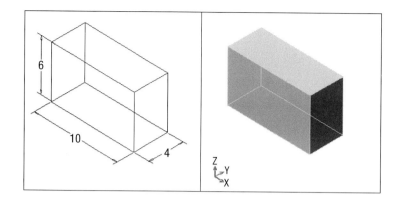

Figure 7.15

Use the **BOX** command to create a simple box, and use **SHADE** to shade the result.

- Entering "c" (for cube) and specifying the length of one edge creates a box with sides of equal length; for example:

```
Command: box
Specify corner of box or [CEnter] <0,0,0>: ce
Specify center of box <0,0,0>: <Press Enter>
Specify corner or [Cube/Length]: c
Specify length: 10
```

- Alternatively, you may enter "l" and specify a length, followed by a width and height (using X, Y, and Z directions, respectively). You'll find this example creates a similar size box as the first example, which specified 10,4,6 coordinate points (see Figure 7.15 for the length, width, and height specifications):

```
Command: box
Specify corner of box or [CEnter] <0,0,0>: <Press Enter>
Specify corner or [Cube/Length]: l
Specify length: 10 (in the X direction)
Specify width: 4 (in the Y direction)
Specify height: 6 (in the Z direction)
```

SPHERE

The **SPHERE** command (equivalent to choosing Draw|Solids|Sphere) constructs a spherical solid; it's one of the easiest solid primitive commands to use. Enter the **SPHERE** command and choose a center location for your sphere. Then, either enter the radius or enter "d" to specify a diameter for the sphere.

The created sphere is positioned with its central axis parallel to the Z axis of the current user coordinate system (UCS). See Figure 7.16. Here's a hint: You'll need to set **ISOLINES** to upgrade the visualization accuracy of the model before you create the sphere. For example:

```
Command: isolines
Enter new value for ISOLINES <4>: 12
```

```
Command: sphere
Current wire frame density:  ISOLINES=12
Specify center of sphere <0,0,0>: <Press Enter>
Specify radius of sphere or [Diameter]: d
Specify diameter: 5
```

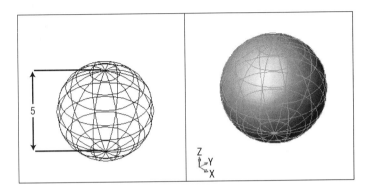

Figure 7.16
Use the **SPHERE** command to create a sphere, and use **SHADE** to shade the result

CYLINDER

The **CYLINDER** command (equivalent to choosing Draw|Solids|Cylinder) constructs either a 3D cylindrical solid or a 3D elliptical solid perpendicular to the base view. Choose the Cylinder icon or the **CYLINDER** command and you'll be prompted to specify the base point of your cylinder. At this start prompt, you can either pick the center point for your circular cylinder or enter "e" to specify an elliptical cylinder:

1. The circular cylinder command requires that you pick your center point followed by a radius or diameter. Start a new drawing with English or metric units. Set your 3D View to SE Isometric and activate the command. (Set your **ISOLINES** to 12 as in the previous example.) To construct a cylindrical solid, specify the center start point (in this example it's set to 0,0,0; see Figure 7.17):

```
Command: cylinder
Current wire frame density:  ISOLINES=4
Specify center point for base of cylinder or [Elliptical]
<0,0,0>: <Press Enter>
Specify radius for base of cylinder or [Diameter]: d
Specify diameter for base of cylinder: 3
Specify height of cylinder or [Center of other end]: 6
```

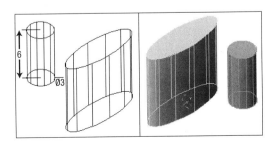

Figure 7.17
Use the **CYLINDER** command to create cylinders, and use **SHADE** to shade the result.

2. When you use **CYLINDER** to produce an elliptical cylinder, you're prompted for three axis endpoints. Alternatively, as you'll see from the example below, you can enter "c" to specify a center and two axis endpoints for the elliptical cylinder. For example, to create the elliptical solid, you first enter "e" for Ellipse. Notice the extra prompts for the minor and major axes of the ellipse:

```
Command: cylinder
Current wire frame density:  ISOLINES=12
Specify center point for base of cylinder or [Elliptical]
   <0,0,0>: e
Specify axis endpoint of ellipse for base of cylinder or
   [Center]: c
Specify center point of ellipse for base of cylinder
   <0,0,0>: <Press Enter>
Specify axis endpoint of ellipse for base of cylinder: @4<0
   (minor axis)
Specify length of other axis for base of cylinder: @12<90
   (major axis)
Specify height of cylinder or [Center of other end]: 20
```

CONE

The **CONE** command (equivalent to choosing Draw|Solids|Cone and shown in Figure 7.18) is similar to the **CYLINDER** command in that it constructs a conical solid that's either circular or elliptical in the plan view. Again, like the **CYLINDER** command, you need to specify a circular or elliptical base first followed by a height, or pick a point to the apex of the cone:

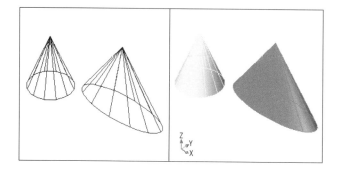

Figure 7.18
Use the **CONE** command to create cones, and use **SHADE** to shade the result.

1. Entering a height draws a vertical cone, whereas using the **Apex** option creates a slanted cone. (Entering a positive value draws the height along the positive Z axis of the current UCS. Entering a negative value draws the height along the negative Z axis.) For example:

```
Command: cone
Current wire frame density:  ISOLINES=12
Specify center point for base of cone or [Elliptical]
   <0,0,0>: <Press Enter>
```

```
Specify radius for base of cone or [Diameter]: d
Specify diameter for base of cone: 10
Specify height of cone or [Apex]: 12
```

2. When you need to produce an elliptical cone (see Figure 7.18), you have a number of axis endpoints. To create the elliptical cone, you first enter "e" for Ellipse. Notice extra prompts for the minor and major axes of the elliptical cone:

```
Command: cone
Current wire frame density:  ISOLINES=12
Specify center point for base of cone or [Elliptical]
  <0,0,0>: e
Specify axis endpoint of ellipse for base of cone or
  [Center]: @5,0
Specify second axis endpoint of ellipse for base of cone:
  @10<90
Specify length of other axis for base of cone: 15
Specify height of cone or [Apex]: 20
```

WEDGE

The **WEDGE** command is similar to the **BOX** command, except that the top slopes to meet the base and constructs a wedge-shaped solid, with the sloping face tapering along the X axis. The wedge height—which can be positive or negative—is parallel to the Z axis. To create a simple wedge, choose Draw|Solids|Wedge. First, specify the original corner of the base; second, specify the opposite corner of the base, and finally, specify the height of the wedge. In each of the three examples that follow, entering a positive value creates the first length about the positive X axis of your current UCS; entering a negative value creates the first length about the negative axis. You can create a wedge using one of these three methods:

- The **Cube** option (see lower-right shapes in Figure 7.19) creates a 45-degree wedge with sides of equal length; for example:

```
Command: wedge
Specify first corner of wedge or [CEnter] <0,0,0>: <Press
  Enter>
Specify corner or [Cube/Length]: c
Specify length: 35
```

- The **Corner** option of the **WEDGE** command specifies the first start corner and then the opposite corner of your wedge. However, if both corner points are at the same Z height, you'll need to specify the height of your wedge. Otherwise, AutoCAD will use the difference in Z height values for the height; for example:

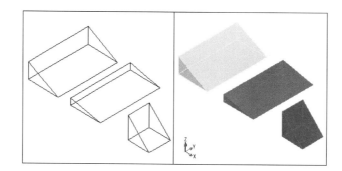

Figure 7.19
Use the **WEDGE** command to
create wedges, and use **SHADE**
to shade the result.

```
Command: wedge
Specify first corner of wedge or [CEnter]  <0,0,0>: <Press
   Enter>
Specify corner or [Cube/Length]: @100,200
Specify height: 50
```

You can easily get the same results using X,Y,Z coordinates; for
example:

```
Command: wedge
Specify first corner of wedge or [CEnter]  <50,50,0>: <Press
   Enter>
Specify corner or [Cube/Length]: @100,200,50
```

- When you have specific X,Y,Z values, the **Length** option is the easiest
  to use. The wedge length corresponds to the X axis, the width to the
  Y axis, and the height to the Z axis; for example:

```
Command: wedge
Specify first corner of wedge or [CEnter]  <100,100,0>:
   <Press Enter>
Specify corner or [Cube/Length]: l
Specify length: 100 (X axis)
Specify width:  200 (Y axis)
Specify height:  20 (Z axis)
```

TORUS

The **TORUS** command (equivalent to choosing Draw|Solids|Torus) constructs
a torus (3D donut or ring) solid. Remember to set **ISOLINES** for better visual
accuracy. You can create plain or self-intersecting torii:

- To create a plain torus (see the upper-left primitives of Figure 7.20),
  choose the Torus icon or the **TORUS** command. Then, locate the center point and enter the radius, or specify "d" for the diameter of the
  torus. Finally, enter the radius or diameter of the circular cross-section:

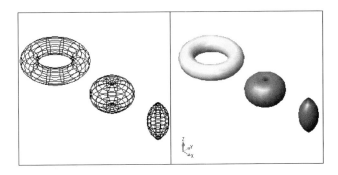

Figure 7.20
Use the **TORUS** command to create torii, and use **SHADE** to shade the result.

```
Command: isolines
Enter new value for ISOLINES <4>: 12
Command: torus
Current wire frame density:  ISOLINES=12
Specify center of torus <0,0,0>:   <Press Enter>
Specify radius of torus or [Diameter]: d
Specify diameter: 150
Specify radius of tube or [Diameter]: 25
```

- As seen in the lower-right corners of both sides of Figure 7.20, a self-intersecting torus is shaped like a football (spheroid) and has no center hole. To create one, you simply make the radius of the tube greater than the radius of the torus. You can create a self-intersecting torus two ways. In the first instance, you set the radius of your torus to be negative and then create a tube with a greater size than the radius of the torus. The result will look similar to a football or sphere with a pointed pole at each end:

```
Command: torus
Current wire frame density:  ISOLINES=12
Specify center of torus <0,0,0>: <Press Enter>
Specify radius of torus or [Diameter]: -12 (negative 12)
Specify radius of tube or [Diameter]: 20
```

- To create another type of self-intersecting torus, you set the radius of the tube to be greater than the radius of the torus. The result looks like a sphere with a depression at each pole. See the central shapes in Figure 7.20:

```
Command: torus
Current wire frame density:  ISOLINES=12
Specify center of torus <0,0,0>: <Press Enter>
Specify radius of torus or [Diameter]: 12
Specify radius of tube or [Diameter]:  20
```

EXTRUDE

EXTRUDE (equivalent to choosing Draw|Solids|Extrude) is one of the most used (and useful) commands in 3D modeling. Just remember that the extrusion is always along the Z axis of the current UCS or construction work plane. Initially, the **EXTRUDE** command constructs a solid by projecting a closed entity along a straight line; alternatively, you can sweep it along a path. Choose the **EXTRUDE** command and at the prompt select the object you want to extrude. You can also select multiple objects, but each object you select must be a closed shape such as a region, circle, closed polyline, or spline. Once you've selected your objects, you have two further options: Either extrude the objects along the Z axis of the current UCS or sweep the objects along a path.

As you use the **EXTRUDE** command, the default is to enter the height of the extrusion along the Z axis. After entering the height, you can enter a taper angle for your extrusion. A zero angle creates a straight extrusion with no taper, a positive angle causes the object to taper toward its centroid, and a negative angle causes the object to taper outward. (When you create complex profiles, don't forget to include fillets, rounds, chamfers, and other details that are difficult to reproduce except in profile.)

Enter "p" to extrude along a path. When prompted, select a line, arc, circle, elliptical arc, ellipse, polyline, or spline as the extrusion path. If necessary, AutoCAD relocates the path to the center of your selected extrusion object and passes the object along the path to generate a 3D solid.

For an example, let's create the drawing shown in Figure 7.21. To do so, start a new drawing, set your view to SE Isometric, and then use a **SPLINE** command:

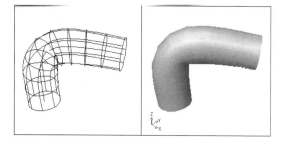

Figure 7.21

Use the **EXTRUDE** command to create an extrusion, and use **SHADE** to shade the result.

```
Command: spline
Specify first point or [Object]: 0,0,0
Specify next point: 0,0,20
Specify next point or [Close/Fit tolerance] <start tangent>:
  20,20,20
Specify next point or [Close/Fit tolerance] <start tangent>:
  <Press Enter>
Specify start tangent: 0
Specify end tangent: 0
```

```
Command: ucs
Current ucs name:  *WORLD*
Enter an option [New/Move/orthoGraphic/Prev/Restore/Save/Del/
  Apply/?/World] <World>: x
Specify rotation angle about X axis <90>: 90 <or press Enter>
Command: circle
Specify center point for circle or [3P/2P/Ttr (tan tan radius)]:
  20,20,20
Specify radius of circle or [Diameter]: 6
Command: ucs
Current ucs name:  *NO NAME*
Enter an option [New/Move/orthoGraphic/Prev/Restore/Save/Del/
  Apply/?/World] <World>: <Press Enter>
Command: extrude
Current wire frame density:  ISOLINES=12
Select objects: (Pick the circle)
Select objects: <Press Enter>
Specify height of extrusion or [Path]: p
Select extrusion path: <Pick the extrusion path>
```

AutoCAD will then indicate the following and create the extrusion for you as seen in the left part of Figure 7.21:

```
Path was moved to the center of the profile.
Profile was oriented to be perpendicular to the path.
```

Change the color of the parametric extrusion and then shade the result. Your result should then be the same as shown on the right of Figure 7.21.

REVOLVE

The **REVOLVE** command (equivalent to choosing Draw|Solids|Revolve) constructs a solid by revolving a closed object about a central axis. You activate the **REVOLVE** command and select the objects to revolve. See Figure 7.22. You can select more than one object, but each object must be closed and will become a separate solid. After selecting the objects to revolve, define your axis of revolution using one of these four methods:

- *Revolve - Locate Endpoints*—The default method. Locate any two points on screen, and the resulting straight line between those points becomes the axis of revolution.

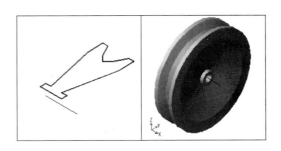

Figure 7.22
Use the **REVOLVE** command to create a revolve example, and use **SHADE** to shade the result.

- *Revolve - Object*—Revolves the object around a selected line or single-segment polyline.

- *Revolve - X*—Revolves the object around the X axis of the current UCS.

- *Revolve - Y*—Revolves the object around the Y axis of the current UCS.

Finally, you specify the angle of revolution. Enter an angle or press Enter to accept the default of a full circle (360 degrees). You'll need to create a line or use an imaginary center point to revolve your object. For example, start a new drawing in metric or English units and then use the listed coordinates below. (Alternately, use the revolve-1.dwg drawing from the CD-ROM and then start at the **REVOLVE** prompt below.) Set your view to SE Isometric; then, respond to the command prompts as follows:

```
Command: pline
Specify start point: 6,28
Current line-width is 0.0000
Specify next point or [Arc/Close/Halfwidth/Length/Undo/Width]:
  4,28
Specify next point or [Arc/Close/Halfwidth/Length/Undo/Width]:
  2,24
Specify next point or [Arc/Close/Halfwidth/Length/Undo/Width]:
  0,22
Specify next point or [Arc/Close/Halfwidth/Length/Undo/Width]:
  -2,24
Specify next point or [Arc/Close/Halfwidth/Length/Undo/Width]:
  -4,28
Specify next point or [Arc/Close/Halfwidth/Length/Undo/Width]:
  -6,28
Specify next point or [Arc/Close/Halfwidth/Length/Undo/Width]:
  -6,22
Specify next point or [Arc/Close/Halfwidth/Length/Undo/Width]:
  -2,4
Specify next point or [Arc/Close/Halfwidth/Length/Undo/Width]:
  -4,4
Specify next point or [Arc/Close/Halfwidth/Length/Undo/Width]:
  -4,2
Specify next point or [Arc/Close/Halfwidth/Length/Undo/Width]:
  4,2
Specify next point or [Arc/Close/Halfwidth/Length/Undo/Width]:
  4,4
Specify next point or [Arc/Close/Halfwidth/Length/Undo/Width]:
  2,4
Specify next point or [Arc/Close/Halfwidth/Length/Undo/Width]:
  6,22
Specify next point or [Arc/Close/Halfwidth/Length/Undo/Width]: c
  <for close>

Command: line
Specify first point: 0,0 (start of the axis)
Specify next point or [Undo]: 12,0 (endpoint of the axis)
Specify next point or [Undo]: <Press Enter>
```

```
Command: revolve
Current wire frame density:  ISOLINES=4
Select objects: <Pick the closed Polyline just created>
Select objects: 1 found
Select objects: <Press Enter>
Specify start point for axis of revolution or
  define axis by [Object/X (axis)/Y (axis)]: o (for object)
Select an object: <Pick the line>
Specify angle of revolution <360>: <Press Enter>
```

Use ZOOM – ALL to see all your revolved drawing. Then, change it to a suitable color and use **SHADEMODE** to shade the finished drawing.

INTERFERE

The **INTERFERE** command (equivalent to choosing Draw|Solids|Interfere) is different from the previous Boolean commands in that it doesn't alter the selected 3D objects. Rather, it identifies (highlights) the area where two selections of 3D solids overlap and gives you the option to create a new 3D solid from the overlapping volumes. If you create a new overlapping solid volume, you may then either erase it (once you've seen the location of the interfering part) or use the **SUBTRACT** command to remove the 3D solid section that interferes with the main component.

At the prompt, pick the first set of solids, press Enter, and pick the second set of solids. AutoCAD then calculates all the volumes where the objects in the first selection overlap the objects in the second selection. You're asked if you want to create new interference solids from the overlapping volumes; the default response is No. The prompt is as follows:

```
Create interference solids? [Yes/No] <N>:
```

If you enter "y" for yes, AutoCAD will create multiple new solids based on the interference volumes. AutoCAD then asks if you want to highlight (identify) pairs of solids that interfere with each other. Entering "y" identifies (highlights) one solid from each group to show which pairs of solids will interfere with each other:

```
Highlight pairs of interfering solids? [Yes/No] <N>:  y
```

If there's more than one interfering pair, AutoCAD displays the following prompt:

```
Enter an option [Next pair/eXit] <Next>:
```

If you enter "n" for no or press Enter, AutoCAD will cycle through the interfering pairs of 3D solids. You can also enter "x" to end the command.

The companion CD-ROM has an interfere.dwg file (see Figure 7.23). Open the drawing, zoom in to the main collar, and notice it's in three colored

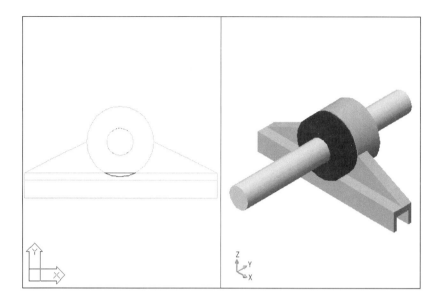

Figure 7.23
Use the **INTERFERE** command, and then use **SHADE** to shade the result.

segments: blue for the main shaft slider, black for the collar, and green for the sliding cylindrical shaft. Activate the **INTERFERE** command and choose the black cylindrical collar as the first set of solids. Then, choose the blue set of solids. Answer "y" for yes to create a new interference solid at the prompt. The result will show a black segment as the interference solid. You can then subtract it from the main shaft. Finally, shade the result as shown on the right side of Figure 7.23.

Creating A Simple Object

The objective of this exercise is to use a number of the solid primitives we've reviewed in this chapter to create a simple object, as shown in Figure 7.24. (A color version of this figure is included in the Color Studio in the middle of this book.) In the exercise, you'll use Boolean commands both to subtract and union all the primitives you create into a whole part. In addition, you'll use **MVSETUP** to create automatic standard viewports in paper space.

Start a new metric drawing, name it clip.dwg, and set your 3D View to SE Isometric. Stay in the World Coordinate System (WCS) and activate the Solids toolbar. (clip.dwg is also available on the CD-ROM). In this example, as shown in Figure 7.24, the five main steps to create the component are as follows:

1. **Create the main box 200x150x38 starting at 0,0,0.** From the Solids toolbar, choose the Box icon and create a box 200x150x38mm:

   ```
   Command: box
   Specify corner of box or [CEnter] <0,0,0>: <Press Enter>
   Specify corner or [Cube/Length]: 200,150,38
   ```

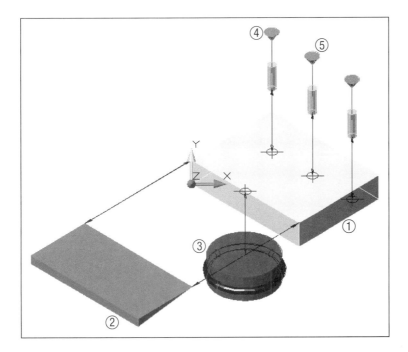

Figure 7.24
The clip.dwg drawing and its various parts.

Zoom as tight into the drawing as possible. Use **ZOOM** Extents or **ZOOM** Window:

```
Command: zoom
Specify corner of window, enter a scale factor (nX or nXP),
  or [All/Center/Dynamic/Extents/Previous/Scale/Window]
  <real time>: e
```

2. **Create an inverted wedge as a cutout.** To create the sloping part, you'll use **WEDGE**. But because **WEDGE** constructs a 3D solid with a sloping face that tapers along the X axis, you'll need to revolve the Z axis of the UCS by 90 degrees:

```
Command: ucs
Current ucs name:  *WORLD*
Enter an option [New/Move/orthoGraphic/Prev/Restore/Save/
  Del/Apply/?/World] <World>: z
Specify rotation angle about Z-axis <90>: 90
```

Creating the wedge from the top down will ensure that the flat part of the wedge follows the top profile:

```
Command: wedge
Specify first corner of wedge or [CEnter]  <0,0,0>: 0,0,38
Specify corner or [Cube/Length]: l
Specify length: 100
Specify width: -200
Specify height: -13
```

Reset your UCS to the WCS:

```
Command: ucs
Current ucs name:  *NO NAME*
Enter an option [New/Move/orthoGraphic/Prev/Restore/Save/
  Del/Apply/?/World] <World>: <Press Enter>
```

3. **Create the main cylinder and its torus.** Create the cylindrical cut-out part of the clip:

```
Command: cylinder
Current wire frame density:  ISOLINES=4
Specify center point for base of cylinder or [Elliptical]
  <0,0,0>: 100,0,0
Specify radius for base of cylinder or [Diameter]: 50
Specify height of cylinder or [Center of other end]: 38
```

Create the torus with the same diameter and center point as the central cylinder:

```
Command: torus
Current wire frame density:  ISOLINES=4
Specify center of torus <0,0,0>: 100,0,15
Specify radius of torus or [Diameter]: 50
Specify radius of tube or [Diameter]: 5
```

4. **Create and array the three cylinders and inverted cones.** Create a single cylinder, as follows:

```
Command: cylinder
Current wire frame density:  ISOLINES=4
Specify center point for base of cylinder or [Elliptical]
  <0,0,0>: 25,125
Specify radius for base of cylinder or [Diameter]: 6
Specify height of cylinder or [Center of other end]: 38
```

Create the inverted cone slightly above the top of the clip (say, 1mm). Doing so ensures that when you subtract the cone part as a countersink hole, AutoCAD will remove it cleanly and not leave dangling edges:

```
Command: cone
Current wire frame density:  ISOLINES=4
Specify center point for base of cone or [Elliptical]
  <0,0,0>: 25,125,39
Specify radius for base of cone or [Diameter]: 10
Specify height of cone or [Apex]: -14
```

Array the hole cylinder and the countersink cone a distance of 75mm:

```
Command: 3darray
Initializing...  3DARRAY loaded.
Select objects: <Pick the small cone and the small cylinder>
Enter the type of array [Rectangular/Polar] <R>: r
Enter the number of rows (—) <1>: <Press Enter>
Enter the number of columns (|||) <1>: 3
Enter the number of levels (...) <1>: <Press Enter>
Specify the distance between columns (|||): 75
```

Before or after using the Boolean commands, you can set the visualization accuracy to the part, especially if you plan to use the **HIDE** or **SHADE** commands. Upgrade **ISOLINES** and **FACETRES** as follows:

```
Command: isolines
Enter new value for ISOLINES <4>: 12
Command: facetres
Enter new value for FACETRES <0.5000>: 5
```

Use the **REGEN** command to see the result of setting **ISOLINES** and **FACETRES**.

5. **Use the Boolean SUBTRACT command to subtract the primitives from the main box.** All your primitives are now created, and you're ready to union and subtract. One way is to union the countersink holes and cones together, union the torus and central cylinder together, and then subtract these from the core component, along with the inverted wedge.

   A more efficient way is to use the **SUBTRACT** command to both subtract and union in one smooth operation. To do so, activate the **SUBTRACT** command and choose the body (the original box is the body) of the clip as the main component and press Enter. Then, in the second half of the command, choose the remaining objects with a crossing window (it doesn't matter if you highlight the main body of the clip again, because your selection set still recognizes it as the part to be kept):

```
Command: subtract
Select solids and regions to subtract from:  <Pick the large
  box as the body of the clip>
Select objects: <Press Enter>
Select solids and regions to subtract: <Pick the rest of the
  primitives> <Press Enter>
Select objects: <Specify opposite corner>: 10 found
```

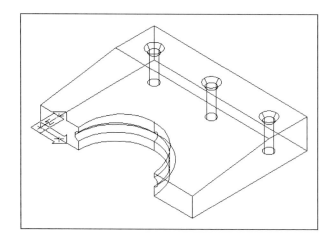

Figure 7.25
The completed clip.dwg drawing prior to using **MVSETUP**.

Now that you've created the component (as shown in Figure 7.25), you're ready to create standard engineering viewports. Pick the Layout1 tab to enter paper space and click on OK to close the Page Setup Layout1 dialog box. If the Isometric drawing appears in the viewport, simply erase the viewport.

You'll see the completed drawing prior to using **MVSETUP** in Figure 7.25. The final result after using **MVSETUP** is shown in Figure 7.26. At the command line, type "mvsetup" and then follow the prompts:

```
Command: mvsetup
Initializing...
Enter an option [Align/Create/Scale viewports/Options/Title
  block/Undo]: c
Enter option [Delete objects/Create viewports/Undo] <Create>: c
Available layout options: . . .
 0:      None
 1:      Single
 2:      Std. Engineering
 3:      Array of Viewports
Enter layout number to load or [Redisplay]: 2
Specify first corner of bounding area for viewport(s): 0,0
Specify opposite corner: 270,210
Specify distance between viewports in X direction <0>: 5
Specify distance between viewports in Y direction <5>: <Press
  Enter>
Enter an option [Align/Create/Scale viewports/Options/Title
  block/Undo]: <Press Enter>
```

Your final result after using **MVSETUP** will be similar to Figure 7.26. You may now use the **MS** command to enter the viewports and use the **ZOOM** command to zoom scale each viewport to .5xp (except the upper-right viewport, which can be left as is). With **SHADEMODE** set to Gouraud, you may also change the color of the pictorial viewport or just shade it. Remember to use the **PS** command to return to paper space before you plot.

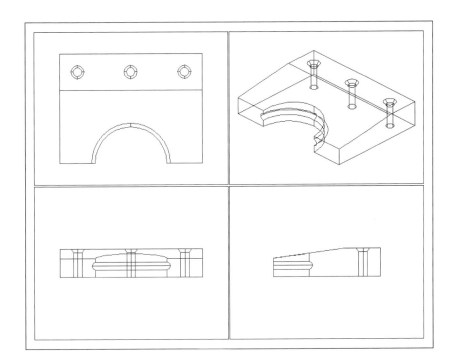

Figure 7.26
The completed clip.dwg
drawing in standard
engineering viewports.

Parametric Design And Associativity

You need to be aware that, in addition to CSG and B-REP modeling, you can use parametric modeling and feature-based design. See Table 7.1 for a list of the different types of modeling engines attached to various CAD software. However, the current approach is to incorporate and integrate parametric features into a 3D model. You do this by using datum points, called Primary, Secondary, and Tertiary Datum (DTM1, DTM2, and DTM3), which you'll see referenced in Figure 7.27.

Also, if you look closely at Figure 7.27, you'll see that the parametric model is defined by a set of parameters (expressions of variable numbers and names), which range from simple dimension values (for example, the radius of a local fillet, or the radius of a circle [as a through hole] to the length of a small flange, as opposed to a global parameter that has an effect on

Table 7.1 Popular CAD packages and their modeling engines.

Software	Wireframe	Surface	Solid Model	Parametric	Solid Modeler
AutoCAD 2000	Yes	Yes	Yes	No	ACIS
Mechanical Desktop	Yes	Yes	Yes	Yes	ACIS
IronCAD	Yes	Yes	Yes	Yes	ACIS
CADKEY	Yes	Yes	Yes	Yes	ACIS
MicroStation	Yes	Yes	Yes	No	Parasolid
Solid Works	Yes	Yes	Yes	Yes	Parasolid
CATIA	Yes	Yes	Yes	Yes	Proprietary
Pro/Engineer	Yes	Yes	Yes	Yes	Proprietary

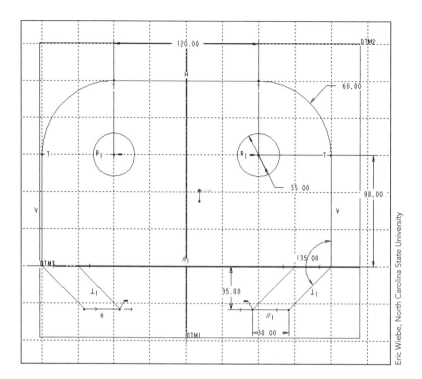

Figure 7.27
A constrained parametric model, which shows a profile with implicit constraints.

Eric Wiebe, North Carolina State University

the entire design, such as the overall length of the part (the length of a crankshaft, for example, would be a global parameter). Nevertheless, parametric models have associativity, and it is usually bidirectional.

Associativity is the ability of a modeler to allow you to change or alter an object through direct editing commands without having to erase and/or redraw the part. (You'll find more information about associativity in Chapter 8.) Thus, parametric models go a step beyond using standard dimensional attributes of a 3D model. Parametric models use names and expressions that relate to dimensional variables and/or to other parametric dimensions. In turn, these expressions can be constrained (attached) and named to a specific part or feature of the model. As a result, if you change the model, the feature(s) are also updated and the model's dimensions are changed according to the value of its attached expression. In turn, this associativity provides you with a true solid model that can be designed according to general shape and topology, and it allows you to attach key features and key variables throughout. Plus, when you attach standard parts (such as fasteners), you can constrain them according to the tolerance ranges within your family of parts.

Feature-based design is another form of parametric design. It lets you form features (fillets and flanges, for instance). Although popular with designers, form features are difficult to implement: You can't define geometric elements in isolation and then add or subtract them in the database. For example, a chamfer requires two planar faces meeting at a straight edge with enough space on each planar face to locate the new plane without touching other objects.

So, how does parametric design help you—the designer? Most drawings are made up of a number of parts called an *assembly*. You can create the assembly model as dynamic or static. A static 3D model has no link to any other drawing or component. A dynamic model includes dynamic linking of features or parts into the drawing, such that this set of parts becomes a family with a specific parent-child relationship. So, if you updated a series of parts as separate entities, the main drawing to which they were dynamically linked would be automatically updated. (The **XREF** and OLE AutoCAD commands allow this dynamic form of linking.) ProE and AutoCAD's Mechanical Desktop (plus other CAD software—see Table 7.1) are parametric modelers and allow you to incorporate and integrate parametric features into a 3D model. Figures 7.27 shows an example of a parametric model profile with implicit constraints and Figure 7.28 shows the completed extrusion.

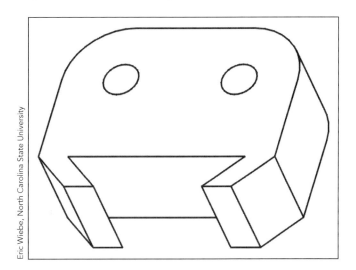

Eric Wiebe, North Carolina State University

Figure 7.28
The completed parametric model, showing the extruded profile.

Moving On

Solid modeling is an exciting method of creating components, and it gets easier the more you use it. This chapter explained some of the theory of solid modeling, along with practical working examples of how to use various primitive commands.

The next chapter will review how some of the solid and surface modeling edit commands function. Then, as you move on to Chapter 9, you'll review the Drawing, View, and Profile setup options. You use the setup commands after you've created the 3D solid and you need to lay out the drawing in paper space before printing. In addition, you'll learn how to create profiles in CAD.

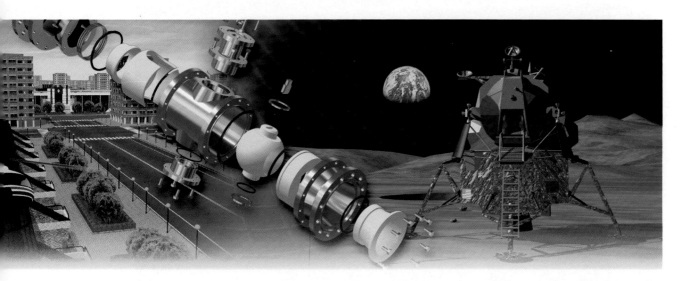

AUTOCAD 2000
3D STUDIO

AutoCAD has emerged into the visual age as an improved tool for both 3D modeling and 3D rendering. In this Color Studio, you'll see some of the photorealistic images that AutoCAD 2000 can produce from 3D surface and 3D solid drawings.

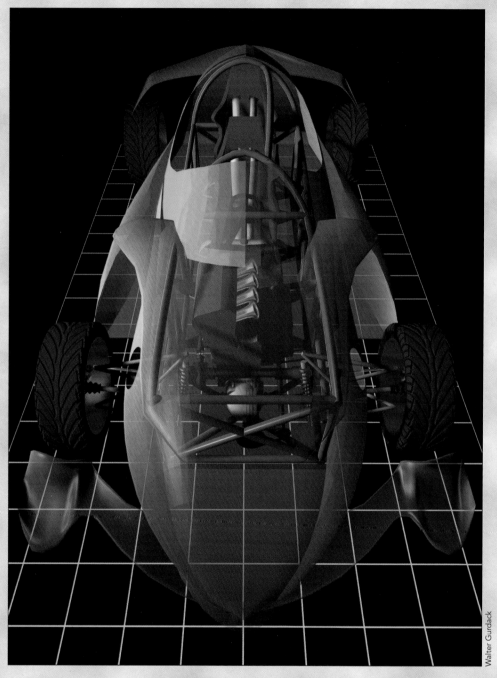

Walter Gurdack

Fully rendered visualization of a frame and chassis with a transparent surface shell. Notice how the lighting is placed to throw subtle shadows onto other parts of the frame, and how the translucency of the shell adds to the overall effect of this 32-bit image. Background color could have been added, but with more than 133,500 colors in the image, it would have over-stimulated the viewer. Instead, your eye is drawn toward the overall effect of the translucent image. (See Chapter 12.)

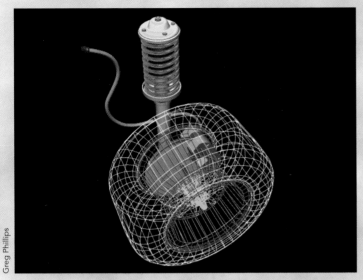

Greg Phillips

Pictorial image that shows part wireframe and part rendered assembly. This image uses multiple attached materials, along with a plain wireframe around the main component. The black background forces your eye to the main part, which shows a subtle hint of shadowing on the opaque parts. (See Chapter 11.)

Joe Ernst

Fully rendered visualization of an assembly with a transparent shell, using both opaque and translucent components. (See Chapters 4 and 12.)

Ju Yeom Mun

Rendered image of a pictorial assembly drawing. In this example of a manufactured component, the use of light, shadows, and background enhance the overall effect of the simple part. (See Chapter 11.)

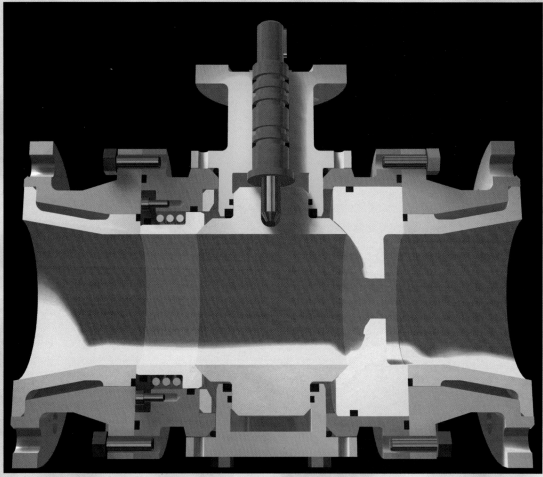

Jan Hill

Rendered cutaway section view of an assembly. For a layperson, section views are often hard to visualize, and rather than using hatching as a presentation technique, one method is to use a simple rendering of the different components that make up the assembly. (See Chapter 9.)

A fully rendered example of a surface model. Prototype models go through various stages of design and conceptualization, which often require intermediate rendering to show the stage reached. (See Chapter 6.)

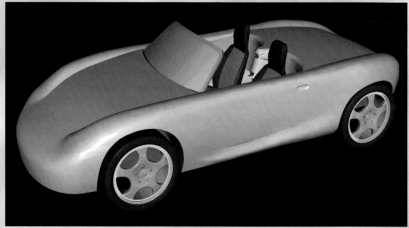

Yann Bertraud, Autodesk, Inc.

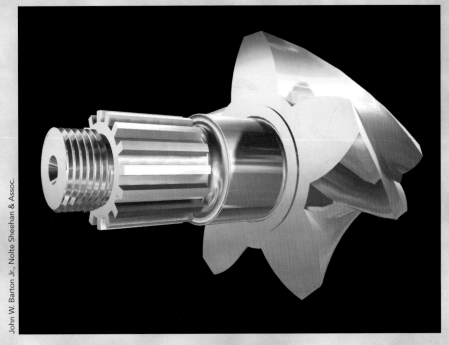

John W. Barton Jr., Nolte Sheehan & Assoc.

A fully rendered 24-bit image of a complex gear. Images of manufactured components are often used in catalogs as visualizations for prospective buyers or as part of a portfolio that shows prospective customers what a manufacturing company can produce. The image in this example uses no background for a more dramatic effect. (See Chapter 4.)

Yann Bertraud, Autodesk, Inc.

Pictorial image that shows a conrod component. The mirroring effect and the background add to the overall effect of the simple part. (See Chapters 9 and 11.)

An exploded assembly drawing is used to depict a sequence of parts and a parts list. You'll notice the list includes detail number, description, size, material, and quantity. (See Chapter 4.)

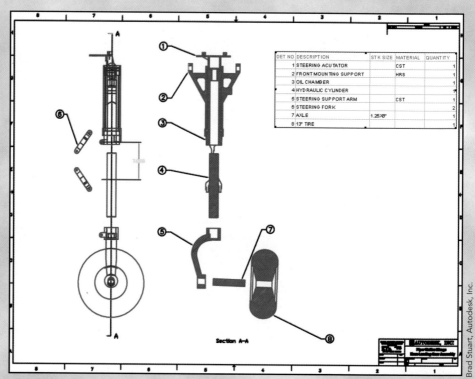

DET NO	DESCRIPTION	STK SIZE	MATERIAL	QUANTITY
1	STEERING ACUTATOR		CST	1
2	FRONT MOUNTING SUPPORT		HRS	1
3	OIL CHAMBER			1
4	HYDRAULIC CYLINDER			1
5	STEERING SUPPORT ARM		CST	1
6	STEERING FORK			2
7	AXLE	1.25X6"		1
8	13" TIRE			1

Section A-A

Brad Stuart, Autodesk, Inc.

Brad Stuart, Autodesk, Inc.

Visualization is used as a tool for solid modeling. In this example, you can visualize from an ink sketch to a 3D isometric wireframe to the finished product. (See Chapter 12.)

Brad Stuart, Autodesk, Inc.

Fully rendered visualization of a front wheel assembly. Notice the attention to detail and the dramatic effect of the background. (See Chapter 11.)

Rendered visualization of Apollo 13. Your eye is immediately drawn to the main image of the Apollo craft, which is placed at an angle for a better visual effect. Your eye tends to ignore the drab moon in the off-center background. (See Chapters 11 and 12.)

Keith Sylvester, University of Houston

Rick Kaplan

Rendered visualization of a lunar landing module. To be more imaginative with lighting, use it to cast long shadows, as seen here. Although this image is drab with a black background, the visual effect is heightened, because the eye is attracted to both the image in the foreground and the earth's image in the background. (See Chapter 12.)

AZ-Tech and Shadow & Light Production, California

Rendered visualization of a rocket booster. Your eye is immediately drawn to the slightly off-center image of the booster rocket, but the jettisoned motor in the upper right is placed for the best visual effect, with the background enhancing the overall visualization effect. (See Chapter 11.)

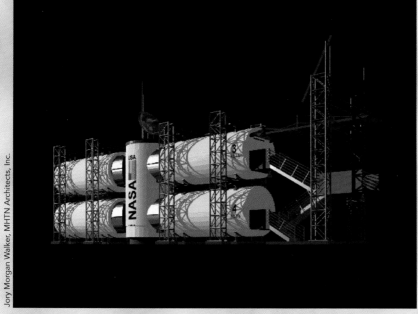

Jory Morgan Walker, MHTN Architects, Inc.

Rendered visualization of a NASA space station component. The image lighting is used to cast shadows in this space station. (See Chapter 11.)

Interior image shots that are lit by diffuse lighting provide flat, uninteresting scenes. In addition to ambient light, this image uses distant lighting in the main section of the design, with extra lighting in the side boxes, which in turn enhances the overall effect of the image. (See Chapter 12.)

Jose Maria de Espona, Triplefactor, Spain

You can make the lighting of a standard office interior interesting by introducing natural light. Add sunlight as a distant light source and make it cast through either a skylight or window. Use spotlights on objects to cast shadows. (See Chapter 11.)

Ron Jong, Autodesk, Inc.

Jose Maria de Espona, Triplefactor, Spain

When the sun is overhead, it can produce a flat, uninteresting feel because there is no variation in shadow. A better technique is to render your image at sunset. This scene, for example, could have had dark skies with brightly illuminated building faces. The use of artificial lighting from the buildings' interiors, plus light from adjacent streetlights and from landscape lighting in the immediate area of the buildings, would have produced a more realistic image. (See Chapter 11.)

Jory Morgan Walker, MHTN Architects, Inc.

Buildings are most interesting at dawn and dusk, when shadow effects are more realistic and dramatic. The enhanced drama produced by the low sun angle causes different faces of the buildings to be produced in different light qualities; some of the buildings' faces are in deep shadow, while other faces are in bright sunlight. Notice how the elongated shadows enhance this effect. (See Chapter 11.)

Rendering and textures are used in this image to enhance what otherwise would have been a mundane part. (See Chapter 11.)

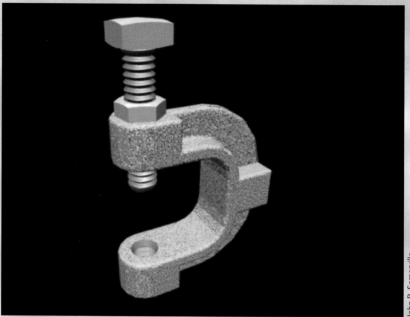

John R. Somerville

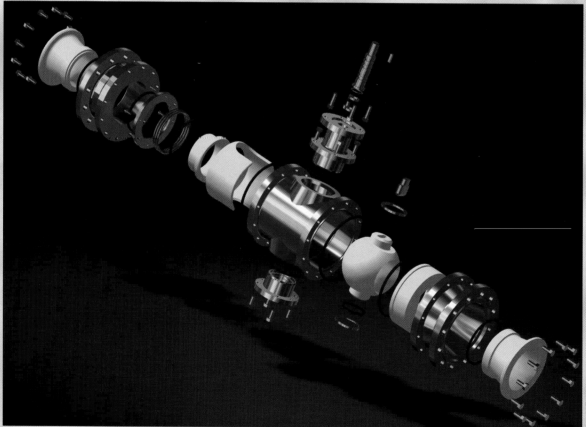

Jan Hill

Example of a fully rendered, exploded pictorial assembly drawing, with approximately 60,000 colors used in the image. The chrome parts and the yellow spacers distinctly show the buildup of the exploded assembly. (See Chapter 4.)

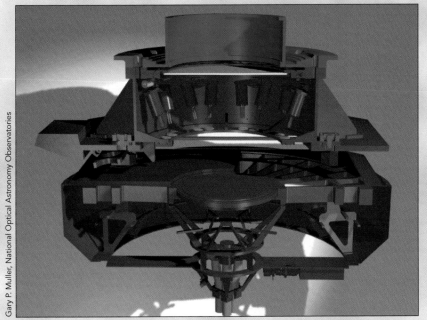

Gary P. Muller, National Optical Astronomy Observatories

Rendered cutaway section view of an assembly model telescope part that raises and lowers. With more than 6,500 colors used in this model, the lighting is used to show shadows and the myriad of details that make up the component. (See Chapter 9.)

Jan Hill

Example of a fully rendered assembly drawing. Notice how the background, the lighting, and the shadows contribute to the overall effect of the image. (See Chapters 4 and 12.)

This translucent image with attached bitmapped materials is an effective image. A yellow spotlight with a fuzzy cone of light can be used to show a flame. (See Chapter 12.)

Scott A. Vonhof

A simple sculptured effect with bitmapped materials and the use of shadowed lighting really enhance the quality of this image. (See Chapter 11.)

Robot Ale

Transparency and translucency contribute to the overall effect of this image, along with the bitmapped attached materials. (See Chapters 11 and 12.)

Scott A. Vonhof

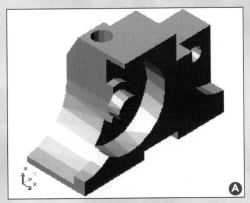

The difference between 1-bit (A), 8-bit (B), and 24-bit (C) images is obvious. One-bit images are extremely plain, 8-bit images have more color and lighting, and 24-bit True color images provide the most dramatic effect. (See Chapter 12.)

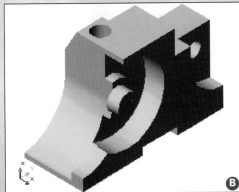

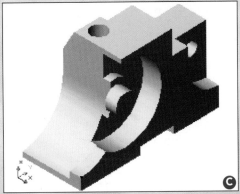

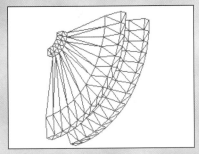

Hidden Line Image

Flat Shaded Image

Gouraud Shaded Image

Rendered With Shadows Image

Flat Shaded + Edges Image

Gouraud Shaded + Edges Image

Hidden wireframe images are the simplest form of image, whereas 24-bit rendered images with shadows are the most complex. The shademodes are as follows: flat shaded (showing facets of the polygonal faces), flat shaded plus edges, Gouraud shaded, and Gouraud shaded plus edges. (See Chapter 12.)

Visualization is used as a tool for solid modeling. Think of the steps you need to take to create the component. In this example, the steps are as follows: (1) create the main box 200×150×38 starting at 0,0,0; (2) create an inverted wedge as a cutout; (3) create the main cylinder and its torus; (4) create and array the three cylinders and inverted cones; and (5) use the Boolean SUBTRACT command to subtract the primitives from the main box. (See Chapter 7.)

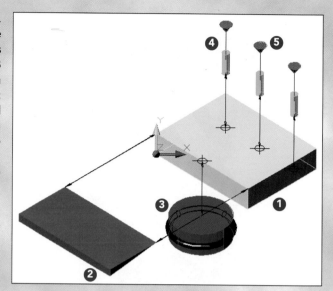

Visualization is a specific thought process for solid modeling. The creation of this 3D model can be broken down into five steps: (1) create first profile in the World UCS and extrude up 19mm; (2) create second profile in the Side UCS and extrude away 24mm; (3) union the two extrusions; (4) create two solid boxes as primitives; and (5) subtract two boxes from the main solid. (See Chapter 7.)

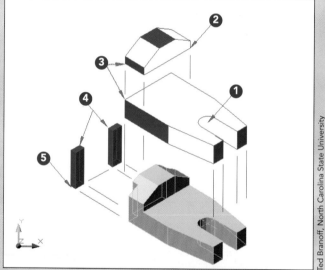

Ted Branoff, North Carolina State University

This flat rendered image is a simple visualization example of a rendered exploded assembly drawing. It could be used, for example, in a publishing document to show the sequence of placing components into a case. (See Chapter 12.)

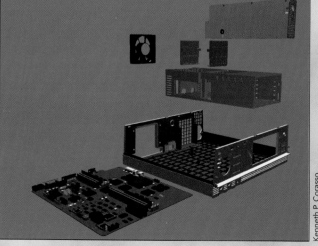

Kenneth P. Corasso

EDITING
3D MODELS

This chapter provides you with background knowledge on both general and specific editing of 3D models, including the editing of surface and solid models and the analysis of completed models.

General Editing Hints For CAD Modeling

AutoCAD 2000's editing capabilities are a huge improvement over the limited editing features of previous AutoCAD releases. Before a part is released for manufacture, three types of editing may occur to a 3D model: geometry, cosmetic, and topology. With *geometry editing*, only a few parameters are changed within the model; these minor edits can include dimensions, angles, the dimensioning style, and the alteration of 2D or 3D tolerances. For example, dimensional and angular changes—such as aligning, bending, moving, rotating, or scaling a part—can alter the size and location of surfaces without altering the topology. *Cosmetic editing* involves a minor change, such as editing a dimension location, a material specification, or notes. With *topology editing*, you need to be careful, because this type of editing often involves changing the number of edges or vertices of some of the faces of the model or the actual number of faces of a part.

AutoCAD 2000 has a new set of editing commands for both surface splines and solid model editing, allowing you more associativity and flexibility as you create and revise your solid models. The 3D solid editing commands allow you to edit the faces, edges, and body of the object you create, including stretching and reducing the solid entities.

Listed below are some general hints for hierarchy and geometry creation of complex 3D geometry:

- Keep your geometry and your design simple.

- Try to create your wireframe geometry first, rather than creating every line, arc, and so on. For instance, you can use commands such as **COPY**, **OFFSET**, and **ARRAY** to produce geometric elements adjacent to each other.

- When you have complex multiple parts and subassemblies, perform all the operations to each single construction first before using the Boolean operations to join or intersect the subassemblies.

- Before using Boolean operations, make a block of each part. The block could be used as a backup of each subassembly, making it easier to alter pieces of the design rather than redraw the whole part.

- Use arcs and lines rather than splines or polyarcs to preserve the original geometry. For example, replacing an arc with a spline in a cross-section profile when you extrude, sweep, blend, or revolve will alter the surface definition produced.

- If your modeler allows it, use the **EXTRUDE** command rather than the **SWEEP** command. For example, when using splines with numerically controlled (NC) programming, the toolpath becomes much more difficult to produce. Thus, if you replace your spline or polyarcs with a standard arc, the **EXTRUDE** command will allow simpler toolpath creation and also reduce file size and complexity.

- If your modeler allows it, use the **SWEEP** command rather than a blend or transition command. Remember, AutoCAD has no commands named blend, transition, or sweep, but this book tries to show you ways around this. For example, to sweep an object, you can use **EXTRUDE** with the **Path** option. (See the "Creating A Swept Curve From A Profile" section later in this chapter. Or alternately, to create a blend or transition, see "Changing Profiles In AutoCAD" later in the chapter.)

- Try to use single curvature modeling as opposed to double curvature modeling. For example, never try to rotate the angle of revolution for a cross-section profile more than 360 degrees. Doing so results in an invalid, self-intersecting solid.

Associative Vs. Nonassociative Elements In A 3D Model

Associativity is the ability of a modeler to let you change or alter an object through direct editing commands without having to erase and redraw the part. Grades of associativity are nonassociativity, one-way associativity, and two-way associativity. Some 3D modelers use associativity through dimensioning (that is, associative dimensioning and hatching)—for example, the dimension changes as you alter the geometry of the part. Other 3D modelers use parametric and constraint-based modeling. AutoCAD will allow you to use dimensioning and hatching associativity, and it will also let you use grips. With nonassociative drawings or CAD systems, you have no link (direct or otherwise) between your 3D model, the part drawings, dimensions, or detail views. Thus, if you wish to edit a part drawing or a dimension, you must redraw it.

One-way associativity lets you update smaller changes in your drawings as you modify them: It's a form of unidirectional link from the 3D model to the assembly drawing, part drawing, or CAD dimension. Thus, if you edited an assembly drawing, part drawing, or dimension, the 3D model would be updated automatically through the link between the geometric part and the dimension. You could stretch the part geometry, for example, and the dimension attached to it would update automatically. On the other hand, you couldn't stretch or alter the dimension and expect the part geometry drawing to be updated automatically, because such a result would require two-way associativity.

Two-way associativity implies a bidirectional link from the 3D model through the dimensions of the drawing assembly and drawing part geometry and back to the 3D model, forming a type of loop. Be careful with two-way associativity, because inexperienced hands can accidentally change the main 3D model without realizing it. By altering a portion of the view or part drawing, for example, an inexperienced operator may alter the main 3D model, thereby stopping production if the model fails to meet production specifications or design tolerances on the shop floor.

Associativity In A Surface Model

The greater the amount of associativity in a surface model, the less you can edit the model through direct surface or curve modifying commands. The challenge with a surface model is to create a model that combines both associative and nonassociative elements. In turn, doing so allows you to modify the model through dimension and/or direct editing commands. Whatever type of 3D surface you design, it will usually have both curves and surfaces, and these will often have some associativity.

Associativity Of A Mesh

Usually, an AutoCAD surface mesh has little associativity. If you need to edit a mesh or a small portion of a mesh, you can move chosen vertex points with its grips. If you need to edit the edges of your model plus edit the internal mesh, you're limited to erasing the mesh, changing the edge curve, and then reapplying the surface mesh to the edges.

Another alternative is to explode your mesh, causing it to revert to individual 3D faces. Alternately, you may use **PEDIT** to smooth the mesh into various surface types. The type of surface may be changed to quadratic B-spline, cubic B-spline, or Bezier surfaces. (See "Editing Smoothness For A Bezier, Quadratic, Or Cubic Mesh" later in this chapter.)

Open the assoc-mesh.dwg from the CD-ROM. As Figure 8.1 shows, it's a simple associative mesh model with nonassociative curves that make up its four edges. Thus, if you try to edit the curves, the surface mesh will not be

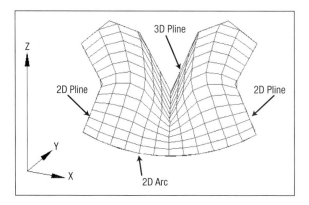

Figure 8.1

Editing mesh surfaces. You may edit this associative mesh but not the edges of this model.

affected—hence, the curves are nonassociative. On the other hand, the mesh, which is associative and created from the four curves, can be adjusted. For example, set the variables **SURFU** to 20, **SURFV** to 30, and **SURFTYPE** to 5. Then, activate **PEDIT** and pick the mesh; at the **Enter an option** prompt, enter "s" for smooth surface, and see the surface change to a quadratic B-spline mesh instead of the Bezier surface mesh, which is its current setting.

Associativity Of A 3D Face

The **3DFACE** command creates individual segments of a mesh. Using an object's vertex grip points, you can grip individual hot spots and move the vertex to a new X,Y,Z location. By pressing the Shift key and choosing multiple vertex points, you can move multiple vertex points of a mesh at the same time. See Figure 8.2.

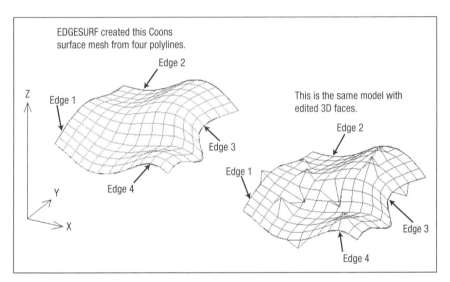

Figure 8.2
Grips allow you to alter individual elements of 3D faces.

Open the coons-mesh.dwg from the CD-ROM. Figure 8.2 shows that it was created with **EDGESURF** as a Coons mesh. Pick anywhere on the unaltered main mesh (the left-hand sketch); notice that blue grips appear. Pick any one of the grip node points and it will change red (to a hot grip). Move your mouse cursor to any new location and pick again; do this five or six times, picking arbitrary node points. You may also press the Shift key and pick a few grip points (to make them hot). Then, release the Shift key, repick any one of the hot grips, and move your cursor to a new location.

Next, set the variables **SURFU** to 30, **SURFV** to 50, and **SURFTYPE** to 5. Activate **PEDIT** and pick the mesh; at the **Enter an option** prompt, enter "s" for smooth surface and see the surface change to a smoothed mesh. Thus, with this Coons mesh, you have general associativity through the variables just mentioned and local freedom via grips to move individual nodes to new locations. Remember, moving the curves that were originally used to create the mesh does not affect the associativity of the mesh, because the curves are a nonassociative element.

Associativity In AutoCAD

Associativity, especially in AutoCAD, is often referred to with reference to how you can edit or modify the dimensioning or the hatching of objects as the associated geometry is modified. Thus, if you alter the geometry of your AutoCAD part (for example, by stretching it) and it has dimensions and/or hatching attached to it, the dimensions and/or hatching will also alter (stretch) and update automatically to the new size. The AutoCAD 2000 ACIS modeler provides a great deal more flexibility that lets you alter (through **SOLIDEDIT**) the face, edge, and body of your 3D solid:

- *Associative dimensioning*—Changing the geometry changes the dimension. Thus, the dimension is updated as the associated geometry is modified.

- *Associative hatching*—Changing the geometry changes the hatching. Thus, hatching conforms to its bounding objects such that modifying the bounding objects automatically adjusts the hatch. AutoCAD uses **BHATCH** as an associated boundary hatch.

- *Smoothed surfaces*—Types of smoothed surfaces available in AutoCAD are quadratic B-spline, cubic B-spline, and Bezier. Use the **SURFTYPE** or **PROPERTIES** command to set the surface type.

Modifier Commands

Most 3D modelers include modifier commands that allow you to translate and rotate your object in 3D space. The purpose of these modifier commands is movement—that is, they let you translate, rotate, or perform a combination of translation and rotation commands on your object either singly or simultaneously.

Choose 3D Operation from the Modify menu; you'll see the **3DARRAY**, **MIRROR3D**, **ROTATE3D**, and **ALIGN** commands. These modifier commands are the AutoCAD interpretation of translation and rotation commands. Before you begin using the commands, you need to understand translation and rotation and what they mean to the modification of an object.

- *Translation*—To *translate* an object means to move it along one, two, or three axes without a change in its angular orientation relative to any of the three axes.

- *Rotation*—To *rotate* an object means to change its angular orientation relative to its UCS (local) or WCS (global) coordinate system, in effect at the time of rotation.

Translation and rotation can occur simultaneously along a curved path, but the object remains aligned with a line between the origin and a fixed point on the object. See Figures 8.3 through 8.6 and the corresponding text for an explanation of this.

Now let's look at the **3DARRAY, MIRROR3D, ROTATE3D,** and **ALIGN** commands within AutoCAD.

3DARRAY

The **3DARRAY** command allows you to copy objects in a 3D array. The translation may be rectangular or polar, but rotation is allowed only in polar mode. The command is similar to the **2DARRAY** command but adds a third dimension: Z height spacing, which AutoCAD calls a *level* (as in *3D level*). The easiest way to understand a 3D rectangular array is to picture a 3D grid, in which you specify the 3D distance between rows and columns along with the Z height/spacing of your levels.

If you use **POLAR** as an array option of this 3D command, be aware that AutoCAD uses the distance from the center point of the array to a specific reference point on the last selected object you've chosen. For example, AutoCAD uses the center of an arc or circle, the endpoint of a line, the start point of text, and the insertion base point to a block or shape. Hint: When you need to choose multiple objects in your 3D Array, use a crossing window to select the objects, and then press the Shift key and unpick (remove) the specific reference object from your selection set. Then, release the Shift key and repick the object, because adding it back forces that object to be the last object chosen in your selection group. You can also rotate the objects as you copy them in a circular translation.

From the CD-ROM, open 3darray.dwg, which shows a circular plate, cylinder, and rib. Your objective is to use the **Polar Array** option of **3DARRAY** to array and rotate the rib about the main cylinder. As you'll see in the left side of Figure 8.3, the UCS is set to **World** at the center of the circular plate, and you should be in an SE Isometric view. Activate the **3DARRAY** command, choose the rib, and then use the **Polar** option of the **3DARRAY** command to array it about the main cylinder. Here's the **3DARRAY** command in more detail:

```
Command: 3darray
Initializing...  3DARRAY loaded.
Select objects: <Pick the rib with the cylinder attachment>
Select objects: <Press Enter>
Enter the type of array [Rectangular/Polar] <R>: p
Enter the number of items in the array: 7
Specify the angle to fill (+=ccw, -=cw) <360>: <Press Enter>
Rotate arrayed objects? [Yes/No] <Y>: <Press Enter>
Specify center point of array: 0,0,0
Specify second point on axis of rotation: @0,0,20
```

Once you've arrayed the rib, use the **UNION** command to combine all the 3D objects in the drawing into a single 3D solid. See the right side of Figure 8.3 for the end result of the command, along with a hidden view of the 3D model.

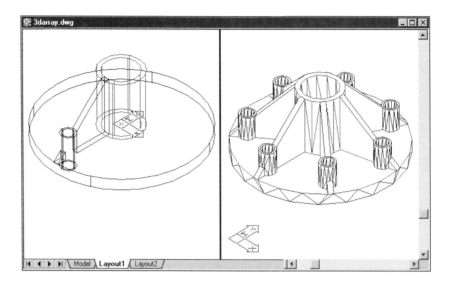

Figure 8.3
The **3DARRAY** command.

MIRROR3D

The **MIRROR3D** modifier command provides a number of options: **Object**, **Last**, **Zaxis**, **View**, **XY/YZ/ZX**, and **3points**. Each of the options allows you to delete your source object:

- *Object*—The **Object** option uses the plane of your chosen (planar) object as the mirror plane. The planar object is a circle, arc, or 2D-polyline segment you've created.

- *Last*—Use the **Last** option only if you previously mirrored an object, because this option uses the last mirroring plane you defined.

- *Zaxis*—Defines the mirror plane by a point on the plane and a point normal to the plane. Simply pick point (1) as a point on the mirror plane, and then pick point (2) as a point on the Zaxis of the mirror plane.

- *View*—The **View** option aligns the mirror plane with the viewing plane of the current viewport through a chosen point.

- *XY/YZ/ZX*—Each of these options (XY, YZ, or ZX) will align the mirror plane with a standard plane through a chosen point.

- *3points*—This option provides you with a very precise method to specify the first, second, and third points of your mirror plane. Hint: Use **OSNAP** tools to snap to exact endpoint locations of your object.

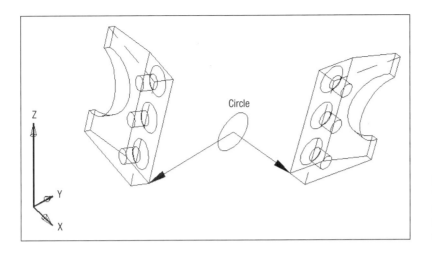

Figure 8.4
The **MIRROR3D** command.
MIRROR3D lets you mirror using a 3D planar object such as a circle, arc, or 2D polyline.

See Figure 8.4 for an example of how to use this command. The original 3D solid on the right of the figure uses a circular object in 3D space to perform the **MIRROR3D** operation.

ROTATE3D

With similar options to **MIRROR3D**, the **ROTATE3D** modifier command provides a number of options: **Object**, **Last**, **View**, **Xaxis**, **Yaxis**, **Zaxis**, and **2points**. See Figure 8.5 for an example of how to use this command. Picking two points is the default method, and the command may be used with the default. Or, pick the first point and then use a rotation angle or reference angle. In the example, the solid was rotated using a first pick point (Point 1) and then a reference angle of 30 degrees.

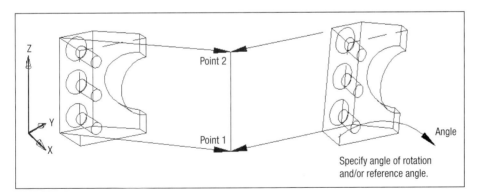

Figure 8.5
The **ROTATE3D** command lets you rotate a 3D object about an axis.

ALIGN

AutoCAD uses the **ALIGN** command to both translate and rotate a 3D object in 3D space. Translation and rotation can occur simultaneously along a curved path, but the object remains aligned with a line between origin and a fixed point on the object. Hint: Use **OSNAP** tools to snap to exact endpoint locations of your object. See Figure 8.6 for an example of how to use this command.

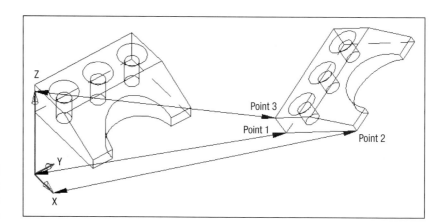

Figure 8.6
The **ALIGN** command is
both a translation and a
rotation command.

Open align.dwg from the CD-ROM and ensure your **OSNAP** tools are set to
Endpoint. Enter the **ALIGN** command and pick the 3D solid (it's the 3D
model on the right in Figure 8.6). Pick the three points as shown in the
illustration. The model will then move and reorient (that is, translate and
rotate) itself to the origin of the UCS settings on the left side of the illustration.

Changing Profiles In AutoCAD

At some stage, you may be called upon to edit or connect two or more
differently shaped profiles in AutoCAD, as you can see in Figure 8.7. So let's
look at how to use AutoCAD to create a square profile at one end of a part
and an ellipse profile at the other end. Alternately, you may create a filleted
square at one end and a circular profile at the other end to provide a variable radius round. In some modelers, this would be referred to as creating a
blend or a transition.

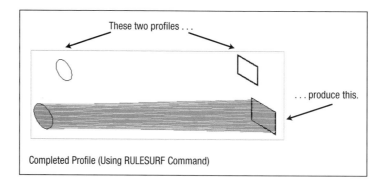

Figure 8.7
Changing profiles in AutoCAD:
creating a variable radius round.

Start a new drawing and name it radius.dwg. (This drawing is also available on this book's companion CD-ROM.) Use either English or metric units.
At the outset, you'll need to create the end shapes in a UCS you can relate
to, set your UCS to X 90 (Front view), and set your 3D Viewpoint to SE Isometric. Then, in the same UCS plane, create a closed polyline that forms a
rectangle or trapezium, and also draw an ellipse at a different location. Set

the **SURFTAB1** variable to a higher value than the default value of 6, such as 16 or 20. Finally, use the **RULESURF** command to join the two objects into surfaces. You may want to try the command with different end profiles. The main limitation with **RULESURF** is that the command connects only in a straight line.

Creating A Swept Curve From A Profile

Instead of creating a profile in a straight line, you may be called upon to create a swept object to a curvilinear path curve with a specific profile shape. You'll complete this exercise in a few easy steps: creating the path in the WCS, creating the profile in the UCS, and then sweeping the profile using the **Path** option of the **EXTRUDE** command. Finally, you'll shade the swept curve.

Start a new metric drawing, name it sweep.dwg, and set your 3D Viewpoint to SE Isometric. (The sweep.dwg drawing is also available on the CD-ROM.) Stay in the World Coordinate System (WCS) and use the **PLINE** command to create a path in 3D space to the following coordinates (see Figure 8.8):

```
Command: pline
Specify start point: 0,0
Current line-width is 0.0000
Specify next point or [Arc/Close/Halfwidth/Length/Undo/Width]:
   0,46
Specify next point or [Arc/Close/Halfwidth/Length/Undo/Width]:
   25,71
Specify next point or [Arc/Close/Halfwidth/Length/Undo/Width]:
   91,71
Specify next point or [Arc/Close/Halfwidth/Length/Undo/Width]:
   116,96
Specify next point or [Arc/Close/Halfwidth/Length/Undo/Width]:
   116,175
Specify next point or [Arc/Close/Halfwidth/Length/Undo/Width]:
   141,200
Specify next point or [Arc/Close/Halfwidth/Length/Undo/Width]:
   220,200
Specify next point or [Arc/Close/Halfwidth/Length/Undo/Width]:
   245,225
Specify next point or [Arc/Close/Halfwidth/Length/Undo/Width]:
   245,285
Specify next point or [Arc/Close/Halfwidth/Length/Undo/Width]:
   <Press Enter>
```

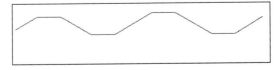

Figure 8.8
Create the path curve in the WCS using **PEDIT** or **FILLET**.

You can now use **PEDIT** to Spline the polyline or, better still, lock in the specific line coordinates by using the **FILLET** command set to a radius of 30. The **FILLET** command is revised in AutoCAD 2000, and when you use it with the p (for polyline) option, it will fillet all your line segments in one operation. Use it as follows:

```
Command: fillet
Current settings: Mode = TRIM, Radius = 10.0000
Select first object or [Polyline/Radius/Trim]: r
Specify fillet radius <10.0000>: 30
Command: fillet
Current settings: Mode = TRIM, Radius = 30.0000
Select first object or [Polyline/Radius/Trim]: p
Select 2D polyline: <Pick the Polyline just created>
```

Remember, you can't create both your path and your profile in the same UCS; one must be perpendicular to the other. So at this point, set your UCS to X 90 in order for the construction or work plane to flip to the Front view. In this vertical work plane, you'll create your profile to the path:

```
Command: ucs
Current ucs name:  *WORLD*
Enter an option [New/Move/orthoGraphic/Prev/Restore/Save/Del/
  Apply/?/World] <World>: x
Specify rotation angle about X axis <90>: 90
```

Depending upon how you made the path, it's usually best to center your profile about the center line of your path. (Remember that the profile may be any closed 2D shape you choose.) Now, create an ellipse profile about the center of the path line as follows (see Figure 8.9):

```
Command: ellipse
Specify axis endpoint of ellipse or [Arc/Center]: c
Specify center of ellipse: <Choose the endpoint of the path>
Specify endpoint of axis: @16,4
Specify distance to other axis or [Rotation]: @-2,10
```

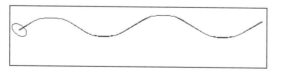

Figure 8.9
Create the ellipse or any other shape.

You're now ready to use the **EXTRUDE** command to sweep your profile into the curvilinear filleted path outline. Prior to sweeping the profile, set **ISO-LINES** to 12 (see Figure 8.10):

```
Command: isolines
Enter new value for ISOLINES <4>: 12
```

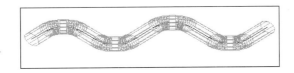

Figure 8.10
Set **ISOLINES** to 12 and use **EXTRUDE** with the **Path** option.

When you extrude an object, it's best to use a standard work plane. So reset your UCS to World:

```
Command: ucs
Enter an option [New/Move/orthoGraphic/Prev/Restore/Save/Del/
   Apply/?/World] <World>: <Press Enter>
```

You're now set to extrude the object along the center line of the curvilinear path:

```
Command: extrude
Current wire frame density: ISOLINES=12
Select objects: <Pick the profile>
Specify height of extrusion or [Path]: p
Select extrusion path: <Pick the curvilinear path>
```

Next, render or shade the end result (see Figure 8.11).

Figure 8.11
Render or shade the end result.

In addition to sweep.dwg on the CD-ROM, you can look at sweep2.dwg, which has a profile and a path in 3D space set up for you. As you'll see in sweep2.dwg, you can also create two or more profiles in the same work plane, both of which you may sweep at one time.

Spline Editing And Spline Variables

You'll remember from Chapter 6 that there are two types of spline: a NURBS spline and a freehand polygonal spline. You create a freehand polygon (or spline-fit polyline) as a series of straight lines set to specific X,Y,Z coordinates, and then spline it as a polyline through the **PEDIT** command. The NURBS spline is a natural spline—it has curved sides, and the spline nodes are its specific spline control points, which sit directly on the spline line.

Four basic editing properties let you modify the spline line: position (of its node points), tension (the sharpness of the curve), bias (the discontinuity of the curve), and continuity (which affects how each of the curves flow into the node points). (AutoCAD allows you editing control of the position and tension properties of your spline; it doesn't allow control of bias or continuity.)

AutoCAD uses one major editing command that allows general editing of spline lines: **SPLINEDIT**. Let's examine the spline properties in more detail before moving on to **SPLINEDIT**.

Position

The position property relates to node placement, as it affects the placement of each of the spline nodes (see Figure 8.12). The basic spline position in AutoCAD is affected by the grip points, which allow you to move the node points of the spline. In turn, these resultant positional changes of your spline affect the overall shape of your splined polygon. The position property is simply where you place or relocate the node points of the spline. Grips easily allow you to alter this property by picking the spline with the left mouse button and then choosing the node of choice and moving it as a hot grip. Position is also affected by the **Move Vertex** option of **SPLINEDIT**.

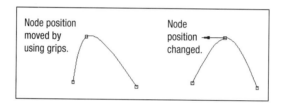

Figure 8.12
The position property.

Tension

The tension property relates to how sharp the bend of the curve to the spline is (see Figure 8.13). (For example, if you increase tension, it sharpens the curve, and the frames of the adjacent node are also pushed toward that vertex.) In AutoCAD, this is usually affected by weight to the node point. **SPLINEDIT** includes a **Refine** option, which, as you'll see from the following example, has a Weight subroutine. Activate AutoCAD and draw a spline (not a polyline); then, use the **SPLINEDIT** command to alter the tension of the nodes:

```
Command: splinedit
Select spline: <Pick the spline>
Enter an option [Close/Move vertex/Refine/rEverse/Undo/eXit]
  <eXit>: r
Enter a refine option [Add control point/Elevate order/Weight/
  eXit] <eXit>: w
```

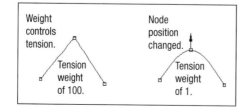

Figure 8.13
The tension property.

At this point you've chosen your spline and also which node point you wish to weight. A high weight factor will increase the sharpness of the spline curve toward 90 degrees. The default value is 1.0 and the Weight value must be positive and nonzero; for example, set a Weight value of 30 and look at what happens to the spline curve and how it moves toward the node point. Once you've set the weight, simply keep entering an "x" at the command line until you exit the command.

(Remember from Chapter 6 that loftsmen originally used spline curves, which were flexible pieces of wood or metal used by ship, aircraft, and automobile designers to draw smooth curves. The splines had "Ducks" weights or control points attached to them, which were used to pull the Spline in various directions through tension or weight.)

Bias

Bias relates to the skew of the spline curve (see Figure 8.14). (It also relates to discontinuity in a spline curve.) But just think of this as skew; it's similar to the histograms you drew in mathematics that had a positive skew bias or a negative skew bias. Thus, bias is simply the amount of skew in a spline.

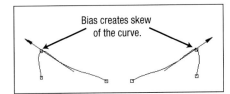

Figure 8.14
The bias property.

So to recap, bias simply creates discontinuity in a curve by overshooting to one side of a spline node. For example, a negative bias should overshoot to the left of a node, a positive bias to the right.

Continuity

Continuity relates to how each curve flows into the node points (see Figure 8.15). AutoCAD allows you editing control of the spline's position and tension properties, but it doesn't let you control bias or continuity.

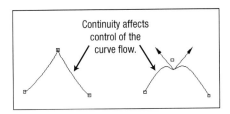

Figure 8.15
The continuity property.

SPLINEDIT

You've just examined spline editing in general. Now, let's review spline editing in AutoCAD. As mentioned earlier, AutoCAD uses **SPLINEDIT** for general editing of spline lines. **SPLINEDIT** also offers a number of suboptions that let you refine your splined lines. Here are some hints and examples regarding **SPLINEDIT**:

- **SPLINEDIT** lets you edit splined lines. The subcommand options are [Fit Data/Close/Move vertex/Refine/rEverse/Undo]. Your splines may be closed or open (that is, the endpoints of the splines may be connected or not connected). When you choose a closed spline, the **Close** option internally adjusts to **Open** and provides you with a choice of opening the spline. If the spline you pick has no fit data, you'll find the **Fit Data** option unavailable. (Fit data consists of all the tangents associated with splines created by the **SPLINE** command, plus all the fit points and the fit tolerance.)

- The control points of polylines are shown in your choice of grip color when you select a spline created with **PLINE** (Polyline). **SPLINEDIT** automatically converts splined polylines to spline objects. You'll automatically convert a splined polyline even if you select it and exit **SPLINEDIT**.

- Your spline may lose its fit data if you aren't aware of some pitfalls. You'll lose fit data if you:

  - Refine your spline curve in any form.

  - Fit the spline curve to a tolerance and then move its control vertices.

  - Use the **Purge** option when editing the spline curves on your model.

  - Fit the spline curve to a tolerance and then open or close the spline curve.

Editing Smoothness For A Bezier, Quadratic, Or Cubic Mesh

Here are some hints and examples for adjusting surface smoothness of a Bezier, quadratic, or cubic mesh surface (for practice adjusting smoothness, bezier.dwg is available on the CD-ROM):

- *PEDIT*—Allows you to edit polylines and 3D polygon meshes. Choose Polyline from the Modify menu or the Edit Polyline button from the Modify II toolbar. Remember that the level of smoothness is determined by system variable **SURFTYPE**, while the number of vertices is determined by system variables **SURFU** and **SURFV**. You can edit two types of meshes:

- *Closed mesh*—When a mesh is closed in a given direction, the number of surface elements and the number of vertices in that direction are equal. When a mesh is open in a given direction, the number of vertices is one more than the number of surface elements.

- *Smooth mesh*—You can smooth a spline mesh by editing it with the **PEDIT** command and selecting the s option. The level of smoothness is determined by the system variable **SURFTYPE**, whereas the number of vertices is determined by system variables **SURFU** and **SURFV**.

- *SURFU*—Used with **PEDIT** to control the number of M elements in a smoothed surface. System variables **SURFU** and **SURFV** control the number of elements in the smoothed surface. **SURFU** controls the number of elements in the M direction of the mesh, **SURFV** in the N direction. High values in **SURFU** and **SURFV** produce a fine, smoothed mesh, but such a mesh also takes longer to regenerate on screen.

- *SURFV*—Used with **PEDIT** to control the number of N elements in a smoothed surface. Don't confuse **SURFU** and **SURFV** with **SURFTAB1** and **SURFTAB2**, which control the number of vertices in the original (unsmoothed) mesh. **SURFU** and **SURFV** apply only to smoothed surfaces.

- *SURFTYPE*—Controls the level of smoothness to create a quadratic, cubic,or Bezier surface.

  - *Quadratic surface*—The **SURFTYPE** system variable setting controls the level of smoothness. A setting of 5 produces a quadratic surface that has a low level of smoothness.

  - *Cubic surface*—The system **SURFTYPE** variable setting controls the level of smoothness. A setting of 6 produces a cubic surface with a medium level of smoothness.

  - *Bezier surface*—The system **SURFTYPE** variable setting controls the level of smoothness. A setting of 8 produces a Bezier surface with a high level of smoothness. The smoothness and conformity are inversely related—the smoother the surface, the less it conforms to the defining mesh.

Let's look at an example. Open bezier2.dwg drawing from this book's companion CD-ROM. The 3D mesh drawing is a standard mesh that you can edit (see Figure 8.16). Remember that AutoCAD mesh drawings have two types of faces: a regular face and an MxN mesh made up of multiple faces. In an AutoCAD drawing, all mesh faces have four vertices (except polyface meshes, which are treated as adjoining triangles). For rendering purposes,

Note: You may want to refer back to Chapter 6 and Figures 6.28 through 6.30, which indicate how to control the level of smoothness to a quadratic B-spline, cubic B-spline, and Bezier surface mesh.

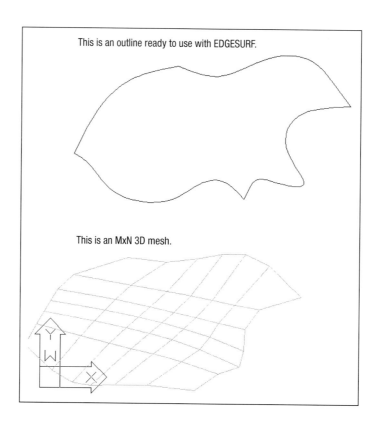

Figure 8.16

Editing bezier2.dwg as a surface mesh.

each quadrilateral face is treated as a pair of triangular faces that share one edge.

The mesh components include normals, faces, vertices, and edges:

- *Normals*—Vectors perpendicular to the face that point outward

- *Faces*—Triangular or quadrilateral segments of a surface object

- *Vertices*—Vertex points that form the corners (nodes) of a face

- *Edges*—The boundaries of a face

For Smooth Shade, use either the Render or Rendering Preferences dialog box to set the density of the mesh so that the angle between the normals of any two adjoining faces of the mesh is less than the smooth angle. For example, if the angle is greater than the smoothing angle, an edge appears between those faces as you render your model, even with Smooth Shade turned on. In addition, if you need to adjust surface smoothness, you can use **FACETRES** to control the density of the faces.

If Smooth Shade is turned on with Gouraud Shading, AutoCAD can either calculate the shading at each vertex or average the shading across each face as in Gouraud shading. Gouraud calculates light intensity at each vertex and interpolates intermediate intensities. If Smooth Shade is turned on with Phong Shading, AutoCAD calculates the shading at each pixel as in

Phong shading. Phong shading generates more realistic highlights; it's just one of the methods used by the photorealistic renderers. Phong uses more sophisticated interpolation than Gouraud to generate shading with more realistic highlights. Phong calculates light intensity at each pixel. When the Smooth Shade option is turned off, the renderer assigns a color or material to each face based on the light that strikes the base of the normal (that is, at the face's centroid). Because this shading is uniform across the faces, edges between faces are often visible.

Solids Editing

This section discusses editing commands for 3D solids and also reviews a few standard editing commands that behave differently when applied to solids. As you'll see, in AutoCAD 2000 Autodesk created a whole new set of commands for solid editing, the purpose of which is to provide you with more associativity (flexibility) to create and/or revise your solid models.

SOLIDEDIT

The purpose of **SOLIDEDIT** is to let you edit faces and edges of 3D solid objects. As you activate the **SOLIDEDIT** command, it starts with a basic listing:

```
Command: solidedit
Solids editing automatic checking: SOLIDCHECK=1
Enter a solids editing option [Face/Edge/Body/Undo/eXit] <eXit>:
  <Enter f, e, b, u, or x>
```

The basic listing of the **SOLIDEDIT** command lets you edit the faces, edges, and/or body of the 3D object you've created. In turn (and in addition to **Undo** and **Exit**, which are self-explanatory), these three editing functions include the following suboptions:

- *Face*—**Extrude**, **Move**, **Rotate**, **Offset**, **Taper**, **Delete**, **Copy**, and **Color**.

- *Edge*—**Copy** and **Color**.

- *Body*—**Imprint**, **Separate Solids**, **Shell**, **Clean**, and **Check**.

You'll find that the **SOLIDEDIT** command allows you to treat your 3D solid model with more associativity—that is, it provides the ability to adjust your model, but with less associativity than a true parametric model. In addition to the **SOLIDEDIT** command, you can use the Solids Editing Toolbar, as shown in Figure 8.17.

Figure 8.17
The Solids Editing Toolbar.

Using The **SOLIDEDIT** Command

Let's work through an exercise that will help you become familiar with some of the basic solid editing functions. Create a new file and name it solidedit-1.dwg, or locate the file on the CD-ROM. If you create your own file, choose English or metric units, set your view to SE Isometric, and draw a solid box primitive 350×95×450:

```
Command: box
Specify corner of box or [CEnter] <0,0,0>: <Press Enter>
Specify corner or [Cube/Length]: l
Specify length: 350
Specify width: 95
Specify height: 450
```

Save the file as solidedit.dwg. You'll need to return to the 3D solid box drawing you created for the next few editing commands.

From the View menu, choose Toolbars and activate the Solids Editing toolbar. Place it in the lower-right corner of your screen. Do a Zoom Extents, and then Zoom .9x. Now, issue the **SOLIDEDIT** command, choose the **Extrude Faces** option of the command or the Face Extrude icon, and pick the thin vertical face of the box drawing you just created. See Figure 8.18; it shows the face to work on. (If you overpick—that is, pick more faces than are required—simply press the Shift key and repick the extra faces, which removes them from the selection set. Then, release the Shift key.) Your objective is to extrude a face outward with a taper angle of 30 degrees. Later, you'll perform a second extrusion with a curved path:

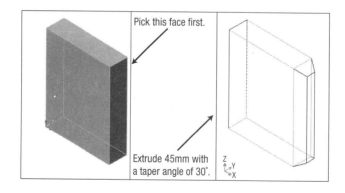

Figure 8.18
Extrude the thin vertical face of the box.

```
Command: solidedit
Solids editing automatic checking:  SOLIDCHECK=1
Enter a solids editing option [Face/Edge/Body/Undo/eXit] <eXit>: f
Enter a face editing option
[Extrude/Move/Rotate/Offset/Taper/Delete/Copy/coLor/Undo/eXit]
  <eXit>: e
Select faces or [Undo/Remove]: <Pick the face> 1 face found.
Select faces or [Undo/Remove/ALL]: <Press Enter>
```

```
Specify height of extrusion or [Path]: 45
Specify angle of taper for extrusion <0>: 30
Solid validation started.
Solid validation completed.
Enter a face editing option
[Extrude/Move/Rotate/Offset/Taper/Delete/Copy/coLor/Undo/eXit]
  <eXit>: <Press Enter>
Solids editing automatic checking: SOLIDCHECK=1
Enter a solids editing option [Face/Edge/Body/Undo/eXit] <eXit>:
  <Press Enter>
```

For extra practice, you can now create an arc and then extrude the portion you just tapered by 30 degrees through the path of the arc (do *not* save the file):

```
Command: arc
Specify start point of arc or [CEnter]: 350,47.5 <The midpoint of
  the end face>
Specify second point of arc or [CEnter/ENd]: 500,400
Specify end point of arc: 300,600
```

Reactivate the **SOLIDEDIT** command and the **Extrude** option, and choose p for path at the prompt. Pick the arc just created as the path.

Close the file without saving it and then reload it back onto your screen. Or, use the **UNDO** command to return all the way back to your original solid box. Try the same command again, this time with a negative taper, and notice the result:

```
Command: solidedit
Solids editing automatic checking:  SOLIDCHECK=1
Enter a solids editing option [Face/Edge/Body/Undo/eXit]
  <eXit>: f
Enter a face editing option
[Extrude/Move/Rotate/Offset/Taper/Delete/Copy/coLor/Undo/eXit]
  <eXit>: e
Select faces or [Undo/Remove]: <Pick the face> 1 face found.
Select faces or [Undo/Remove/ALL]: <Press Enter>
Specify height of extrusion or [Path]: -45 <negative 45>
Specify angle of taper for extrusion <0>: 30
Solid validation started.
Solid validation completed.
Enter a face editing option.
[Extrude/Move/Rotate/Offset/Taper/Delete/Copy/coLor/Undo/eXit]
  <eXit>: <Press Enter>
Solids editing automatic checking:  SOLIDCHECK=1
Enter a solids editing option [Face/Edge/Body/Undo/eXit] <eXit>:
  <Press Enter>
```

Notice that the taper has moved inwards. Do *not* save the file; just close it.

Face Editing

You have many options when working with faces and the **SOLIDEDIT** command. Your immediate choices are Extrude, Move, Rotate, Offset, Taper, Delete, Copy, Color, Undo, and Exit. Let's take each of these options in turn.

You just tested the **Extrude** option, so it's obvious to say that it will extrude one of the faces of your 3D object a certain distance or along a path, and your path may be curved or straight. While the **SOLIDEDIT** command is active, you may also enter "u" for Undo to cancel the selection set, "r" for Remove to remove a face(s) from the selection set, "a" for Add to add a face to the selection set, or "all" to include all the faces in the selection set. Your reason for using the **ALL** option, for example, at the selection set stage, may be to simply enlarge a part or feature equally in all directions. Here are the other face-editing options:

- *Extrude*—The Face|Extrude option extrudes either a positive or a negative distance along a face. To add a specified slope to the face, you have the further option of using a taper angle. The standard option of entering the Height of Extrusion as a distance and/or P for Path allows you to extrude a face through an arc or a straight line path.

- *Move*—The Face|Move option allows you to move a 3D solid object within a 3D object. For example, you may have created a 3D countersink or a 3D counterbore hole as a feature, and now you need to move the feature. Use the Move subcommand to select the feature and then move it to a new location. Move also has a second use similar to the **EXTEND** command. If you need to extend a whole face, for example, and not just move a single feature, use Move and pick the face you wish to extend; then, either pick the distance or use coordinates to enter the distance.

- *Rotate*—The Face|Rotate option rotates a face or feature(s) about an axis point. Hint: For complex rotations, it's easier to rotate and align the feature with an object such as a line, an arc, or a spline.

- *Offset*—Similar to the Face|Extrude|ALL option, the Face|Offset option reduces or enlarges a face or feature equally in all directions. Entering a negative value reduces the offset of the feature, and entering a positive value enlarges the feature.

- *Taper*—The Face|Taper option is useful for tapering a feature such as a countersink. To taper a selected face to the outside of the feature, enter a negative angle; to taper it inward, use a positive angle. (Thus, your values are: to taper in use a positive value, and to taper out use a negative value. The default of 0 will simply extrude the face.) You need to select or enter two points and an angle of taper. For example, you must first specify a base point, which is static (that is, the center of a feature). Then, enter or pick a second point (the other end or the center of the feature). The distance between these two points on the feature will be enlarged or reduced by the amount of taper angle you specify. The angle used must be between +90 degrees and –90 degrees—it can't go beyond 90, and it must also be nonzero.

- *Delete*—This option is useful for deleting a face or a feature such as a chamfer, round, or fillet that simply has to be removed for editing purposes.

- *Copy*—The **Copy** option copies a face or series of features a specified distance from the part.

- *Color*—**Color** simply changes the color of faces or part features. In addition to the 9 standard colors, the AutoCAD Color Index (ACI) allows you to change to any of the 255 ACI colors, including the gray color numbers 250 through 255.

- *Undo*—Just like the standard **UNDO** command, this subset simply reverses back to the beginning of **SOLIDEDIT**.

- *Exit*—This option exits the face-editing options.

Let's work through a second exercise to become familiar with some of the basic solid editing functions. You can create a new file called solidedit-2.dwg or locate it on the CD-ROM. See the left side of Figure 8.19. If you create it, choose metric units, set your view to SE Isometric, and check to ensure the file has a solid box primitive 350×95×450, with two cylinders set within the front face of the body of the solid.

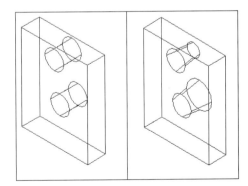

Figure 8.19
Subtract the two cylinders from the box; then, taper the cylinders. Note that the pick point is the base.

If you chose to locate solidedit-2.dwg on the CD-ROM, notice two cylinders set into the front face of the box you used before. They're set to a local front UCS. From the Solids Editing toolbar, choose the Color Faces icon and set the two cylinders to different colors. If you're creating your own drawing, you'll need to set the UCS to X 90 to the Front work plane. Then, choose the Taper icon and taper the cylinders. (Use the center of each cylinder as its base point.) Taper one cylinder to –10 and the other to +10 degrees, to create two tapered holes. See the right of Figure 8.19. Save the file; you'll use it again in the next section.

Edge Editing

You have only a few minor editing options when working with edges and the **SOLIDEDIT** command. Your immediate choices are **Copy**, **Color**, **Undo**, **Remove**, and **Exit**. You may also add edges to the selection set. The **Undo**, **Remove**, and **Add** options are mainly to work with the AutoCAD selection set and how you pick, unpick, or repick your solid edges. Here's a rundown of the edge-editing options:

- *Copy*—The **Copy** option copies solid edges. All your 3D solid edges are copied as an arc, circle, ellipse, line, or spline. In turn, the **Copy** option prompts you to either select edges or enter an **Undo/Remove** option. Do so or press Enter and specify a base point of displacement. After picking a base point, specify a second point of displacement. (AutoCAD then displays the previous prompt.)

- *Color*—The **Color** option lets you change the color of edges. After you select your edges, AutoCAD displays the Select Color dialog box, which allows you to define the color of an AutoCAD object by letting you choose from among the 255 AutoCAD Color Index (ACI) colors.

- *Undo*—**Undo** cancels the selection of the edges you added most recently to the selection set. AutoCAD then displays the previous prompt. If all edges have been removed, AutoCAD will indicate that the edge selection has been completely undone.

- *Remove*—This option removes a previously selected edge from the selection set. AutoCAD then displays the previous prompt to let you remove edges or use **Undo/Add**. Simply select an edge(s), enter an option, or press Enter.

- *Add*—The **Add** option adds edges to the selection set. You may also use **Undo** and **Remove** with this option.

- *Exit*—The **Exit** option simply exits the edge editing options and returns to the main **Enter a solids editing option** prompt.

Let's continue with the edge editing functions just mentioned. Reopen the solidedit-2.dwg you just saved. See left side of Figure 8.20. Choose the Copy icon and copy the cylinders' edges away from you by 100mm. See the right side of Figure 8.20. Save the file so you can use it with the body editing options covered next.

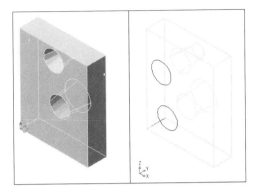

Figure 8.20
Use **SOLIDEDIT** to copy the two cylinders; then, copy the two cylinder faces and change the color of the new face.

Body Editing

The purpose of body editing is usually one of the following:

- To edit the entire 3D solid entity and imprint alternative geometry on the 3D solid

- To separate the solid into individual components

- To create a shell (a small thin wall of constant thickness)

- To clean redundant edges and vertices

- To check the selected solid

The body-editing options are as follows:

- *Imprint*—This option imprints an object on the selected solid. The object to be imprinted must intersect one or more faces on the selected solid in order for Imprint to be successful. It's limited to arcs, circles, lines, 2D and 3D polylines, ellipses, splines, regions, and 3D solids.

- *Shell*—Shell is a type of 3D Offset command. Often, you need to create a shell, which is basically a hollow, thin wall with a specified thickness. With the **Shell** option, you can specify a constant wall thickness for all the faces of your object. In addition, if you select certain faces of your object, you can exclude those faces from the resultant shell. Remember that a 3D solid can have only one shell. AutoCAD creates new faces by offsetting existing ones outside their original positions. If you specify a positive value, AutoCAD creates a shell from the outside of the perimeter; if you specify a negative value, it creates a shell from the inside.

- *Clean*—Sometimes you'll overdraw lines, arcs, curves to your edges, or vertices. The **Clean** option is a way of removing unwanted or shared edges or vertices that have the same surface or curve definition on either side of an edge or vertex. It removes all redundant edges and vertices, plus imprinted as well as unused geometry.

- *Check*—The purpose of the **Check** subroutine is to validate the 3D solid entity as a well-founded ACIS solid model. The **Check** option is independent of the **SOLIDCHECK** setting. Simply select a 3D solid and the prompt (**Select a 3D solid**) will indicate whether the object is a valid ACIS solid (**This object is a valid ACIS solid.**).

Let's continue with the body-editing functions just mentioned. Reopen the solidedit-2.dwg you just saved and refer to the left side of Figure 8.21. Choose the Shell icon and create a thin 10mm shell to the box with the two cylinders, as seen in right sight of Figure 8.21. Remember that with the **Shell** option of **SOLIDEDIT** a positive value creates an inward shell, a negative value creates an outward shell. Save the file and then exit.

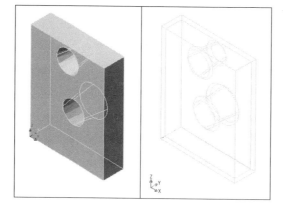

Figure 8.21
Use **SOLIDEDIT** to shell the body of the box; then, use the **Shell** option to create a thin shell from the box.

General Editing Commands

In addition to using **SOLIDEDIT**, there are other forms of solid model editing, including Boolean operands, the commands that provide you with derivative surfaces such as fillet and chamfer, and other commands, including **SECTION** and **SLICE**. So let's move on to more general editing commands, starting with Boolean operands and how they work in AutoCAD 2000.

Boolean Operations

AutoCAD uses Boolean operations as a means of combining, removing, and/or associating 3D solid models into cohesive combinations. It's a simple fact that without Boolean operations you cannot create solid models. Yet what is a Boolean operation and where is it derived from?

In 1854 an English mathematician, George Boole (1815-1864), defined Boolean algebra in the text *An Investigation of the Laws of Thought*. He was a mathematics professor at University College, Cork, Ireland. His logical propositions in Boolean algebra are denoted by symbols and can be acted on by abstract mathematical operands that conform to the laws of logic. (With

Boolean algebra, it's possible to denote the operation $\oplus$ with +, $\vee$, or $\cup$ instead, and the operation $\otimes$ with $\times$, $\wedge$, $\cap$, or O.) Boolean algebra is used in the study of pure mathematics, physical science, electric-circuit theory, modern computer design, and CAD modeling software. In AutoCAD, it's used to edit and build up individual components of a solid model into a composite model. Thus, most solid modelers including AutoCAD use Boolean operands, which allow you to create 3D models through three basic commands: **UNION**, **SUBTRACT**, and **INTERSECT**. Let's look more closely at how Boolean algebra is used in AutoCAD.

UNION

UNION, one of the main Boolean commands, lets you create a new solid by merging two or more 3D solids. Your initial 3D solids may be created by extruding 2D profiles in different work planes, revolving objects, combining 3D primitives, and/or combining multiple extruded profile, revolved, and primitive objects. The **UNION** command is located under the Solids Editing section of the Modify menu or in the Solids Editing toolbar, and it prompts you to select two or more solid objects. The objects are then welded into a single 3D object.

Open the edit-1.dwg file from this book's companion CD-ROM and use the **UNION** command to combine the elements into a single solid. Use **SHADE** to shade the result. See Figure 8.22.

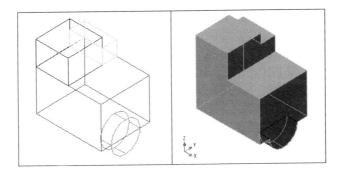

Figure 8.22
Use the **UNION** command to union all the 3D solids into one main solid model, and use **SHADE** to shade the result.

SUBTRACT

SUBTRACT is another Boolean command that allows you to create a new 3D solid by subtracting one selection set of solid(s) from a second selection set of solid(s). Where more than one object is selected and they overlap with a third (or more) object to be removed, it will also union the first two objects. Again, the command is located under the Solids Editing section of the Modify menu or in the Solids Editing toolbar.

The prompt is in two parts: Kept and Cut. (After entering the Kept portion, you press Enter to move to the Cut portion.) In the first half of the prompt, you select the 3D solid(s) you need to keep and that require parts to be subtracted from them. (This is the Kept part of your selection set—AutoCAD will union these objects.) In the second half, you select the 3D solid(s) you need to remove from the first selection set (the Cut objects). The result is a single new 3D solid that's the union of the Kept objects after the Cut objects have been removed.

Open the edit-2.dwg file from the CD-ROM and use the **SUBTRACT** command to subtract the main box primitive from the two small box primitives into a single solid object. (Pick the main box first, press Enter, and then pick the two smaller boxes. Press Enter again.) Then, reactivate **SUBTRACT** and use it to subtract the main box from the cylinder. Use **SHADE** to shade the result. See Figure 8.23.

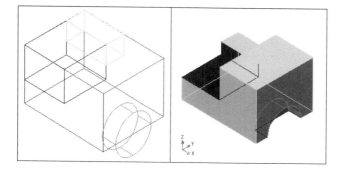

Figure 8.23

Use the **SUBTRACT** command to subtract the two small boxes and cylinder from the main box, and use **SHADE** to shade the result.

INTERSECT

INTERSECT, yet another Boolean command, lets you create a new composite 3D solid or region from the resultant volume where two, three, or more 3D solids or regions overlap. It simply removes the overlapping areas outside the intersection. The command is located under Solids Editing on the Modify menu or in the Solids Editing toolbar. It prompts you to select two or more solid objects, which AutoCAD then intersects into a single composite 3D entity. Simply pick the **INTERSECT** command and, at the prompt, select two or more 3D solids that overlap. The resultant new 3D solid is the volume shared by all your selected solids.

Open the edit-3.dwg file from the CD-ROM. Activate the **INTERSECT** command and choose all three of the extrusions. The resultant volume created by **INTERSECT** is where the regions overlap into a single composite solid. Use **SHADE** to shade the result. See Figure 8.24.

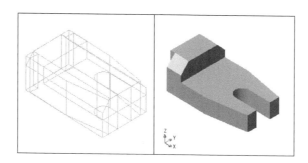

Figure 8.24

Use the **INTERSECT** command and choose all three of the extrusions, and use **SHADE** to shade the result.

INTERFERE

INTERFERE is an identifier command. It's different from the Boolean commands already covered in that it doesn't alter the selected 3D objects—rather, it identifies (highlights) the area where two selections of 3D solids overlap and gives you the option to create a new 3D solid from the overlapping volumes. This command is useful to create new overlapping solid volumes that can then be subtracted from the main solid, thereby preventing interference of a part with the main object. In addition, the command may be used for error checking.

To use the **INTERFERE** command, at the prompt, pick the first set of solids. Press Enter and pick the second set of solids. AutoCAD then calculates all the volumes where the objects in the first selection set overlap the objects in the second selection set. You're then asked if you want to create new interference solids from the overlapping volumes. (You'll find more a more in-depth discussion of this command in Chapter 7.)

Open the interfere.dwg file from the CD-ROM. Activate the **INTERFERE** command and choose the black cylindrical collar as the first set of solids. Then, choose the blue set of solids. Answer "y" for yes to creating a new interference solid at the prompt. The result will show a black segment as the interference solid. You can then use the **SUBTRACT** command to subtract the interfering solid from the main shaft. Use **SHADE** to shade the result. See Figure 8.25.

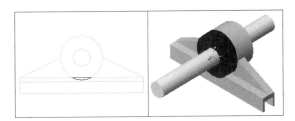

Figure 8.25
The **INTERFERE** command.

FILLET

The **FILLET** command is similar to the **FILLET** command for 2D drawings. With it, you can create fillets and rounds on a 3D model. (Remember that a *fillet* is an internal rounding of edges or corners and a *round* is an external edge or corner, typically used on castings. AutoCAD's **FILLET** command creates both fillets and rounds on a 3D model.) It fillets the edges of your solid objects a specified radius distance. When you're prompted to select the first object, select a solid. You'll then be prompted to enter a fillet radius. After entering a radius, you have two options:

- Select individual edges and press Enter to fillet the selected edges.

- Enter "c" to select an edge chain. Selecting a single edge in Chain mode causes AutoCAD to find and select all edges that are tangent to the selected edge.

Open the fillet.dwg file from the CD-ROM and activate the **FILLET** command. Pick one of the top edges (as shown on the left side of Figure 8.26) and, at the first prompt, set the Radius to 5. Next, at the **Select an edge or [Chain/Radius]** prompt, pick the rest of the top edges singly. Shade your result. Your result should be similar to the right side of Figure 8.26.

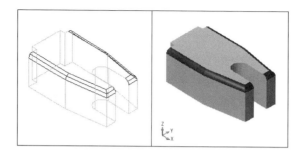

Figure 8.26

Use the **FILLET** command and pick the top edges singly, or use the **Chain** option. Then, use **SHADE** to shade the result.

CHAMFER

The **CHAMFER** command is similar to the **CHAMFER** command for 2D drawings. It chamfers or bevels the edges of your solid objects a specified distance(s). The bevel distance may be equal on both edges to produce a 45-degree corner, or you can set unequal bevel distances for an alternative result.

At the prompt, instead of selecting a first line (as in 2D drawings), select your solid. The prompt will then ask you to identify the base surface. You do so to define which edges of your object are valid for chamfering, because only those edges that surround the base surface can be chamfered.

After selecting the base surface, you're prompted to enter the base surface distance (similar to the first distance on a 2D chamfer) and then to enter the other surface distance (similar to the second distance). Note that the angle method of chamfering isn't available for solids.

Once you specify the distances, you have two options for selecting edges to chamfer:

- Select edges one at a time and then press Enter to chamfer only the selected edges.

- Enter "l" (for Loop) and then select a single edge to select all the connected edges that surround and loop the base surface.

Open the chamfer.dwg file from the CD-ROM and activate the **CHAMFER** command. At the first **Select first line or [Polyline/Distance/Angle/Trim/Method]** prompt, enter "d", set the distance to 2, and accept the second chamfer distance by pressing Enter. You have now set both the distances to 2mm.

Reactivate the **CHAMFER** command, but this time at the **Select...** prompt, pick one of the top edges, as shown in Figure 8.27. Keep pressing "n" for next until AutoCAD has highlighted the whole of the top surface of the solid. Then, press Enter until you reach the **Select an edge or [Loop]** prompt. At the prompt, enter "l" and, as shown in Figure 8.27, pick the top edge of the 3D model as a loop. The command should highlight the top surface, so press Enter. Shade your result.

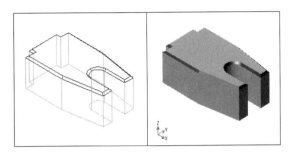

Figure 8.27
The **CHAMFER** command.

SECTION And SLICE

The **SECTION** and **SLICE** commands have similar options. They both create a 2D region based upon a section plane passing through a 3D solid.

The **SECTION** command uses the same prompts as **SLICE**. With either command, at the prompt, you select one or more solid objects. The **SLICE** command then cuts the selection of solids along a specified plane. The difference between **SLICE** and **SECTION** is that **SECTION** doesn't alter the original selected solids—instead, it creates 2D regions to represent the cut surface of the objects. See Figure 8.28. You specify a plane with one of the following options:

- *3points*—The default method. Pick three points on your screen that will explicitly define the desired cutting plane.

- *Object*—Aligns the cutting plane with a 2D object such as a circle, arc, ellipse, or polyline.

- *Zaxis*—Pick two points that define your Zaxis, which should be perpendicular to the cutting plane. The first point locates the origin of the axis and the cutting plane.

- *View*—Aligns the cutting plane with the current viewport. You may then pick a point to locate the position of the cutting plane.

- *XY/YZ/ZX*—Aligns the cutting plane with the selected axes of the current UCS. You then pick a point to locate the position of the cutting plane.

The **SLICE** command cuts a selection of solids along a specified plane. At the prompt, select one or more solid objects. The cutting plane you specify with one of the options cuts the selected objects. After specifying the cutting plane for the **SLICE** command, pick which part of the selected objects to keep, or enter "b" to retain both sides of the objects after cutting. See Figure 8.28.

Figure 8.28 shows both the **SECTION** and **SLICE** commands. The figure on the left has the UCS set to the MIDpoint of the 3D solid and is sectioned about the YZ plane. The right-hand figure has been sliced about the ZX plane and both sides have been kept.

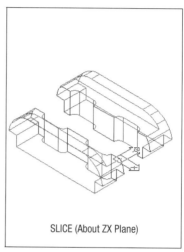

SECTION (About YZ Plane) SLICE (About ZX Plane)

Figure 8.28
The **SECTION** and **SLICE** commands.

Analysis Of 3D Computer Models

In many electronic 3D models, it's important to define the inner and outer elements and surfaces of the 3D object. Likewise, with CAD/CAM models, you're often called upon to define and compute the properties of mass and volume. Other uses for electronic models include FEA stress and temperature analyses via the use of Finite Element Modeling. In addition, you can also use the model to test interference of adjacent parts, simulate (animate) components and how they interact with other components, or simulate how a milling tool will cut the part and then define the stress placed upon both the cutting tool and part. A satisfactory conclusion generates the cutting tool path for the computer-controlled machine in order to generate the part.

Design constraints come in many forms, and most solid modelers provide you with the ability to obtain mass property information such as volume, density, and surface area. The information provided in AutoCAD gives you simple data about your solid model. AutoCAD uses **MASSPROP** to calculate mass, volume, a bounding box, centroid, moments of inertia, products of inertia, radii of gyration, principal moments, and X-Y-Z directions about the centroid.

Although the electronic 3D model itself has no mass, you can apply the algorithm $F = m\ dv/dt = ma$ to the model to find the model's mass and volume. Note that certain 3D geometric modelers allow you to input the density of a material. They allow you to assign a specific type of material to the part—for example steel, aluminum, or bronze—through a material lookup table (LUT). The LUT is a form of appendable material library, usually placed in an ASCII file.

AutoCAD commands for the analysis of computer models include: **MASSPROP**, **AREA**, and **LIST**. Let's work through an exercise using the **MASSPROP** command. Start a new drawing and name it mass.dwg (this drawing is also available on the CD-ROM). With your 3D View set to SE Isometric, create a cylinder with a two-unit radius and five-unit height. Set **ISOLINES** to 24 and **FACETRES** to 5. Then, use the **MASSPROP** command on the cylinder, and you should get these results:

```
Command: massprop
Select objects: <Pick the Cylinder>
Select objects:
    ---------------   SOLIDS   ----------------
Mass:                   62.8319
Volume:                 62.8319
Bounding box:       X: -2.0000  --   2.0000
                    Y: -2.0000  --   2.0000
                    Z: 0.0000   --   5.0000
Centroid:           X: 0.0000
                    Y: 0.0000
                    Z: 2.5000
Moments of inertia: X: 586.4306
                    Y: 586.4306
                    Z: 125.6637
Products of inertia: XY: 0.0000
                    YZ: 0.0000
                    ZX: 0.0000
Radii of gyration:  X: 3.0551
                    Y: 3.0551
                    Z: 1.4142
Principal moments and X-Y-Z directions about centroid:
                    I: 193.7315 along [1.0000 0.0000 0.0000]
                    J: 193.7315 along [0.0000 1.0000 0.0000]
                    K: 125.6637 along [0.0000 0.0000 1.0000]
Write analysis to a file? [Yes/No] <N>:
```

From the results of the **MASSPROP** command, you can see that AutoCAD allows you to view a number of properties: Mass, Volume, and so on. Next, we'll look at some possible uses for these properties.

Uses for **MASSPROP**

Let's look at some uses for the properties of the **MASSPROP** command:

• *Volume of a product*—Manufacturers who create containers for industrial or consumer use may need to know the volume of the receptacles they create. The receptacles may be bottles, plastic containers, or even fluid containers for automobiles. Remember that if you model a container in AutoCAD, the **MASSPROP** command will give you the volume of the container solid, not the volume that the container can hold.

- *Volume of a product*—If a manufacturer uses injection molding to create plastic parts, the manufacturer needs to know the exact volume of the product in order to complete a production run.

- *Surface area of a product*—If a manufacturer has to paint (or galvanize) a series of parts (especially large parts), you can calculate the area and then use it to determine the cost of both painted or galvanized finishes. In turn, doing so lets you calculate the amount of paint or application of the finish required, along with the application cost.

- *Surface area of a product*—An airplane manufacturer, for example, dealing with airflow over a curved surface, can determine the effects of surface friction over a specified shape. Another use would be in boat building, to examine fluid flow over a specific surface shape.

The following list shows the mass properties AutoCAD displays for solids:

- *Mass*—A constant measure that uses the equation *Mass = Density x Volume*. It's often equated to weight, but it doesn't rely on gravitational force. It's a measure of resistance to linear acceleration or the inertia of a body at rest. (However, AutoCAD uses a density of one, so the mass and volume you compute in AutoCAD have the same value.) Usually, you look up the value of your material in an engineering material table. You'll also need to check that the mass units equate to your units in use—that is, if you're using inches or millimeters as compared to mass density units of slugs or milligrams per cubic millimeter.

- *Volume*—Measured in cubic units. Volume is the amount of 3D space your solid encloses, regardless of the type of material it's made from.

- *Bounding box*—The smallest box that can contain your 3D solid. In AutoCAD, it's the diagonally opposite corners of a 3D box that will enclose your solid. The sides of the box are parallel to the three principal planes of your current UCS. So, changing the UCS can make a difference to the bounding box of your 3D solid.

- *Centroid*—The center of an object's mass or center of gravity. The centroid is the theoretical point that your object could be suspended from and at which all gravitational forces would cancel each other out. According to your current UCS, AutoCAD provides you with an X,Y,Z point that's the center of mass of your solid object with a solid of uniform density.

- *Moments of inertia*—Relates to rotational/angular acceleration. Inertia, on the other hand, relates to linear acceleration. Thus, you use moments of inertia when you need to compute the force required to start an object spinning about a given axis, such as a wheel rotating about an axle. The formula for mass moments of inertia is:

mass_moments_of_inertia = object_mass * radius²

The property will vary according to the location and mass of the object and the location and orientation of the axis. For example, if your axis runs through the centroid of your object, it will emit a lesser moment of inertia than an object whose axis runs parallel or perpendicular to the object's length, but away from the centroid.

- *Products of inertia*—A property of dynamic balance, as opposed to static balance. Similar to moments of inertia, it's used to determine the forces causing the motion of an object. Take wobble, for example. If you rotate a statically balanced object, and during the rotation it wobbles. The force that causes it to wobble is its product of inertia. It's always calculated with respect to two orthogonal planes. The formula for product of inertia for the YZ plane and XZ plane is:

product_of_inertiaYZ,XZ = mass * distcentroid_to_YZ * distcentroid_to_XZ

This XY value is expressed in mass units times the length squared. The product of inertia is dynamically balanced when it is 0.

- *Radii of gyration*—The distance from an object's rotational axis to the point at which its mass can be concentrated (or its centroid) without changing its moment of inertia. The formula for the radii of gyration is:

radii_of_gyration_(k) = the square root of (moments_of_inertia/body_mass)

which is derived from the formula $I=mk^2$ and expressed in distance units.

- *Principal moments*—Calculated as maximums and minimums, with reference to the orientation of the principal axes and coordinate system in effect at the time. Thus, your object's principal moments are determined as the maximum moment of inertia around a centroidal axis, such that its orientation produces a zero product of inertia. For example, at the centroid of your object is an axis about which the moment of inertia is highest. In addition, there's a second axis, which is normal to your first axis. It, too, runs through the centroid, and the moment of inertia to this second axis is lowest. If you then calculate a third value, the result will be somewhere between the high and the low value. Thus, the moments of inertia are principal moments when the product of inertia is zero.

Moving On

This chapter provided you with background knowledge on both general and specific editing of surface and solid 3D models, plus analysis of completed models. In addition to associativity and spline editing, the chapter reviewed commands that provide you with derivative surfaces, such as **FILLET** and **CHAMFER**. It also moved into the new editing commands for solids through **SOLIDEDIT**, which permits you to adjust and edit the faces, edges, and/or body of your 3D object.

The next chapter demonstrates various commands that assist you in creating sections of your 3D models. In addition, these commands allow you to quickly set up any number of orthographic, isometric, or perspective views.

3D SECTION VIEWS

9

This chapter describes the different types of section views in conventional practice, along with many examples of each type of section view.

Rules Of Section Views

A *section view* is a type of 2D graphic or visualization that helps portray the inner details of a 3D model. These inner details can otherwise be hidden if you don't create the section. Using a variety of methods and techniques, you can create section views from a 3D solid model as a 2D view. The color section in the middle of this book contains examples of cut-away section views, plus fully rendered exploded pictorial assembly drawings.

A number of standard engineering methods represent sections, and this chapter begins with a review of the different types of sections. We'll then examine the **SECTION**, **SLICE**, **SOLDRAW**, **SOLVIEW**, and **SOLPROF** commands, and discuss how you use them in AutoCAD to create section views.

Listed here are a few rules that apply to both CAD drawn sections and conventional drawn sections:

- *Thin parts*—Instead of using the **HATCH** command, thin parts are usually blacked in.

- *Section-lining*—Use outline sectioning of large parts for clarity (outline each separate part with a bold line).

- *Symbols*—A standard section symbol ANSI31 is used to represent most sectioned materials.

- *Hatch lines*—The hatch lines appear at 45 degrees or an angle that isn't parallel or perpendicular to the part it depicts.

- *Hidden lines*—Hidden lines are omitted in all section views (unless needed to add clarity to the model).

- *Assembly views*—The hatch lines should be in the same direction for a given part and in a different direction or angle for all other parts.

- *Scale*—In small parts, the scale of the section lines should be close together; in large parts, the scale of the section lines should be farther apart.

- *Standard parts*—You don't need to section standard parts, such as bolts, rivets, washers, set screws, gear teeth, dowels, pins, and ball and roller bearings.

- *Phantom or ghost sections*—Use this technique only for clarity. It creates a main section with faint dashed lines instead of continuous lines and works around main features as standard lines. (Think of it as viewing the part by x-ray.)

Types Of Section Views

Often, a standard orthographic view using Top, Front, and Right Side views may not show true details of your model, so you need to supplement the views. A model may, for example, show hidden lines, but the hidden lines may be so complex that they create confusion as opposed to clarity. In Figure 9.1, the 3D model would have been easier to understand with a section view instead of a Front view. When you use sections, you should do so to add clarity to your model.

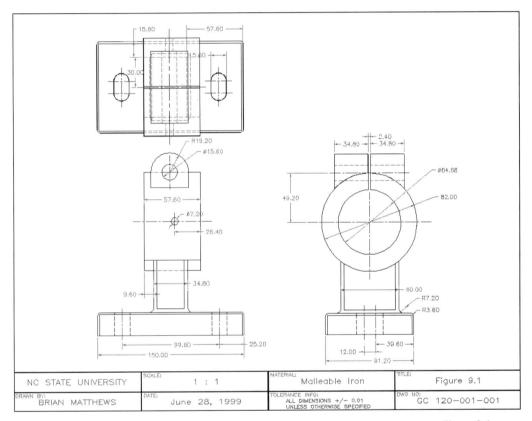

Figure 9.1

To show the model's complexity, the lower left Front view of this three-view model would be better depicted with a section view.

So, what is a section? It's simply a cutaway view (there are many forms of cutaway views). The section view will also have a *cutting plane*, a heavy dashed line that indicates where the section cut passes through the model, along with arrows pointing to the line of sight.

The types of section views are as follows:

- Full

- Half

- Broken-out

- Revolved

- Removed

- Offset

- Assembly

- Auxiliary

- Aligned

- Phantom or ghost

You use standard positions to place sections along with standard cutting planes. Figure 9.2 shows the Top view, Front view, and Right Side view, along with cutting planes and the directions in which the arrows point.

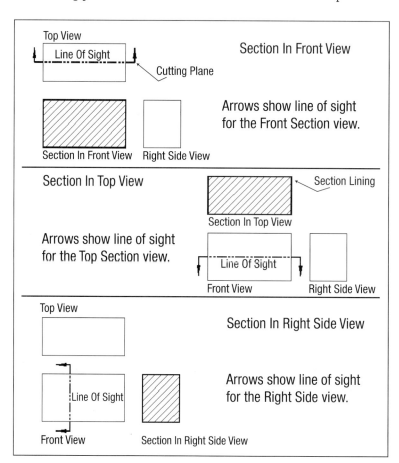

Figure 9.2

The standard positions to place section views of your 3D model.

Full Sections

You create a full section view by passing the imaginary cutting plane through your model, so that all the hidden features of your model (as intersected by the cutting plane) will have physical lines in the created section view. Remember that any surface touched by the cutting plane will display section lines drawn at a 45-degree angle to the horizontal, and your hidden lines are omitted in all section views unless they're used to add clarity to the model. The Top view of the section drawing (as seen in Figure 9.2) shows the cutting plane line, with arrows pointing in the direction of the line of sight necessary to view the sectioned half of the object. In a multiview drawing, a full section view is placed in the same location that the unsectioned view would normally occupy. (In most situations, section views augment the standard views but do no replace them.)The standard positions to place sections along with standard cutting planes are the Top view, Front view, and Right Side view, along with cutting-plane lines and indications of where arrows point. For example, Figure 9.3 shows a full section view. Here's a hint: In AutoCAD, use the **SECTION** command with the **XY** option to produce a full section of your model. Alternatively, use the **SOLVIEW** command with the **Section** option to create a full section view; then, use **BHATCH** to hatch the section using ANSI31 to represent your sectioned material.

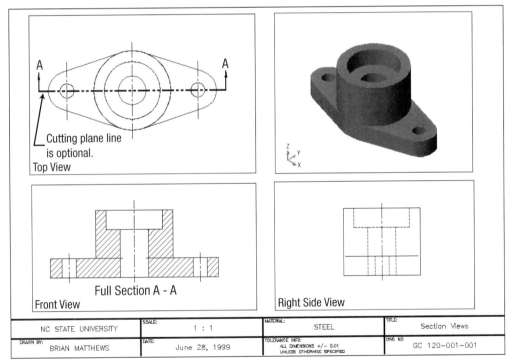

NC STATE UNIVERSITY	SCALE: 1 : 1	MATERIAL: STEEL	TITLE: Section Views
DRAWN BY: BRIAN MATTHEWS	DATE: June 28, 1999	TOLERANCE INFO: ALL DIMENSIONS +/− 0.01 UNLESS OTHERWISE SPECIFIED	DWG NO: GC 120−001−001

Figure 9.3
A typical full section view of a model.

Half Sections

You'll use half section views on symmetrical parts and sometimes on assembly drawings when you must show external features. By passing an imaginary cutting plane only halfway through your model, you create a half section. You omit hidden lines on both halves of the section view. If they're crucial, you may add hidden lines to the unsectioned half for dimensioning or clarity. External features of the part are drawn on the unsectioned half of the view. You can use a center line to separate the sectioned half from the unsectioned half of the view. Figure 9.4 shows an example of a half section. Here's a hint: Further on in the chapter, we'll look at some methods of half sectioning a model in AutoCAD by simply using the **SUBTRACT** command over a completed 3D model. You can also use the **BOX** command. For example, to create the pictorial for this type of half section view, you first copy the 3D solid; then, using the **BOX** command, create a Box from the quadrant of the minor axis to the quadrant of the major axis, and pick or enter the height to complete the Box. Finally, use **SUBTRACT** to remove the box from the pictorial section, as shown in Figure 9.4.

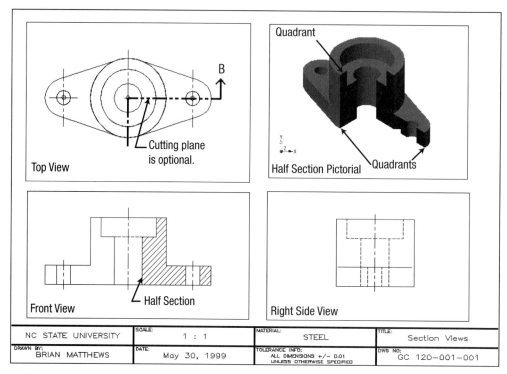

Figure 9.4

A half section view. (Use the quadrants as pick points to create a Box, then subtract.)

Broken-Out Sections

Broken-out sections are used when only a portion of an object needs to be sectioned—for example, to show further details about an interior feature that could not be shown without using a broken-out section view. As shown in Figure 9.5, you simply remove or break away a portion of the object to reveal the interior features or qualities. A broken-out section saves time, as opposed to using a full or half section view. You use a freehand (jagged) break line to separate the sectioned portion of the object from the unsectioned view. Hint: Hidden lines aren't used in an unsectioned part of your drawing unless required for clarity. In the AutoCAD system, you may use the **SKETCH** or **POLYLINE** command to draw a closed freehand break line. Alternatively,

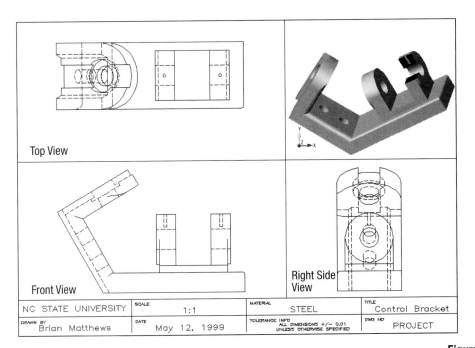

Top View

Front View

Right Side View

NC STATE UNIVERSITY	SCALE 1:1	MATERIAL STEEL	TITLE Control Bracket
DRAWN BY Brian Matthews	DATE May 12, 1999	TOLERANCE INFO ALL DIMENSIONS +/− 0.01 UNLESS OTHERWISE SPECIFIED	DWG NO PROJECT

Figure 9.5

A broken-out section.

to create the particular illustration shown in 9.5, follow these steps: Copy the solid in the Pictorial view and, using a Box primitive, create a Box from the lower quadrant of the cylinder to the upper quadrant. Then, use **SUBTRACT** to remove the Box primitive from the 3D model and so create the broken-out section.

Revolved Sections

Don't confuse revolved sections with the **REVOLVE** command. A revolved section is a rotated cross-section view of your model. Use the **SECTION** or **SLICE** command to create a cross-section of a feature; then, rotate the cut section 90 degrees, placing the cut section in the center of the main component. You use a revolved section to show more detail of a model with a single view. For example, the model could have an elongated width. As you can see in Figure 9.6, the 3D pictorial of the model lacks detail apart from the end features. The simplest way to describe the part is through a revolved section. Thus, you take a cross-section of the part and rotate it 90 degrees on its height or Y axis. Then, the section can be seen from where it's placed in the Front view. To create a prerotated section of the conrod.dwg (which can also be found on this book's companion CD-ROM), as seen in Figure 9.6, proceed as follows:

1. Set the UCS to the Side plane, and then set the Origin of the UCS to the upper midpoint of the Conrod. (Do this by restoring the UCS to Side.) You can also set the UCSICON to Origin to see it move to the new origin, as shown in Figure 9.6.

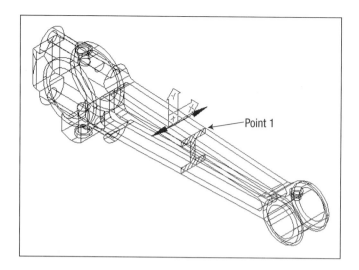

Point 1

Figure 9.6
A typical revolved section.

2. Use the **SECTION** command with the **XY** option (which depends upon the orientation of the hidden features you need to see), choose the Conrod as the object, and when the XY prompt is returned (as **Specify a point on the XY-plane <0,0,0>:**, press Enter or pick Point 1, as shown in Figure 9.6.

Using this UCS method, you will not need to rotate the result 90 degrees. See the Color Studio in the middle of this book for a fully rendered example of a conrod drawing.

Removed Sections

Similar to a revolved section, a removed section shows a feature, or highlights or enlarges a part when there's no room on the orthographic view as a revolved section. The removed section simply provides you with a complete or partial section view, which can clarify details. Figure 9.7 shows an example. You pass an imaginary cutting plane perpendicular to a feature or part and then revolve the resulting cross-section 90 degrees, which simply depends upon the orientation of the hidden features you need to see. Ideally, the section may be moved and placed as a view anywhere on the drawing; because it's a removed section, it isn't aligned with any of the principal views.

Take, for example, the complex shape of a turbine blade or an airplane wing. If you obtain equidistant sections of the parts and then remove those sections to other locations on the drawing, you'll have a true cross-sectional visual representation of the model. You can also scale up your removed sections to show better cross-sectional details of the part (remembering to show the new scale below the view). Here's a hint: In AutoCAD, one option is to use the **SECTION** command with the **XY** option. Let's use it to produce

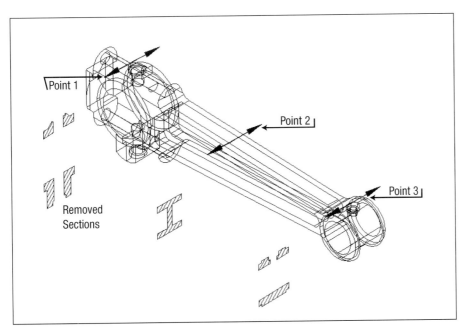

Figure 9.7
A removed section.

a revolved section of the conrod.dwg 3D model; then, use the **MOVE** command to produce a removed section. Here are the steps to create removed sections with the conrod.dwg, as you'll see in Figure 9.7:

1. Open conrod.dwg and restore the UCS to Side.

2. Set the UCS origin to the center of Point 1 (that is, the through hole) and use the **SECTION** command with the **XY** option; pick Point 1 at its center at the prompt, **Specify a point on the XY-plane <0,0,0>:** choose the center of the through hole).

3. The section will be created and rotated to the Side plane. Repeat for Points 2 and 3.

4. Use the **MOVE** command to move the sections away from the model, and use **BHATCH** with ANSI31.

Offset Sections

An offset section is a kind of full section that uses a cutting plane bent at one or more 90-degree angles to pass through important features of a particular object or part. You use this type of sectioning when a straight cutting plane or a full section can't show important features of the object. When sectioned, the front portion of the object is removed to create a type of full section view, which also includes any or all features that may not be seen in a full section view or in a normal multiview drawing. Figure 9.8 shows an example. One method of creating an offset section in AutoCAD is to create a closed polyline at a desired location and then to extrude it via the **Path**

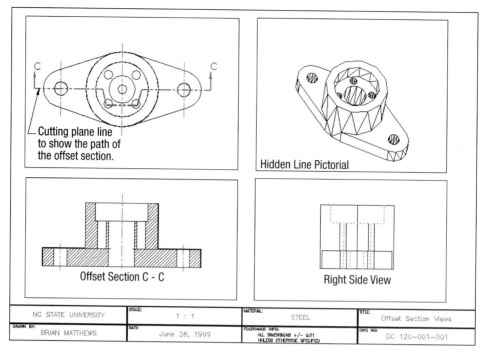

The figure contains the following labels:

C — C

Cutting plane line to show the path of the offset section.

Hidden Line Pictorial

Offset Section C - C

Right Side View

| NC STATE UNIVERSITY | SCALE: 1 : 1 | MATERIAL: STEEL | TITLE: Offset Section Views |
| DRAWN BY: BRIAN MATTHEWS | DATE: June 28, 1999 | TOLERANCE INFO: ALL DIMENSIONS +/− 0.01 UNLESS OTHERWISE SPECIFIED | DWG NO: GC 120−001−001 |

Figure 9.8

An offset section.

option of the **EXTRUDE** command. (The polyline and resulting extrusion are in different UCS work planes, and you'll need to Boolean **SUBTRACT** the extruded polyline from the 3D model.)

Assembly Sections

When you section an assembly as an assembly view, you must treat it differently than a single part view. This is the case because you're seeing multiple components in the same section view, each of which has to be treated as a separate part. You do so by applying the hatch lines at a different scale and angle, and/or applying different hatch symbols. The main rule is that the hatch lines should be in the same direction of slope for the same part and in a different direction or angle for all other parts, as illustrated in Figure 9.9. (Hint: One way to create assembly sections is to assemble and place all the singular parts into a whole without unioning the parts together; then, use the **SECTION** command.)

Auxiliary Sections

Auxiliary sections supplement the main views in an orthographic projection. For example, they apply where the type of part could be shown at an oblique angle; such parts include spokes, flanges, webs, or ribs in cross-section. In turn, you can pass the auxiliary section cutting plane through the Front view to project an auxiliary view from the cutting plane. The resulting auxiliary section provides a true cross-section of the part, as shown in Figure 9.10. (AutoCAD has an **Auxillary** option as a subset of the **SOLVIEW** command.)

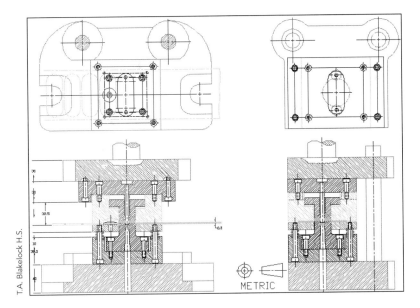

Figure 9.9
Assembly sections of a model.

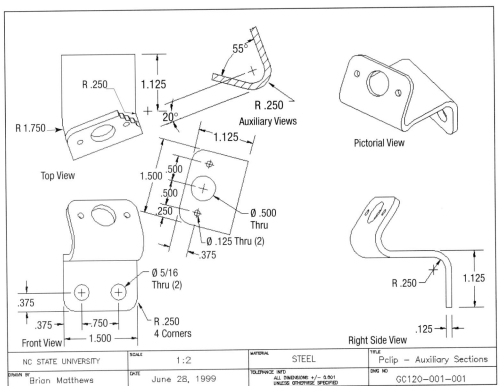

Figure 9.10
An auxiliary section of a model.

Aligned Sections

Aligned sections are special types of orthographic drawings that revolve or align special features of parts to clarify them or make them easier to represent in section. You use aligned sections when it's important to include details of a part by bending the cutting plane. The cutting plane and the features are imagined to be aligned or revolved before the section view is created. In other words, the principal or orthographic projection is violated in order to provide more clarity for the features of your model. Normally, the alignment is placed along the center line of the vertical or horizontal axis, and the re-alignment is always less than 90 degrees. The aligned section view provides more clarity toward a complete geometric description of the part. The cutting plane line may be bent to pass through all the nonaligned features in the unsectioned view. Figure 9.11 shows examples of aligned sections.

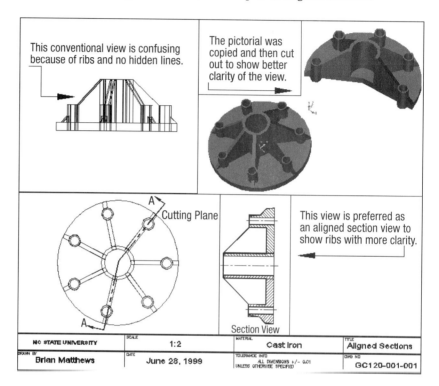

Figure 9.11
An aligned section.

Phantom Or Ghost Sections

If you could x-ray a section through a part as a view and produce it as faint lines, the result would be a *phantom section* or *ghost section*. You simply take a standard Top, Front, or Side view and create a section with faint dashed lines instead of continuous lines. You leave main features—through holes, keys, and so on—in position as standard lines and work around them.

Creating Sections In AutoCAD

As outlined at the beginning of the chapter, a section view is a type of 2D graphic that helps you show the inner details of a 3D model. The section lets you portray inner details that may otherwise be hidden. So, using a variety of methods and techniques, you can create 2D section views from your 3D solid model. We just reviewed a number of standard engineering methods that let you represent sections as graphics. Now, we'll move on to AutoCAD and take a practical look at how to create section views.

On the CD-ROM is a drawing named conrod-sect.dwg (alias connection-rod). It's a solid model that requires a number of section views in order to show the part with more clarity. Using this drawing plus conrod-slice.dwg and tailstock.dwg, you'll look at how to create sections with AutoCAD. The main commands that grab your attention to create sections in AutoCAD are **SECTION** and **SLICE**. These two basic commands allow you to create simplistic section views, but to create some of the more complex sections, you'll have to use additional techniques. Other commands you'll use include **SOLVIEW**, with its **SECTION** subcommand, along with **SOLDRAW** and **SOLPROF**, both of which allow you to create a profile from a solid model.

SECTION

As you pick a 3D solid you need to section, the **SECTION** command creates a 2D region based on your chosen section or cutting plane. Without the need for duplication, you'll find the command uses the same prompts as the **SLICE** command described in the next section. The main difference between **SLICE** and **SECTION** is that **SECTION** doesn't alter the original selected 3D solid. Instead, it creates a 2D region, which represents the cut surface of your 3D model. Figure 9.12 shows an example of using **SECTION**.

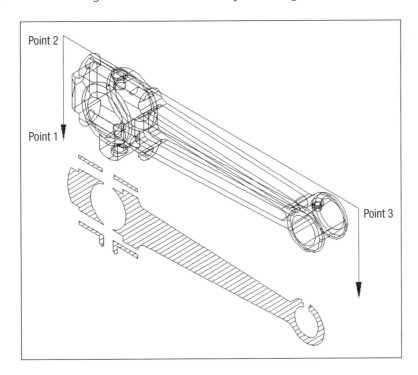

Figure 9.12
Use conrod-sect.dwg to create a cross-section.

Here are the steps to create the section as shown in Figure 9.12:

1. From the CD-ROM, open the conrod-sect.dwg and set the UCS to the Front plane (front is X 90 degrees)—that is, activate UCS and restore it to Front.

2. Use the **SECTION** command with the 3points default option and pick Points 1, 2, and 3 (as shown in Figure 9.12).

3. Move the section away from the 3D solid and hatch the section (using **HATCH** with ANSI31 set to a scale of 10).

Using the **SECTION** command, you can also create a cross-section through a solid as a region or an anonymous block. The default method is to specify three points to define the plane. Other methods define the cross-sectional plane by another object, the current view, the Z axis, or the XY, YZ, or ZX plane. Remember that AutoCAD places the cross-sectional plane on the current layer, so you should first change to the layer on which you want the section created.

To create a default cross-section of a solid, follow these steps:

1. From the Draw menu, choose Solids|Section.

2. Select the 3D model to cross-section.

3. Specify three points to define your cross-sectional cutting plane.

Remember, the first point you choose defines the origin point (0,0,0) of the cutting plane. The second point defines the X axis, and the third point defines the Y axis.

Hint: If you're applying hatching to the cross-sectional cutting plane, you must first align the UCS with the cross-sectional cutting plane. You should use the **SECTION** command with the **View** suboption first; doing so sets up the view for you as a UCS view.

SLICE

The **SLICE** command cuts a section of solid along a specified 3D plane. The specified plane may be picked as three points, an object, a Z axis, or in alignment with an XY, YZ, or ZX plane. The **SLICE** command is also useful with assembly drawings, because you may select one or more 3D solid models or objects. Remember that the **SLICE** command won't create more than two new composite solids for each 3D solid you select.

The main options for **SLICE** (which also apply to **SECTION**) are as follows:

- *3points*—This default method prompts you to pick three points on screen that specifically define your cutting plane.

- *Object*—The **Object** option lets you align the cutting plane with a simple 2D object (that is, an arc, circle, ellipse, or polyline).

- *Zaxis*—The **Zaxis** option lets you pick two points to define the Z axis, which is perpendicular to your cutting plane. Remember, your first pick point locates the axis origin and the cutting plane of your Z axis.

- *View*—The **View** option first aligns the cutting plane with your current viewport. You then pick a point to locate the position of your cutting plane.

- *XY/YZ/ZX*—These three options let you align the cutting plane with the selected axes of your current UCS. You then pick a point to locate the position of the cutting plane.

Remember this further point about the **SLICE** command: After you've chosen the cutting plane, pick which part of the 3D model you wish to keep. Alternately, enter "b" to retain both sides of the 3D model after cutting. Figure 9.13 shows an example of a sliced model.

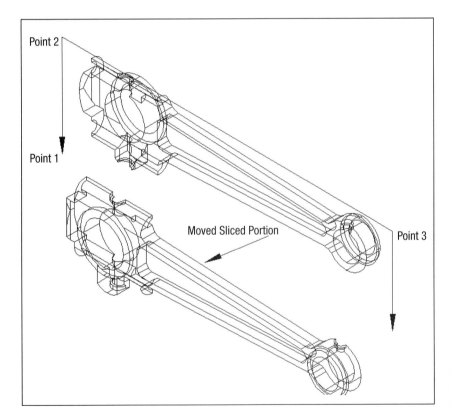

Figure 9.13
Use conrod-slice.dwg to create a sliced model.

Here are the steps to create a sliced model as shown in Figure 9.13:

1. From the CD-ROM, open the conrod-slice.dwg and set the UCS to the Front plane (that is, activate UCS and restore it to Front).

2. Use the **SLICE** command with the **3points** default option and pick Points 1, 2, and 3 (as shown in Figure 9.13).

3. Enter "b" at the prompt (for both) to retain both sides of the slice and move one of the slices away from the 3D solid, as shown in Figure 9.13.

SOLVIEW, SOLDRAW, And SOLPROF

If you choose Solids from the Draw menu and then choose Setup, you'll see three options: Drawing, View, and Profile, as shown in Figure 9.14. The corresponding AutoCAD commands are **SOLDRAW**, **SOLVIEW**, and **SOLPROF**. Here are the general steps for using these menu commands:

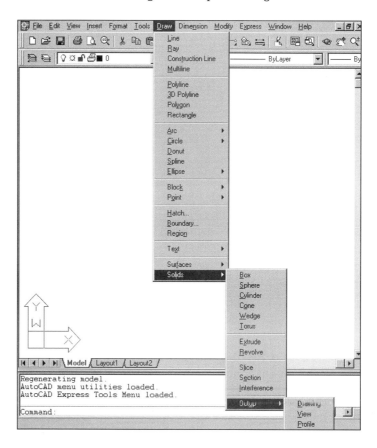

Figure 9.14
The Drawing, View, and Profile menu options.

1. Always create your 3D solid model before using these commands. They're mainly setup commands that let you place and create multiviews of your 3D solid model before you send the drawing to the plotter or printer.

2. Use the **SOLVIEW** command at the outset to create First-Angle Projection and Third-Angle Projection views and/or Pictorial views of your model. Remember, the **SOLVIEW** command creates layers (see Table 9.1), so you must name each projected view differently, such as Top, Front, R-side, L-side, Pict, or Iso.

3. Run the **SOLDRAW** command to create the model's hidden lines. Remember to change the color of your *Layer name*-HID layer to Green or Red in order for it to plot at a finer lineweight than the Black lineweight of 0.7, or whatever you have set.

Table 9.1 Layers created by the **SOLVIEW**, **SOLDRAW**, and **SOLPROF** commands.

Layer Name Created	Object Or Entity Type	Command
Layer name-DIM	Layer for dimensions	**SOLVIEW**
Layer name-HID	Layer for hidden lines	**SOLVIEW**
Layer name-VIS	Layer for visible lines	**SOLVIEW**
Layer name-HAT	Layer for hatch lines	**SOLVIEW**
PV-*viewport handle*	Layer for Profile Visible block	**SOLPROF**
PH-*viewport handle*	Layer for Profile Hidden block	**SOLPROF**

4. Use the **SECTION**, **SLICE**, or **SOLPROF** command if you need further clarity or views.

Now, let's look at how to use **SOLDRAW**, **SOLVIEW**, and **SOLPROF** for 3D solids.

SOLVIEW

The **SOLVIEW** command lets you create floating viewports using standard orthographic projection. This process, in turn, lets you lay out multiview and section view drawings of your 3D solid model, especially while you're in a Layout tab or paper space.

Most CAD systems today provide automatic methods of creating multiviews and sectional drawings. The **SOLDRAW**, **SOLVIEW**, and **SOLPROF** commands of the Setup submenu are AutoCAD's answer as an automatic method to create multiviews.

The **SOLVIEW** command determines each orthographic projection you need and intuitively guides you through an on-screen process to create orthographic, auxiliary, and/or section views of your model. As you can see in Table 9.1, it also creates layer names for each view you create of your model, including DIM (for DIMension), HID (for HIDden), and VIS (for VISible) layers for each named orthographic view you create. For example, if you use the American Third-Angle projection, your first view would be the Top view in the upper-left corner of the viewport. In turn, you'd name this view TOP and the **SOLVIEW** command would automatically create three extra layers: TOP-Dim, TOP-Hid, and TOP-Vis (plus the layer VPORTS if it didn't already exist).

Nevertheless, the purpose behind this view-specific information—which is saved with each orthographic view you create—is to create layer names used by the **SOLDRAW** command. **SOLDRAW** uses the layer names to place hidden and visible lines for each view.

As you can see in Table 9.1, **SOLVIEW** creates a number of standard layers as you set up each of your views. (Hint: Never put or draw any information on the VIS, HID, and/or HAT layers. These layers are deleted and/or updated when you activate **SOLDRAW**.)

SOLDRAW

SOLDRAW creates profiles and/or section views in the viewports created with the **SOLVIEW** command. You can't use the command on its own: You must have set up viewports with **SOLVIEW** first.

The command takes a snapshot image of your solid model and places visible and hidden lines as an edged silhouette to represent your solid model.

When you create section views, you need to remember that cross-hatching is created using any settings of the **HPNAME**, **HPSCALE**, and **HPANG** system variables.

If you have an existing profile and/or section in the viewport you're using, it will be deleted and then updated as a new profile and/or section is generated.

The **SOLDRAW** command automatically sets (freezes/thaws) layers in the active viewport. For example, all layers except those required to display the profile or section are frozen in the viewport in which you're working. Never put or draw any information on the created VIS, HID, and/or HAT layers. These layers are deleted and/or updated when you activate **SOLDRAW**.

SOLPROF

SOLPROF creates a profile image of your solid model when you're working in paper space or a Layout tab. You must be active within the model space of a floating viewport of a Layout tab. Like **SOLDRAW**, **SOLPROF** displays a profile image of edge and surface outlines of your solid model's current view.

As you activate the command and select the solid model, you'll choose from a number of Yes/No options:

```
Display hidden profile lines on separate layer? [Yes/No] <Y>:
Project profile lines onto a plane? [Yes/No] <Y>:
Delete tangential edges? [Yes/No] <Y>:
```

If you answer Yes to the first prompt, AutoCAD will create two blocks: one for visible lines and the other for hidden lines of your selected solid model. When you create hidden lines, some solids can partially or completely hide other solids. In addition, remember to preload your HIDDEN linetypes.

At the same time **SOLPROF** is creating the two blocks of visible lines and hidden lines, it's also creating extra PV and PH layers to place the blocks on, as described previously in Table 9.1.

Remember that **SOLPROF** doesn't change the display of layers: If you want to view the profile lines you created, simply turn off the layer containing your solid model. A second prompt asks if you want to project profile lines:

```
Project profile lines onto a plane? [Yes/No] <Y>:
```

A Yes answer will make AutoCAD use your profile lines as visible lines and then create a block for the profile lines of your solid model. The visible profile blocks **SOLPROF** generates are drawn in the same linetype as the original solid and placed on a unique named layer. A final prompt refers to tangential edges:

```
Delete tangential edges? [Yes/No] <Y>:
```

This final tangential prompt determines whether tangential edges are displayed or not (for most drafting applications, you don't show tangential edges).

A *tangential edge* is the transition line between two tangent faces, the imaginary edge at which two faces meet and are tangent to each other. For example, if you fillet the edge of a wedge or a box, you'll have tangential edges created where the cylindrical face of the fillet blends into the planar faces of the wedge or box.

Hint: Any solid models that overlap each other produce dangling edges, especially if you request hidden-line removal. These dangling edges occur because edges must be broken at the point where they enter another solid, to separate them into visible and hidden portions. Use **UNION** to eliminate dangling edges by combining the overlapping solids before you create a profile.

Using **SOLVIEW** To Create Orthographic Views

SOLVIEW is superior to some of the other options (such as **MVSETUP** or **MVIEW**) because it sets up layers according to your named views. After you've created the 3D model, **SOLVIEW** helps you develop alternative orthographic views. Here are a few hints:

- Create your AutoCAD 3D solid model in model space and make a backup copy of it (that is, make a hidden block copy of the model within the drawing and/or make a backup copy of the drawing file).

- Access the **SOLVIEW** command by choosing Draw|Solids|Setup|View (or enter "solview" at the keyboard prompt and then follow the keyboard prompts at the command line).

- Remember, when you use **SOLVIEW**, you'll pick corner location points on your drawing sheet as you create each view. It's best to do this visually by using your grid and snap.

- Provide a scale for the views (remember that a scale should show a relationship such as 1=1 or 0.5 = 1).

- Provide a name for each view, such as Top, Front, Rside, or Lside.

- Remember to leave room for dimensions as you create each orthographic viewport.

- If you have complicated parts, you can also place a pictorial as an isometric, trimetric, section, or auxiliary view with the **SOLVIEW** command. Then, use the AutoCAD 2000 **VPOINT** command to change the view.

- Set lineweight by using the new Lineweight option of the object's properties through the **DDMODIFY** or **PROPERTIES** command. Or simply set lineweight in the Layer Properties Manager dialog box.

Let's work through an example. From the CD-ROM, open tailstock.dwg, which is a metric drawing. Figure 9.15 shows the completed drawing. Figure 9.16 shows a number of profiles in two profile planes: Top and Front.

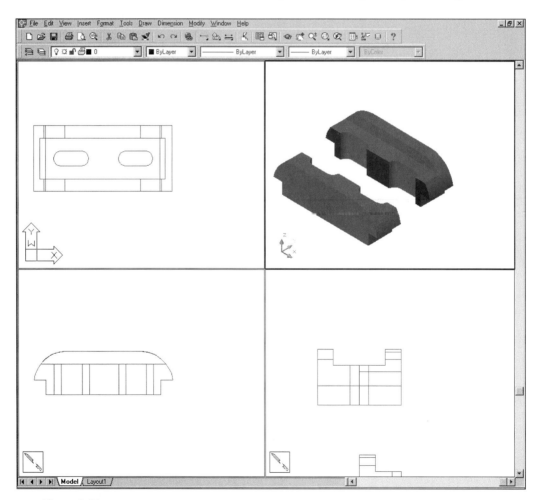

Figure 9.15
The completed Tailstock section drawing.

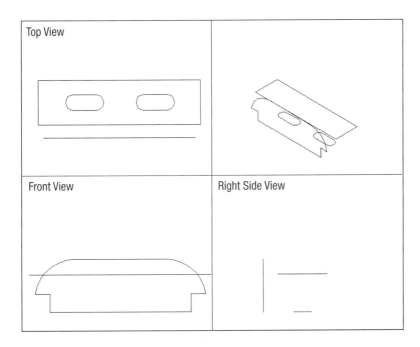

Top View

Front View

Right Side View

Figure 9.16
The Tailstock drawing profiles.

The objective of the exercise is to extrude the profiles and then create Top, Front, and Right Side views, with a pictorial section view as a bonus to aid your final presentation drawing. Initially, you'll extrude the profiles within two UCS views (Top and Front) and use the **SUBTRACT** command to create a solid model. You'll then create the Top, Front, and Right Side views and finally the sliced pictorial section view. Follow these steps:

1. In tailstock.dwg, check to ensure you are in the Model Space tab (that is, **TILEMODE** should be set to zero, Snap should be turned off) and access the upper-right SE Isometric viewport. The profiles are colored red for the front UCS work plane and green/blue for the top UCS work plane. Notice the current UCS is set to the World Coordinate System and its location is at 0,0,0.

2. Using the **EXTRUDE** command, extrude the two blue profile slots up 40mm. Then, extrude the green profile rectangle up 12mm.

3. Restore the UCS to the Front UCS view and then extrude the red profile a negative distance of –58mm. Reset your UCS to the World Coordinate System.

4. Using the **SUBTRACT** command, subtract the main front profile from the remaining profiles (that is, at the first **Select objects:** prompt, choose the main Front profile and press Enter; then, at the second **Select objects:** prompt, pick the 12mm rectangular object and the two profile slots, and press Enter to complete the **SUBTRACT** command). You're now ready to use the **SOLVIEW** command and create the orthographic views.

5. Choose the Layout1 tab. Using the **ZOOM** command, do a Zoom
   Extents to the boundary of the title block that's pre-inserted in the
   Layout1 space.

6. At the keyboard, enter the **SOLVIEW** command or activate it by
   choosing Draw|Solids|Setup|View. (You can also jump straight into
   the **SOLVIEW** command by opening the tailstock-1.dwg drawing on
   the CD-ROM.) Then, respond to the prompts as follows:

```
Command: solview
Enter an option [Ucs/Ortho/Auxiliary/Section]: u
Enter an option [Named/World/?/Current] <Current>: <Press
    Enter>
Enter view scale <1>: 1
Specify view center: <Choose a location on screen at 90,160>
Specify view center <specify viewport>: <Press Enter>
Specify first corner of viewport: <Choose a location on
    screen at 20,200>
Specify opposite corner of viewport: <Choose a location on
    screen at 170,120>
Enter view name: top
UCSVIEW = 1   UCS will be saved with view
Enter an option [Ucs/Ortho/Auxiliary/Section]: O
Specify side of viewport to project: <Choose the midpoint of
    the viewport border at 95,120>
Specify view center: <Choose a location on screen at 95,80>
Specify view center <specify viewport>: <Press Enter>
Specify first corner of viewport: <Choose a location on
    screen at 20,110>
Specify opposite corner of viewport: <Choose a location on
    screen at 170,40>
Enter view name: front
UCSVIEW = 1   UCS will be saved with view
Enter an option [Ucs/Ortho/Auxiliary/Section]: s
Specify first point of cutting plane: 90,40
Specify second point of cutting plane: 90,0 100
Specify side to view from: 120,20
Enter view scale <1>: 1
Specify view center: <Choose a location on screen at 0,100>
Specify view center <specify viewport>: <Press Enter>
Specify first corner of viewport: <Choose a location on
    screen at 180,110>
Specify opposite corner of viewport: <Choose a location on
    screen at 270,40>
Enter view name: r-sect
UCSVIEW = 1   UCS will be saved with view
Enter an option [Ucs/Ortho/Auxiliary/Section]: u
Enter an option [Named/World/?/Current] <Current>: <Press
    Enter>
```

```
Enter view scale <1>: <Press Enter>
Specify view center: <Choose a location on screen at
  225,165>
Specify view center <specify viewport>: <Press Enter>
Specify first corner of viewport: <Choose a location on
  screen at 180,200>
Specify opposite corner of viewport: <Choose a location on
  screen at 270,120>
Enter view name: iso
UCSVIEW = 1  UCS will be saved with view
Enter an option [Ucs/Ortho/Auxiliary/Section]: <Press Enter
  to complete>
```

The upper-right viewport will show the wrong view: As shown in Figure 9.17, it should be an Isometric pictorial, not an orthographic view. Here's how to change it:

1. Use the **MS** command to change to model space; enter the upper-right viewport.

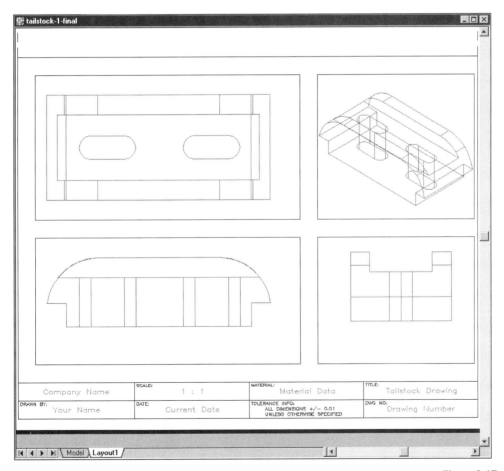

Figure 9.17

Complete viewport placement for the Tailstock drawing.

2. Choose View|3D Views and select the SE Isometric preset view. If this activates the View dialog box, choose Southeast Isometric preset view in the dialog box and click on Set Current; then, pick OK.

3. Instantly, your upper-right viewport will change to the SE Isometric view. You're now ready to dimension and then turn off the VPORTS layer in the Layer dialog box. Remember to use the **PS** command to return to paper space before you plot the drawing.

Using **REVOLVE** To Create A Section View

Let's look at another method of creating a section view, by using the **RE-VOLVE** command. Start a new revolve.dwg file using Standard English units (or use the revolve.dwg on the CD-ROM, as shown in Figure 9.18, which is ready for you to revolve and shade).

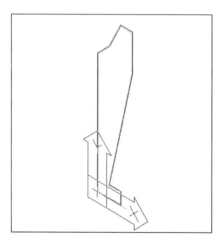

Figure 9.18
Create the outline using
a polyline.

If you start a new drawing, the steps are as follows: Change your view to SE Isometric. In the default World UCS, draw a line from 0,0 to 5,0. (This line will be the axis of rotation line.) Set the UCS to a Front work plane as listed below, and then use a polyline to draw the outline of the part you're going to revolve:

```
Command: ucs
Current ucs name:  *world*
Enter an option [New/Move/orthoGraphic/Prev/Restore/Save/Del/
  Apply/?/World]
<World>: x
Specify rotation angle about X axis <90>: 90
```

Create the outline of the part as shown in Figure 9.18. Then, do a Zoom Extents:

```
Command: pline
Specify start point: 0,0,0
Current line-width is 0.0000
Specify next point or [Arc/Close/Halfwidth/Length/Undo/Width]: 4,0
Specify next point or [Arc/Close/Halfwidth/Length/Undo/Width]: 4,2
Specify next point or [Arc/Close/Halfwidth/Length/Undo/Width]: 2,2
Specify next point or [Arc/Close/Halfwidth/Length/Undo/Width]:
  6,20
Specify next point or [Arc/Close/Halfwidth/Length/Undo/Width]:
  6,26
Specify next point or [Arc/Close/Halfwidth/Length/Undo/Width]:
  4,26
Specify next point or [Arc/Close/Halfwidth/Length/Undo/Width]:
  2,22
Specify next point or [Arc/Close/Halfwidth/Length/Undo/Width]:
  0,20
Specify next point or [Arc/Close/Halfwidth/Length/Undo/Width]: c
Command: zoom
Specify corner of window, enter a scale factor (nX or nXP), or
  [All/Center/Dynamic/Extents/Previous/Scale/Window]
  <real time>: e
```

Prior to revolving, you may want to change the color of the component to blue; then, you can shade it as a finished product.

Use the **REVOLVE** command to perform a sectional revolve on the component. If you use 270 degrees instead of 360 degrees as the value, the component will appear as if it's had a corner segment cut out of it, and the cut portion will be facing you:

```
Command: revolve
Current wire frame density: ISOLINES=4
Select objects: <Choose the closed polyline just created>
Specify start point for axis of revolution or
  define axis by [Object/X (axis)/Y (axis)]: O
Select an object: <Choose the axis of rotation line, drawn from
  0,0 to 5,0>
Specify angle of revolution <360>: 270
```

After you've revolved the component, you may need to do a Zoom Extents. Then, use the **SHADE** command and use **Shademode** to change the shading to Gouraud. See Figure 9.19. Alternatively, if you enter **Shademode** first, and change the shading type to Gouraud, it will shade the object itself. (The revolve-finish.dwg file is available on the CD-ROM, ready to shade.)

An alternative method is to use the **REVSURF** command, choosing the closed polyline as the object to revolve, and the line you drew from 0,0 to 5,0 as the axis of revolution.

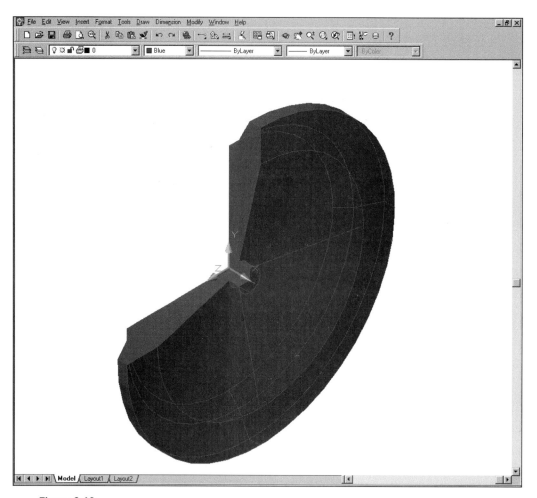

Figure 9.19
The revolved and shaded sectional drawing.

Moving On

Sectioning and slicing solid models as 2D and 3D graphics helps you show inner details of a 3D model—details that can otherwise be hidden. The next chapter moves into dimensioning and the many methods available to you in AutoCAD.

DIMENSIONING
AND
GEOMETRICS
10

An essential communication task of every designer is to enter the dimension and tolerance information of a part or series of parts and thereby indicate how the component geometry fits together. Without understanding dimensioning, you can't communicate your design intent to the manufacturer, who, in turn, will assemble the designed component.

Understanding Dimensioning And Geometrics

An engineer, architect, or draftsperson has to guarantee two vital components to produce a CAD drawing: a true shape description and a true size description. Thus, dimensions and annotations are vital graphical components of a drawing. They show overall measurements of a model and include measurements of features such as counterbore diameter and depth, or the radius of fillets and rounds. This chapter begins by discussing dimension basics, dimension style sheets, and dimension creation commands to refresh your memory. It moves on to outlining geometric dimensioning and tolerancing commands plus leader and ordinate dimensioning. Final sections discuss dimension editing and associative dimensioning.

Dimensioning is a tool you use to provide a client or a colleague with size and location information about the object being drawn. In turn, dimensioning is used with *geometrics*, which identifies the tolerance or accuracy required for each dimension. Geometry, in turn, can be associated with geometric dimensioning and tolerancing (GD&T), as an association of the shape. In other words, GD&T measures the three-dimensional cylindricity, flatness, and/or parallelism of the features that make up the part and their 3D tolerance relationship to other components. Correct dimensioning is an important aspect of a drawing, because dimensions communicate and show exact measurements, distances, tolerances, and X and Y geometric and datum coordinates. Dimensioning is especially important with mechanical parts and geometric tolerancing, especially when communicating the geometrics of a feature—that is, in order to understand its shape, size, location accuracy, and 3D tolerancing to the main component.

As just mentioned, *geometrics* is another tool: the science of specifying and tolerancing the shapes and locations of features for your model. For example, as a designer, you use geometrics along with the practice of dimensioning and tolerancing to specify the shape of a part, the roundness of a shaft, or the radius of a round or a fillet.

In addition, with the practice of concurrent engineering, dimensioning and geometrics help you achieve effective communication in the triangle of design, manufacturing, and quality control as your part is being created. (If your company is using concurrent engineering, you'll find that it's also a form of quality control.) In this concurrent engineering environment, the designer's intent is thus relayed through adequate and standardized dimensioning practice to other members of the product development team, so it's essential to know how to dimension correctly.

Size And Location Of Dimensions

AutoCAD 2000 has a new quick dimensioning command (**QDIM**), but the program doesn't take into account the fact that dimensions are initially based on two criteria of communication:

- The basic size and location of features

- The details of construction, for manufacturing

Both of these criteria are important communication items for the designer. When you start to dimension, one of the first items to note is the unit of measure—that is, English or metric. In the United States, most drawings are in Third-Angle Projection and dimensioned in English (imperial) inches. Other countries generally use First-Angle Projection and the metric or the Systeme Internationale d'Unites (SI) system.

Be aware there are different dimensioning practices within different industries. For example, within both the sheet-metal and the locomotive design industries, all dimensions (regardless of length) are usually placed in inches. In other industries, if you draw in inches and the part is 72 inches or longer, the part should be dimensioned within the drawing as feet and inches. In the architectural and structural design and drafting industries, any dimension under 12 inches is expressed in inches, and any dimension over 12 inches is expressed as feet and inches. Alternately, if your drawing is completely in metric, just place the capitalized word "METRIC" in the drawing's upper-right corner, or place it prominently on the drawing and underscore it or place it within a box.

Now, let's take a look at the rules for size and location of dimensions. In mechanical drawings, a standard dimension text size is 3mm high, with dimension placement usually starting in the Front view or your most descriptive view with the smallest features. The dimension placement then moves on to the overall size of the part and to other views. You need to place your first row of dimensions a minimum of 10mm (0.40 in or 3/8") away from your model or part, and then place successive rows of dimensions at least 6mm (0.25 in or 1/4") from that first row. You should refer to fillets and rounds with a leader attached to a radius dimension, and to through holes with a leader attached to a diameter dimension. Never repeat dimensions in successive views; however, where dimensions apply to two views, it's good practice to place the dimensions between the views. It's also good practice to dimension visible lines as opposed to hidden lines. It isn't good practice to have extension lines cross each other, but if it's absolutely necessary, you can do so.

Unidirectional And Aligned Dimension Basics

The two basic dimension types for drawings are *unidirectional* and *aligned* (see Figure 10.1). The unidirectional method of dimensioning (used in mechanical drawings in automotive, aircraft, and other industries because of its ease of use) allows you to read a blueprint without turning it in any direction. Architectural drawings use the aligned method, which allows you to rotate the blueprint once to the right. For the sake of clarity, Figure 10.1 shows a simple mechanical part copied twice within the same drawing. The left drawing is set to the unidirectional (also called horizontal) method of dimensioning, and the right is set to the aligned method, in which you'll notice the text is aligned with the dimension lines.

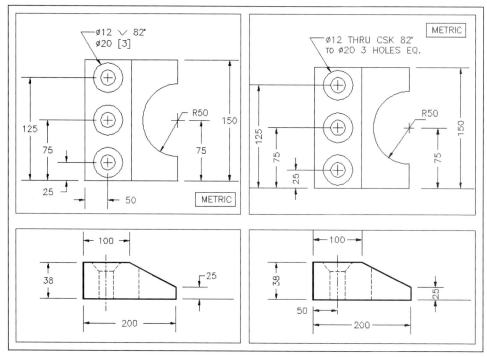

Figure 10.1

The basic dimensioning types: unidirectional (in the two left panes) and aligned (in the two right panes).

The Dimension Style Manager

When you create dimensions, they always associate themselves with a dimension style name, even if it's the default name of Standard. AutoCAD 2000 includes the dimension styles ANSI, DIN, JIS, and ISO, which are located in different drawing templates. For example, if you start a new drawing and select English units, AutoCAD assigns the default dimension style of Standard. (Standard is based on—but doesn't exactly conform to—the American National Standards Institute [ANSI] dimension standards.) If you start a new drawing and select metric units, the default dimension style in this template is based on the metric ISO-25 (the International Standards

Organization). The AutoCAD DIN and JIS drawing templates use the DIN (German) and JIS (Japanese Industrial Standard) styles.

The Dimension Style Manager dialog box, shown in Figure 10.2, lets you set current, create new, modify, override, and compare dimension style(s). You activate it by picking the Dimension Style icon on the Dimension toolbar (extreme right icon) (shown later in this chapter in Figure 10.11), choosing Dimension|Style, or entering "ddim" or "dimstyle" at the command prompt. The Dimension Style Manager also allows you to make global changes to a drawing or use a dimension override command to suppress a single feature to a dimension. When you need to edit a dimension, you can use **DIMEDIT** or **DIMTEDIT**, or use the Properties dialog box.

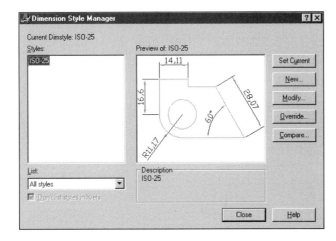

Figure 10.2
The Dimension Style Manager dialog box.

By creating a dimension style , you provide control for the dimension standards within your drawing. (You're simply changing the dimension system variables and then saving those changes as a name along with the other settings.) The Dimension Style Manager dialog box allows you to modify and create family dimension styles without having to learn all the dimension system variable settings.

Now, let's take a brief journey through the Dimension Style Manager. Don't save any settings on the way—just cancel each dialog box as you look through it and get an idea what it will do. Activate the Dimension Style Manager dialog box and notice to the right a series of buttons. The Set Current button lets you assign the current settings to all newly created dimensions from a named dimension style; the New, Modify, Override, and Compare buttons access further dialog boxes.

Clicking on New activates a Create New Dimension Style dialog box, shown in Figure 10.3. This dialog box provides built-in flexibility to allow you to create dimension (parent and child) subsets of the main dimension style name; you can also set different dimension fonts as you dimension drawing components. You start with this dialog box and enter a New Style Name

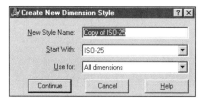

Figure 10.3

The Create New Dimension Style
dialog box.

and what you'll use the style for. Take a peek at the Use For drop-down list, which includes All Dimensions, Linear, Angular, Radius, Diameter, Ordinate, Leaders, and Tolerance options. Just remember to keep new style names simple—ARCH, MECH, ANSI, DIN, and JIS are good parent name examples because of their simplicity.

Now, close the Create New Dimension Style dialog box and click on Modify. Figure 10.4 shows the resulting Modify Dimension Style dialog box. This multipurpose dimension dialog box has six tabs: Lines And Arrows, Text, Fit, Primary Units, Alternate Units, and Tolerances.

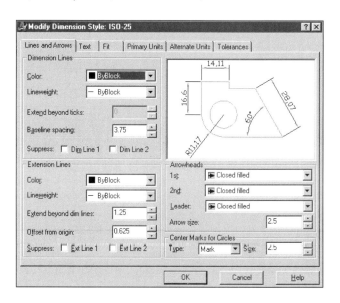

Figure 10.4

The Modify Dimension Style
dialog box.

Close the dialog box and click on Compare. You'll see a listing of dimension variables, their descriptions, and their current settings, as shown in Figure 10.5. Close the dialog box and then close the file without saving it. Now, we'll see how to set up an ANSI dimension style sheet.

ANSI Dimension Style Sheet

In this section, you'll learn how to set up an ANSI dimension style sheet in AutoCAD. Start a new drawing in metric units. Then, follow these steps:

1. Activate the Dimension Style Manager dialog box. Click on New. In the Create New Dimension Style dialog box, enter "ANSI" in the New Style Namebox, as shown in Figure 10.6, and then click on Continue.

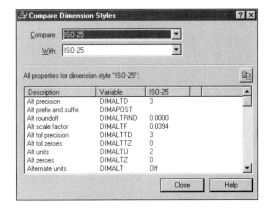

Figure 10.5
The Compare Dimension Styles dialog box.

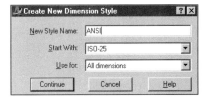

Figure 10.6
The Create New Dimension Style dialog box for ANSI.

2. The main New Dimension Style dialog box opens with the ANSI name in the header, as shown in Figure 10.7. Click on the Lines And Arrows tab and enter the following settings according to Figure 10.7:

- In the Dimension Lines area, set Baseline Spacing to 10.

- In the Extension Lines area, set Extend Beyond Dim Lines to 2 and Offset From Origin to 1.

- In the Arrowheads area, set Arrow Size to 3 and check that all the arrowheads are set to Closed Filled.

- In the Center Marks For Circles section, set Type to Line.

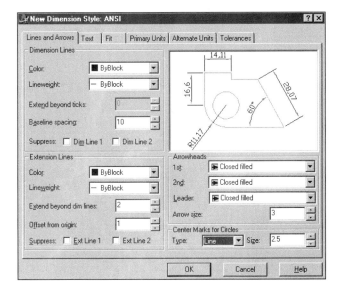

Figure 10.7
The New Dimension Style: ANSI dialog box.

3. Click on the Text tab of the New Dimension Style dialog box. See Figure 10.8. Set the following:

• In the Text Appearance area, to the right of the Text Style drop-down list, click on the ellipsis (...) button. Doing so activates the Text Style dialog box. In the Font Naming box of the Font area, set Font Name to romans.shx; then, click on Apply and Close. You'll be returned to the Text tab.

• In the Text Appearance area, set Text Height to 3.

• In the Text Placement area, set both the Vertical and Horizontal boxes to Centered and the Offset From Dim Line to 1.

• In the Text Alignment area, ensure that the Horizontal radio button is selected.

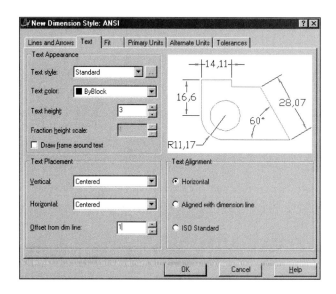

Figure 10.8

Settings for the Text tab of the New Dimension Style dialog box.

4. Click on the Fit tab in the New Dimensions Style dialog box. This tab allows you to set up the fit format for arrows and text. See Figure 10.9 and enter the following settings:

• In the Fit Options area, ensure that the Either The Text Or The Arrows, Whichever Fits Best radio button is selected.

• In the Text Placement area, ensure that the Beside The Dimension Line radio button is selected.

• In the Scale For Dimension Features area, choose the Scale Dimensions To Layout (Paperspace) radio button.

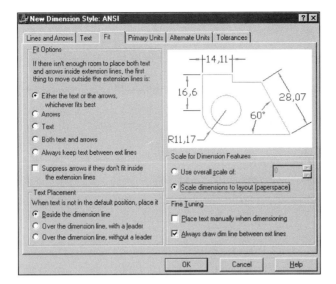

Figure 10.9

Settings for the Fit tab of the New Dimension Style dialog box.

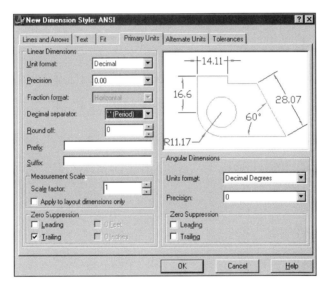

Figure 10.10

The Primary Units tab of the New Dimension Style dialog box.

5. Click on the Primary Units tab of the dialog box. See Figure 10.10. In the Linear Dimensions area, make sure Unit Format is set to Decimal, Precision is set to 0.00, and Decimal Separator is set to "." (Period).

6. Click on OK to return to the Dimension Style Manager dialog box. Click on Close, and AutoCAD will save your ANSI settings.

Now that you've created a dimension style, you can start dimensioning some parts. On the CD-ROM, you'll find several drawings to work with: qdim-1.dwg, hanger-1.dwg, plate-1.dwg, profile-1.dwg, and panel-1.dwg. The CD also contains the dimension-1.dwg file, which is a version of Figure 10.40, shown later in this chapter; you can quickly dimension the simple part.

Dimension Commands

As you can see in Figure 10.11, the AutoCAD 2000 Dimension toolbar has a number of dimension icons: Linear, Aligned, Ordinate, Radius, Diameter, Angular, Quick Dimension, Baseline, Continue, Quick Leader, Tolerance, Center Mark, Dimension Edit, Dimension Text Edit, Dimension Update, Dim Style Control, and Dimension Style.

Figure 10.11
The Dimension toolbar.

If you activate the AutoCAD 2000 Dimension menu (as opposed to the toolbar), you'll see dimension options in a different sequence:

- *Qdim*—Creates a set of quick dimensions to a part.

- *Linear*—Creates three types of dimensions: horizontal, vertical, and rotated.

- *Aligned*—Creates dimensions at an angle .

- *Ordinate*—Creates ordinate-style dimensions from a set UCS origin point (you'll use this feature later to create a quick series of dimensions).

- *Radius*—Draws radius dimensions to arcs and circles.

- *Diameter*—Draws diameter dimensions to arcs and circles.

- *Angular*—Creates angled degree dimensions to objects. In addition to degrees, they can also be Radians or Gradians.

You'll deal with the rest of the commands as you work with dimensioning. As you saw in Figure 10.11, the AutoCAD 2000 Dimension toolbar provides a number of dimension commands. Table 10.1 lists the AutoCAD dimension commands that will allow you to dimension or edit the dimensions on your model.

Linear Dimensions

DIMLINEAR is a multipurpose command. Use it to create horizontal, vertical, and/or rotated dimensions. To use **DIMLINEAR**, simply choose your object or location—such as an intersection or endpoint of the part—and then place your dimension.

You can enter the command at the command line

```
Command: dimlinear
```

or choose the Linear Dimension icon on the Dimension toolbar. At the command prompt, you'll see:

```
Specify first extension line origin or <select object>:
```

Table 10.1   Quick reference listing of the most used dimension commands.

Command	Dimension Type	Explanation
DIMLINEAR	Linear dimension	Creates vertical, horizontal, or rotated linear dimensions.
DIMALIGNED	Aligned dimension	Creates an aligned linear dimension. The dimension line is parallel to the extension line source points.
DIMORDINATE	Ordinate dimension	Creates an ordinate dimension from a specific X or Y datum.
DIMRADIUS	Radius dimension	Indicates the radius of an arc, fillet, or circle.
DIMDIAMETER	Diameter dimension	Indicates the diameter of an arc or circle.
DIMANGULAR	Angular dimension	Produces an angular measurement between two connected angles.
QDIM	Quick dimension	Lets you select multiple objects at once to create automatic baseline, continued, and ordinate dimensions.
DIMBASELINE	Baseline dimension	From the same origin point, creates angular, linear, and ordinate dimensions.
DIMCONTINUE	Continuing dimension	From a common dimension line, continues an aligned, linear, angular, and/or ordinate dimension.
QLEADER	Leader annotation	Links text and/or tolerance notation with a leader line.
TOLERANCE	Tolerance dimension	Creates a geometric tolerance dimension.
DIMCENTER	Center mark	Creates center lines or marks and/or center points of arcs/circles.
DIMEDIT	Dimension edit	Lets you edit text via **Home**, **New**, and **Rotate** options, or extension lines via the **Oblique** option.
DIMTEDIT	DimensionText edit	Lets you move, rotate, and justify dimension text.
DIMUPDATE	Dimension update	Updates any picked dimension to a new dimension style.
DIMSTYLE	Dimension style	Shows and sets the dimension style for new and existing dimensions.
DDIM	Dimension Manager	Lets you modify and set dimension styles to various standards.

At this point, you can press Enter to select an object for automatic dimensioning; try pressing Enter and then selecting the line, polyline, arc, or circle that you want to dimension, and AutoCAD will find the extension line origins automatically. You then place the dimension.

Or at the prompt for first and second extension line origin, use Object Snap and select two specific points. If you choose the first and second extension line origins, the next command prompt is as follows:

```
Specify dimension line location or
  [Mtext/Text/Angle/Horizontal/Vertical/Rotated]: <Specify an
  option or pick a location>
```

From this point you can pick a location for the dimension line. If you pick a location, the command will end and AutoCAD will place the dimension in position.

Alternatively, at the command prompt, enter "m", "t", "a", "h", "v", or "r". These subcommand prompts are as follows:

• *M (Mtext)*—Produces the Multiline Text Editor dialog box in which you can change, customize, and/or add tolerance symbols to your dimension text. (See "Dimension Text Editing" later in the chapter.)

- *T (Text)*—Lets you alter and edit your dimension text at the command line. You simply change the text at the command prompt.

- *A (Angle)*—Lets you change and customize the angle of your dimension text. It doesn't change the angle of the dimension line (that's what the **Rotated** option is for). The **Angle** option will, for example, allow you to align the text with an angular feature on your model.

- *H (Horizontal)*—Forces horizontal dimensions. The option simply overrides the **DIMLINEAR** command and forces it into a horizontal dimensioning mode.

- *V (Vertical)*—Allows only vertical dimension creation. This option overrides the **DIMLINEAR** command and forces it into a vertical dimensioning mode.

- *R (Rotated)*—Lets you customize the angle at which you want to create the dimension line. Using this option simply forces your dimension line to be rotated to a specific angle.

For practice, use the **DIMLINEAR** command to dimension the horizontal and vertical components of the dimension-1.dwg as shown in Figure 10.12. Open the dimension-1.dwg file from the CD-ROM, and reproduce the dimensions as shown in Figure 10.12.

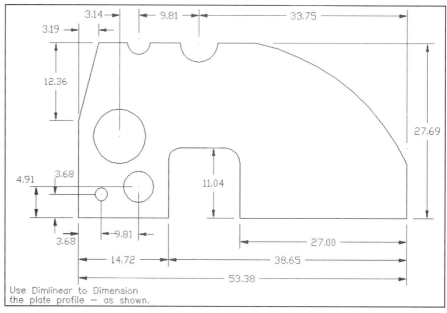

Figure 10.12

Use **DIMLINEAR** to dimension the drawing.

Aligned Dimensions

The **DIMALIGNED** command creates an aligned linear dimension, such as a feature for an angled part. Similar to the **Rotated** option of the previous **DIMLINEAR** command, you can use **DIMALIGNED** to create dimension lines that are aligned with specific features of your model. To activate the command use:

```
Command: dimaligned
```

Or choose the Aligned Dimension icon on the Dimension toolbar, and you'll see the following prompt:

```
Specify first extension line origin or <select object>:
```

At this point, you can either press Enter and select a line for automatic dimensioning, or pick the first endpoint of a line. After picking the first endpoint, you'll see this further prompt:

```
Specify second extension line origin:
```

Pick the second endpoint. Note that for the first and second extension line origins, it's best to use OSNAP to accurately select two specific endpoints.

The next prompt is as follows:

```
Specify dimension line location or
  [Mtext/Text/Angle]: <Specify an option or pick the dimension
  location >
```

This prompt expects you to specify an **M**, **T**, or **A** option or pick the dimension location and accept the default dimension shown at the prompt line.

The **M (Mtext)**, **T (Text)**, and **A (Angle)** options are explained in the "Linear Dimensions" section earlier in this chapter.

For practice, use the **DIMALIGNED** command to dimension the angled component of the profile-1.dwg as shown in Figure 10.13. Open the profile-1.dwg file from the CD-ROM and create the dimensions for the drawing as Figure 10.13 illustrates. The example uses the **DIMLINEAR**, **DIMRADIUS**, **DIMDIAMETER**, and **DIMANGULAR** commands.

Radius Dimensions

You use the **DIMRADIUS** command to create radius dimensions to arc and circular features, such as fillets and rounds. The text displays R and the measured radius. (You can also display a center mark if the **DIMCEN** variable is nonzero.) At the command line, enter "dimradius". Or, choose the Radius Dimension icon on the Dimension toolbar, and the following prompt sequence will appear:

```
Select arc or circle: <You pick the arc or circle>
Enter Dimension text = (The correct dimension will appear here)
Specify dimension line location or [Mtext/Text/Angle]: <Specify
  an option or pick the location >
```

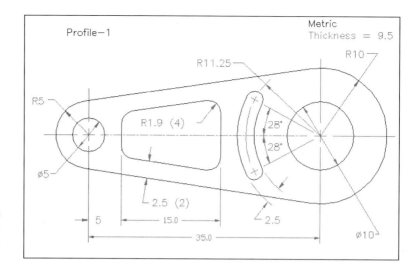

Figure 10.13
Use **DIMLINEAR** and
DIMALIGNED to dimension
the feature.

Enter the command and select your radius feature to dimension. To place the text, move your cursor about the feature and choose a suitable text location. The R for Radius is automatically added to the object's dimension.

You also have the **M (Mtext)**, **T (Text)**, and **A (Angle)** options, which are explained in the "Linear Dimensions" section earlier in this chapter. You'll see examples of using **DIMRADIUS** in Figure 10.14.

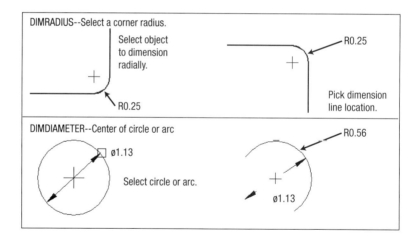

Figure 10.14
Use **DIMRADIUS** and
DIMDIAMETER to dimension
a feature.

Diameter Dimensions

Using the **DIMDIAMETER** command, you can create diameter dimensions for arc and circular objects. AutoCAD will automatically place a diameter symbol in the text line. The cursor position determines the type and placement of diameter dimensions. To activate the command, type "dimdiameter" at the command line or choose the Diameter Dimension icon on the Dimension toolbar. The following prompt sequence will appear:

```
Select arc or circle: <You pick the arc or circle>
Dimension text = (The correct dimension will appear here)
```

Specify dimension line location or [Mtext/Text/Angle]: *<Specify an option or press Enter>*

Use your pick cursor to choose the diameter object for dimensioning. You can move your cursor around or in/out of the object to be dimensioned in order to locate the placement of text.

The position of your end pick point determines the text location. For example, checking the Fine Tuning checkbox of the Fit tab (in the Dimension Style dialog box) to place text manually when dimensioning will allow you either to produce a hook line from the leader to the text or to place the text inline (aligned) with the leader line. Thus, for horizontal dimension text, if the angle of the diameter line is greater than 15 degrees from the horizontal, and you place the text outside the circle or arc, AutoCAD will draw a hook line one arrowhead unit long next to the dimension text, as illustrated in Figure 10.15.

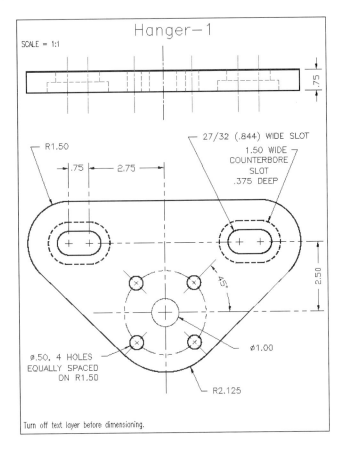

Figure 10.15
Use **DIMRADIUS** and **DIMDIAMETER** to dimension the features.

You also have the **M (Mtext)**, **T (Text)**, and **A (Angle)** options, which are explained in the "Linear Dimensions" section earlier in this chapter. The command is completed after you place the diameter dimension line.

For practice, use the **DIMRADIUS** and **DIMDIAMETER** commands to dimension the components of the hanger-1.dwg as shown in Figure 10.15. Turn off the text layer before you dimension.

Angular Dimensions

The **DIMANGULAR** command creates an angular dimension in degrees. (Remember, you are not limited to degrees; you may also dimension in Radians, Gradians, or Degrees/Minutes/Seconds.) You can create angular degree dimensions between three pick points to two angular lines and a vertex point, or between two adjacent angular lines, or to arcs or circles. To activate the command, type "dimangular" at the command line or choose the Angular Dimension icon on the Dimension toolbar. You'll see the following sequence of prompts:

```
Select arc, circle, line, or <specify vertex>: <Pick the first
  line or endpoint>
Select second line: <Pick the second line or endpoint>
Specify dimension arc line location or [Mtext/Text/Angle]:
  <Specify option or pick the dimension location >
  Dimension text = (The actual angle text is shown here)
```

Dimensioning An Angle Vertex And Two Lines

If you're dimensioning angular lines, you select three points. After pressing Enter at the command line, your three chosen points are first the vertex point (the intersection of the angle), then the endpoint of line one, and then the endpoint of line two. See the top part of Figure 10.16.

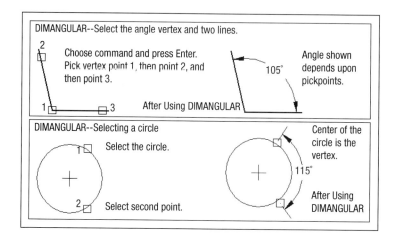

Figure 10.16
Three pick points and circle methods.

Your command line sequence would be as follows:

```
Command: dimangular
Select arc, circle, line, or <specify vertex>: <Press Enter to
  specify vertex>
Specify angle vertex: <Pick the intersection of a vertex point
  between two lines>
```

```
Specify first angle endpoint: <Pick the endpoint of the first
  line>
Specify second angle endpoint: <Pick the endpoint of the second
  line>
Specify dimension arc line location or [Mtext/Text/Angle]:
  <Specify an option or place the dimension >
Dimension text = (The actual angle text is shown here)
```

After you've picked the location, the radial and angular degree dimension lines are placed in the drawing, as shown in Figure 10.16.

Dimensioning A Circle With An Angular Dimension

If you select a circle to which you need to add an angular dimension, AutoCAD automatically determines the center of the circle as the vertex definition point. The first point you pick on the circle is the origin to the first extension line. See the bottom part of Figure 10.16. Your command line sequence would be as follows:

```
Command: dimangular
Select arc, circle, line, or <specify vertex>: <Pick the circle>
Specify second angle endpoint: <Pick a second point>
Specify dimension arc line location or [Mtext/Text/Angle]: <Pick
  the location>
Dimension text = (The actual angle text is shown here)
```

After you've chosen a second pick point, a dimension line arc is produced with angular degrees. At this point, you need to locate the dimension text.

Dimensioning An Arc With An Angular Dimension

If you select an arc with angular dimensions, AutoCAD automatically defines the arc center and arc endpoints. A dimension line arc is produced with angular degrees. See Figure 10.17.

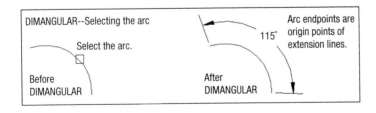

Figure 10.17
Arc entry method.

The location prompt is finally returned. Here is how the command prompts appear on screen:

```
Command: dimangular
Select arc, circle, line, or <specify vertex>: <Pick the arc>
Specify dimension arc line location or [Mtext/Text/Angle]: <Place
  the angular dimension>
Dimension text = (The actual angle text is shown here)
```

Dimenioning A Line With An Angular Dimension

To dimension an angular line, choose one of the two lines you want to dimension. See Figure 10.18. If you've selected a line, the prompt

```
Select second line:
```

is returned. Select the other line and the location prompt is finally returned.

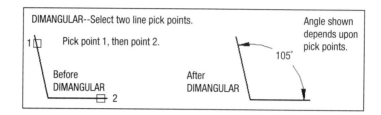

Figure 10.18
Line entry method.

For practice, open the profile-1.dwg drawing from the CD-ROM and dimension it as shown in Figure 10.13. Use the **DIMLINEAR**, **DIMRADIUS**, **DIMDIAMETER**, and **DIMANGULAR** commands. It's set to dimension on the dims layer, so you'll need to turn off the text layer before you start.

Quick Dimensions

The new **QDIM** command lets you quickly create a dimension by choosing an object. Options to access the command include:

- Picking the Quick Dimension icon from the Dimension toolbar.

- Choosing Qdim from the Dimension menu.

- Entering "qdim" at the command line prompt.

You'll find the **QDIM** command useful for creating a sequence of baseline or continued dimensions, and also for dimensioning a sequence of arcs and circles.

If you enter the **QDIM** command or choose the Quick Dimension icon, this prompt is returned:

```
Select geometry to dimension: <Pick the object to dimension and
    then press Enter>
```

After you've picked the object, the next prompt specifies these options:

```
Specify dimension line position, or [Continuous/Staggered/
    Baseline/Ordinate/Radius/Diameter/datumPoint/Edit] <Current>:
    <You need to enter an option or press Enter>
```

The options are as follows:

- ***Continuous***—Produces a succession of continued dimensions.

- ***Staggered***—Makes an array of staggered dimensions.

- *Baseline*—Creates an array of baseline dimensions.

- *Ordinate*—Produces a series of ordinate dimensions.

- *Radius*—Creates a series of radius dimensions.

- *Diameter*—Generates a series of diameter dimensions.

- *Datum Point*—Sets a new datum point for baseline and ordinate dimensions. AutoCAD prompts you for the new datum point. After you've picked the new datum point, the command then returns you to the main option prompt. Then, you choose the **Baseline** or **Ordinate** option and pick the side to dimension.

- *Edit*—Edits a series of dimensions. AutoCAD prompts you to add or remove points from existing dimensions. After activating the **QDIM** command and picking the geometry to dimension, enter "e" for edit. Doing so produces vertex points and the following prompt:

```
Indicate dimension point to remove, or [Add/eXit] <eXit>:
```

To use the e for **Edit** option within **QDIM**, enter "r" to remove or "a" to add a dimension point. (Entering "x" will exit the option.) Notice as you choose the **Edit** option that vertex points (small x's) appear at each of the node points on your geometry. This is the vertex selection set or what AutoCAD has found as your selection set; it is these vertex points that you remove or add. If you enter "r", you simply move about the drawing and pick which vertex points you wish to remove. (Pick as many as needed.) If you pick more than you intended, simply use "a" for **Add** option; then, repick the points to add them back to the selection set. Finally, enter "x" to complete the selection, and then place your quick dimensions.

AutoCAD 2000 lets you open multiple drawings at once. So while you retain the dimension-1.dwg, you can also access the qdim-1.dwg from the CD-ROM. Use the **QDIM** command to place three sets of quick dimensions on the qdim-1.dwg drawing, as shown in Figure 10.19.

Baseline Dimensions

Often, you need to continue a horizontal, vertical, angular, or ordinate dimension with a baseline or parallel dimension. The **DIMBASELINE** command expects that you'll create baseline dimensions from previous horizontal, vertical, angular, and/or ordinate dimensions. This command lets you produce a series of related dimensions, each of which are measured from the same origin point or baseline. To access the command from the

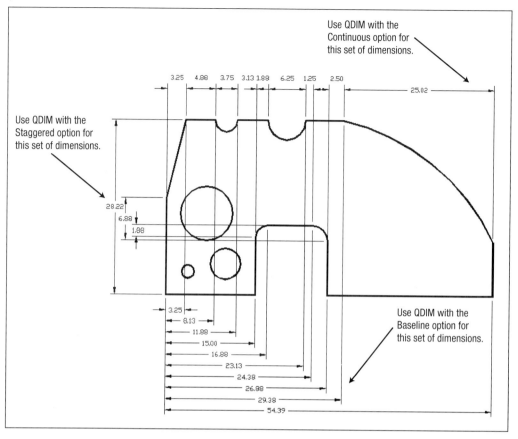

Figure 10.19

Use Quick Dimension to dimension multiple features.

command line, enter "dimbaseline". Or choose the Baseline Dimension icon on the Dimension toolbar. The prompt

```
Select base dimension:
Specify a second extension line origin or [Undo/Select] <Select>:
```

is returned at the command prompt line.

At this point, if you press Enter, the command expects you to pick a base dimension and then the second point; alternatively, if you've been working with a dimension, you can choose a second extension line origin. Remember, the previous dimension you pick must be either a linear, angular, or ordinate dimension. Once you've picked the dimension and dimension point, the second extension line prompt is returned again to let you pick further baselines. To end the command, press Esc. (Alternatively, use a right-click of the mouse and press Enter.)

For practice, use the **DIMBASELINE** command to continue the baseline feature components of the panel-1.dwg, as shown in Figure 10.20. Remember to press Enter to pick the base dimension (only if you want to change the base dimension currently being used) and then pick the second point of the chosen extension line origin. Don't save the file—you'll use it again.

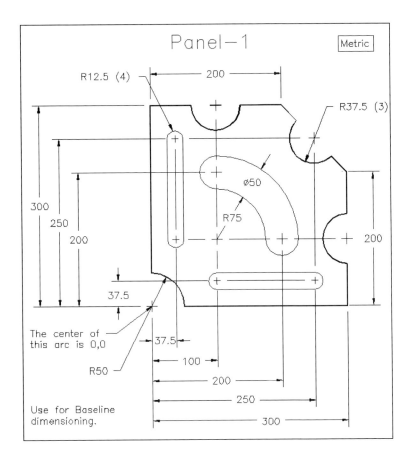

Figure 10.20

Use **DIMBASELINE** to dimension the feature.

Continuing Dimensions

The **DIMCONTINUE** command continues a horizontal, vertical, angular, or ordinate dimension into a sequential chain of dimensions. You can also continue dimensions between previously created horizontal, vertical, angular, and ordinate dimensions. This command produces a series of interrelated dimensions, each of which is measured from the previous origin point. To access the command from the command line, enter "dimcontinue". Or, choose the Continue Dimension icon on the Dimension toolbar. The prompt

```
Specify a second extension line origin or [Undo/Select] <Select>:
```

is returned.

You can select a dimension by pressing Enter or choose a second extension line origin. The previous dimension you choose must be linear, angular, or ordinate. The select extension line prompt is then returned to allow you to choose further baselines. Press Esc to end the command. See Figure 10.21.

Reopen the panel-1.dwg drawing and use the **DIMCONTINUE** command to continue the sequential components of the drawing as shown in Figure 10.18. Remember to press Enter to pick the dimension to be continued, and then pick the second point of the chosen extension line origin.

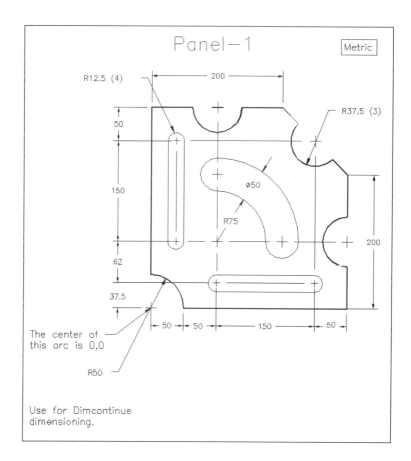

Figure 10.21
Use **DIMCONTINUE** to dimension the feature.

Center-Mark And Center-Line Dimensions

The **DIMCENTER** command creates center-mark points or center-line points for an arc or circle. After you've created the arcs and circles, you'll need to enter settings in the Lines And Arrows tab of the Modify Dimension Style dialog box, which controls the settings for center-mark points and center-line points. The difference between a center mark and a center line is the size. A center mark is a small plus mark placed in the center of the arc or circle, whereas a center line reaches the outer edges of the arc or circle, as illustrated in Figure 10.22. To access the command from the command line,

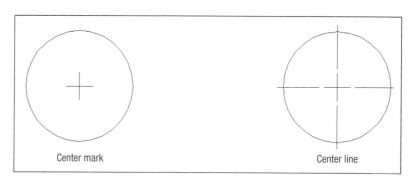

Figure 10.22
Center mark and center line of a circle or arc.

enter "dimcenter". Or choose the Center Mark icon from the Dimension toolbar. The prompt

```
Select arc or circle:
```

is returned. You can now select an arc or a circle in which to produce a center mark or a center line.

You can open any of the drawings in this chapter and use the **DIMCENTER** command to place center marks and center lines.

Ordinate Dimensions, Leader Lines, And Geometric Tolerancing

Ordinate or *datum* dimensions refer to the lines that extend from an object in the drawing to the dimension text as leader lines. A small amount of setup is required before you create ordinate dimensions, because AutoCAD measures the ordinates from an origin point (0,0,0) of the current UCS. Use the "o" for **Origin** option of the **UCS** command to move the current UCS origin to a chosen dimension origin. Any text placed is aligned with the leader.

Geometric dimensioning and tolerancing (GD&T) refers to a series of geometric tolerance symbols and datum planes that are used to dimension a 3D feature or part. You can create geometric tolerances to define allowable variations such as profile, location, orientation, and runout of an AutoCAD 3D object.

A *leader line* and its text connect to a dimension feature. The **LEADER** command lets you create complex leader lines. The annotation attached to the leader line can be edited through the Modify|Text command. You can choose the **LEADER** command at any time and create complex leaders.

DIMORDINATE Dimensions

Ordinate dimensions are used between X and Y datum points on a feature. Before using the **DIMORDINATE** command, you first set the UCS to an origin point on the part to be dimensioned; then, you create your dimensions. The origin setting can be the lower-left corner of the part or a locator hole, for example. The resultant new UCS is the origin point for the **DIMORDINATE** command. Remember that if you don't set the UCS to a new origin, the default WCS origin will be used. See Figure 10.23.

For practice, you can open the plate-1.dwg file from the CD-ROM and use the **DIMORDINATE** command to place ordinate dimensions as shown in Figure 10.23.

To access the command, you can enter "dimordinate" at the command line or choose the Ordinate Dimension icon on the Dimension toolbar. The prompt

```
Specify feature location:
```

Note: You can also use the **DIMCEN** variable. If you set the variable to a positive number (for example, 0.09), it sets a center-mark point. If you set it to a negative number (for example, 0.-09), it creates center lines. Figure 10.22 has a center mark on the left and a center line to the right. (The arbitrary numbers of 0.09 and –0.09 just mentioned are relative numbers; your default setting is 0.09.)

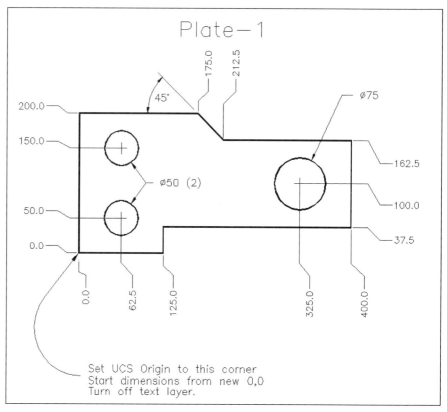

Figure 10.23
Use **DIMORDINATE** to specify multiple features.

is returned. Now, you can select the feature(s) you want to dimension. As you choose the feature, the prompt

```
Specify leader endpoint or [Xdatum/Ydatum/Mtext/Text/Angle]:
```

is returned. You can either pick a point, enter "x" and a point, or enter "y" and a point:

- *Leader endpoint*—Simply choose any endpoint, and AutoCAD will determine if it's an X or Y datum leader point and create the dimension text accordingly.

- *X (Xdatum)*—If you enter "x", you force AutoCAD to use the UCS origin as a start point, to measure the distance in the X direction, and to prompt you for a leader endpoint.

- *Y (Ydatum)*—If you enter "y", you force AutoCAD to use the UCS origin as a start point, to measure the distance in the Y direction, and to prompt you for a leader endpoint.

After you've chosen the leader endpoint and X or Y origin, the prompt

```
Specify leader endpoint or [Xdatum/Ydatum/Mtext/Text/Angle]:
```

is again returned. At this point, you can simply pick a location for the dimension line. Or, at the command prompt, enter the **M (Mtext)**, **T (Text)**, and **A (Angle)** options, as explained in the "Linear Dimensions" section earlier in this chapter.

Quick Leaders

AutoCAD 2000 has two types of leader: a standard leader (**LEADER** command) and a quick leader (**QLEADER** command). They both produce leader lines, but of varying complexity. The **LEADER** command produces simple leader lines, and the **QLEADER** command allows you to access a dialog box that gives you more control over the text, the leader line and arrows, and how you attach the text to the leader.

You use quick leaders to create a leader line and text to connect to a dimension feature. You can create quick leader lines for any type of object or dimension. The **QLEADER** command also allows you to create complex leader line (as opposed to the **LEADER** command, which creates simplified leader lines). Any annotation you attach to the leader line can be edited by choosing Modify|Edit Text. You can choose the **QLEADER** command at any time and provide multiple pick points to create complex leaders.

To access the command, enter "qleader" at the command line. Or, choose the Quick Leader icon on the Dimension toolbar. The resulting prompt is as follows:

```
Specify first leader point, or [Settings]<Settings>:
```

It allows you to select a series of points for the leader line. It keeps prompting as

```
Specify next point: <Enter point>
Specify text width <0.000>: <Enter width>
Enter first line of annotation text <Mtext>:
```

At this last prompt, you can either enter the new text at the command prompt or press Enter to access the Multiline Text Editor, and then place your specific text.

Alternatively, if you press Enter after starting the **QLEADER** command, the Leader Settings dialog box will open. Within the body of the Leader Settings dialog box are three tabs: Annotation, Leader Line & Arrow, and Attachment. You use the Leader Setting dialog box to force AutoCAD to set up its leader lines in a specific way or method. The options on the various tabs of the dialog box are described in the following sections.

Leader Settings Dialog Box, AnnotationTab

The Annotation tab of the Leader Settings dialog box, shown in Figure 10.24, allows you to insert text at the end of the leader line. It has three main

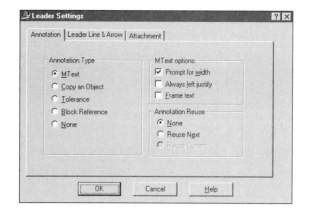

Figure 10.24

The Annotation tab of the Leader Settings dialog box.

sections: Annotation Type, MText Options, and Annotation Reuse. Each of the three sections has multiple radio buttons and checkboxes.

The Mtext Options section is self-explanatory apart from Frame Text, which places a text frame around the mtext annotation. The Annotation Reuse section simply sets options for reusing the leader annotation. The Annotation Type section contains the following radio buttons:

- *MText*—Activates and enters the Multiline Text Editor dialog box.

- *Copy An Object*—Simply prompts you to copy multiline text, single text, a tolerance, or a block to the leader line termination point.

- *Tolerance*—Provides access to a Geometric Tolerance control frame and a Symbol dialog box that allow you to set a datum for a geometric tolerance. See the "Geometric Dimension And Tolerancing" section later in this chapter.

- *Block Reference*—Lets you insert a block as a reference at the end of the leader line.

- *None*—Ends the command and doesn't place any text. (Notice that if you choose None in both the Annotation Type and Annotation Reuse areas of the dialog box, AutoCAD removes the Attachment tab. This action forces the **QLEADER** command into a leader option only without text.)

Leader Settings Dialog Box, Leader Line & Arrow Tab

The Leader Line & Arrow tab of the dialog box, shown in Figure 10.25, provides control over the leader line, arrowhead, and angle constraints with multiple options. Options you can set include:

- *Straight radio button*—Creates a leader line in straight line segments.

- *Spline radio button*—Creates a leader line as a splined (smoothed) curve, using pick points as control points.

- *Number Of Points section*—Refers to how many pick points you want the leader line to have before the text is attached. (The default is three, so

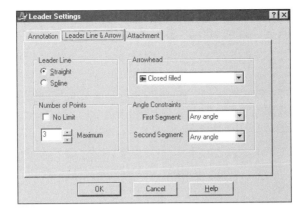

Figure 10.25

The Leader Line & Arrow tab of the Leader Settings dialog box.

after two leader pick points AutoCAD prompts for the text as the third pick point.)

- *Arrowhead drop-down list*—Creates a leader line with an arrowhead attached to the start point. You can choose from 21 options for arrowheads.

- *Angle Constraints section*—Forces AutoCAD to draw the first and/or second segments of the leader line to a specific angle. Choices include Any Angle, Horizontal, 90, 45, 30, and 15 degrees.

Leader Settings Dialog Box, Attachment Tab

The Attachment tab of the dialog box, shown in Figure 10.26, is used as a justification prompt. It forces the multiline text attachment into a left or right justification and into a top, middle, or bottom mode. The tab also includes an Underline Bottom Line option.

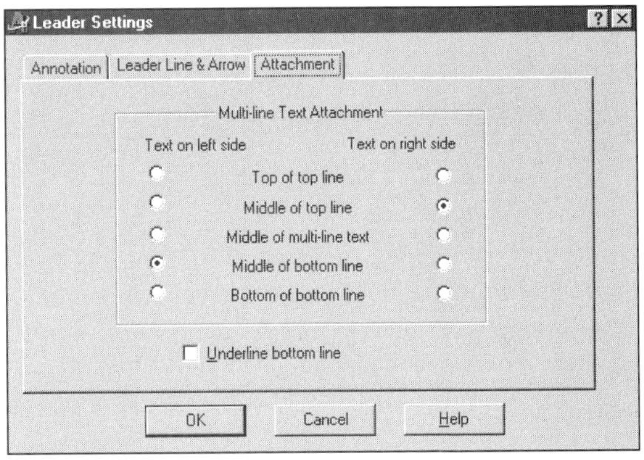

Figure 10.26

The Attachment tab of the Leader Settings dialog box.

Geometric Dimensioning And Tolerancing

So far, you've looked at location dimensions and their use to locate features and parts, which often use 2D plus/minus tolerances, along with general notes attached to leaders and tolerance limits. But 2D location dimensions don't take into account the 3D shape description of the tolerance zone. You often need to indicate by how much the 3D shape of the perfect part you've drawn can vary, to what 3D shape is acceptable when it's actually produced. You do this through the international language of geometric dimensioning and tolerancing (GD&T). Simply think of GD&T as a 3D tolerancing tool. The purpose of GD&T is to allow you to accurately describe the perfect geometry of the part you're tolerancing in three dimensions. GD&T uses international symbols to describe the model and uses the geometric tolerancing to define the allowable shape variations of features or to define the position of features. See Figure 10.27.

Feature Type	Tolerance Type	Characteristic	Tolerance Symbol	2D/3D	Controls	
					Surface	**Axis/Median Plane**
Individual Feature	Form	Straightness	———	2D/3D	2D Surface (Line Element)	3D Axis/Median
		Flatness	▱	3D	3D Surface	
		Circularity	○	2D	2D Surface	
		Cylindricity	/○/	3D	3D Surface	
Individual or Related Feature	Profile	Line Profile	⌒	2D	2D Surface	
		Surface Profile	◠	3D	3D Surface	
Related Feature	Orientation	Angularity	∠	2D/3D	2D Surface (Line Element)	3D Axis/Median
		Perpendicularity	⊥	2D/3D	2D Surface (Line Element)	3D Axis/Median
		Parallelism	//	2D/3D	2D Surface (Line Element)	3D Axis/Median
	Location	Position	⊕	2D/3D	2D Surface Boundary	3D Axis/Median
		Concentricity	◎	3D	(Opposite Median Points)	3D Axis/Median
		Symmetry	⌰	3D	(Opposite Median Points)	3D Axis/Median
	Runout	Circular Runout	↗	2D	2D Surface	
		Total Runout	↗↗	3D	3D Surface	

Figure 10.27

GD&T tolerance characteristic symbols for shape and position of a feature.

In the world of visual graphics, GD&T has been around only since the 1930s. Stanley Parker of the Royal Torpedo Factory in Scotland U.K., among others, started to devise GD&T after realizing that the limited type of tolerancing he was using had problems and limitations with 3D features. The tolerancing needed to be more precise. From that early beginning, both ANSI and ISO have produced standards that reflect GD&T principles and methods of tolerancing. It's simply another form of mathematical language. The GD&T system is based on the ANSI Y-14 standards, which in turn are based on the metric system and the millimeter as the unit of measurement. If required, inch units with decimal fractions can be used as a substitute. As you can see in Figure 10.28, the profile of the surface of the part shows how a .005 tolerance zone would be viewed by GD&T. The dimensions within the boxes, called basic dimensions, indicate the dimensions of the perfect part. The shaded portion around the profile of the part indicates the theoretical tolerance limits to which the part could be shaped and still pass inspection.

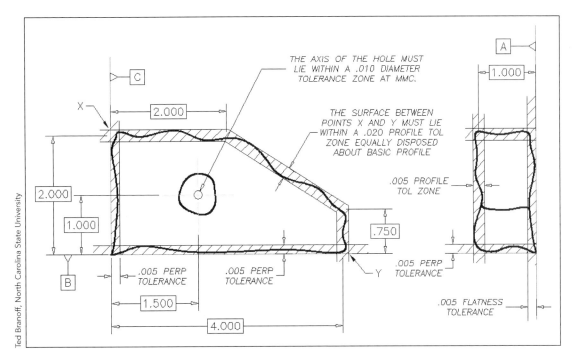

Ted Branoff, North Carolina State University

Figure 10.28

The profile of a surface showing how a .005 tolerance zone is viewed by GD&T.

In AutoCAD, you'll use the **TOLERANCE, QLEADER,** or **LEADER** command to create a geometric tolerance as a dimension feature. In addition, you can choose between two divisions or types of geometric dimension and tolerance symbols:

- *Form tolerance*—Defines the shape of the feature.

- *Position tolerance*—Defines the location of the feature. Further indicators describe whether the feature is an individual feature or a datum-referenced related feature.

Individual features include the form, profile, location, orientation, and runout of an AutoCAD object as a geometric tolerance dimension. Within AutoCAD, a series of dialog boxes (Geometric Tolerance, Symbol, and Material Condition) helps you create specific tolerance symbols and geometry.

You can use a number of methods to activate the **TOLERANCE** command:

- At the command line, enter "tolerance".

- Choose the Qleader icon, press Enter, and set the Annotation Type to Tolerance on the Annotation tab of the Leader Settings dialog box.

- Choose the Tolerance icon from the Dimension toolbar.

In each case, the Geometric Tolerance dialog box opens (see Figure 10.29). Let's start to enter data (as shown in Figure 10.29) to create a feature control frame. Figure 10.30 shows the different parts of the completed tolerance feature control frame. This dialog box is split into six parts from left to right:

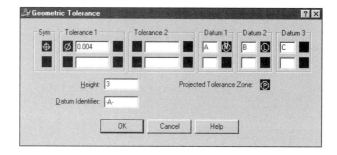

Figure 10.29
The Geometric Tolerance
dialog box.

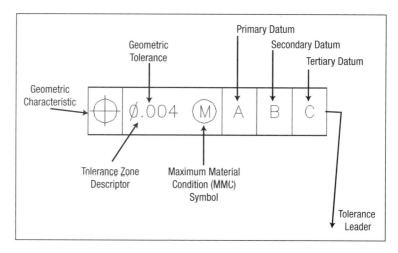

Figure 10.30
A typical tolerance feature
control frame.

Figure 10.31
The Symbol dialog box for
geometric tolerance.

- *Sym*—This section displays the Symbol dialog box, shown in Figure 10.31. If you pick the Sym area, you should then pick one of the 15 symbols from the Symbol dialog box (the default is a blank). Repicking the Sym part of the dialog box allows you to change the symbol.

- *Tolerance 1 & 2*—These sections set up the first and second tolerance values to be viewed in the feature control frame.

- *Datum 1, 2, and 3*—GD&T works on a three-datum plane concept. A *datum plane* is an exact geometric reference used to establish the specific origin for the toleranced dimension of the feature. In the three-datum plane concept, three mutually perpendicular datum planes are used to accurately dimension the object. The three datums create primary, secondary, and tertiary datum references in the feature control frame. The primary datum can have three contact points with the datum, the secondary can have two points, and the tertiary can have a single point. (These could simply be labeled A, B, and C for priority.) Each datum reference consists of a value and a Material Condition (MC) modifying symbol. The symbol options—available from the Material Condition dialog box, shown in Figure 10.32—are M (maximum material condition), L (least material condition), and S (regardless of feature size [RFS]).

Figure 10.32
The Material Condition dialog box.

In addition to containing six parts, the Geometric Tolerance dialog box includes three options:

- *Height*—Used in the feature control frame as a projected tolerance zone value. This value controls the height of the extended portion of a fixed vertical part. You simply enter the value in the text box.

- *Projected Tolerance Zone*—Used to insert a projected tolerance zone symbol, P, after a zone value has been entered.

- *Datum Identifier*—The reference letter used as a datum identifying symbol. It may have a dash placed before and after it (for example, -B-).

Click on OK when you've inserted all the geometric tolerance symbols into the dialog box. Doing so provides a final response of:

```
Enter tolerance location:
```

You then place the feature control frame reference symbol into the drawing.

For practice with GD&T symbols and dimensions, open the angle-block.dwg file from this book's companion CD-ROM. Figure 10.33 shows the complete dimensions and the location of each A, B, and C datum to the simple part. Remember to check that the Tolerance tab of the Dimension Style dialog box is set to the Basic Method. This should be preset for you in the angle-block.dwg file. I suggest that you should start with the basic dimensions first (the dimensions in boxes), then apply the tolerance dimensions to each A, B, C datum, then place the leader tolerance dimensions, and finally create the diameter dimensions.

Rules Of Geometric Tolerancing

Here are three general rules for geometric tolerancing:

- *Position tolerance*—When a tolerance of position is specified on an object—such as MMC, LMC, or RFS—it should be specified in respect to the tolerance, the datum, or both the tolerance and the datum.

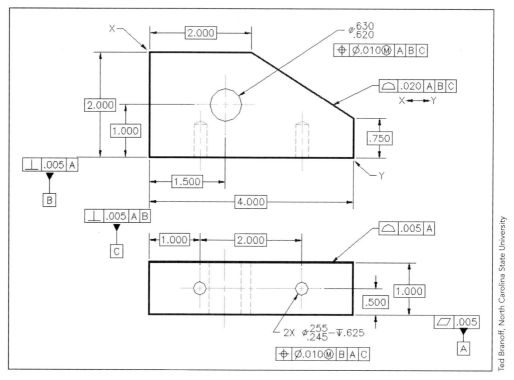

Figure 10.33

The completed GD&T tolerances to the angle-block part.

- *Feature size*—When only a tolerance of size is specified on a part, the limits of size prescribe the amount of variation allowed in its geometric form.

- *Other geometry*—RFS applies to all other geometric tolerances, especially to individual tolerances and datum references if no modifying symbol is used in the feature control symbol. If a feature is at MMC, it should be specified as MMC.

Editing Dimensions

The Properties and Text options of the Modify menu allow you to edit dimensions and text. Thus, you can edit dimensions in a number of ways: through the Properties dialog box, the single-line Edit Text dialog box, or the Multiline Text Editor dialog box. AutoCAD commands to activate these include **DIMEDIT**, **DIMTEDIT**, **DDEDIT**, **DDMODIFY**, and **PROPERTIES**.

Both the **DIMEDIT** and **DIMTEDIT** commands allow you to alter text and dimension extension lines at a command prompt. On the other hand, the **DDEDIT** command uses either the Edit Text or the Multiline Text Editor dialog box, depending on whether you wish to edit single-line text or multiline text. The **PROPERTIES** and **DDMODIFY** commands allow further editing functions through the Properties dialog box.

Dimension Editing with **DIMEDIT**

DIMEDIT provides **Home**, **New**, and **Rotate** options to let you edit dimension text. The **Oblique** option of the command lets you adjust the angle of the dimension lines attached to the dimension text. This command allows you to edit both dimension text and extension lines. You can use **DIMEDIT** on more than one dimension object at a time; you can also rotate and adjust the oblique angle of the dimension text and the dimension lines.

You can access the **DIMEDIT** command using three methods:

- Entering "dimedit" at the command line prompt.

- Choose Oblique from the Dimension menu.

- Pick the Dimension Edit icon from the Dimension toolbar. The main **DIMEDIT** prompt

```
Enter type of dimension editing [Home/New/Rotate/Oblique]
   <Home>:
```

is returned. At this point, you select an option and then pick a dimension object. The options are as follows (see Figures 10.34 and 10.35):

- *H (Home)*—Returns the dimension text to its original location. This default option works with previously altered dimension text. Enter "h" at the prompt and press Enter. Then, at the **Select objects** prompt, choose the text and once again press Enter.

- *N (New)*—Allows you to alter the dimension text or dimension symbols via the Multiline Text Editor dialog box. Within the dialog box, you change the text and then click on OK. A **Select objects** prompt then allows you to choose the dimension text to change. Entering "n" at the prompt activates the Multiline Text Editor, with a pair of <> brackets, as a symbol of the original text. Simply enter the new text in the dialog box and delete the <> brackets. Click on the OK button and then choose the dimension text you wish to adjust.

- *R (Rotate)*—Allows you to rotate dimension text. (This option is similar to the **Angle** option of **DIMTEDIT**.) The **Specify angle for dimension text** prompt allows you to specify an angle, such as 0, 15, 30, 45, 90, 135, 180, or 270. You enter an angle and then select a dimension text object. It works as follows: Entering "r" for rotate will supply the prompt of **Specify angle for dimension text**. Simply enter a suitable angle as previously suggested, press Enter, and then pick the text.

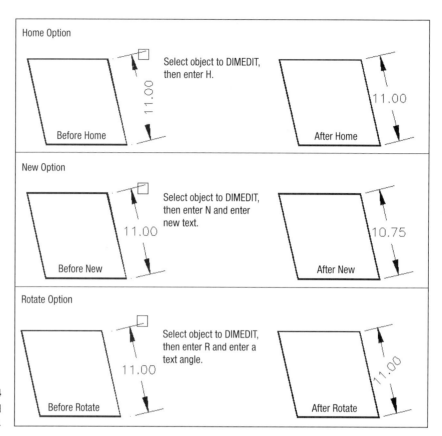

Figure 10.34
The **DIMEDIT Home**, **New**, and **Rotate** options.

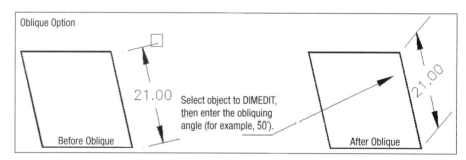

Figure 10.35
The **DIMEDIT Oblique** option.

- *O (Oblique)*—Lets you force the dimension extension lines to an oblique angle. To use it, enter "o" for oblique, pick the dimension you wish to alter, and then press Enter. The resultant prompt is **Enter obliquing angle <Press ENTER for none>**. At this point, simply enter a new oblique angle and press Enter. Both your dimension text and dimension lines are then adjusted to the new angle.

An alternate option is to choose Oblique from the Dimension menu, which forces the **DIMEDIT** command into an Oblique mode. The **Oblique** option lets you alter the obliquing angle of the linear dimension extension line. See Figure 10.35. Hint: Use the **Oblique** option when you have feature and extension line conflicts. It will move the extension lines away from the feature.

Dimension Text Editing With **DIMTEDIT**

The **DIMTEDIT** command only allows you to move and rotate dimension text; you need to use **DIMEDIT** to actually edit the text. Its features allow you to justify (move) text to the left, right, center, or home. It also lets you adjust the angle of the dimension text. The **Left** and **Right** options work only with linear, radius, and diameter style dimensions. Your activation options include:

- Enter "dimtedit" at the command line.

- Choose the Dimension Text Edit icon from the Dimension toolbar.

- Alternatively, choose Align Text from the Dimension menu, which uses the preset options of **Home**, **Angle**, **Left**, **Center**, and **Right**.

If you enter **DIMTEDIT** at the command line, the prompt

```
Select Dimension:
```

is returned. You select a single dimension. A further prompt of

```
Specify new location for dimension text or [Left/Right/Center/
   Home/Angle]:
```

is returned. At this point, you enter an option and move your cursor to drag and position the dimension text to a new location. It drags dynamically, letting you view the new position point as you move the cursor. The options are as follows (see Figure 10.36):

- *Left*—Acts as a justifier and allows you to move the dimension text to the left. Use for Linear, Radius, and Diameter dimensions. Turn **DIMSHO** to ON to see dimension being dragged.

- *Right*—Acts as a justifier and lets you move the dimension text to the right.

- *Center*—Acts as a justifier and forces the text to be in the center of the dimension line.

- *Home*—Returns the dimension text to its original position.

- *Angle*—Alters the angle of the dimension text. The prompt **Enter Text Angle** is returned. Enter an angle such as 0, 45, 90, 135, 180, or 270, and then select the dimension.

Dimension Text Editing with **DDEDIT**

DDEDIT allows you to edit dimension text. You can edit single-line text, paragraphs of text, and single text characters. Depending upon the type of

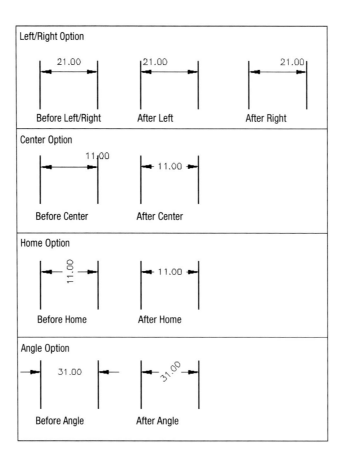

Figure 10.36
Editing with **DIMTEDIT**.

text you need to edit, the command will use one of two types of dialog boxes: a single-line text editor or a multiline text editor. The options to activate the command are as follows:

• Enter "ddedit" at the command prompt.

• Choose the Properties icon from the Standard Toolbar.

• Choose the Text command from the Modify menu.

The prompt

```
Select an annotation object or [Undo]:
```

is returned. If you have normal single-line text editing, the **DDEDIT** command activates the Edit Text dialog box. See Figure 10.37. If you've used dimension and multiline paragraph type text, the **DDEDIT** command opens the Multiline Text Editor dialog box. The Multiline Text Editor creates or

Figure 10.37
The Edit Text dialog box.

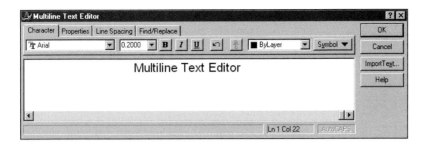

Figure 10.38
The Multiline Text Editor
dialog box.

modifies multiline text objects. It also lets you import and paste text created from other files (TXT and RTF). See Figure 10.38.

The Multiline Text Editor has four tabs:

- *Character*—Lets you control character formatting for text entered at the keyboard or for text imported into the Multiline Text Editor. It includes options such as choosing a font, setting text height, bolding text, italicizing text, underlining text, stacking text, assigning a text color or AutoCAD Color Index, and setting a symbol.

- *Properties*—Lets you alter text style, justification, width, and rotation.

- *Line Spacing*—Lets you control line spacing for new or selected multiline text.

- *Find/Replace*—Lets you search for specified text strings and replace them with new text.

The Stack button (indicated by a/b) converts the selected region into stacked text or stacked fractions. Select any text you want to convert and then click on the Stack button. It converts the selected text into stacked text or stacked fractions.

The Symbol drop-down list lets you select any type of symbol you need. If you pick the Other option, it opens the Unicode Character Map dialog box. Hint: If you select the GDT font within the Unicode Character Map dialog box, you can place GDT symbols into your drawing.

The Import Text button activates the Open dialog box. This dialog box lets you select an ASCII (TXT) text file or a Rich Text Format (RTF) file to import into the Multiline Text Editor.

Dimension Variables And DIMOVERRIDE

DIMOVERRIDE allows you to override any dimension system variable's setting. It doesn't affect the dimension style the dimension is attached to. Listed as Override in the Dimension menu, the **DIMOVERRIDE** command overrules and invalidates prior settings used to dimension chosen objects.

You have a number of options to activate the command: enter "dimoverride" at the command line, pick the Override button in the Dimension Style Manager dialog box, or access the **OVERRIDE** command from the dimension menu.

When you start the command from the dimension menu, the prompt

```
Enter dimension variable name to override or [Clear overrides]:
```

is returned. Enter a system variable name or the letter c. If you enter "c" and then select objects, the command will clear any overrides on dimensions on the chosen object. If you enter a system variable name, a further prompt of

```
Enter new value for dimension variable < >:
```

is returned. At this point, you can enter a new value for the dimension system variable or press Enter to exit.

If you enter a value, the

```
Enter dimension variable name to override:
```

prompt will appear. If you press Enter, the next prompt

```
Select objects:
```

will ask you to select an object to change. After you select the object(s) to override, the command exits.

You can press Esc at any point to exit the command. See Figure 10.39 for a visual explanation of the dimension variables and their uses.

To find out which dimension variables have overrides, use the **LIST** command on each dimension you need to check. Open the qdim-2.dwg file from the CD-ROM and use the **LIST** command on a few of the dimensions. You'll see the overridden dimension variables listed in the text window.

Associative Dimensions

Using associative dimensioning, or the more complex ordinate and geometric dimensioning and tolerancing, you can create any type of dimension in AutoCAD. An *associative dimension* in AutoCAD is a type of dimension that automatically adjusts as you alter the geometry of the part the dimension is attached to (system variable **DIMASO** is set to ON for associative dimensions). AutoCAD's associative dimensions are unique because you create them the same way as regular dimensions, and they have special properties that allow you to use them as you edit your drawing. If you treat them as a single object, they can be stretched, scaled, or rotated at the same time your object is being stretched, scaled, or rotated. The dimension is

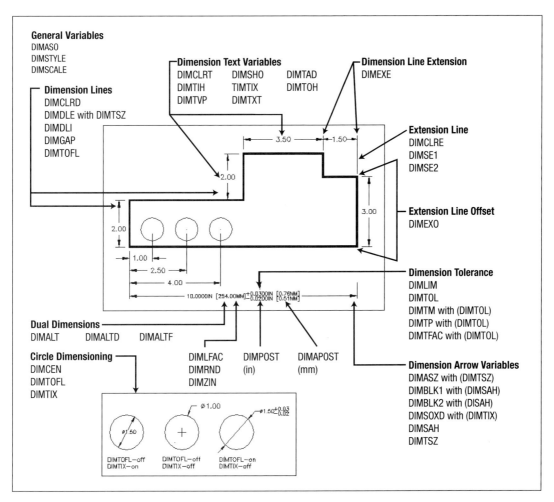

Figure 10.39

Visual explanation of AutoCAD's dimension variables.

automatically realigned, and its text is updated as you stretch, scale, rotate, and/or revise your drawings.

There are some limitations when using associative dimensions in AutoCAD; remember that they are not parametric, just associative, and that they work with only certain command types. For example, the Linear, Radius, and Angular styles of dimension commands let you create associative dimensions, whereas the **LEADER** and **CENTER** commands can't generate associative dimensions. See Figure 10.40. In addition, you can edit your associative dimensions or change your drawings through the dimension structure.

An *associative dimension* is a dimension that adapts as the associated geometry is modified around it. For example, if you stretch an object, the dimension is also stretched and automatically updated to the new dimension. (Think of the dimension as being hot linked to your object, so if the object is stretched or shrunk, the dimension stretches or shrinks accordingly and in doing so will display the true dimension of the new adjusted size.)

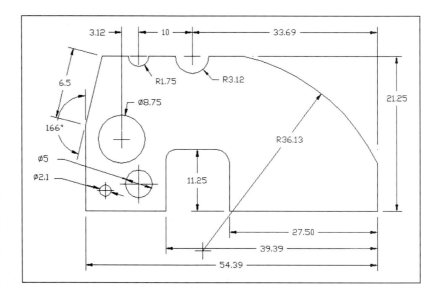

Figure 10.40
Only the **DIMLINEAR**,
DIMRADIUS, and
DIMANGULAR commands are
used to dimension associative
features, not the **LEADER** or
DIMCENTER command.

(Note: Don't think of the dimensions as being parametric, because they aren't. You're either stretching the definition points with grips or the **STRETCH** command.)

Associative dimensions are controlled by special definition points (small dots called *grips*). For example, a **DIMLINEAR** horizontal, vertical, or aligned dimension has grip definition points located at the origin point of the witness lines, at the first end of the dimension line, and at the midpoint of the text. Two of these grips (definition points) lie under object lines, so they should be automatically included in the selection set when you stretch an object using a crossing window. If you pick any dimension, you see the definition points simply as its grips.

You must remember certain rules when using associative dimensions:

• You can stretch a dimension's text to a different place along the dimension line or even outside the dimension line, and the dimension line will adjust itself.

• When you want only one end of a dimension stretched, the end of the grip dimension point must be included in a stretch crossing window.

• Besides Stretch, Move, Rotate Scale, and Mirror, other editing commands—including Trim, Extend, and Array—can affect associative dimensions.

• If you scale or rotate some objects and select them individually with the pick box, you must remember to include the grip definition points; otherwise, the associated dimensions won't be adjusted automatically. As you edit a dimensioned object, notice whether the dimensions are highlighted (mainly to check if they've been selected).

- When you explode an associative dimension, its elements revert back to lines, arc, and text.

- Definition points are placed on a layer called Defpoints. AutoCAD automatically creates this layer and makes it nonplotting the first time you create an associative dimension. As you'd expect, while the Defpoints layer is off, the definition points won't plot. However, the screen visibility of definition points is determined by the on/off status of the layer containing the actual dimensions, not by the Defpoints layer.

To find out how easy it is to edit with associated dimensions, open the plate-1.dwg drawing from the CD-ROM and use the **STRETCH** command as shown in Figure 10.41. Make sure you use a crossing window on the picked object; then, stretch it 50mm to the right.

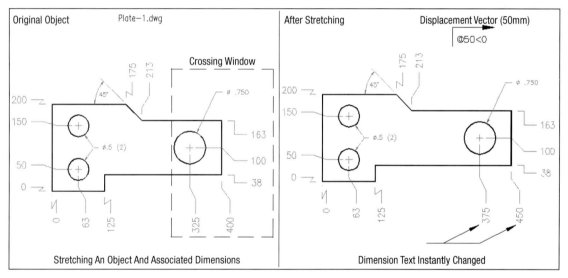

Figure 10.41

Stretching an object with dimensions.

At the prompt

```
Specify base point or displacement:
```

enter the base point as "0,0". At the next prompt

```
Specify second point of displacement:
```

enter your second point of displacement, "@50<0". Doing so stretches the object 50mm to the right.

The dim3d.lsp Program

The example program dim3d.lsp, available on this book's companion CD-ROM, dimensions automatically in 3D. It sets multiple Object Snaps to ENDpoint or INTersection and sets the UCS and direction of X by the order in which you pick the points. At the command prompt, use the **NOTEPAD** command and name the file dim3d.lsp. Then, create the file as shown in Listing 10.1.

Listing 10.1   The dim3d.lsp program.

```
(defun C:dim3d (/ cme osm e pnt1 pnt2 pnt3 a1 b1 c1)
  (setq cme (getvar "cmdecho"))
  (setvar "cmdecho" 0)
  (command "undo" "mark")
  (setq osm (getvar "osmode"))
  (setq e (car (entsel)))
  (command "ucs" "v")
  (setvar "osmode" 33)
  (setq pnt1 (getpoint "\nPick the first point  "))
  (setq pnt2 (getpoint "\nPick the second point  "))
  (setvar "osmode" 0)
  (setq pnt3 (getpoint "\nPick the dimension line location  "))
  (command "point" pnt1)
  (setq a1 (entlast))
  (command "point" pnt2)
  (setq b1 (entlast))
  (command "point" pnt3)
  (setq c1 (entlast))
  (command "ucs" "3point" pnt1 pnt2 "")
  (setq pnt1 (cdr (assoc 10 (entget a1))))
  (setq pnt2 (cdr (assoc 10 (entget b1))))
  (setq pnt3 (cdr (assoc 10 (entget c1))))
  (setq pnt1 (trans pnt1 0 1))
  (setq pnt2 (trans pnt2 0 1))
  (setq pnt3 (trans pnt3 0 1))
  (command "dim" "hor" pnt1 pnt2 pnt3 "" ^c)
  (command "erase" a1 b1 c1 "")
  (command "ucs" "p")
  (setvar "osmode" osm)
  (setvar "cmdecho" cme)
  (princ)
  )
```

To load the file, choose Load Application from the Tools menu or enter **APPLOAD** at the command prompt. Either of these actions activates the Load/Unload Application dialog box. You may want to copy the file into a suitable folder, such as the AutoCAD 2000 folder, and then load it via the dialog box. Then, to activate the LISP file, enter "dim3d" at the command prompt.

Note that the 33 **OSMODE** value (setting for the multiple object snaps) was derived by adding the code 32 for Intersection and the code 1 for Endpoint from Table 10.2. Therefore, if you want to set multiple Object Snaps, add the numbers together for the groups you want to use. For example, if you want to create a dimension tool for linear objects, which will pick either the Endpoint or the Intersection, use the 32 + 1 value. Or, you could set it for circular objects by using the 4 + 16 value (Center or Quadrant), and so on.

Table 10.2 Codes for the **OSMODE** system variable.

Code	Description
0	None
1	Endpoint
2	Midpoint
4	Center
8	Node
16	Quadrant
32	Intersection
64	Insert
128	Perpendicular
256	Tangent
512	Nearest

Moving On

One of the essential tasks of every designer is visual communication, especially through dimension and tolerance information, and how a component and its adjacent geometry fit together. From this chapter, you learned that true shape and true size descriptions are two main components needed to produce accurate CAD drawings. To achieve that end, from simple lineal to complex GD&T, AutoCAD provides a number of dimension commands.

The next chapter describes how to set up your drawings to render, shade, and hide 3D models. It explores what you need to do to render a 3D model and how to set scenes, materials, and lighting. It also reviews how to work with the **SHADE** and **RENDER** commands, how to attach materials through layers, colors, or objects, the different types of lighting, and how to set up lighting. Finally, in Chapter 12 you'll see how to import, export, and manipulate images. You'll also find tips for greater productivity with setting up scenes, views, and lighting within your drawing.

PART III

RENDERING AND IMAGE PRESENTATION

RENDERING
3D MODELS

11

*Rendering can be confusing the first
time you open AutoCAD 2000. To help you
overcome this confusion, this chapter provides
an easy, step-by-step explanation of the terms
and concepts used in AutoCAD's render package.*

Rendering Considerations

To trained technicians and draftspersons, standard orthographic drawings and wireframe models have a meaning and beauty that only they or the architects/engineers for whom they're preparing the drawings can appreciate and understand. Nontechnical persons need more training before they can begin to grasp what the 2D drawing or the 3D model represents. Fortunately, rendering can take a plain old technical drawing and make it appear to be a photograph of the finished item—so anyone who looks at it can appreciate it.

Besides visual representation, what are some of the reasons why you should draw in 3D? As just stated, on the one hand, you might wish to make a drawing more realistic so laypersons can understand it. Alternatively, many mechanical engineers use a 3D model with Computer Numerical Control (CNC) machines, or they create presentation and visualization drawings for their clients. You might also use kinematics to determine how the design of a part and its connecting joints are affected by motion and time. By using the Boolean **INTERSECT** operation, the simple animation may also be used to evaluate how parts intersect with each other for conceptualization and/or error and conflict checking to ensure that drawn parts don't conflict with each other.

The renderer in AutoCAD 2000 allows you to create visual effects and use features such as fog, scenes, photorealism, raytracing, background colors, shadow casting, reflectivity, translucency of materials, a materials library, and texture mapping. Plus, you can use true materials such as granite, wood, and marble. Lighting effects include ambient, distant, point, and spotlights. In addition, you can control colors of entities as well as the lights using both the RGB (red, green, and blue) and the HLS (hue, lightness, and saturation) methods. With the materials library and material-editing dialog box, you can control facets of any material to give it a reflection, roughness, transparency, or refraction, as well as color.

The minimum computer configuration required for a good rendering program is a Pentium-II or III with a minimum clockspeed of 350MHz and with a 4.5GB hard drive and 64 to 128MB of RAM. High speed and plenty of RAM are the keys to working with rendering programs, because rendering is an intensive operation for a computer. One piece of advice is to get the fastest computer possible. If doing so is out of your reach, then put as much RAM in your computer as possible. It has been said that you can get a 50 percent increase in speed every time you double the RAM in your computer.

Rendering Terms

Here are some of the rendering terms I'll be using in this chapter:

- *Light sources*—AutoCAD provides a number of light sources (ambient, point, distant, and spotlight), and you can adjust all four types of light sources for color and intensity. Some light sources can also be adjusted for attenuation (Inverse Square) and shadow options, plus the angle of the sun and geographic location.

- *Background illumination*—Ambient light (which is always present in a scene) represents general background illumination. Ambient light illuminates all surfaces with equal intensity and from all directions. Most of your scenes require a small amount of ambient light, which is a preset value of approximately 0.3. Setting it higher produces a flat, washed-out effect.

- *Color*—Color in the renderer serves two purposes: to supply color and to group objects with the same material and texture.

- *Diffuse reflection*—Rough or matte surfaces produce diffuse reflection and scatter light in all directions. With diffuse reflection, the surface will appear to have the same amount of brightness, no matter where the viewer is located in relation to the source of light.

- *Distant light*—You should aim distant lights at your model, because the light won't diminish regardless of the distance of travel (even though the source is an infinite distance away). You can equate a distant light source to the sun: The emitted light rays are parallel and come from one direction.

- *Polygonal shading*—For the purpose of rendering, all 3D objects in your model are converted into face meshes because face meshes consist of many small, flat faces. The smoothing controls of **SHADEMODE** in AutoCAD 2000 allow you to determine when the edges of faces should be blended into a smooth surface.

- *Point light* —A point light is similar to a light bulb, where the rays of light spread out in all directions from a single source. However, because the light rays from a real light bulb diminish as they move farther from their source, AutoCAD allows you to control this special effect by letting you set an attenuation value.

- *Rendering speed and face normals*—Rendering speed often depends upon the number of faces in your model that need to be rendered. To save time and increase speed, AutoCAD will calculate and discard the back faces of your model and not render them. It does this by checking face normals—a simple process for 3D solid and 3D mesh models, because AutoCAD automatically orients the face normals to point from the center of the object outwards. Thus, if a face normal points away from the viewport, it's on the rear or back face of your model and won't need to be rendered—so AutoCAD discards this back face. Be aware that if you construct 3D models from 2D profiles (by using **EXTRUDE**, for example) or if you manually draw 3D faces, their face normals may not be oriented correctly. For this reason, AutoCAD lets you disable face normal calculations. (See the More Options button under the Rendering Options section of the Render dialog box. Picking the button gives you access to the Face Controls section in the Render dialog box, at which point you can pick the Discard Back Faces checkbox.) The resulting rendering is slower, but at least all the faces render. Alternately, use the Rotate Faces option, located on the Modify|Solids Editing menu.

- *Scenes and views*—When you save a view (usually with several light sources), it's called a *scene*. A scene represents a full or partial view of your drawing along with any named light sources. You may have an unlimited number of scenes in a drawing, and within each scene you place views and lights. A scene can include up to 500 lights, but a good rule of thumb is to use no more than three of each type—otherwise, you lose control of the lighting. Use **3DORBIT**, **DVIEW**, **VIEW**, or **VPOINT** to set up new scenes, along with one or more named views and one or more lights. For example, a view may have no light source, one specific light source, or several light sources consisting of any of the four types of light

- *Screen color palette*—Rendered images require many colors to represent the effects of light and shade on the surface of an object. When you're rendering on systems that support only 256 colors, you must tell AutoCAD how you want to manipulate the limited color palette. The fewer colors available on your system, the less realistic your rendered images will be. If you have a system that supports 16-bit or 24-bit color, you don't have to worry about this limitation.

- *Specular reflection*—On a shiny surface, light rays follow this rule: The angle of reflection is equal to the angle of incidence. This means that light coming from a point source is reflected in one particular direction. If the viewer is located in that direction, the place where the light hits the surface appears very bright. In the extreme case, specular reflection behaves just like light bouncing off a mirror. Specular reflection is most noticeable with convex surfaces on which only a very small portion of the surface reflects the light directly to the viewer, causing a bright highlight.

- *Spotlight*—The spotlight light source provides a cone of light with a hotspot cone and a falloff cone angle. These cone angles of light, which range from 0 to 160 degrees, define how the hotspot and falloff diminish along the main cone of light. The *hotspot* is the brightest part of the light beam. The *falloff* is the area of *rapid decay* (soft shadow), which starts at the outer edge of the hotspot and stops where the full cone of light becomes maximum shadow. You can aim spotlights at your model like distant lights, because they diminish over distance like point lights. They can also be focused and limited to a certain area by adjusting the hotspot and falloff settings.

- *Shadows and lighting*—With rendering, it's important to use shadows and light, so remember to place objects in front of a light source so they will cast a shadow.

The Render Commands

Most of the commands in this chapter are located in the Render toolbar, shown in Figure 11.1. You can display the toolbar by choosing View|Toolbars|Render. In addition to the Render toolbar, you'll also find the Hide, Shade, and Render commands located under the View menu.

Figure 11.1
The AutoCAD Render toolbar.

The Render toolbar includes these options: Hide, Render, Scenes, Lights, Materials, Materials Library, Mapping, Background, Fog, Landscape New, Landscape Edit, Landscape Library, Render Preferences, and Statistics. Table 11.1 provides a quick reference to the main commands you'll need to learn to get started with 3D shading and rendering. As the chapter progresses, they'll be explained in more depth.

HIDE, SHADE, And RENDER

Now, let's discuss the differences among the **HIDE**, **SHADE**, and **RENDER** commands, and examine the various components of a rendered model. Rendering is a 3D function; the only items you can shade or render in AutoCAD are extrusions, faces, and meshes. You don't and can't render 2D arcs, lines, hatching, or text. One of the first points to note when using **RENDER** is that the color you apply to your AutoCAD objects, entities, or 3D models is unimportant. The **RENDER** command lets you designate the color. Just be aware that **RENDER** uses color in a different way, by using color to attach materials.

Table 11.1 Quick reference listing of commands used in rendering.

Command	Explanation
HIDE	Creates a suppressed hidden line image of your 3D model.
SHADE	Shades your wireframe model in the current viewport. Use **SHADEMODE** to return.
SHADEMODE	Lets you select the proper shading type to apply to your scene.
RENDER	Creates a photorealistic shaded image of your 3D model.
SCENE	Allows you to set new or modify preset scenes with lights and 3D views into named scenes in model space.
LIGHT	Manages lights and lighting effects.
RMAT	Manages your rendering materials.
MATLIB	Imports and exports materials to and from a library of materials.
SETUV	Mapping coordinate command that maps materials onto objects.
BACKGROUND	Lets you set up a background image, color gradient, or solid color for your scene.
FOG	Creates fog and depth: White color produces fog, black produces depth.
LSNEW	Useful for adding realistic landscape items (such as trees and bushes) to your rendered images.
LSEDIT	Lets you edit a landscape object.
LSLIB	Maintains libraries of landscape objects.
RPREF	Allows you to set up render options in the Rendering Preferences dialog box.
STATS	Displays rendering statistics.

The **HIDE** command simply removes the hidden lines of your model to produce a 3D image. **SHADE** is basically a flat coloring system with a single source light—it uses a light source that starts from over your shoulder to provide light for your model. So, when you shade your 3D model as an image, any entity that's blue is shaded blue, any entity that's red is shaded red, any entity that's cyan is shaded cyan, and so on. The **SHADE** command is simply a paint command that paints color as a shaded image onto your 3D model. On the other hand, the **RENDER** command moves into more complexity and realism by adding color, material texture, lighting, and shadows. Realize that unlike the **SHADE** command, **RENDER** has nothing to do with the colored entities of your model, but it does use color or layers to attach texture or material to the entities of your model. Later, you'll study these aspects of rendering more closely. Nevertheless, both 3D surface models and 3D solid models can be displayed using the **HIDE**, **SHADE**, and **RENDER** commands.

The **HIDE** Command

For more clarity and to clear up complex details of your models, you often need to hide background components. The **HIDE** command lets you temporarily remove hidden lines from a 3D surface or a 3D solid model. It creates a temporary hidden line image of your 3D model in your current viewport. The results remain visible only until you issue the **REGEN** command. Basically, the **HIDE** command is similar to the **SHADE** command except that when you shade a 3D surface or face, you highlight with a color instead of the surface being represented by a face. **HIDE** doesn't regard items on frozen layers. Here are some considerations when using the **HIDE** command:

- *Text*—If your model includes text, the text will probably have a thickness of zero and obviously won't hide. Although you can change text thickness, whether you'll want to do so depends upon your chosen text style. For example, standard fonts such as romans.shx, gdt.shx, and txt.shx can be changed to 3D through thickness, whereas most other font styles can't.

- *Layers*—If objects or elements of your model are on a layer that's currently turned off, they may obscure objects on layers that are still on; the result may not show your true hidden 3D model. Instead of turning off the layers, freeze the layers that are off.

- *Intersections*—When applied to edges, **HIDE** may not correctly show true edges and where objects intersect (it may give slightly false results).

- *Polylines*—When you assign thickness to polylines, solids, and circles, they have both a top and a bottom, so they can be hidden in 3D models.

- *Polygon meshes*—In addition to polygon meshes, **HIDE** also reviews solids, polylines, circles, regions, 3D faces, and the extruded edges of objects that have a nonzero thickness. It regards them as opaque surfaces in order to hide objects.

- *Extruded objects*—If a model includes extruded objects, AutoCAD reviews solids, polylines, and circles as solid objects with both top and bottom faces.

- *Views*—When you use the **VIEW**, **VPOINT**, or **DVIEW** command to create a 3D view of your model, AutoCAD simply produces a wireframe within your current viewport. All the lines are present, including those hidden by other objects; the **HIDE** command simply removes hidden background lines from your screen and replaces them as a temporary screen image.

The **SHADE** Command

Unlike the **HIDE** command, **SHADE** is a flat coloring system that also takes minimal lighting into account. It uses a single over-the-shoulder light source that starts from directly behind you; as you shade your model, each entity uses its assigned color. As you'll see from the **SHADEMODE** variable choice list in the next section, the **SHADE** command in AutoCAD uses two basic algorithms: flat shading and Gouraud shading.

FLAT, GOURAUD, AND PHONG SHADING ALGORITHMS

As you look at the surface of an object away from the computer screen, you'll see the color of the object change continuously across the object's surface, with high tones, irregularities, and gradual color changes. The color of the object throughout never stays exactly the same depth or hue. Yet calculating such changes with a computer would be memory intensive. So instead of scanning the entire object, the computer looks at the colors at various points and uses a shading tool in a number of ways. The three main shading modes or algorithms are flat, Gouraud, and Phong (a Z-buffer algorithm is also used for the back faces of 3D images). AutoCAD uses all three methods in various ways and in different commands.

Flat shading is also known as *face* or *polygonal* shading because it shades each face. With flat shading, the computer calculates the color of each facet by sampling it at one vertex and then using that color for the entire facet.

Henri Gouraud, a native of France, developed a shading technique to render smoothly shaded curved surfaces from a faceted sample. The Gouraud shading method, also called *vertex shading,* has the advantage of providing a smooth appearance instead of a faceted appearance (that is, polygonal faces). It works by smoothly blending the color across the facets using linear interpolation between the edges of each facet or vertex.

Bui-Tong Phong developed an improvement on the Gouraud shading technique—Phong shading (also called *pixel shading*). Although Phong shading is similar to Gouraud shading because it uses faceted polygonal sampling, this method achieves accurate computer calculations by means other than smoothing the color across the polygons. Phong shading smooths the surface normals and applies lighting to each pixel with an interpolated normal to achieve the simulated effect of a smooth surface. It does so at a cost of speed, because the shading computations calculate each pixel.

To control **SHADE**, you use a number of system variables: **SHADEMODE**, **SHADEDIF**, and **SHADEDGE**. You'll find that the **SHADEMODE** variable provides you with a number of instant images as you adjust its simple settings. On the other hand, the **SHADEDIF** variable controls the contrast or the ratio of reflective light to ambient light (70 being the default). The **SHADEDGE** variable (which you can set from 0 to 3) controls visibility to the edges of the faces of your 3D model and whether you want to simply draw with hidden lines or to color and shade your model. As you can see in Figure 11.2 (with the exception of the Render option), the **SHADEMODE** variable provides you with multiple options, as follows:

- *Wireframe*—Shows your 3D model in either a 2D or 3D wireframe view, with lines and curves representing the boundaries of your model. Any material applied to the flat geometry is visible, whereas material applied to solid objects isn't visible. You'll find the main difference between 2D and 3D is the UCS icon. The 2D icon is the standard UCS, and the 3D icon is the colored icon.

- *Hidden*—Shows your 3D model in a 3D wireframe view, but the back edges of your 3D model are hidden.

- *Flat Shaded*—The faceted polygonal faces of your 3D model are shaded, which provides your model with a less smooth, flatter appearance.

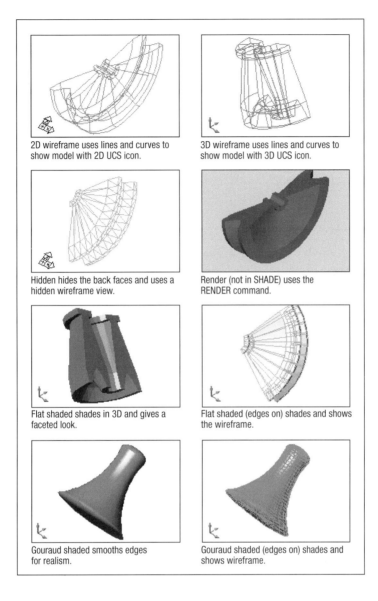

2D wireframe uses lines and curves to show model with 2D UCS icon.

3D wireframe uses lines and curves to show model with 3D UCS icon.

Hidden hides the back faces and uses a hidden wireframe view.

Render (not in SHADE) uses the RENDER command.

Flat shaded shades in 3D and gives a faceted look.

Flat shaded (edges on) shades and shows the wireframe.

Gouraud shaded smooths edges for realism.

Gouraud shaded (edges on) shades and shows wireframe.

Figure 11.2
SHADEMODE options as applied to the **SHADE** command.

- *Gouraud Shaded*—Provides a smoother, more realistic appearance. Besides shading your 3D model, this option also smooths the edges between faceted polygon faces.

- *Flat Shaded, Edges On*—A combination of the flat shaded and wireframe options, with the 3D model flat shaded in wireframe mode.

- *Gouraud Shaded, Edges On*—A combination of the Gouraud shaded and wireframe options, with the 3D model Gouraud shaded in wireframe mode.

Thus, the **SHADE** command simply colors your 3D model to provide a basic flat color as a simple rendered image. You'll find that **SHADE** operates realistically with either the 16-color palette of the standard VGA card or the

256-color palette of the super VGA cards. Usually, **SHADEMODE** is the only variable you'll need to adjust, but in case you need to change the **SHADEDGE** or **SHADEDIF** variables, they are explained in more detail here:

- *SHADEDGE*—With a 16-color palette, the **SHADEDGE** variable's default is 3. This setting simply fills the surface of your model with its assigned color, while using the background color of your screen to draw the edges. If you set the variable to 2, it will emulate the **HIDE** command—rather than shading your surface, it will simply fill the surface with your background screen color. If you use a 256-color palette and you wish to produce a realistic but basic colored image, set the **SHADEDGE** variable to 0 or 1. For example, the 0 setting will shade the surface of your model but not the model's edges. The 1 setting will shade the surface of your model, and the edges of your model will use the screen's background color.

- *SHADEDIF*—When **SHADEDGE** is set to a 0 or 1 the **SHADEDIF** variable controls the contrast (the amount of light reflective to ambient light). It's a contrast setting with a default value of 70, but you can set it from 1 to 100. A low value provides a small amount of contrast, and a higher value provides a higher contrast. The default—and best—image contrast is at about 70, which provides a medium to high contrast. So, leave **SHADEDIF** set at 70.

From this book's companion CD-ROM, open shade.dwg, which is a 3D solid model in a single color. Activate the **SHADE** command; then, use the **SHADEMODE** variable to cycle through and check out the options 2D, 3D, H, F, G, L, and O (that is, 2D wireframe, 3D wireframe, Hidden, Flat, Gouraud, fLat+edges, and gOuraud+edges). **SHADEMODE**, for example, has these options:

```
Command: shademode
Enter option [2D wireframe/3Dwireframe/Hidden/Flat/Gouraud/
  fLat+edges/gOuraud+edges] <Flat+Edges>:
```

The **RENDER** Command

You've looked at the advantages of and differences between the **HIDE** and **SHADE** commands, so now let's see the advantages of using the **RENDER** command. You'll find the main advantage of **RENDER** is that it adds more elements of sophistication than you can achieve by using the plain **SHADE** command alone, such as:

- HLS and RGB color through the **LIGHT** command

- Background imaging effects via the **RENDER** and **BACKGROUND** commands

- Fog and shadow effects through the **FOG** and **RENDER** commands

- Material and texture attributes through the materials library's **MATLIB** and **RMAT** commands

- Mapping of texture, reflection, opacity, and bump maps through the **SETUV** command

RENDER Vs. SHADE

Here's a simple exercise to test the **SHADE** command versus the **RENDER** command. Open the bkt-iso.dwg file from the CD-ROM; it's an isometric pictorial of a 3D solid model. Without altering any settings, use the **SHADE** command and then immediately use the **RENDER** command, pressing Enter to accept the default values. Notice the lack of sophistication with the **RENDER** option (see Figure 11.3). You might also wish to use **SHADEMODE** and see what effect it may have on the shaded isometric drawing.

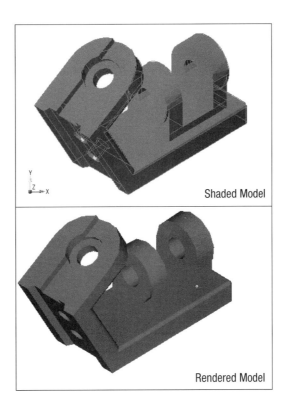

Shaded Model

Rendered Model

Figure 11.3
Comparison of **SHADE** and **RENDER** with bkt-iso.dwg.

Let's now move on and look at using the **RENDER** command in more depth. But before we review the Render dialog box, let's take a quick look at some color basics, including the importance of using color as a tool within your 3D model and how you can change and access RGB and HLS color settings.

The Render Dialog Box

You need to remember that the only things you can shade or render in AutoCAD are extrusions, faces, meshes, and regions—you can't render arcs, lines, text, or hatch patterns. Rendering is strictly a 3D function, which you achieve through the Render dialog box, shown in Figure 11.4. Choose Render from of the View menu to open the Render dialog box.

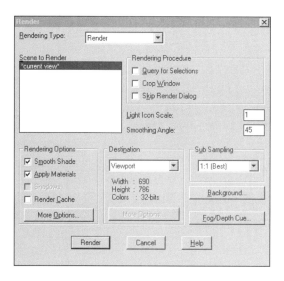

Figure 11.4

The Render dialog box.

The first thing you'll notice when you open the Render dialog box is its simplicity. The Rendering Type drop-down list offers the following three options:

• *Render*—AutoCAD's basic rendering option. You may use this basic algorithm without setting lights or scenes or applying materials or other effects.

• *Photo Real*—AutoCAD's photorealistic scanline renderer. With this algorithm, AutoCAD can display both bitmapped and transparent materials, plus generate volumetric and mapped shadows. (Generates images one horizontal scanline at a time.)

• *Photo Raytrace*—AutoCAD's photorealistic raytraced renderer. This algorithm uses raytracing to generate reflections, refraction, and more precise shadows. (Generates images one horizontal scanline at a time.)

Ensure that the Photo Real option is selected in the Rendering Type drop-down list. In the lower-left of the dialog box, notice the Rendering Options: Smooth Shade, Apply Materials, Shadows, and Render Cache. For a more realistic rendering, choose Smooth Shade, and when you've defined your materials, select the Apply Materials checkbox. (If you don't select this option, your model assumes the color, ambient, reflection, transparency, refraction, bump map, and roughness definitions of the *GLOBAL* material of the materials library.) You choose Shadows only with the Photo Real and Photo Raytrace optional Rendering Types. The final option, Render Cache, writes the rendering data to a cache file on your hard drive and saves you time if you're constantly testing various lights, materials, and special effects.

If you click on More Options, you'll see that two types of dialog boxes are available, depending upon which Rendering Type you select. The Render option offers a minimal Render Options dialog box, whereas Photo Real and Photo Raytrace make available an advanced dialog box.

The Destination drop-down list in the center of the Render dialog box offers three options: Viewport, Render Window, and File. These options are self-explanatory—that is, they render to the current viewport, a separate render window, or an electronic file output. If you set your rendering to a render window and then choose to render your model, AutoCAD will render it to a separate window. If you choose File|Options in this render window, another dialog box will open, in which you can set file output size in pixels, along with 8-bit or 24-bit color depth.

If you choose File from the Destination list, the More Options button will become active below it. Click on More Options to activate the File Output Configuration dialog box, shown in Figure 11.5. The default File Type output is set to BMP output at 640×480 (VGA); the five available outputs are BMP, PCX, Postscript, TGA, and TIFF. As you choose any of the file outputs, the dialog box activates the specific options for that file type and lets you choose 8-, 16-, or 24-bit color output options. (See Chapter 12 for an explanation of these types of color outputs.)

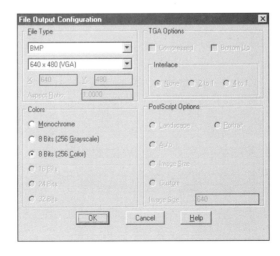

Figure 11.5

The File Output Configuration dialog box.

Returning to the Render dialog box, the Sub Sampling field is simply a series of algorithms (from 1:1 to 8:1) for rendering speed. These algorithms let you quickly set up and render a rough image to see how the lights, background, and so on look prior to sending the file to disk at a 1:1 speed.

Below that is the Background button, which activates the Background dialog box, shown in Figure 11.6. The Background dialog box sets up how the rear projection of your image will look with your model in the foreground. You may either set a solid color, a gradient color, an image, or merge files. The dialog box defaults to solid color with the AutoCAD Background option selected. With the Solid option selected, unchecking the AutoCAD Background option activates the Color System RGB slider bar or lets you use the Select Custom Color button. With the Gradient option selected, again you have the option of the RGB slider or the Select Custom Color button, but you can also set how far the horizon, height, and rotation of the gradient should be set and use the Preview box for visual assistance. Selecting the Image option in turn activates the Image section of the dialog box, in which you can select the background file you wish to use. With any of these options, you can use the Environment section and select a file.

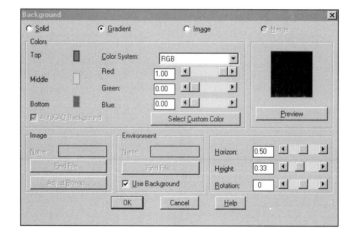

Figure 11.6
The Background dialog box.

Returning to the Render dialog box, click on the Fog/Depth Cue button to open the Fog/Depth Cue dialog box. Choosing the Enable Fog checkbox (as shown in Figure 11.7) activates the Color System option's RGB or HLS slider bars. Further options include the Select Custom Color button and Select From ACI (AutoCAD Color Index) button. Further slider bars for Near Distance, Far Distance, Near Fog Percentage, and Far Fog Percentage also appear in the dialog box.

Returning to the Render dialog box for the last time, note the Rendering Procedure field, with its Query For Selections, Crop Window, and Skip Render Dialog checkbox options. Placing a check in the Query For Selections checkbox lets you select individual model components to render. The Crop Window option allows you to select or crop a specified coordinate

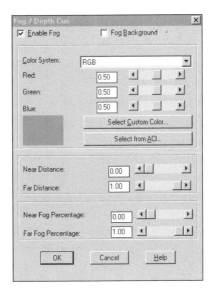

Figure 11.7
The Fog/Depth Cue dialog box.

render window, and the Skip Render Dialog option bypasses the Render dialog box each time you use it. The only way to return to the Render dialog box is to open the Rendering Preferences dialog box and deactivate the Skip Render Dialog checkbox, as shown in Figure 11.8.

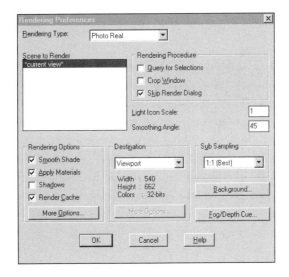

Figure 11.8
The Rendering Preferences dialog box.

To set up render preferences for the **RENDER** command, use the Rendering Preferences dialog box. Enter "rpref" at the command line to display the dialog box, or click on the Render Preferences icon.

In the Rendering Options section of the dialog box, you can choose the Smooth Shade, Apply Materials, Shadows, and Render Cache options. Hint: If you intend to do a lot of complex rendering, you need to select the Render Cache option, because it specifies that your rendering information is written to a cache file on your hard drive. In turn, the cache file is used for further renderings, which improves rendering performance.

In the Rendering Procedure section, you determine the rendering procedure, such as rendering selected objects or the entire scene.

In the Destination section of the dialog box, you determine where to send the rendered image: to the current viewport, a separate render window, or a graphic file on disk. You also determine a choice of viewport size and whether to use 8-bit or 24-bit color depth. (See Chapter 12 for an explanation of 8-bit and 24-bit and the different file types.) See Figure 11.8 for further options of the AutoCAD Render Preferences dialog box.

Color And Lighting

In a CAD system, color (or lighting) serves a dual purpose: to supply the color and to group objects that have the same material and texture. If you use the **RENDER** command without any settings, it will render your model with basic colors for each component within the drawing and use very little light. (Refer back to Figure 11.3, which shows a comparison of **SHADE** versus **RENDER**.) That's because the only light setting in the image is ambient light—no distant light or spotlights are set up. So, if you render your model at this stage, you don't have much more than a simple shade file. (In fact, it's worse than a simple shade file.) To provide your rendered image with a more realistic appearance, you'll need to add material and texture, as well as lighting.

Pigment Color Vs. Light Color

Be aware that there is a difference between pigment color and light color, and they use different color rules. If you look away from your computer screen for a short time, you'll notice *pigment* colors attached to objects about you. If you see an object that absorbs all the spectrum colors, you'll see the object as the color black. Alternately, if you see an object that reflects all the spectrum colors, you'll see it as the color white. You'll remember from art classes at school that the primary *pigment* colors are red, yellow, and blue, and that from these primary colors you make secondary colors by mixing two equal parts of primary colors: orange (red and yellow), green (yellow and blue), and purple (red and blue). These, then, are the simple color rules outside your computer screen. They are not the same color rules that apply within your computer screen, however.

Now, move back to the computer monitor, where you don't see *pigment* color—instead, you see *light* color, and the color rules change. For example, if an object is a source of light, it emits color rather than reflects color. Every pixel on your modern computer monitor has a red, green, and blue phosphor. Electrons are used to vary the excitement of the phosphors in your computer screen to produce a large range of colors. Thus, on screen an object is a light source emitting the primary *light* colors of red, green, and blue (RGB). These colors are termed the *additive primaries*; for if you add different colored light the result is a color that's a mix of the RGB values. Yet what happens when you want to plot color images is that instead of using additive primaries the computer goes one step further and uses *subtractive primaries*, also known as CMY: cyan (green and blue), and magenta (red and blue), and yellow (red and green). Remember, if you combine all the light colors, the result will be white, whereas any absence of light color will produce black. When you need to print or plot your color images, the computer uses CMYK (cyan, magenta, yellow, and black) instead of RGB for a better result.

In addition to RGB, a computer uses hue, lightness, and saturation (HLS). On screen you don't mix primary colors, so you choose from a range of hues and vary the lightness of the color (often referred to as *brightness*) and saturation of the color (also referred to as *purity* of the color). When you set a lighting color, you can use either the RGB or HLS method.

Colors in the renderer are different from the standard colors in AutoCAD, because AutoCAD has a fixed 255-color palette. Each color has a different color number. If you enter "color" at the command line, the Select Color dialog box will open (it's the 255 AutoCAD Color Index [ACI]); here you set color by layer or by number, but you don't customize the color. (You simply set the color either by layer or by number, which is a restriction.) Within the renderer, you have more control over the shade of a color in your model, because you can control color by either RGB or HLS.

Hue, Lightness, And Saturation (HLS)

HLS allows you to use RGB to add or control color. For example, you can produce the same color using either HLS sliders or RGB sliders. Most rendering programs that use HLS and RGB are correlated, so that as you move one set of slider bars or numbers, the other set will move correspondingly. Activate the **LIGHT** command and pick the Select Custom Color button in the Lights dialog box to locate both the RGB and HLS number boxes.

Here are the definitions of HLS terms:

- *Hue*—Hue is simply color. If you cycle the number slider from 0 to 255, you'll move through the basic color spectrum. You move not by adding red, green, or blue, but by simply progressing through the 255 basic colors provided on your palette. Once you have the basic color (hue), you can add lightness and/or saturation.

- *Lightness*—Lightness, often referred to as *luminance*, determines the intensity or brightness of the color. Each color includes 255 levels of lightness. So, if you set the lightness to 255, the result will be white, regardless of the hue. If you set the lightness to 0, the result will be black, regardless of the hue.

- *Saturation*—Saturation is purity of color. Let's say you were choosing paint for a room in a certain brightness, but the brightness needed to be toned down. You'd tone it down by adding gray without actually changing the color itself, which is where saturation comes in. The higher the saturation (that is, the purity), the less gray in the color; the lower the saturation, the more gray in the color.

Red, Green, And Blue (RGB)

By mixing degrees of red, green, and blue, you can create a full palette of colors. You have two options with RGB: the standard AutoCAD Color Index option or the Select Custom Color option with its RGB numbered sliders. (Note: These are the same options as HLS and are accessed from the Light dialog box.)

Most programs display a slider bar for each of the primary colors. You can move each slider with your mouse from 0 to 255. AutoCAD's Lights and Color dialog boxes work a bit differently. In the Lights dialog box, you can move the slider from 0 to 1. In the Color dialog box, you can enter a value in a number box from 0 to 255 but is has no slider bar. Table 11.2 shows typical 0 to 255 value settings.

You need to understand three important principles when working with RGB sliders:

- If you set all three color components to 0, you create black.

Table 11.2 RGB value settings for primary and gray tones.

	Red	Green	Blue
Colors			
Red	255	0	0
Yellow	255	255	0
Green	0	255	0
Cyan	0	255	255
Blue	0	0	255
Magenta	255	0	255
White	255	255	255
Black	0	0	0
Gray Tones			
10%	233	233	233
20%	204	204	204
30%	178	178	178
40%	153	153	153
50%	127	127	127
60%	102	102	102
70%	77	77	77
80%	26	26	26

- If you set all three color components to 255, you create white.

- If you set all three color components to exactly the same number, you create gray. You determine the shade of gray by the number to which you set the three components. For example, the higher the number, the lighter the gray; the lower the number, the darker the gray.

Using RGB sliders, you can add or subtract one or more of the primary colors. If you want pure red, then you set red to 255 and green and blue to 0. The same would be true with the other two primary colors. When you move red and green to 255 and blue to 0, the result is yellow. Table 11.2 shows the RGB settings that create various colors and grays. Hint: Don't try randomly moving the number in the hope of finding the correct color mix; instead, use the Color Palette in the Color dialog box that AutoCAD provides.

Setting RGB And HLS

Here's how to set RGB and HLS colors. Open AutoCAD 2000 and enter the **LIGHT** command to open the Lights dialog box. You'll see the buttons Select From ACI (the standard 255 AutoCAD Color Index) and Select Custom Color. Click on Select Custom Color to open the Color dialog box, shown in Figure 11.9. In the lower-right portion of the Color dialog box are six boxes labeled Hue, Sat (Saturation), Lum (Luminance), Red, Green, and Blue. You'll also notice a vertical slider bar on the far right of the dialog box above these boxes that you can slide up and down. If you enter any of the RGB settings from Table 11.2 in the RGB boxes, you'll get the colors listed; plus, the equivalent HLS numbers will appear in their boxes. The colors are usually applied to lighting in order to provide lighting effects, which provide your images with feelings of warmth (orange/yellows), cold (blues), daylight (off whites), and so on. RGB and HLS also appear in the Fog, Background, and Material dialog boxes, but the slider bars use decimal division from 0 through 1, as opposed to 0 through 255.

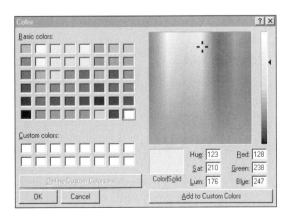

Figure 11.9
The Color dialog box.

Understanding Lighting

The **LIGHT** command allows you to add dramatic lighting effects to your model. AutoCAD uses four types of light: point, distant, spotlight, and ambient. If you render your model without adding any lights, it uses the default ambient lighting, which in AutoCAD is minimal. Normally, ambient light is a constant illumination to all surfaces. As you add lights to your model, you'll begin to notice more realism.

In addition, you can add different shadow types. The shadows you add can be as simple as a depth shadow, where the object appears darker the further it moves away from the light source, to true shadow casting, which casts shadows in all directions. The purpose of lights is threefold within a rendered image:

- *Ambient light*—Ambient light produces both light and color for your 3D surface or solid model.

- *Light and dark*—Lighting is a source of both lightness and darkness, which add a degree of realism to your 3D model.

- *Shadows*—Light can cast volumetric shadows, shadow maps, or raytraced shadows. Remember, using and adding shadows increases rendering time.

Working with lights can be confusing at first to an AutoCAD user, especially one who is just beginning to use a rendering program for the first time. Nevertheless, you must create, name, and set lights once you've finished working on your 3D model. If you don't set lighting before you render, you may get a totally black screen. To start you off, AutoCAD places an ambient light within the program. The Lights dialog box in Figure 11.10 shows the types of lighting.

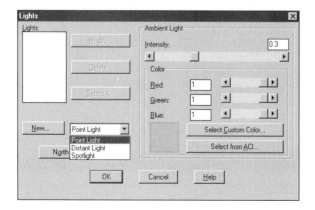

Figure 11.10
The Lights dialog box.

Ambient Light

All rendering programs include ambient light. Ambient light by itself doesn't produce realistic images, and that's because in ambient light all the adjacent faces of an object are equally lit, so they appear to blend with each other. The main application for ambient light is to provide fill light to surfaces not directly lit by other light sources, such as point, distant, or spotlight. The best way to understand ambient light is to sit in a totally dark room; as you know, it's nearly impossible to make a room totally dark, because once your eyes adjust, you can still see something. So it appears as if light enters the room from somewhere, but you can't pinpoint its origin; yet if you were to turn up the intensity of the imaginary light, you'd probably see better. The room has light, but no identifiable light source—and therefore no shadow. Ambient light has no direction because it simply illuminates a scene as background lighting. It has no other use. See Figure 11.11.

Figure 11.11
Ambient lighting diagram. The model is lit by background ambient lighting. Ambient lighting is a constant illumination to all the surfaces.

Although AutoCAD sets the intensity of ambient light to 0.3, you can control its brightness, intensity, and color. The 0.3 default happens to be a good value—don't set it much higher than 0.4, because doing so will produce a low-contrast, washed-out effect in the rendered image of your model.

Point Light

The *point light*, or *omni light*, is a specific point of light. As you'll see in the point lighting diagram in Figure 11.12, this light—which you can place in a scene—doesn't shine in a specific direction. In the New Point Light dialog box, shown in Figure 11.13, you can control brightness (intensity), attenuation, color, and shadow options. Unlike AutoCAD, some general rendering programs that use point lights don't let you cast shadows.

Point lights emulate incandescent light bulbs, and for special lighting effects you should use a combination of point lights and spotlights. In addition, you need to set the attenuation level, mainly because a point light will reduce in intensity due to its distance from the source. Hint: Don't use more than three or, at the most, four point lights in a rendering or you'll lose control of your image. However, you may use point lighting for effect with the attenuation (Inverse Linear or Inverse Square) option.

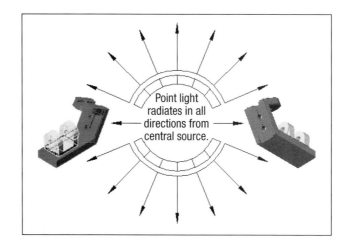

Figure 11.12
Point lighting diagram. The models are lit by point light.

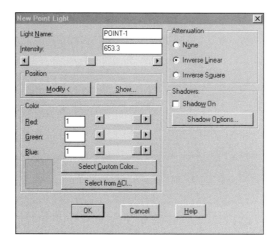

Figure 11.13
The New Point Light dialog box.

Distant Light

Distant lights or *directional lights* are similar to ambient lighting only in that the exact point and placement of the lights aren't critical—it's the direction of the light rays that's important. See Figure 11.14. Sunlight is an example of an AutoCAD directional light source; if you look at Figure 11.15, you'll see the Sun Angle Calculator button. Within the Sun Angle Calculator dialog box is the Geographical Location button. Pick it to activate the built-in Geographical Location dialog box. Hint. Always position distant lights at your drawing extents, because the direction of a distant light in your drawing is what's critical, not the location.

As Figure 11.15 shows, you have the option of turning on shadows by selecting the Shadows On checkbox. Because a distant light will strike your model uniformly and in a specific direction (refer back to Figure 11.14), you can use distant lights to cast shadows. Further, you don't need to set attenuation with a distant light because the intensity of distant light isn't lost with distance from the source.

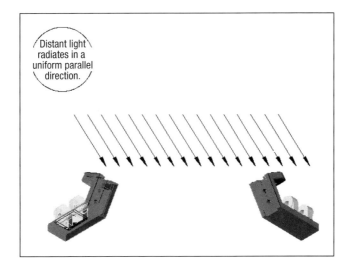

Figure 11.14
Distant lighting diagram. The models are lit by distant lighting.

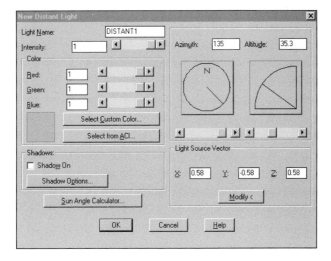

Figure 11.15
New Distant Light dialog box.

Spotlight

A spotlight creates a directional, cone-shaped light that will diminish in intensity over a distance. As you can see in Figure 11.16, within a spotlight is an inside circle of light that's bright (a *hotspot*) and an outside circle of light that gradually decreases in intensity. That is, a spotlight is an area of maximum illumination surrounded by an area of less intense illumination (the *falloff zone*). The region between the hotspot and falloff angles is often referred to as the *rapid decay* area or *soft edge*.

The spotlight is directional (it can be oriented toward the object to be lit), casts a shadow, and operates in a similar manner to a wall spotlight or a stage spotlight, which has a bright center. Further, you can reduce the intensity of the spotlight through its attenuation rate, and you can also use it for special effect with the Inverse Linear or Inverse Square attenuation options in the New Spotlight dialog box, shown in Figure 11.17.

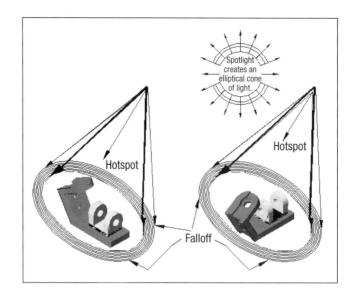

Figure 11.16
Spotlight diagram. The hotspots are the bright areas, and the falloffs are the decay areas of the hotspots.

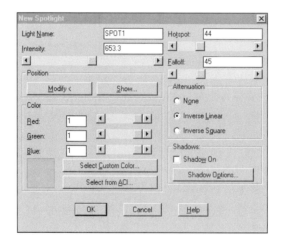

Figure 11.17
The New Spotlight dialog box.

Attenuation

Attenuation is an intensity level relative to the distance from the source to your model. The New Point Light (Figure 11.13) and New Spotlight (Figure 11.17) dialog boxes both allow attenuation settings. You can reset attenuation in one of four ways:

- 0 intensity turns intensity off.

- 1 sets the intensity to none.

- The Inverse Linear setting's value is half of the extent's distance. Thus, AutoCAD indicates that it decreases illumination in inverse proportion to the distance from the light source. For example, as light travels 2, 4, 6, and 8 units, its brightness becomes 1/2, 1/4, 1/6, and 1/8 as strong.

- The Inverse Square's setting value is the square of half of the extent's distance. Thus, AutoCAD indicates that it decreases illumination in inverse proportion to the square of the distance from the light source. For example, as light travels 2, 4, 6, and 8 units, its brightness becomes 1/4, 1/16, 1/36, and 1/64 as strong.

Putting Lights In Your Model

Listed here are quick steps for setting up lights within your model using the Lights dialog box:

1. In AutoCAD, the Lights dialog box will allow you to set up a number of different lights within your model. Enter "light" at the command line or choose the Lights icon from the Render toolbar. (Refer back to Figure 11.1.) In the Lights dialog box, set the Intensity slider bar to an Ambient Light level between 0.3 and 0.4.

2. Select Point Light, Distant Light, or Spotlight from the light drop-down list and click on New. Doing so opens a New Light dialog box of your choice. (Refer back to Figures 11.13, 11.15, and 11.17.) In the Light Name box, enter a name (up to eight characters) such as Point1, Distant1, or Spot1. In the upper-left of the dialog box, set the intensity level. Be careful, because an intensity setting of 0 will turn off the light. You'll notice that the light has a preset intensity level and a default location in your drawing.

3. According to the type of light, refer to the appropriate item below:

   - *Point light*—Through the Inverse Linear and Inverse Square options, you can set attenuation. You can also set shadow volume.

   - *Distant light*—You can set the Azimuth and Altitude angles. For example, if you're in the Northern hemisphere, you can set Altitude to around 70 or 110 to emulate time (that is, before or after noon). Set the Azimuth angle to emulate the sun's position from the East, the South (180), or the West. Also, set the Intensity and color level.

   - *Spotlight*—You need to set the Hotspot and Falloff angles via the slider bars. Hint: If you want a sharp, crisp cone or light circle, set both angles to be equal. If you want a softer and more dramatic effect to the edge of the cone of light, set the Hotspot cone angle a few degrees less than the Falloff angle.

4. To alter the light target and/or light location, choose the Modify button to set the X, Y, and Z coordinates.

5. Click on OK to return to the Lights dialog box. Then, click on OK again to exit the dialog box; or create another light and repeat the steps.

Shadows, Fog, And Sunlight

You can now place shadows, fog, and sunlight with AutoCAD's render program:

- *Shadows*—In addition to adding materials and texture to your model, you can add shadows. Generally, the main types of shadow are volumetric, shadow maps, and raytraced.

- *Fog*—The **FOG** command can create fog that appears in the background or foreground of your image. Set the near and far distance percentage from 0 to 100 percent fog saturation. (AutoCAD indicates that the values are percentages of the distance from the camera to the back clipping plane.) The **FOG** command allows you to create fog and depth effects. For example, using a white color produces a fog effect, whereas black color produces depth. You're not limited to white or black—you can use other colors.

- *Sunlight*—Using a distant light, you can create sun shadow effects for architectural design. See "Simulating Sunlight To An Architectural Model" later in the chapter.

Shadow Mapping

Volumetric shadows compute the volume of space cast by the shadow of each object. The shadows are hard-edged with approximate outlines. (Color affects shadows cast by translucent and transparent objects.) Be careful, because shadow maps increase rendering time—although the volumetric shadows are faster than raytraced. Volumetric shadows are a default type of shadow. Turn on shadow volumes as follows:

1. Check that you've selected Photo Real or Photo Raytrace in the Render Preferences dialog box. Activate the Shadows-On toggle in the Render Preferences dialog box by selecting the Shadows checkbox. Click on OK.

2. Move to the Lights dialog box. Create any new light type and name or modify it. Select the Shadow On checkbox in the New Light dialog box; then, click on Shadow Options.

3. Select Shadow Volumes/Raytraced Shadows in the Shadow Options dialog box. See Figure 11.18. Click on OK to accept all the settings as you back out of each dialog box.

Shadow maps are bitmaps; the larger the shadow map, the greater the accuracy. Shadow maps don't show colors cast by translucent and transparent objects. You may create soft-edged shadows for spotlights using the Shadow Map option. (Shadow-mapped shadows override the default shadows—volumetric for Photo Real or raytraced for Photo Raytrace.) Within each light,

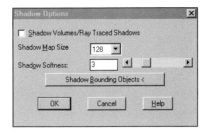

Figure 11.18
The Shadow Options dialog box.

you can set the size of the shadow map from 64 pixels up to a maximum of 4096 pixels square; the default is 128. The renderer generates the shadow map during a pre-rendering pass as it renders a view. The steps to turn on shadow maps are as follows:

1. Check that you've selected Photo Real or Photo Raytrace in the Render Preferences dialog box. Activate the shadow-on toggle in the Render Preferences dialog box by selecting the Shadows checkbox. Click on OK.

2. Move to the Lights dialog box. Create any new light type and name or modify it. Select the Shadow On checkbox in the New Light dialog box; then, click on Shadow Options.

3. Toggle off Shadow Volumes/Raytraced Shadows in the Shadow Options dialog box. See Figure 11.18. Click on OK to accept all the settings as you back out of each dialog box.

Raytraced shadows have accurate outlines and hard edges. They're similar to the default volumetric shadows. They transmit color from translucent and transparent objects. To create sunlight shadows through a distant light, turn on the shadow toggle, use the sun angle calculator, and then render the model. Raytraced shadows are extremely accurate, so they're ideal for use with complex geometry. Select the Photo Raytrace option in the Render dialog box. If you've selected the Shadows option and you choose the Photo Raytrace renderer, AutoCAD will generate raytraced shadows for each light that has shadows turned on, except lights that are set to generate shadow-mapped shadows.

Simulating Sunlight To An Architectural Model

When you're working with architectural models, you create simulated sunlight shadows using distant lights. For practice, you'll find the arch-model.dwg file on the CD-ROM. Remember that you can use **SHADE** and/or **HIDE** to give you an idea of how the 3D model will appear before you use the **RENDER** command. Here are the simplified steps to set shadows for an architectural model:

1. First, orient your architectural model to the site—that is, locate it to North, South, East, or West.

2. Activate the Lights dialog box and create and name a new distant light.

3. In the New Distant Light dialog box, pick the Sun Angle Calculator; in the dialog box that appears (see Figure 11.19), you'll select a date and time of day (including GMT, PST, EST, and Daylight Savings).

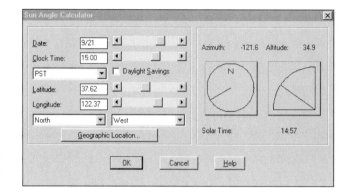

Figure 11.19
The Sun Angle Calculator dialog box.

4. Click on Geographic Location to open the Geographic Location dialog box (see Figure 11.20) and locate your city and its latitude and longitude. Click on OK when you're finished to return to the Sun Angle Calculator dialog box.

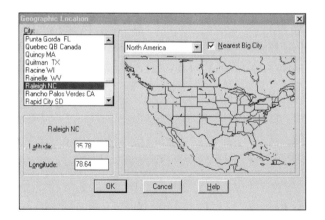

Figure 11.20
The Geographic Location dialog box.

5. Set the Azimuth. For example, AutoCAD indicates that to emulate the sun's position at noon in the northern hemisphere, enter 180 for Azimuth—that is, due south. But remember, you don't normally set a shadow to noon time; you set it before or after to get the benefits of the shadows.

6. Set the Altitude. For example, AutoCAD indicates that to emulate the sun's angle at noon, enter 80 to put the sun almost overhead. Again, remember that a noon setting will not result in a dramatic image. When you've finished, click on OK to return to your model.

7. Be sure you select either the Photo Raytrace or Photo Real option, plus the Shadows option in the Render dialog box; then, render your model. Save the drawing; you'll use it in the "Landscape Materials" section to place landscaping materials.

Setting Up For An AutoCAD Rendering

To prepare to render a model in AutoCAD, follow these general steps:

1. Create your 3D surface or solid model and make a backup copy to disk.

2. Place and name lights in your drawing (prior to making views). Realize that you can accompany each view with any number of light sources. Usually, in addition to ambient lighting, you combine distant lights and spotlights for dramatic effects, with point lights.

3. Set up, create, and name views within the drawing and save them in the Views dialog box. Use the 3D Views preset option and the **3DORBIT** command to set up different views around your model and name them. (The names are used with the scenes later.) Hint: Use the **SHADE** command to check your 3D view presets. If you have doubts about whether you can render your model, try shading it first—obviously, if your model won't shade, it certainly won't render. This way, you'll get an idea of the general shape and form of the final product. However, you won't be able to tell if you're missing any texture on the surfaces of your model.

4. In order to recall a scene at a later time, save each named view with its named lights into a scene. The renderer in AutoCAD uses your named saved views. (See "Setting Up Scenes And Views" later in this chapter.)

5. Apply material to the faces of your model. For more specialized effects, think about creating or importing materials. (See "Attaching A Material By Object" later in the chapter.)

6. Set up the rendering preferences you wish to use—such as the photorealistic algorithm or the raytrace algorithm—along with the smoothing parameters. Then, test-render the model. At this point, you can adjust views, lighting, and finish to improve the final appearance; then, re-render. Finally, save your finished rendering to a file, along with a suitable size and compression ratio. (See "Setting Render Preferences" later in this chapter for an in-depth look at rendering file types.)

Here's a hint: If you have a large 3D model to render, sometimes it's good practice to test it with the **HIDE** command and check for the removal of hidden surface normals. If your results are satisfactory, you'll save rendering time if you toggle on Discard Back Faces in the Render Options dialog box, as shown in Figure 11.21. You can turn on this option by clicking on More Options in either the Render dialog box or the Rendering Preferences dialog box. The time you subsequently save depends upon the total number of faces in your 3D model as compared to the back faces it discards.

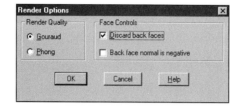

Figure 11.21
The Render Options dialog box.

Setting Up Scenes And Views

The renderer within AutoCAD can use preset AutoCAD views, which you preset into scenes with both background and foreground lighting. The **SCENE** command allows you to place AutoCAD-created views with embedded lighting into rendered scenes before you render. That way, you don't have to set up new viewpoints and new lights each time you render an object. It's also a good idea to set up several views, so you simply choose a scene using the New Scene dialog box shown in Figure 11.22.

Figure 11.22
The New Scene dialog box.

Now, let's look at the steps for setting up scenes:

1. Create and save a number of different views. Use the **VPORTS** and **3DORBIT** commands to set up different views of your model. You also need to use the **LIGHT** command to place different lights in your 3D model.

2. Either click on the Scene icon, choose Scene from the View menu, or at the command line type "scene" to open the Scenes dialog box.

3. In the Scenes dialog box, choose New to open the New Scene dialog box. (Refer back to Figure 11.22.) In the Scene Name box, enter a name no more than eight characters long. Doing so will save the view settings and your light sources to a scene name.

4. In the Views list box, select either a named AutoCAD view (one of your previously saved views) or *CURRENT*.

5. In the Lights list box, select a series of lights (or simply *ALL*, but it's better to be selective with your lights).

6. Click on OK to exit and save the scene.

You can also modify a scene by reactivating the Scene dialog box and then clicking on Modify. The Modify Scene dialog box will open, in which you can rename a scene, change a view, and add or remove lights to a scene. Remember, the maximum number of lights in a scene is 500.

Attaching Materials To Your 3D Model

Within AutoCAD, you need to make decisions ahead of time. You must decide whether to *render by object*, *render by color*, or *render by layer*, as well as what colors and materials you'll use in the final rendered product and which items in your 3D model will share the same materials. Still, whatever you decide, you have total flexibility, so at any point you can change the color of your model. A material can also have properties such as dullness, shininess, transparency, bumpiness, or luminance; these properties and attributes simulate real material texture.

Throughout this section on materials, you'll use the render-1.dwg drawing from this book's companion CD-ROM to help you attach and understand materials. Open the file, which is an exploded 3D assembly with three components, each having a different color and layer. Try shading the model; then, use **UNDO** to back out of the **SHADE** option. Next, use the step-by-step listing later in this section, along with the 3D model, to attach materials to their simple components.

Attaching A Material By Object

AutoCAD has a standard material library. A *material* is something such as aluminum, brass, brick, granite, marble, plastic, wood, and so forth. A material can be modified with different attributes such as color/pattern, ambient, reflection, roughness, transparency, refraction, and a bump map. You can also adjust the RGB and HLS values for each material. To define the material, you specify the material's color and any reflective parameters you want the material to have, such as a reflective shiny or transparent dull face. Work in two steps: Define the material with its color, along with its reflection and transparency; and then attach the material to your model.

Clicking on the Materials icon or entering "rmat" at the keyboard displays the Materials dialog box, shown in Figure 11.23. The dialog box contains a list of materials defined in your current drawing, along with buttons for accessing the Materials Library and modifying and attaching materials. You can also click on Preview to see what a material looks like before you attach it to your model or components of your model.

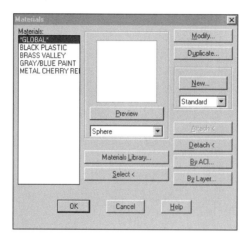

Figure 11.23
The Materials dialog box.

Attaching A Material By Color

Color is important in preparing your 3D model to be a final rendered image. AutoCAD allows you the option of applying materials and texture to a color, a block, a layer, or an object.

Remember that the actual colors you apply to your AutoCAD entities and objects are meaningless. In AutoCAD, don't be concerned with what color each object is going to be—just pay attention to the color numbers. Let's see how you attach a material by color.

If you plan to render by color and you want unique textures or different materials on individual parts of your model, you should use a different color number for each of the different components in your model. With this method, you can change the actual color in the rendering package and apply unique textures. Remember that with this method, every different material you use will require a different color number.

Click on the Materials icon and then click on Materials Library to open the Materials Library dialog box, shown in Figure 11.24. This dialog box provides functions for managing material textures, such as importing, exporting, deleting, purging, and saving materials. Think of this dialog box as divided into three parts: library controls on the right, transfer controls in the center, and drawing material controls on the left.

Note: Be aware that if you choose to render by color number, you'll limit yourself to the number of materials and textures you can use in any given scene. As pointed out, AutoCAD supports 255 colors, which seems to indicate that the maximum number of materials to use in a scene is 255—but most scenes won't use up to 255 materials at any one time.

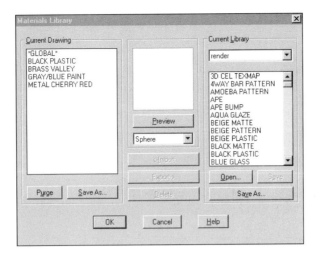

Figure 11.24
The Materials Library dialog box.

The Current Library list contains materials using the AutoCAD Standard rendering library file. You choose a pattern in this column and then click on Import to place it into the Current Drawing column.

Here's how to attach materials by the AutoCAD Color Index to objects within your 3D model. Open render-1.dwg from the CD-ROM, if you haven't already, and then save it under a different name on your hard drive. Now, follow these steps:

1. Enter "rmat" at the command line or pick the Material icon to open the Materials dialog box. Click on Materials Library to open the Materials Library dialog box. In the Current Library list, highlight one of the materials; click on Import to copy the material to the Current Drawing list. Repeat the procedure for all the materials you need to import, and then click on OK to retain the material. You'll return to the Materials dialog box.

2. In the Materials list of the Materials dialog box, highlight a material. After choosing a material (other than *GLOBAL*), click on By ACI to open the Attach By AutoCAD Color Index dialog box, shown in Figure 11.25. Select a material in the Select A Material list and then select a number from 1 to 255 in the Select ACI column. Click on Attach, and the material will appear in the Select ACI list against your chosen number.

3. Click on OK once again in the Materials dialog box. At this point, you can either click on Attach and choose a specific component within your model to attach the material to, or click on OK. The material then attaches itself. Now, you can render the file.

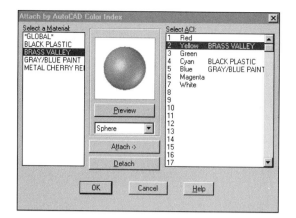

Figure 11.25

The Attach By AutoCAD Color Index dialog box.

Using Layers To Attach A Material

You've just looked at how to attach a material through a color number, but using color isn't the most productive method of rendering 3D models. When you render a model, it's often hard to visualize the parts of your model that need a certain type of material, especially if all you have are different color numbers. It's even harder to remember that color number 123 was the texture for the base of the 3D model or some other part. So, let's look at another method of attaching materials. Again, use the render-1.dwg from the CD-ROM; you may want to attach materials by layer and then save the file as a different name on your hard drive. Follow these steps:

1. Use **RMAT** at the keyboard or click on the RMAT (rendering materials) icon to open the Materials dialog box. Then, highlight a material from the Materials list. If you haven't yet placed any materials in the list, pick them from the Materials Library.

2. After highlighting a material from the Materials list, click on By Layer to open the Attach By Layer dialog box. (See Figure 11.26.) The dialog box is split into three parts: Select A Material, Select Layer, and Attach, Detach, or Preview. Highlight a material from the

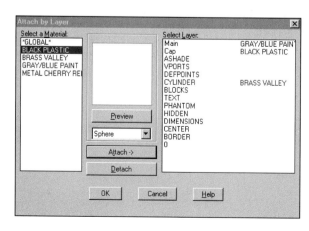

Figure 11.26

The Attach By Layer dialog box.

Select A Material list; then, in the Select Layer column, select a layer to attach it to. Click on Attach, and the material will appear in the Select Layer listing next to the chosen layer. Check to ensure you have the same layer attachments as listed in Figure 11.26.

3. Click on OK to exit the dialog box and return to the Materials dialog box. You may either click on Attach and choose a specific object in your drawing to attach the material to, or click on OK. The material then attaches itself. Now, you can render the file.

Modifying A Material

Open render-2.dwg from the CD-ROM and notice that it's a 3D single model. Using this drawing, we'll look at how to modify materials. At the keyboard, enter "rmat" or click on the Materials icon to open the Materials dialog box. Click on Materials Library, choose BLUE GLASS from the Current Library list, and click on Import to move it to the Current Drawing list. Click on OK to accept the material. Then, ensuring it's still highlighted, click on Modify to open the Modify Standard Material dialog box. (See Figure 11.27.) Notice the series of attributes, such as Color/Pattern, Ambient, Reflection, Roughness, Transparency, Refraction, and Bump Map, plus, in the Color section of the dialog box, the RGB and HLS sliders for each material. The name BLUE GLASS will appear in the Material Name text box. While you're in the Modify Standard Material dialog box, pick the Transparency radio button; then, pick OK to return to the Materials dialog box. Next, use the Attach button to attach the material to the 3D model. Finally, pick OK again to complete the modification, and then Render the drawing. (When you start to render, don't forget to set the Rendering Type to Photo Real or Photo Raytrace.) For practice, you may want to experiment with changing some of the other attributes of the Modify Standard Material dialog box. Hint: To make an illusion of shadowy areas without activating the shadow toggle, you can make Ambient a darker shade than the color of the chosen material.

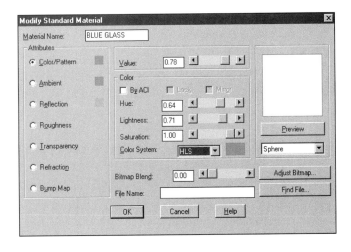

Figure 11.27
The Modify Standard Material dialog box.

2D Mapping Of A 3D Model

Mapping simply refers to the projection of a 2D image onto the surface of a 3D object. For example, photorealistic rendering maps are simply 2D images in a BMP, TGA, TIFF, PCX, or JPEG file format. That's exactly what a bitmap material is: a computer graphic reproduction in a graphic file format. The general format is a GIF, a TIFF, or a TARGA file. In most cases, applying a bitmap material to an object is as simple as loading the GIF, TIFF, or TARGA file and applying it to the object, which can be applied via the Mapping dialog box, shown in Figure 11.28. Under the ACAD2000/ Textures folder, you'll find a supply of about 150 TARGA files, which you can use as bitmaps. Material maps fall into two basic categories: bitmap and parametric.

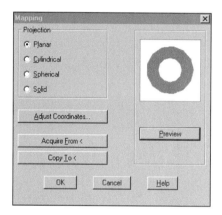

Figure 11.28
The Mapping dialog box.

Bitmaps

To create background scenes (such as clouds, mountain and lake vistas, beach scenes, city skylines, and so forth), you can always take a 2D digital picture of the particular scene you want to use and then map that picture onto your 3D model. With this method, you'll find that the kind of textures and backgrounds you'll be able to manufacture may be endless.

You need to understand a couple of things about texture files. First, you should know how big the file was to begin with—that is, the scale and resolution used to create the file. This information is important because the rendering program needs to know how to scale the bitmap file in order to apply it to the object in your drawing. You generally scale by using a mapping coordinate technique or providing the map scale coordinate factors. After picking a projection type in the Mapping dialog box, simply click on the Adjust Coordinates button to bring up the appropriate coordinates dialog box (see Figure 11.29 for an example). In many programs, mapping simply amounts to putting a window around the object so that the program can see the appropriate scale. At the very least, you can enter a numeric scale factor in some programs.

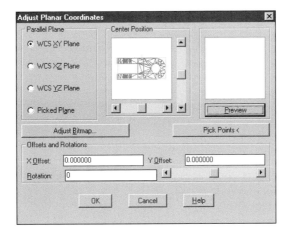

Figure 11.29
The Adjust Planar Coordinates dialog box.

The second consideration is how often, if at all, you'll replicate the pattern over your object and in what direction and format this wrapping will take place. If you want to create a tiled appearance on a floor, you don't want to create one huge tile representing the entire floor—you want tiles placed similarly to an array in AutoCAD. If you're wrapping a texture around a sphere or curved area, you don't want it to lie flat on the sphere. Rendering packages that use bitmaps for texture files can define the format in which you apply the texture file.

Parametric Materials

Parametric materials are the materials and textures that the rendering package itself is capable of creating. The program will create the materials internally. Most rendering programs enable you to create your own materials library without the use of texture maps, external files, scanners, or any other peripheral devices. Parametric materials may go by a variety of names, but they all do much the same thing.

When building a parametric material, you generally start with the base color of the material and add certain properties to the material. There might be some primitive properties in a material library already built in to your package, including brick, tiles, transparency, stripes, shininess, bumps, or reflection, just to name a few. If you combine color with any of these materials from the library list, along with how the material reacts to light, you can produce an almost infinite variety of materials within the rendering package itself. AutoCAD's Render.mli file stores the main library list of materials. Once you've created your materials, you can save them to a new material library file for future use by other models.

Importing A 2D Material Into A 3D Model And Modifying It

Now, let's look at how you can select 2D materials from the Materials Library and import them into your 3D model. For practice, you can reopen the render-2.dwg from the CD-ROM, and then attach a material to it by following these steps:

1. Enter "rmat" at the keyboard or click on the Materials icon to open the Materials dialog box. Click on Materials Library to access the Materials Library dialog box. Select a material from the Current Library list, such as BLUE GLASS, and import it into the Current Drawing list. Then, click on OK to accept the material. (The material is simply copied from AutoCAD's Render.mli file.)

2. To apply the material, choose a material from the Materials list. Click on Attach and choose a specific object in your drawing to attach the material to (or attach it by Layer or Color number), and then click on OK. Attachment of the material is automatic. You're now ready to render.

Landscape Materials

To provide more realism to your renderings, AutoCAD provides a library of 3D landscape plants. You can add trees, plants, bushes, and people as rendered images to final rendered scenes. Landscape plants are generated by fractal-style algorithms; they may also cast shadows and appear in reflections.

Three icons or commands activate landscape materials—**LSNEW**, **LSEDIT**, and **LSLIB**—which in turn open three dialog boxes. Use the dialog boxes to insert new plant images, access plant images from a plant library list, and modify plant images. A landscape object is extended-entity geometry with an image mapped onto to it. You can align it with a view in order to maintain its aspect, or you can use it nonaligned in order for its appearance to change as you change the view of the model.

LSNEW

The **LSNEW** command allows you to choose and place new plants from a Landscape New dialog box, as shown in Figure 11.30.

LSLIB

The **LSLIB** command allows you to modify premade plants from the library list. You can add to the list by using an initial plant from the list, modifying it, and then changing its name.

LSEDIT

The **LSEDIT** command allows you to edit plants you have placed. As you activate the **LSEDIT** command, it prompts you to pick the placed item (such

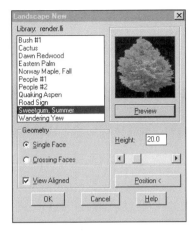

Figure 11.30
The Landscape New dialog box.

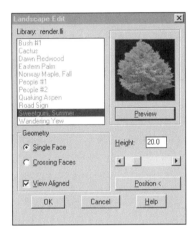

Figure 11.31
The Landscape Edit dialog box.

as a bush or tree). The editing is limited to the position, the height, or setting Geometry to Single Face, Crossing Faces, or View Aligned. Figure 11.31 shows the Landscape Edit dialog box.

Quick Steps To Create And Place Landscape Objects

For practice placing landscaping objects, use the arch-model.dwg file on this book's companion CD-ROM. You should have previously saved it with its shadow setting from the "Simulating Sunlight To An Architectural Model" section earlier in the chapter. To create and place a new landscape object in your drawing, follow these steps:

1. Open your drawing and enter "lslib" or pick the LSLIB icon from the Render toolbar.

2. Click on New in the Landscape Library dialog box, shown in Figure 11.32. In the Landscape Library New dialog box, enter a name such as Sweetgum-1 (without any spaces).

Figure 11.32

The Landscape Library dialog box.

3. Now, you have to provide two files: an image file and an opacity map file. In the Image File box, click on the Find File button, which places you in the Find Image File dialog box. Choose a tree (such as 8tree32i.tga) from the \Textures directory. Remember that all the images are in TGA format, so set the Files Of Type box to *.tga. (All landscape objects need an image and opacity map.) Next, set Opacity Map File to its counterpart, such as 8tree32o.tga.

4. In the Geometry section of the dialog box, choose the Crossing Faces radio button. Doing so makes a 3D object appear more realistic. Also, select the View Aligned checkbox. Click on the Preview button to see the image of your chosen tree. Click on OK to exit the Landscape Library New dialog box. This returns you to the Landscape Library dialog box. Click on the OK button to accept the tree you just created. This may result in the Landscape Library Modification dialog box, which indicates that the current landscape library has been changed. Choose the Save Changes button, which saves your changes to the render.lli file under the \Support directory. Choose the Open button to complete saving and altering the file.

5. To place a landscape or one of the other items from the render.lli library file, pick the LSNEW icon, which activates the Landscape New dialog box. From the render.lli listing box, choose Dawn Redwood or the tree you just created, or one of the other trees of your preference, and pick Preview to view its image. If you are using the arch-model.dwg from the CD-ROM, set the height to 150, and then click on the Position button and place the tree in position. (Its position will default to the UCS, so position it near to the building.) Ensure that Crossing Faces and View Aligned are checked in the Geometry section of the dialog box, and then click on OK. You can copy or array it as needed, so copy the landscape item a few times in the drawing. Finally, pick the triangular apex of each landscape item and drag its apex to a suitable height, but no higher than the height of the building.

6. Set the Render Preferences dialog box to render the landscape items you just placed. Click on the RPREF icon to access the Render Preferences dialog box and set the Rendering Type to Photo Real or Photo Raytrace. Then, in the Rendering Options section of the dialog box, choose the More Options button and set Anti-Aliasing to Medium and Texture Map Sampling to Mip Map Sample. Keep choosing OK to exit the dialog boxes. Use the **RENDER** command to render the simple model.

7. If you click on the Statistics icon in the Render toolbar, a Statistics dialog box will open. It advises you about rendering parameters within your drawing, as you can see in Figure 11.33. These parameters include the scene name, last rendering type, rendering time, and total faces and triangles. Use the command after you've rendered the arch-model drawing and view your statistic results. The value of this dialog box is self-explanatory. If you forget the scene name, it reminds you. An obvious use is to compare rendering times: If you're comparing rendering times within different scenes, the information in this dialog box is the best way to make the comparison. It's also useful if you need to know the number of faces or triangles within the rendering.

Figure 11.33
The Statistics dialog box.

Moving On

Rendering an image can be both time consuming and rewarding, especially when you achieve the image realism of the component you're trying to depict. The key to rendering is practice, practice, practice. In the next chapter, we'll look at more images, but with a view to Web design. We'll explore how to save images for the Web, along with writing animation scripts and adding sound to simple animations.

IMAGE AND ANIMATION FILES

12

Whether you use single images or combine images into animation files and link sound and voice-overs, they all have the same common thread: They're all communication devices that can convey your design ideas to a client or to an end user who will use your product.

Images

In the field of graphics, images are simple communication tools used to convey messages and ideas. In addition, they can be used for eye and brain stimulation and as mnemonic devices to let you communicate more effectively in this visual age. The principle behind this enhanced communication is that your eyes are able to scan images and take in their meaning at a faster rate than you can by reading words alone (as you read, you form mental pictures to understand the words' description). Here are some of the reasons to use images for communication:

- *Problem solving*—To communicate and present your engineering team ideas and solutions to design problems, you may need to import and/or export electronic raster and/or vector files (often into Web Page or multimedia presentations).

- *New customers*—Often, you may need to place images onto your Web site for overseas customers and potential new customers to access.

- *Existing customers*—You can transfer images or drawings to a client's secure server site via FTP for either of two reasons. First, the client may have contracted with you to work up technical solutions as a consultant. Or, you may need to send a solution to remedy an unforeseen problem to the client's remote site plotter; the remote site can then plot out the revised blueprints of the design solution, saving you both time.

- *Desktop publishing*—You can place images and text into technical presentation documents.

- *Presentations*—To enhance PowerPoint or other forms of presentations to potential and new clients, AutoCAD 2000 lets you import and export images in multiple formats. In this chapter, you'll learn how both raster and vector files can be imported or exported. In addition, you'll see how to use the Image Manager and some of the alternate Import and Export commands located on the File and the Insert menus.

Image Quality And File Types

Before you learn how to import or export files, you need to understand image quality and some of the computer terminology associated with it. At the outset, the quality and color depth of the images you export will depend upon your graphics card and the frame buffer in your computer. You have a choice of 8-, 16-, 24-, or 32-bit cards, and subsequent file output, so when you start to think about exporting your images to a file or to the Web, you need to keep a few considerations in mind. An 8-bit graphics card limits you to 256 colors. A 16-bit graphics card provides you with 65,536 colors, which is great if you remember that the human eye can see only 65,000 colors. And a 24-bit or a 32-bit card provides a whopping 16,777,216 colors. Why do you need a 24-bit or 32-bit graphics card if you can only see 65,000 colors? The simple answer is that with the availability of up to 16.7 million colors, you get a smoother transition in the color portions of your image, and you can include gradations of color without banding (lines across your image), thus providing a higher-quality image. (Remember, for faster file access and more compatability, you don't need that much color depth with a Web file.)

Here are some things you need to consider before you export an image file to disk:

- *Resolution of the image*—320×200, 640×480, 800×600, or 1024×768

- *Color depth of the image*—8-bit or 24-bit (see Table 12.1)

- *File storage type*—Raster image or vector image

- *Purpose of the image*—Printing, posting on the Web, or serving as an electronic graphic illustration slide

- *File format or type*—BMP, GIF, TIF, or TGA (see Table 12.1)

Calculating Color Depth

You've looked at a few different file types and reviewed simplified color depth. Now, let's examine the difference between 1-, 8-, 24-, and 32-bit color and how you should decide which to use.

The first bitmapped images were limited in color depth and were basically either black or white. These images were called *1-bit* because one pixel was mapped to a single bit in the memory of the computer. This mapping isn't the situation with more modern systems, which use multiple bits of memory

Table 12.1 File formats.

File Type	Extension	Maximum Bit Depth	Description
BMP	.bmp	8-bit	Standard Windows bitmap file, suitable for low color-depth images
GIF	.gif	8-bit	Graphics Interchange Format, good for Web work at low resolution (for example, 72 or 96dpi)
PCX	.pcx	8-bit	Paintbrush graphics file, suitable for low color-depth images
PostScript	.ps or .eps	24-bit	Stores files in a vector format; great for scaling without image loss
JPEG	.jpg	24-bit	Joint Photographic Expert Group file; great compression for Web work
RGB	.rgb	24-bit	Silicon Graphics Image (SGI) image file, good for high color-depth, without an Alpha channel
TARGA	.tga	32-bit	Great for CAD images, due to its color depth, resolution, and compression
TIFF	.tif	32-bit	Great for desktop publishing and screen captures
PICT	.pct	32-bit	Standard Macintosh graphics file

per pixel and in doing so achieve a higher color depth—such as 8-bit, 15-bit, 16-bit, 24-bit, and 32-bit. But what is 8-bit or 24-bit color?

As indicated, a 1-bit image was mapped as one pixel per one bit of black or white image. But 8 bits are equivalent to eight 1s (or bits) in binary. If you multiply 2 to the power of 8 ($2 \times 2 \times 2 \times 2 \times 2 \times 2 \times 2 \times 2$), the result is 256 colors. Then, if you take 2 to the power of 24, the answer becomes 16,777,216 colors for 24-bit files. And that's the limit—32 bits won't give you any more colors. These numbers mean that the video card or graphics file you use will maintain 256 colors when you use an 8-bit graphics card, 65,536 colors with a 16-bit graphics card, and 16.7 million colors with a 24-bit graphics card. See Figure 12.1 for a comparison of 1-, 8-, and 24-bit color.

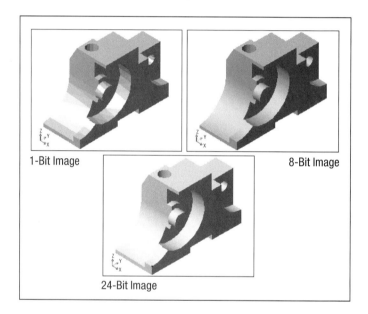

1-Bit Image

8-Bit Image

24-Bit Image

Figure 12.1

Comparison of 1-bit, 8-bit, and 24-bit color.

Your final consideration is the output format of the file and whether the output is 8 bit, 24 bit, or 32 bit. Obviously, *8-bit* and *24-bit* refer to the number of colors or color depth you can display at one time. The best color depths are 24- and 32-bit, which both use 8 bits each to represent the red, green, and blue (RGB) components; 24-bit and 32-bit files are said to use *true color*. Still, you can't get any more color depth from 32-bit output than from 24-bit ouput—so what does 32-bit output provide?

The 32-bit file has an extra *Alpha channel*. A 32-bit file with the Alpha blending file is a combination of the 24-bit true color plus 8 alpha bits, which amount to some 256 levels of translucency. The extra Alpha blending channel is used if you need translucency in your image. It's an overlay technique; instead of seeing all colors as opaque, you also have 8 alpha bits of translucency that allow your color depth to range from translucency to opaque. Fog, for instance, is a form of translucency and would fit into this category—

15-BIT COLOR

The mid range of 15-bit color isn't used much anymore. It stores 5 bits of color per channel (RGB component) to provide 32,768 colors and uses a subsequent trade-off called *dithering* to improve image quality. You appear to get 65,536 colors, due to the trade-off.

Dithering is a trade-off of spatial resolution to color resolution. This technique was used by graphic display adapter cards, with a limited color depth. Dithering tricks the eye into seeing more colors than there actually are. For example, if a color is chosen that the graphics system does not have, it would use a checkerboard pattern of higher and lower color values around the required shade to form a color blend that appeared similar to the shade. Compared to 24-bit, it would be less crisp. So the trade-off is spatial resolution to color resolution.

if you needed to apply fog to one of your files, you'd have to use a 32-bit format and a file type (such as TIFF or TARGA) that supports Alpha blending.

Examples of the types of output files to which AutoCAD lets you render are 8-bit BMP or PCX files or 24-bit TIFF or TARGA files. Let's see where these are situated. Open the Render dialog box by clicking on the Render icon. In the Destination section of the dialog box, choose File from the drop-down list. Now, click on the More Options button below the drop-down list. In the resulting File Output Configuration dialog box, click on the arrow by the top drop-down list in the File Type section and notice that you have five file types to choose from: BMP, PCX, PostScript, TGA, and TIFF. If you look back at Table 12.1, you'll find that the BMP and PCX file types allow 8-bit color; the PostScript, JPG, and RGB allow 24-bit color; and the TARGA, TIFF, and PICT files allow 32-bit color. However, the drop-down list below that indicates the file type specifies file image resolution sizes; values range from 320×200 to 4096×3072, plus a User Defined option. Close the File Output Configuration dialog box, and we'll look at other types of images. So far, you've reviewed just a few types of standard files that AutoCAD lets you save to.

Vector Vs. Raster Files

Within AutoCAD, you can import and/or export both raster and vector files. First, let's consider a *raster* image, which is simply another name for a bitmapped image. A raster file is controlled pixel by pixel and stored as a grid of pixels. (In the past, it was stored with one bit per pixel, and the pixel was either black or white.) On the other hand, a more precise vector (or CAD) image is created as a series of X and Y coordinates from points, lines, and so on. You'll find that raster images use and store more pixel-based data; therefore, they're larger in file size than their vector-based cousins.

The terms *vector* and *raster* originated in the dark ages of cathode ray tube (CRT) displays, in which one type of display used electron beams to paint lines (called *vectors*) directly onto the CRT, and another type of display used a raster scan technique. The process of converting computer vector images into a series of pixels was termed *rasterization*. Because raster images were already in a form as required by the raster displays (that is, *rasterized*), bitmapped images stored in a computer came to be known as raster images. Hence, today's computer displays use a technique called *raster scanning*.

What is raster scanning? Consider a noninterlaced computer display like that shown in Figure 12.2. If you have such a display screen, the raster-scan lines will start in the upper-left corner of your screen, move to the right of the first line pixel by pixel, at the end of the line fly back, start again on the next line down, and so on. At the bottom of the screen, the raster-scan lines will fly back once more, but this time from the lower-right corner to the original upper-left corner, starting the whole process again. Your TV set, on the other hand, uses an interlaced display to scan first the set of odd lines and then the set of even lines on your screen; it keeps repeating this procedure.

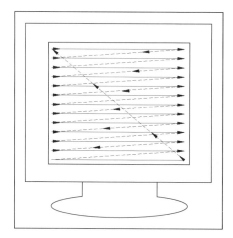

Figure 12.2
Noninterlaced display.

Screen Resolution

When you begin to create images, one of your first tasks is to think of the quality and the resolution—that is, the number of pixels you want to represent your image (such as the pixel width by the pixel height—for example, 640×480), the amount of color depth (such as 8- or 24-bit), and the number of layers you'll use for different colors and textures. Also, consider how much memory your frame buffer contains, because the higher the color depth, the more memory is required in the frame buffer (see Table 12.2).

Table 12.2 Memory and color depth for 2D graphics.

Resolution Color Depth	8-Bit 256 Colors	16-Bit 65,536 Colors	24-Bit 16.7M Colors	32-Bit 16.7M Colors	Memory Size
640×480	0.29MB	0.59MB	0.88MB	1.17MB	Min 1MB
800×600	0.46MB	0.92MB	1.37MB	1.83MB	Min 2MB
1024×768	0.75MB	1.50MB	2.25MB	3.00MB	Min 4MB
1280x1024	1.25MB	2.50MB	3.75MB	5.00MB	Min 8MB

Three factors determine output speed and quality of your images: resolution, file output (type), and color depth. Most image programs give you a choice of resolution from as low as 320×200 to 640×480, 800×600, 1024×768, and higher. For the most part, the higher the resolution you use, the better the quality of the final product and, conversely, the more rendering time it will take (640×480 is a good starting point).

Thus, if you were to create a file with a resolution of 1280 and 32-bit color depth, you'd calculate its file size using the formula $1280 \times 1024 \times 24$ bits—you'd need 5 megabytes of memory just to handle it. So the minimum memory size of your card should be 8MB. Alternately, if you were to create a file with a resolution of 768 and 24-bit color depth, you'd calculate its file size using the formula $1024 \times 768 \times 24$ bits—you'd need a minimum of 4MB of memory to handle it. Similarly, a $640 \times 480 \times 8$-bit file would require a minimum of 1MB of memory. From these simple mathematical equations, it's easy to figure out that the low-end 8-bit file requires less time and is smaller than the electronic computation for a true-color high-end 24-bit file.

Comparing 8-Bit And 24-Bit Color-Depth Files

Let's walk through an example that compares files with different color depths. Open the cross-head.dwg file from this book's companion CD-ROM. This file contains a 3D solid model set to color 140 in the AutoCAD Color Index (ACI) or—in the graphics world—the color lookup table (LUT). Your objective with the drawing is to render it as an 8-bit color-depth file, and also as a 24-bit color-depth file. You'll compare the quality between the two files, as illustrated in Figure 12.3, and then export the 24-bit file (which is better quality) to disk. Here are the steps to do so:

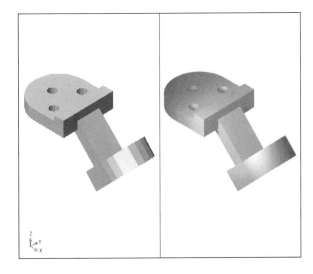

Figure 12.3

Comparison of 8-bit shaded file and 24-bit color-depth file.

1. Open the cross-head.dwg file and pick the Layout1 tab at the bottom of your screen to enter the Layout or paper space, which should be a blank screen. (If a single viewport appears, simply erase it before the next step.)

2. Choose View|Viewports|2Viewports and press Enter to accept the vertical viewport default, and then press Enter again to accept the **Fit** option of the **VPORTS** command you just entered.

3. To ensure that you can see both vertical viewports, choose View|Zoom|Extents. Then, at the keyboard or command prompt, enter "ms" (for model space) and choose the left viewport.

4. Set the left viewport to an NE Isometric view and the right viewport to a mirrored SE Isometric view. Remember to Zoom in tight into the solid 3D model in both viewports. Also, in both viewports, set the **VIEWRES** to 20000; otherwise, you'll have polygonal facets on display as you shade and render.

5. Use **SHADEMODE** with the **Gouraud** option in the left viewport. (Gouraud shading is also referred to as smooth shading, to differentiate between flat and smooth shaded files.) Even though a file's color depth is dependent on the type of file saved and its assigned options, this is just an image on the screen and it can be saved in many file formats that would set its color depth. Its on-screen color depth would be determined by the user's video card setting. You now have the equivalent of an 8-bit shaded file on the left.

6. Choose the right viewport to make it active. Use the **MATLIB** command at the command prompt or click on the Materials Library icon to open the Materials Library dialog box. Scroll down the Current Library list box and choose the Gray/Blue Paint; click on Import. Click on OK to accept the material.

7. Choose the Materials icon to open the Materials dialog box. In the Materials list, select the Gray/Blue Paint material and then use the Attach button to attach it to the model in your right viewport.

8. Use the Light icon to open the Lights dialog box. Select a new spotlight and give it the name "Spot1" in the Light Name field. Set the Hotspot value to 25 and Falloff to 50. Select the Shadows On checkbox; then, keep clicking on OK until you're back at the command prompt.

9. Choose the Render icon to open the Render dialog box. Choose Photo Real as the Rendering Type. In the Destination section, select

File from the drop-down list; then, click on More Options to open the File Output Configuration dialog box.

10. In the File Type section, choose TGA from the top drop-down list and 800×600 from the bottom drop-down list. Choose 24 Bits in the Colors section. Make sure that Compressed is checked in the TGA options, None is selected in the Interlace, and click on OK to return to the Render dialog box.

11. Click on Background. In the Background dialog box, pick the Image radio button and then click on Find File to open the Background Image dialog box; you should be in the ACAD 2000 folder. Select *.TGA in the Files Of Type drop-down list. Next, double-click on the Textures folder and notice all the TARGA texture files in the folder. Choose the Cloud.tga (TARGA) file as the background image. Click on Open and then on OK to return to the Render dialog box.

12. Return to the Destination section and choose Viewport. Click on Render to see your result. You'll see both an 8-bit shaded file and a 24-bit render file on your screen at the same time (refer back to Figure 12.3).

13. Once you've seen your render result, return again to the Render dialog box. In the Destination section, reset the drop-down list to File. In the File Output Configuration dialog box's File Type section, choose TGA from the top drop-down list and 800×600 from the bottom drop-down list. (You're resetting the file type as you did in Step 10.) Click on Render and render the file to disk. If your model is too dark, you'll need to place a light or two. You'll find the completed rendering file—cross-head-rend.tga—on the CD-ROM if you want to see the result of this simple exercise.

QUICK METHOD TO IMPORT AND ADJUST AN IMAGE

Before you move on, let's examine two useful commands you can enter at the command line or choose from the Reference Toolbar. The **IMAGEATTACH** and **IMAGEADJUST** commands both open dialog boxes. You'll find them to be quick, useful ways to attach images and adjust the brightness, contrast, and fade quality of a single image. You may want to open a new file and try attaching the cross-head-rend.tga file from the CD-ROM.

At the command line, enter "imageattach" to open the standard Select Image File dialog box. Select cross-head-rend.tga from the CD-ROM and place it at 0,0,0 on your screen, with a scale of 100. Then, Zoom to the Extents. Once you have the image on screen, enter "imageadjust" at the command line (or pick the icon from the Reference toolbar, or select Modify|Object|Image) and pick the border of the cross-head-rend.tga image. The Image Adjust dialog box will open, as shown in Figure 12.4; it allows you to adjust the Brightness, Contrast, and Fade quality of the image. In the dialog box, set Brightness to 60, Contrast to 55, and Fade to 10. Keep the file open; and let's use Object Linking and Embedding to link another file into it.

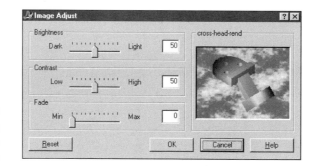

Figure 12.4

The Image Adjust dialog box displaying the cross-head-rend.tga file.

Tips For Improving Image Quality

To improve image quality, you must use lighting effectively. The way you approach lighting varies with the scale of the objects you're modeling:

- *Lighting an object*—The standard learning object is a teapot. A spotlight is the easiest light to place for an object; you could place three 150-watt spotlights 2 meters (6'-6") above the object. You should have two of the spots illuminating the viewing face from different angles. To cast a shadow toward the viewer, position a third spot behind the object.

- *Lighting a building*—Lighting buildings can be challenging because when the sun is overhead, it can produce a flat, uninteresting look on a building because the illumination of two different sides is similar—there's no variation in the shadow or simulated depth. Buildings are much more interesting at dawn and dusk when shadow effects are more realistic and dramatic. For a dramatic effect, photograph the building when the sun angle is low. The low sun angle causes different faces of the building to be produced in different light qualities. Elongated shadows will be enhanced, and some faces of the building will be in deep shadow, whereas others are in bright sunshine. A further advanced technique is to render an image at sunset. The scene, for example, could have dark skies with a brightly illuminated building face, along with artificial lighting from the building's interior, from adjacent streetlights, and landscape lighting in the immediate area of the building, all producing a realistic image.

- *Lighting an interior*—The standard office interior can be very challenging. Offices lit by diffuse lighting provide flat, uninteresting scenes. You can introduce natural light by adding sunlight as a distant light source. Make it cast light through either a skylight or window. Use spotlights on objects to cast shadows. You could place five or six 150-watt spotlights 2 meters (6'-6") above the objects. Remember that you should have two of the spots illuminating the viewing face from different angles. Then, to cast a shadow toward the viewer position, use a third spot behind the object. To be more imaginative, you can also place lights to cast shadows behind columns and to simulate wall sconces.

Placing Images Into Presentation Documents

At this point of the chapter, you've exported an image file to disk, and you've also imported an image file. Let's look at other methods of working with files, plus embedding or placing sound files using Object Linking and Embedding. (In AutoCAD 2000, you're limited to using WAVE sound files—that is, files with .wav extensions; you'll find two royalty-free copyright files on the CD-ROM.)

One of Windows' greatest features is the ability to copy and paste elements from one program to another. For example, if you have both AutoCAD 2000 and Word for Windows open at the same time, you can copy drawing files within AutoCAD and then paste them into a Word document. Object Linking and Embedding (OLE) is a useful method; if you use it and later update the drawing file and reopen the Word document, the document will also be updated and reflect the changes made to the drawing.

Windows also lets you cut and paste images (WMF, EPS, TIFF, GIF, BMP, and JPEG files) and animations (AVI files) into a PowerPoint presentation document. The files can be inserted as picture files or linked objects. Now, let's look at how to use AutoCAD to carry out OLE using the Windows Insert Object dialog box, shown in Figure 12.5.

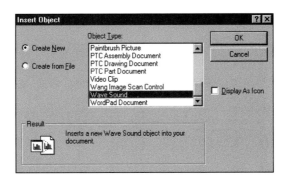

Figure 12.5
The Insert Object dialog box.

Object Linking And Embedding

OLE is a means of *hot linking* files within a Windows environment. The method of placing files is similar to external referencing, or *XREF*, as AutoCAD refers to it. OLE differs from the Windows options of Copy and Paste only in that if you change the original image or file, the target file will automatically be updated. This is a great method for inserting image or spreadsheet files, for example—instead of copying and pasting a file, you simply embed or link the file. Then, as you update the original file, AutoCAD passes along the updated information to the target file within your document.

In AutoCAD, discussing the difference between an embedded file and a linked file is like comparing the Insert and XREF functions. You can think of an embedded file as an inserted file—but there's no hot linking if you embed. If you link a file, on the other hand (through OLE), you create a hot link with the mother program that created the file. If you were in Word for Windows, for example, and you linked an AutoCAD drawing into your document, you could simply double-click on the AutoCAD drawing in Word to open AutoCAD and edit the drawing file.

You can use three methods to open the Insert Object dialog box:

- Choose Insert|OLE Object.

- Choose the insertobj icon on the Insert toolbar.

- Enter "insertobj" at the command prompt.

Open the Insert Object dialog box and notice the many formats you're allowed to link and embed in the Object Type list box. Scroll through the list and you'll see formats from Adobe Acrobat Document, AutoCAD Drawing, and Bitmap Image, to Wave Sound and WordPad Document files. Check to ensure the Create New radio button is selected, choose Wave Sound, and then choose the Create From File radio button to activate the file locator. Click on Browse to open the Browse dialog box; browse to the CD-ROM and choose one of the two WAVE files: sport1a or sport2a. Click on Open to return to the Insert Object dialog box; click on OK to accept the WAVE file. (At this point, you can also click on Link to link the file into the drawing.) The OLE Properties dialog box appears, as shown in Figure 12.6. Click on OK to return to your drawing. You can now double pick the sound icon within the drawing (it's attached or linked to the WAVE file), and it will play within the drawing file. This is a great way to start a presentation, because the WAVE file can be playing in the background. To stop it, simply press the Esc key. (If the OLE dialog box appears, simply pick the Cancel button.) You've now both exported and imported an image file, plus linked sound

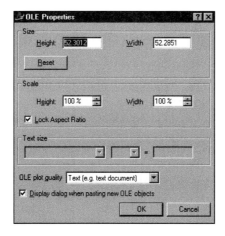

Figure 12.6
The OLE Properties dialog box.

into your image file. You can either save the file to disk or discard the file by picking the File|Close option.

Next, we'll review the more important AutoCAD import and export commands, including the methods of creating and importing DXF and PostScript files. Then, you'll explore the Image Manager, which is a useful method of importing and working with images—especially via the new File Details dialog box and its easy-to-use interface.

Importing And Exporting Images

AutoCAD allows you to import many types of file formats, most of which you'll find on the Insert menu, shown in Figure 12.7. On the other hand, to export files, you'll use the Export and Save As commands located on the File menu.

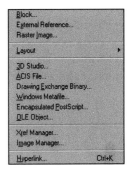

Figure 12.7
The Insert menu.

In addition to the Insert menu, you can also use the Insert toolbar. To activate the Insert toolbar, shown in Figure 12.8, choose View|Toolbars|Insert. The toolbar gives you access to the following commands:

- *INSERT*—Lets you insert a block or another drawing

- *XREF*—Controls external references to drawing files

- *IMAGE*—Inserts images into an AutoCAD drawing file

- *IMPORT*—Imports various types of file formats into AutoCAD

- *INSERTOBJ*—Inserts a linked or embedded object into AutoCAD

Figure 12.8
The Insert toolbar.

IMPORT

The **IMPORT** command allows you to import four file formats—Windows metafile (.wmf), ACIS solid object file (.sat), Encapsulated PostScript file (.eps), and 3D Studio file (.3ds)—into AutoCAD as interchange files. (An *interchange file* is a file used to share drawing data with other applications.) You access and use **IMPORT** as follows:

```
Command: import
```

To open the Import File dialog box, shown in Figure 12.9, choose Import from the File pull-down menu (or enter "import" at the command line).

To import a file, you simply enter the name of the interchange file in the dialog box. Choose the file extension and either click on Open or press Enter to accept the selection.

Choosing the Metafile file format makes available the Options button, which opens the WMF In Options dialog box, shown in Figure 12.10. (Alternately, you can enter "wmfopts" at the command prompt to display this dialog box directly.) Notice it displays two checkboxes: Wire Frame and Wide Lines.

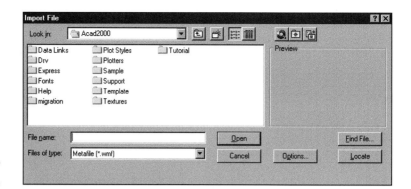

Figure 12.9
The Import File dialog box.

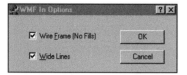

Figure 12.10
The WMF In Options dialog box.

EXPORT

The **EXPORT** command allows you to export various file formats as interchange files:

- Windows Metafile (.wmf)

- ACIS solid object file (.sat)

- Solid object stereolithography file (.stl)

- Encapsulated PostScript file (.eps)

- Attribute extract DXF file (.dxx)

- Device-independent bitmap file (.bmp)

- 3D Studio file (.3ds)

- AutoCAD drawing file (.dwg)

You access **EXPORT** from the command prompt as follows:

```
Command: export
```

To open the Export Data dialog box, shown in Figure 12.11, choose Export from the File menu. To export a file, you simply enter the name of the interchange file in the dialog box. Choose the file extension and either click on Save or press Enter to accept the current (default) drawing name as the interchange file name.

DXFOUT

The **DXFOUT** command allows you to export a drawing exchange file (DXF ASCII text file) from an existing drawing. These drawing interchange files can be used with post-processing programs for a wide range of applications,

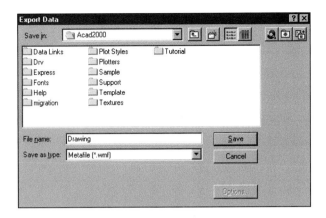

Figure 12.11
The Export Data dialog box.

from finite element analysis to finite element modeling. 3D Studio Max also lets you import both surface and solid models, plus STL and DXF files. Using DXF is a great way to import geometry into animation software and other programs. In AutoCAD 2000, DXF files are now written to disk using the **SAVE, SAVEAS, WBLOCK,** and **DXFOUT** commands, and they may also have thumbnail preview images associated with them.

To DXF a drawing file out to disk, you have a number of options:

- Use the **DXFOUT** command prompt.

- Use the File|Save As command.

- Use the **WBLOCK** command.

The first two options open the Save Drawing As dialog box. The dialog box lets you save AutoCAD 2000 drawings in various formats: DWG, DWT, and DXF, plus prior AutoCAD releases. (The **WBLOCK** command uses the Write Block dialog box. In this case, change the File Name extension from .dwg to .dxf, plus select your units.)

Any files you create with the **DXFOUT** command have the extension .dxf. Simply enter the name of the drawing exchange file (without the .dxf extension). Or, press Enter to accept the default (drawing name) as the drawing exchange file name. You may also save the drawing file into Release 12, 13, 14, or 2000 DXF format.

Notice that when you choose the DXF file type (in the Save Drawing As dialog box), an Options button becomes active that you can click on to display the Saveas Options dialog box, shown in Figure 12.12. This dialog box provides a number of options. It has radio buttons that let you choose the DXF format (ASCII or Binary), along with Select Objects and Save Thumbnail Preview Image checkboxes. You can also enter the precision accuracy (0 to 16) for floating point numbers. The general rule is to keep the accuracy default value of 6 if you're sending the DXF file to an earlier release of AutoCAD or saving it as 2D. If you have 3D models, use 16

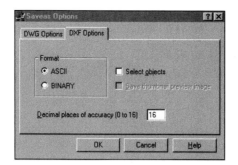

Figure 12.12
The DXF options of the Saveas Options dialog box.

decimal places. AutoCAD indicates that ASCII format DXF files can be read with a text editor and are compatible with a wider range of applications. Binary-format DXF files contain all the information of an ASCII DXF file but in a more compact form. You can read and write to binary-format files faster than to ASCII-format files.

DXFIN

The **DXFIN** command allows you to import a DXF file and creates an AutoCAD drawing file from the drawing exchange file. (In AutoCAD 2000, you can create optional thumbnail images with DXF files using the **SAVE**, **SAVEAS**, and **WBLOCK** commands. DXF images can be previewed using **OPEN** and **INSERT**.)

To DXF a drawing in from disk, you have three options:

- Use the **DXFIN** command line prompt.

- Use the File|Open command.

- Use the **INSERT** command.

The first two methods open the Select File dialog box. The **INSERT** command uses the Insert dialog box. The dialog boxes let you open AutoCAD 2000 drawings from various formats: DWG, DWT, and DXF, plus prior AutoCAD releases.

When prompted, enter the name of the drawing exchange file (without the .dxf extension). Remember to set the extension name to .dxf.

PSOUT

The **PSOUT** command creates an Encapsulated PostScript (EPS) file from an existing drawing. You have two options to create PostScript files:

- Use the **PSOUT** command, which opens the Create PostScript File dialog box.

- Use the File|Export command.

Both methods let you output your drawing as an EPS file, which can be printed on a PostScript device or imported into desktop-publishing software.

Note: If you use the DXFIN command as the first command in the drawing editor, the drawing interchange file is converted into an AutoCAD drawing. If you use the DXFIN command after you've already created part of a drawing, only the objects section from the drawing interchange file is added to the drawing.

Be aware that **PSOUT** doesn't produce any **HIDE** and **SHADE** output. You'll notice that when you choose the EPS file type, the Options button is active; it will open the PostScript Out Options dialog box, shown in Figure 12.13.

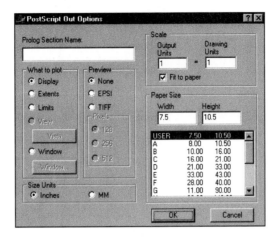

Figure 12.13
The PostScript Out Options dialog box.

Using the PostScript Out Options dialog box is similar to plotting. In the What To Plot section, you can choose a specific view portion of your drawing:

- *Display*—Lets you export a view from the current viewport and the current display if you're in model space, or from the current view if you're in paper space.

- *Extents*—Lets you export the equivalent of the View Zoom Extents option, within the current display. The display amount of the Extents option depends if your display is in model space or paper space.

- *Limits*—If you're in Top view, similar to the Zoom Extents option, this option lets you export the entire drawing.

- *Window*—Lets you simply pick two opposite corner points.

- *View*—Save and name views within your drawing before using this option.

In the Preview section, you can choose None, EPSI, or TIFF headers, along with a Pixels size of 128, 256, or 512, which means you'll have a screen preview image of 128×128, 256×256, or 512×512. You also have Scale and Paper Size options, plus a Size Units choice of Inches or MM. These are all typical plot options.

Now, let's look at the steps needed to create a PostScript file. You'll use two dialog boxes—the Create PostScript File dialog box and the PostScript Out Options dialog box:

1. Enter "psout" at the command prompt to open the Create PostScript File dialog box.

2. Enter the name of the file and locate the folder. Then, choose the Options button, which activates the PostScript Out Options dialog box.

3. In the What To Plot section of the PostScript Out Options dialog box, select one of the radio buttons: Display, Extents, Limits, View, or Window.

4. It's normal to include a screen preview image in a PostScript file. In the Preview section, select the EPSI or TIFF radio button.

5. With either the EPSI or TIFF radio button selected, the Pixels section is activated. The screen preview image size of 128×128 is standard, but you can select 128, 256, or 512.

6. From the Size Units section, select the Inches or Millimeters radio button. The default is Inches.

7. In the Scale section, set the Output Units equal to the Drawing Units or check the Fit To Paper checkbox. The default is Fit To Paper.

8. In the Paper Size section, enter Width by Height components. The User option of 7.50×10.50 is the default, so use the scroll box to choose a letter for size; or, click on OK to accept the options and exit the PostScript Out Options dialog box, which returns you to the Create PostScript File dialog box. Click on Save to write the file to disk.

PSIN

The **PSIN** command imports an EPS file into AutoCAD. Simply enter the command at the command prompt. This command opens the Select PostScript File dialog box, shown in Figure 12.14, which imports and scales an EPS file as a block. Two system variables also control PostScript input and output:

- *PSDRAG*—Value is 0 or 1

- *PSQUALITY*—Default value is 75; uses an integer between –32768 and 32767

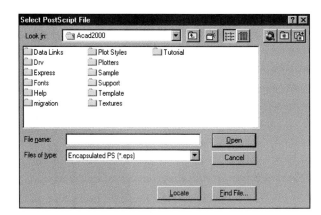

Figure 12.14
The Select PostScript File dialog box.

In the Select PostScript File dialog box, enter the name of the EPS file you wish to import into your AutoCAD file. (You don't need to enter the .eps extension.) Then, choose an insertion point and enter a scale.

Now, let's look at the steps needed to import a PostScript image file using the Select PostScript File dialog box. On this book's companion CD-ROM, you'll find two PostScript files: solid-bell.eps and hand2.eps. You can choose either of these for the exercise:

1. Enter "psin" at the command prompt to open the Select PostScript File dialog box.

2. Enter the name of the file to import and click on Open.

3. At the bottom of the screen, a blue memory banding progress bar will appear to show that AutoCAD is importing the file.

4. Enter the insertion point. 0,0,0 is your default; simply pressing Enter will accept 0,0,0.

5. Enter a scale factor by either stretching the attached image with the mouse (by picking a point on screen) or entering a number. If you use the **LIST** command on the PostScript image you just imported, you'll find that it is now classified as a block within your drawing file.

AutoCAD offers other ways to import images, and AutoCAD 2000 has a new set of tools to do so. For example, the Image Manager, discussed next, can import most kinds of image files (except PostScript images), and it can be used for other purposes as well.

Using The Image Manager

The Image Manager is a new feature of AutoCAD 2000. It lists all the image files attached to your current drawing. Using it allows you to attach, detach, locate, reload, and unload raster images, such as 8-bit (bitmapped bitonal or color) and 24-bit color files. Different raster formats include BMP, TIFF, JPEG, PCX, and TARGA. You'll find no limit to the number and size of images, and you can use more than one image per viewport. Other new image adjustment tools include tools such as Imageadjust, Imagequality, Transparency, and Imageframe. The Image Manager also provides details such as the resolution, color depth, and pixel width of images.

You can access the Image Manager dialog box, shown in Figure 12.15, three ways:

• At the command prompt, type "image".

• Choose Insert|Image Manager.

• From the Standard toolbar, choose the Image Manager icon.

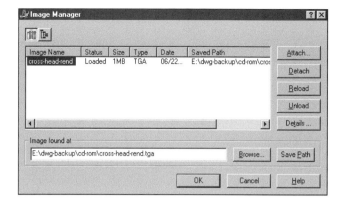

Figure 12.15

The Image Manager dialog box.

When you open the Image Manager dialog box, you'll see that it contains nine components (very similar to those in the XREF Manager dialog box): a list of images; Attach, Detach, Reload, Unload, Details, Browse, and Save Path buttons; and an Image Found At field. In addition, at top left you'll notice two icon buttons: The left List View button displays a list of image file names attached to the drawing; the right Tree View button displays a tree view of this image list. (You can also press F3 to toggle on the list view and F4 to toggle on the tree view in the dialog box.) Here are descriptions of the Image Manager's components:

- *List View button*—Shows a list of images used in the drawing. The list is sorted by Image Name, Status, Size, Type (such as GIF, TIF, TGA), Date, and Saved Path. If you need to select multiple images, press the Shift or Ctrl key as you pick.

- *Tree View button*—Shows image definitions and the nesting levels of images. The top level of the tree view shows images attached directly to the drawing. Edit an image name by picking it, or select it and then press F4. You can then Detach, Reload, Unload, or see the Details of the image.

- *Attach button*—Activates the Image dialog box, which lets you specify an image file.

- *Detach button*—Removes the selected image definition from the drawing database and deletes all the associated image objects from the drawing and from the display.

- *Reload button*—Reloads the most recent version of an image. Reloading doesn't control whether the image is displayed, but it ensures display of the most current image.

- *Unload button*—Displays only the border of the image to conserve memory while maintaining the link to the image—that is, this button unloads image data from working memory without erasing the image objects from the drawing. Here's a tip: To improve performance, un-load any images you don't need.

- *Details button*—Activates the Image File Details dialog box. As shown in Figure 12.16, the dialog box shows the image name, path, file creation time and date, file size and type, color system, color depth, pixel width, height and resolution, default size in units, and a preview image.

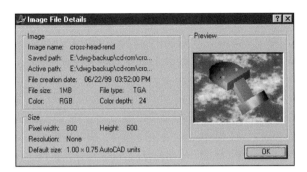

Figure 12.16
The Image File Details dialog box of the Image Manager.

- *Image Found At field*—Shows the path of the selected image. If you select multiple images, this field remains blank. The path shown is the actual path where the image resides.

- *Save Path button*—Stores any new path information. Hint: Remember to click on Save Path after editing the path, or AutoCAD will use the old path the next time you load the drawing; if you need to restore the old path, press Esc.

- *Browse button*—Activates the Select Image File dialog box, which allows you to select an image from a different folder. You can also open this dialog box from the command prompt by entering "imageattach". Then, you can view and attach raster or bitmapped bitonal, 8-bit gray/color, or 24-bit color image files to a drawing. Attaching an image creates an image definition, loads the image into memory, and displays the image.

Now, open the shaded-image.dwg file from the CD-ROM. The objective is to use the Image Manager to place an image into the file. The image formats, found on the CD-ROM, are saved as image1.bmp, image2.tif, image3.tga. Choose one of these files and then follow these steps:

1. Open the shaded-image.dwg file.

2. Access the Image Manager dialog box and click on Attach to activate the Select Image File dialog box. In this dialog box, you'll load the image files.

3. Insert one of the image files into the upper-right corner of the drawing. (It has a blank rectangle in paper space.) Your objective is to

attach the image from the lower left corner to the upper right corner of the blank rectangle. When the Image Manager prompts you for a scale factor, enter "90". (Do not pick the upper-right corner of the rectangle at the scale prompt, because it will be too large for the drawing.)

Creating Electronic Files For The Internet

From within the Plot dialog box, you can save and plot drawing files as Internet-ready, vector-based files in a Drawing Web Format (DWF). Because a DWF file is highly compressed, you can transmit and open it faster than a standard drawing file. You can use either your Netscape or Internet Explorer browser with the Windows High Performance (WHIP) driver plug-in to open and control layers, view and use named views, embed hyperlinks, plot, pan, and zoom. To create the DWF file, there are three ways to open the Plot dialog box:

- Choose Plot from the File menu.

- Choose the Plot icon from the Standard toolbar.

- Enter "plot" at the command prompt.

The Plot dialog box contains two tabs: Plot Settings and Plot Device. Choose the Plot Device tab, and you'll see a Plotter Configuration section as shown in Figure 12.17. Click on the arrow to open the Name drop-down list.

In addition to the configuration for your specific plotting device, the list contains two preconfigured ePlot pc3 plotter configuration files, which are used to create DWF files: DWF Classic.pc3 and DWF ePlot.pc3. The DWF ePlot.pc3 file creates AutoCAD 2000 DWF files with a white background, whereas the DWF Classic.pc3 configuration file creates DWF files similar to AutoCAD 14 DWF files, with a black background.

Hint: Remember that a .06-inch default lineweight is used when you plot a DWF drawing. To control the lineweight option, go to the Plot Settings tab of the dialog box and uncheck the Plot Object Lineweights checkbox in the Plot Options section. (To access the box, remember to uncheck the Plot With Plot Styles checkbox first—it's situated directly beneath the Plot Object Lineweights checkbox.)

DWF Files

Placing a DWF file into your Web page gives authorized users the ability to zoom, pan, and print noneditable versions of your drawing. You can also use the **HYPERLINK** command to create links between DWF files and other drawings or Web pages.

In addition to using the Plot dialog box to create DWF files, you can enter "dwfout" at the command prompt and then follow the steps on the com-

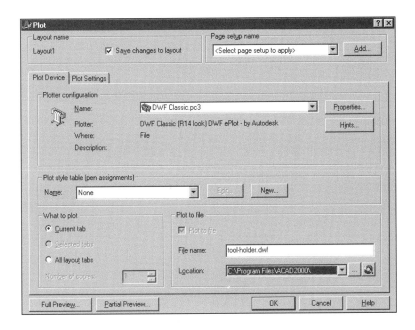

Figure 12.17
The Plot dialog box.

mand line to create a DWF file. Doing so passes all the information to the plot function to create a DWF file from your current file on screen.

Plotting A DWF File

Let's look at how to plot a drawing into a Web-format file. From the CD-ROM, open the tool-holder.dwg file, which is a metric drawing of a solid 3D model. Your objective with the drawing is to plot it into a DWF file. Here are the steps to do so:

1. Open the Plot dialog box by choosing the Plot icon from the Standard toolbar, by choosing File|Plot, or by entering "plot" or "print" at the command prompt.

2. Choose the Plot Device tab. In the Plotter Configuration section, choose the DWF eplot.pc3 plotter configuration file from the Name drop-down list.

3. In the File Name field in the lower-right corner of the dialog box, enter a name for the DWF file. It should be preset to tool-holder-Layout1.dwf. (tool-holder-Layout1.dwf is also available on the CD-ROM.)

4. In the Location drop-down list, you should do one of the following: Enter the location to plot the file to or enter an Internet or intranet URL to plot the file to. (Because you can only plot DWF files to the Internet using the FTP protocol, you'll plot this particular file to disk for this exercise.)

5. Click on OK. Note that as you do so, a Plot Progress dialog box will appear to indicate AutoCAD is writing the DWF file out to disk.

At this point, you have a basic tool-holder-Layout1.dwf file, but you still need to set the compression and resolution options, and any other settings that might be necessary. Next, let's look at how to set the resolution and compression options, along with any additional settings that might be required for DWF files. Then, you'll learn how to view DWF files with an external browser.

Setting Compression And Resolution For DWF Files

You should still have tool-holder.dwg on screen. Open the Plot dialog box and choose the Plot Device tab. In the Plotter Configuration section, select DWF ePlot.pc3 from the Name drop-down list; then, click on Properties. Doing so activates the Plotter Configuration Editor - DWF ePlot.pc3 dialog box shown in Figure 12.18.

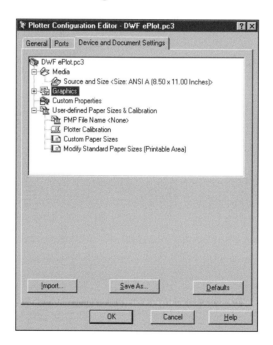

Figure 12.18
The Plotter Configuration Editor dialog box.

Within this dialog box, you'll notice three layout option tabs: General, Ports, and Device And Document Settings. On the Device And Document Settings tab, double-click on the Graphics icon. Below the Graphics icon, the Vector Graphics icon will appear; click on it. Doing so will activate the Resolution And Color Depths section of the dialog box, shown in Figure 12.19.

You may find that the Color Depth value is preset to 32-bit in your system; in the drop-down list, set it to 256 [8-bit] Colors.

Now, look back at the main area of the dialog box and choose Custom Properties (it's below the Graphics and Vector Graphics you just worked with); then, click on the Custom Properties button that instantly appeared below it. Doing so activates the DWF Properties dialog box, shown in Figure 12.20,

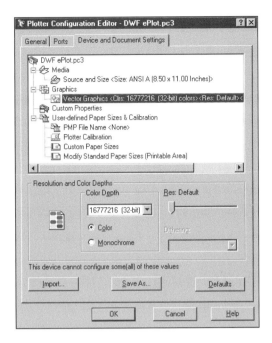

Figure 12.19

The Resolution And Color Depths section of the Plotter Configuration Editor dialog box.

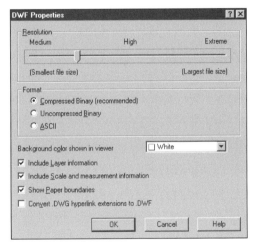

Figure 12.20

The DWF Properties dialog box.

which allows you to specify the resolution of the DWF files you plot. The higher the resolution of the DWF file, the greater its precision and the larger the file size. For example, medium resolution and precision uses 16-bit integer numbers, high precision uses 20-bit integers, and extreme resolution and precision uses 32-bit integers. Using a medium default setting is about 40 percent faster and smaller than the high to extreme settings. For most DWF files, a medium resolution setting is sufficient. For now, keep it at medium, and keep the format as Compressed Binary; then, click on OK to return to the Plotter Configuration Editor. Choose the Save As button and save the file as DWF ePlot256, with Save As Type set to *.pc3. Finally, keep picking OK to save your edits and write the DWF file to disk.

Note: If the Change To A Printer Configuration File dialog box appears, it will indicate that you have made changes to a PC3 printer configuration file. Ensure that the radio button is checked for Apply Changes To The Current Plot Only; then, click on the OK button. Choose OK to write the DWF to disk.

Viewing DWF Files With An External Browser

Using an external Internet browser such as Netscape Communicator or Microsoft Internet Explorer and the installed WHIP plug-in on your system, you can view DWF files.

You have certain options and limitations with DWF files:

- *Cursor menu*—Right-clicking the mouse over the DWF file opens a cursor menu with AutoCAD style commands. Using the menu you may pan, zoom, fit to window, access layers and named views, view the mouse location coordinates, copy, print, saveas, and move forward and back.

- *Layers*—You can control layers or named views within the external browser. You may turn them on or off.

- *Named views*—Any named views specific to the UCS when the DWF was created are written to the DWF file. Other named views specific to other UCS orientations are excluded from the DWF file.

- *Plotted area*—If a named view falls outside the plotted extents of a DWF, it isn't included in the DWF file.

- *Clipped area*—If a named view is partially clipped by the plotted extents of a DWF, only the unclipped portion is viewable in the DWF file.

- *Model space*—If you plot a DWF in model space, only model space-named views are written to the DWF file.

- *Paper space*—If you plot a DWF in paper space, only paper space-named views are written to the DWF file.

Hyperlinks

Hyperlinks are indicators you create in your AutoCAD drawings that provide connections to other files. You can attach hyperlinks to any graphical object in an AutoCAD drawing.

When you create a hyperlink in an AutoCAD drawing and specify a named view to connect to, AutoCAD restores that view when the hyperlink is opened. Views created in model space are restored in the Model tab. Views created in paper space are restored in the last active layout tab.

In addition, you can create a hyperlink to launch a word-processing program and open a specific file, or a hyperlink that activates your Web browser and loads a particular Hypertext Markup Language (HTML) page. You can also specify a named location to connect to in a file, such as a view in AutoCAD or a bookmark in a word-processing program. Hyperlinks provide a simple and powerful way to quickly associate a variety of documents (such as other drawings, bills of materials, or project schedules) with an AutoCAD drawing.

Hyperlinks connect to files stored locally, on a network, or on the Internet. By default, AutoCAD provides cursor feedback so that you know when the crosshairs are positioned over a graphical object that has an attached hyperlink. You can then select the object and use the Hyperlink shortcut menu to open the file associated with the hyperlink. You can also turn off the hyperlink cursor and shortcut menu display from the Options dialog box.

To activate the Insert Hyperlink dialog box, shown in Figure 12.21, choose Insert|Hyperlink, press Ctrl+K, or enter "hyperlink" at the command prompt. Here are the steps to hyperlink an object within your model:

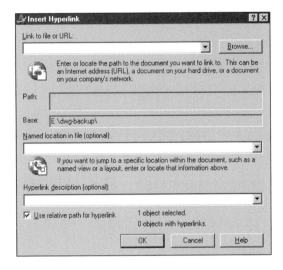

Figure 12.21
The Insert Hyperlink dialog box.

1. From the Insert menu, choose Hyperlink.

2. In the drawing area, select one or more objects to which you want to attach the hyperlink and press Enter or the right mouse button.

3. In the Insert Hyperlink dialog box's Link To File Or URL field (URL is short for "uniform resource locator"), enter the path and name of the file that you want to connect with your hyperlink. Or, click on Browse and navigate to the location of the file that you want to connect with your hyperlink. Click on Open. You also have the option of specifying a named location to connect to in the Named Location In File field. If you connect to an AutoCAD named view, you must enter the name of the view you want to show on screen.

4. Click on OK.

You've gone through the steps to create DWF files and how to work with hyperlinks. Let's finally connect all the steps into the full process you need to follow. Here are the combined, simplified steps to use with DWF and hyperlink:

1. Open an AutoCAD 2000 drawing and attach URL hyperlinks with the Edit Hyperlink dialog box.

2. Plot the drawing as a DWF file and copy the DWF file to your Web site.

3. Open the Web browser by entering "browser" at the command prompt; then, view the DWF file and pick the hyperlink spot you created.

After activating your browser from the AutoCAD prompt, you can open the DWF file you created earlier. See Figure 12.22.

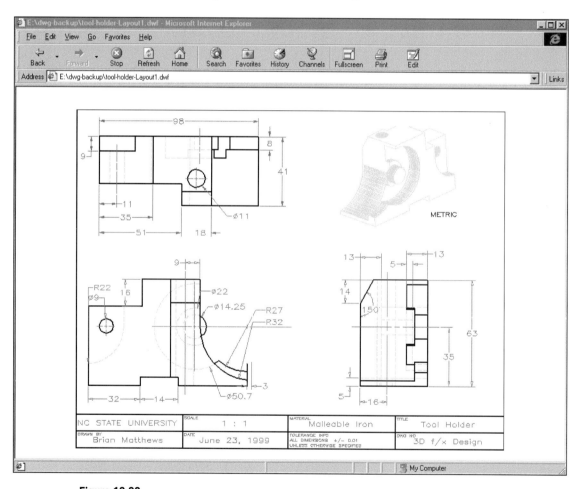

Figure 12.22

The tool-holder-layout1.dwf file from the Web browser.

Rendering Algorithms

Before preparing your images for rendering or animation, you'll need to understand how to work with rendering algorithms. An *algorithm* is the specific programming code used to render a 3D model. There's a constant swap between quality of the final rendered output and the speed of the algorithm being used. How do you make an educated guess as to which algorithm to use for which file output? Quality and speed levels depend on the algorithm used; plus, you must consider the file resolution and the number of special effects, such as lights, shadows, materials, and so on, and the type of file to which you're rendering. Let's start with the algorithm itself.

While working on and testing the various options of material, color, and light, you don't necessarily have to render with the most time-consuming algorithm on your rendering program. You can always render at a lower resolution using a lesser algorithm to run tests on lights and materials and to position the objects and viewpoint. Once everything is as you want it, you can perform the final renderings at a higher resolution with a superior algorithm. The following sections outline the various algorithms from the lowest quality to the highest quality of image resolution:

- *Wireframe algorithm*—At the absolute bottom of the list is a wireframe algorithm. This algorithm simply shows your 2D or 3D model and the placement of the objects in a colored wireframe. It's an efficient and fast method of regenerating files, but it has no use for rendering. Look for this algorithm in the **SHADEMODE** command as 2D and 3D wireframe.

- *Flat shade algorithm*—Next up the ladder is the flat shade algorithm. Just like the **SHADE** command in AutoCAD, it produces a shaded image, providing you with some degree of light and material imaging. You wouldn't use this level of algorithm for anything more than fast previews. Look for this algorithm in the **SHADEMODE** command as Flat and Flat+Edges.

- *Z-buffer algorithm*—Also known as the depth-buffer algorithm because it discards the back faces of a model and renders only what is seen. Look for it in the Render Options dialog box under Face Controls, by picking the More Options button of the Render dialog box. One of the fastest algorithms created, it has the capability of producing high-quality renderings with a low rendering time.

  The Z-buffer algorithm takes a lot of shortcuts. It begins by sorting all the faces relative to the viewpoint of the user. It identifies only those faces seen from this specific viewpoint, and it throws away any other faces. This is where it gets its name—when rendering, it considers only the faces visible from positive Z. As a result, the Z-buffer algorithm works on fewer faces than some of the other, more accurate rendering algorithms. This algorithm may render at speeds up to 10 times faster than other algorithms.

CHOOSING AN ALGORITHM

While performing any given rendering, you'll render a scene several times as you adjust light, materials, and colors. Most programs offer you a choice of rendering algorithms so that you can choose the appropriate one in terms of time and quality to give you the information necessary to make a decision on color, light, and material. If you arbitrarily choose the highest rendering algorithm at the highest resolution for each test, the time expense can be intolerable. You must understand the relative swap of speed and quality when performing each test.

- *Gouraud algorithm*—The Gouraud algorithm smooths the facets around a multifaceted surface. Thus, it isn't a full rendering algorithm; it's known as a smooth shading algorithm, because it can be used to smooth out the jagged-edge appearance of a 3D model. The Gouraud algorithm calculates the intensity of the color at each vertex and interpolates intermediate intensities—that is, it will blend color across the surface of your 3D model to simulate a smoother appearance. In many programs, using Gouraud gives you the ability to control the degree of smoothness and the angle at which smoothing will or won't take place. The biggest drawback of Gouraud is the limited degree to which you can create specular highlights. These highlights are necessary to produce shiny objects. Therefore, you can't use Gouraud exclusively when you want a true reflection. Look for this algorithm in two places in AutoCAD: under the **SHADEMODE** command and in the **RENDER** command.

- *Phong algorithm*—Phong is the best compromise for the highest quality rendering, although it's not as fast a speed as the Gouraud algorithm. Phong permits full specular highlights and true reflection mapping.

- *Raytracing algorithm*—The most costly of the algorithms in terms of speed is raytracing, which compares every triangular face with every other triangular face. Although it can produce the ultimate in features and functionality, the time costs to render grow exponentially as the size of the model grows. AutoCAD uses the **Photo Raytrace** option as a photorealistic raytraced renderer. Use ray tracing in AutoCAD to generate reflections, refraction, and more precise shadows in your 3D models. To use raytracing at its best, set Anti-Aliasing to High. See Figure 12.23.

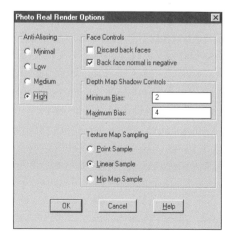

Figure 12.23

The Photo Real Render Options dialog box.

The AutoCAD renderer has both the Gouraud and Phong algorithms. To set the algorithm of your choice, choose the Rendering Preferences icon to open the Rendering Preferences dialog box. Click on More Options to open the AutoCAD Render Options dialog box. Here you can choose either the Gouraud or Phong algorithm.

Once you've created your images, there's a simplified method to do concept animation in AutoCAD by writing a script and using slides. This method uses a few simple commands, **SCRIPT**, **MSLIDE**, and **VSLIDE**, which will be discussed next, in the section on animation.

Computer Animation Or Computer Simulation

By creating multiple single images in AutoCAD and combining them, you can use it to create simple computer animations or presentations. Often, computer presentations become so sophisticated that you need to model the data in motion. There are two methods—computer simulation modeling and computer animation modeling—with precision being the main difference between the two methods. A computer simulation is precise because it is modeled to specific data and over a specified time period—as in a computer prototype of a real product. A computer animation is imprecise because it describes a sequence of movement or events to get an idea across to an audience of laypersons for a complex subject, again over a specified time period. So whether you're sending a DXF or a drawing file to 3D Studio Max or creating slides and writing a script file within AutoCAD, you're able to create simple animations.

Computer simulation is a precise method that can also involve a time element; instead of using a physical model, you produce a precise computer model in order to simulate specific data over a specified time period. You assign material to the different components of the model so the model behaves in a realistic way. Take the examples of an airplane surface model and a boat surface model, as mentioned in Chapter 6. If you create exact scaled models in the computer and then apply wind tunnel testing, you can get simulated performance within the computer, without the initial expense of prototyping. Thus, you can determine the aerodynamic properties of the airplane by applying the precise fluidic properties of air to the airplane's shape, or determine the amount of uplift to a boat's aerodynamic shaped sail or the amount of resistance to the hull shape.

Computer animation is also known as concept animation or simulation modeling, which still involves a time element, because it's an imprecise (although not less costly) method. Remember that precision is the major difference between computer simulation and computer animation. If you want to determine the aerodynamic properties of a simulated airplane, use computer simulation, because it can emulate true fluidic airflow over the airplane's surface skin. If all you need is a visual representation of a boat sailing or an airplane flying, then computer animation is adequate, but it's still approximating a real situation. A modern use for computer animation is training people to make a product, especially when you have to work through a certain sequence of steps to create a complex component or part. You can also use computer animation during the documentation phase of a product, which supports marketing, production, and service. In marketing, the animations are used for advertising the product; in production, they're used for assembly-line techniques of the product; and in service, they're used to train service technicians.

There are three basic types of animation: single path, kinetic, and key frame. Whichever type of animation you use, remember that it's nothing but a series of individually rendered frames that are shown quickly one after the other. To create an animation, you usually start with a storyboard and a script, which is simply a series of rough notes and sketches in outline form. The storyboard illustrates key scenes and the elements that make up the scene at that key point in the animation. Examples of single path animation include the use of sun studies for architectural models and the walk-through of an architectural model for a client. Both are invaluable in the study of building performance (energy use), aesthetics, and landscaping.

Single Path Animation

Single path animation is the fastest and least difficult of any animation program to produce. It's the basis of the walk-through or the fly-by type of animation. Usually, one object in the scene moves, and it's generally the camera. For a basic single path animation, draw a splined polyline path around and through your model to create the path for the camera, the number of control points, and the number of frames. Indicate how many frames the program should place between control points, and the program will generate camera angles required for each frame to create a smooth animation. The program renders each frame and creates a script to run it.

Kinetic Animation

Examples of kinetic animation include the animation of revolving parts, such as mechanism analysis, which is concerned with the study and calculation of loads and motion in mechanical systems. Kinetic animation can be used, for example, to study the joints that connect the rigid bodies of a mechanical system. There are three forms of mechanism analysis:

- *Assembly analysis*—Used to define individual components that make up an assembled mechanism and to analyze velocity input/output of the assembly.

- *Kinematic analysis*—Used to determine the range of motion of an assembly without stress loads.

- *Dynamic analysis*—Often a computer simulation, which is used to determine the loads that create or drive the motion of a mechanism.

Kinetic animation is similar to single path animation in that you set up a path of movement, but due to its complexity, it's used with more than one object. For example, you may wish to animate a mechanism and check it for interference with other parts of the assembly, so you need to move the camera around the mechanism while a specific part of the mechanism moves in an arc motion or, alternately, up and down. With kinetic animation, you create a path of movement for each of the objects, indicate the number of frames between the vertices of the path, and let the animation program create and render the scenes.

Key Framing

The most sophisticated animation procedure is *key framing*, a method developed to expedite the production process. Warner Brothers and then Walt Disney performed much of the pioneer work for animation, especially when animation first became popular. Prior to computers, animation was a labor-intensive and time-consuming process: Artists would draw thousands of images by hand in order to produce a full-length movie. Because of the expense of producing so many drawings, mistakes could be costly. But not all the artists working at the studios were equal in stature—Warner Brothers and Walt Disney didn't want their most talented and expensive senior animators tied to the drawing board. This is what key framing is all about. Over a given segment, a senior animator would draw *key frames*, showing how the movement of all the objects in a scene progressed. The junior animators would then draw the thousands of in-between frames, as the key frames were worked out and approved.

The benefit of key frame animation over single path and kinetic path animation is that there's no limit to the change of movement of one object or even multiple objects over a single path. You simply take into account all the changes from one key frame to the next key frame, including changes in scale, rotation, movement, and shape (morphing).

For example, if you animate a baseball player who's about to hit a baseball, the key frames would be the pull-back of the baseball bat and the follow through. Other parts of the swing (for example, the player waving the bat in the air behind his back to keep up the momentum) would not be key frames. As you can imagine, you carefully analyze the information needed to change from one key frame to another in order to create a smooth transition for the in-between frames to arrive at the next key frame. Also, the number of in-between frames becomes critical not only to the smoothness but to the timing of the animation.

When the key frame is put in place, the key frame animator doesn't take those things into consideration. Adjustment of movement is made through the creation of additional in-between frames until the timing of the baseball bat swing is perfect. As you can see, the sophistication of key frame animation is far superior to path direction animation.

Key frame animation lends itself very nicely to the help of a computer. This technique, more than anything else, separates the animation capabilities of 3D Studio Max over other rendering programs, because 3D Studio Max uses key frame animation

Creating Animations From Single Images

A number of software programs allow you to both use and join single rendered images into a smooth animation sequence. One of the better programs is Adobe Premiere, which lets you import single rendered images onto different tracks, join them into an animation sequence, and place sound and voice-overs onto multiple sound tracks. It also lets you stretch a single image to a multiple image using time coding—that is, it extends the image from a single second to whatever length of time you wish to see it on screen. It also provides a transition track, which lets you transition between single images using a variety of transition techniques (such as fade in and out, or zoom in and out) between each of the single images. See Figure 12.24. The final sequence is compiled into a standard (AVI) animation file, which may be inserted into a PowerPoint presentation, played as an animation on your PC, or sent over the Web. Within Adobe Premiere, you also have the option of adding sound and voice-overs onto separate tracks. Here are some quick tips for the sound and voice tracks:

- *Sound*—Adding sound and/or voice-overs can greatly improve your animation presentation. The Internet has many royalty-free sound clips that you can download. Companies such as Corel Corporation have stock music library clips you can purchase royalty-free. Often, the purchased music clips are in different segment lengths from a few minutes to a few seconds, which provides great flexibility as you place them.

- *Script writing for voice-overs*—To get your message across, animation training clips need voice-overs, and you shouldn't expect your voice-over be perfect the first time. Using a concise script, you need to remember that 3 simple paragraphs can take up 30 seconds, so you also have to speak clearly and use a good-quality microphone and sound program. Sonic Forge is a program that springs to mind, because it lets you do as many takes as you need, edit the sound, replay it, tune it to remove high spots (such as lisping problems), and then save it to disk.

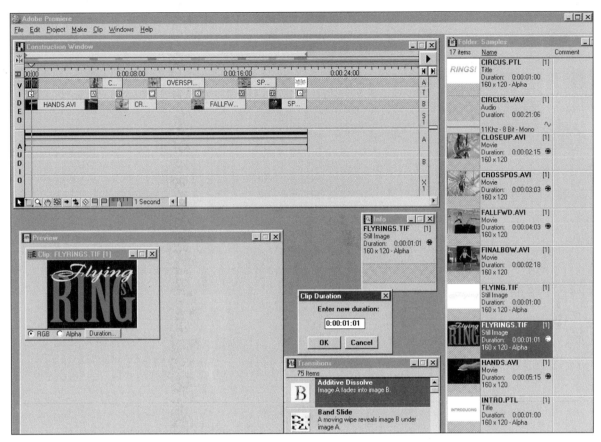

Figure 12.24

Adobe Premiere lets you combine single rendered images.

Calculating Animation Frames

Do you remember the old cartoons you saw as a child? They appeared jerky instead of smooth and were played at speeds as low as 12 frames per second (fps). Modern cartoons and motion pictures appear smoother because they're played at 24fps, whereas television is played at 30fps.

You can create a relatively smooth playback animation in 8-bit color depth with as few as 15fps. But how many frames do you need, how do you calculate the number, and what length of time does it take to animate? Whatever the answers are to these questions, an animation requires a lot of frames, and it's computationally intense with respect to color depth, resolution, and the complexity of the subject. Let's consider a 30-second animation as a calculation example.

If you wanted to create a 30-second animation using 15fps instead of 30fps, you'd have to create and render 900 finished frames. To give you an idea of the rendering time, if you use the Phong algorithm and a resolution of 320×200, plus an approximate rendering time of 10 seconds per frame, it will take about 2 hours and 25 minutes to create a 30-second animation.

Note: To simplify the difference between VHS and S-VHS tape, think of VHS tape as the equivalent of 8-bit and S-VHS the equivalent of 24-bit, with its better quality RGB color-depth.

On the other hand, if you're doing a 32-bit raytraced rendering at a resolution of 800×600 to an uncompressed TGA file and it takes an average of 5 minutes per frame, then the animation will take 25 hours to render—and that may be on a 400MHz Pentium with 128MB of RAM and a 12GB hard-drive.

The storage device of VHS or S-VHS videotape, on the other hand, runs at 30 frames per second. This consideration for videotape is necessary only if you're planning to lay down a frame-by-frame transfer to videotape. If you're going to videotape live from the computer screen, your VHS or S-VHS records whatever looks good to you.

Creating Scripts And Viewing Slide Files

One of AutoCAD's greatest strengths is its adaptability. For example, you can use a script file, which is created sequentially as a series of steps. When you run a script file, the commands are executed in a sequence, one after the other, just as if you entered the commands at the command prompt. The sequence list you create in a script can allow you to manipulate layers, such as turning them on and off, loading linetypes, inserting blocks, setting text styles, and showing a sequence of slides as a presentation. Let's look at how you'd use scripts to deliver a slide show.

To work with the **SCRIPT** command, use the following sequence:

1. Write the script file using an ASCII editor (such as Notepad) and save it with a .scr extension.

2. Use **MSLIDE** to create slides as a series or sequence of images. Each slide has a different name.

3. Run the script file and debug it.

4. Show the completed slide show.

Three commands are associated with script files: **SCRIPT**, **MSLIDE**, and **VSLIDE** (besides using Windows Notepad, you must also write a script file as a sequence of commands):

- *SCRIPT*—Lets you choose a script file of your choice. (It doesn't create a script file. The script file you previously create must have the extension .scr; otherwise, AutoCAD won't recognize the file.)

- *MSLIDE*—Makes a slide. It simply copies the display of the vector image you have in the drawing editor and lets you save it with the .sld extension.

- *VSLIDE*—Views the chosen slides one at a time. It won't view a sequence of slides (a sequence has to be written as a script as an ASCII file in Notepad).

Here's a hint: When you're creating a script, type a space or press Enter for each time you use the Enter key as a command line response.

Creating And Showing Slides With A Simple Script

The objective of this exercise is to write a simple script, create a series of slides, and show the set of slides. To make the exercise quick, you'll turn on four layers and make a slide of each, write the script, and then play it back. Open the plan.dwg file from the CD-ROM. The file has a series of built-in layers: 0, Border, Center, Dimensions, Front, Hidden, Side, Text, and Top. You'll simply turn on the layers and take slides, and then run it as a script. Follow these steps:

1. At the command prompt, type "mslide" and press Enter to display the Create Slide File dialog box. In the File Name box, type "plan-1"; then, click on Save to create the first slide. (Place this file in a directory you can easily locate.)

2. Pick the Layer icon to activate the Layer Properties Manager, and turn on the Top, Front, and Side layers.

3. Enter "mslide" to display the Create Slide File dialog box. In the File Name box, type "plan-2"; then, click on Save to create the second slide. (Place the file in the same directory as plan-1.)

4. Pick the Layer icon and turn on the Dimension layer.

5. Enter "mslide" to display the Create Slide File dialog box. In the File Name box, type "plan-3"; then, click on Save to create the third slide. (Place the file in the same directory as plan-1 and plan-2.)

6. Pick the layer icon and turn on the Hidden and Center layers.

7. Enter "mslide" to display the Create Slide File dialog box. In the File Name box, type "plan-4"; then, click on Save to create the fourth slide. (Place the file in the same directory as the previous slides.)

8. You now have four slides but no script to run them. At the command prompt, type "notepad" to activate the Windows Notepad editor. Enter the following five lines and save the script as plan.scr:

```
vslide plan-1
vslide plan-2
vslide plan-3
vslide plan-4
rscript
```

9. To run plan.scr, type "script" at the command prompt. From the Select Script File dialog box, choose the plan.scr file and click on

Open. Now, let's debug it. It's cycling through the slides too quickly—
you need to go back and adjust the timing to the slide sequence,
using a **DELAY** command. Reopen Notepad and the plan.scr file.
Change the file as follows and save it:

```
vslide plan-1
delay 2500
vslide plan-2
delay 2500
vslide plan-3
delay 2500
vslide plan-4
delay 2500
rscript
```

Because the **DELAY** command is in microseconds, it's written as
2500 to give you a delay of 2.5 seconds. (This is an arbitrary figure
used for the exercise; you can set the delay at whatever value you
like.) This version of the completed plan.scr and the four slides are
on the CD-ROM.

10. Again from the Select Script File dialog box, locate the file plan.scr
    you just edited and click on Open to run the slide show script.

11. Press either the Esc or the Backspace key when you've finished
    watching the simple script, and enter "regen" to redraw the screen.

Preloading And Showing 12 Slides With A Simple Script

You know that scripts are useful for creating slide shows. But normally the
speed at which you're able to access and display slides is limited by your
computer's access rate to both load and read each slide file. You can, however, preload the next slide from disk into memory while the audience is
viewing the current slide, and then quickly display the new slide from
memory. You've written a simple script, so let's move on and look at how to
preload slides as you're viewing them. Open Notepad and write the following script, naming it script-1.scr:

```
vslide slide-1
delay 2000
vslide *slide-2
delay 2500
vslide
vslide *slide-3
delay 2500
vslide
vslide *slide-4
delay 2500
vslide
```

```
vslide *slide-5
delay 2500
vslide
vslide *slide-6
delay 2500
vslide
vslide *slide-7
delay 2500
vslide
vslide *slide-8
delay 2500
vslide
vslide *slide-9
delay 2500
vslide
vslide *slide-10
delay 2500
vslide
vslide *slide-11
delay 2500
vslide
vslide *slide-12
delay 2500
vslide
delay 2500
rscript
```

You'll find the completed script-1.scr script file and 12 slides located on the CD-ROM. Copy the 12 image slide files from the CD-ROM into a new folder and run the script.

Let's look at how the preload function works, referring back to the script file above:

- *vslide slide-1*—Loads and views the slide-1.sld file

- *vslide *slide-2*—Preloads the slide-2.sld file

- *delay 2000*—Delays the slide-1.sld slide by two seconds

- *vslide*—Runs slide-2.sld, because it was preloaded

- *vslide *slide-3*—Starts to preload slide-3.sld into memory

The sequence activates the **VSLIDE** command and then asks the script to show slide-1 for two seconds. The line **delay 2000** keeps the slide on screen with a delay of two seconds. (Remember that the delay is in microseconds.) To preload a slide, you place an asterisk before the slide-2.sld file after the **VSLIDE** command. Then, when the **VSLIDE** command is run again, the command senses that a slide has been preloaded and displays it without asking for a file name.

Whichever of the two methods you use to create and show slides, you'll find AutoCAD is adaptable. You're also not limited to just a few slides or a few seconds of simple animation, you'll be able to create simple sequential animations of work. Remember, in addition to showing a sequence of slides as a presentation, the sequence list you create in any script will also allow you to turn on and off layers, load linetypes, insert blocks, and set text styles.

Moving On

This chapter explored the world of image quality and how to manipulate images and post them on a Web site. It also delved into the various forms of animation and basic slide show scripts. Whatever you use images for, they're a simple communication tool needed to convey messages and ideas more effectively in this visual age.

INDEX

2D graphics, representing in 3D, 12-16
2D mapping of 3D models, 346-348
    Adjust Planar Coordinates dialog box, 347
    bitmaps, 346-347
    importing materials, 347-348
    Mapping dialog box, 346
    overview, 346
    parametric materials, 347
2D objects, extruding, 18-19
2D sketching. *See* Ideation.
3D clamp, creating via perspective views, 90-93
3D drawings, 33-56. *See also* Drawing in 3D.
    ideation, 34
    model space, 36-39
    multiview drawings, 34-35
    orthographic projections, 34, 41-42
    overview, 34-35
    paper space, 36-41
    viewports, 46-55
    VPORTS command, 42-46
3D faces. *See also* **3DFACE** command.
    associativity and, 207-208
3D graphics overview, 3-31
    assembly drawings, 13-14
    basic primitive shapes, 19-20
    coordinates, 7-8
    creating 3D models, 16-20
    DDMODIFY command, 16-19
    drawing in 3D, 21-30
    ECS (Entity Coordinate System), 11-12
    ELEVATION command, 9
    engineering and, 4-6
    extruding 2D objects, 18-19
    EXTRUSION command, 11
    fields of use, 4-6
    Front view (Frontal plane) vs. elevation, 9-10
    Horizontal plane vs. Top view or Plan view, 8-9
    ideation, 12-13
    local vs. world coordinate systems, 11-12

MASSPROP command, 15
model types, 14-16
new features, 7
OCS (Object Coordinate System), 11-12
orthographic projections, 13-14
plan views, 9
Profile plane (Right Side view) vs. side elevation, 10
PROPERTIES command, 10-11, 16-19
representing 2D in 3D, 12-16
revolving objects about cylindrical axes, 19
right-hand rule, 8
sculpted surfaces, 14
solid modeling, 15-16, 18-20
SOLVIEW command, 20
surface modeling, 14-15
terminology, 8-12
THICKNESS command, 11
thickness vs. extrusion, 10-11
UCSs (User Coordinate Systems), 8-12
viewports, 20
WCS (World Coordinate System), 8, 9, 11-12
wireframe modeling, 14, 15
work plane (construction plane) of UCS, 12, 13
3D meshes and geometric generated surfaces, 141-156. *See also* Surface modeling.
    3DMESH command, 145-147
    alternative 3D mesh applications, 160-165
    associativity, 206-207
    commands overview, 143-144
    Coons surfaces, 143
    EDGE command, 144-145
    EDGESURF command, 153-156
    editing smoothness, 218-221
    primitive shapes, 144
    REVSURF command, 147-148
    RULESURF command, 150-153
    SOLID command, 141-143
    TABSURF command, 149-150

3D models
  2D mapping of, 346-348
  analysis of, 234-237
  attaching materials to, 341-345
  creating with profiles, 66-71
  editing. *See* Editing 3D models.
  rendering. *See* Rendering 3D models.
3D section views. *See* Section views.
3D views
  multiview drawings and, 34-35
  perspective views, 88, 97-99
3D wireframe modeling from 2D geometry, geometric modeling, 116-120
3d-model.dwg, **VPORTS** command, 42-43
3d-orbit.dwg, UCS Per Viewport and 3D Orbit, 99-100
3DARRAY command
  editing 3D models, 209-210
  solid modeling, 197
3DFACE command. *See also* 3D faces.
  alternative 3D mesh applications, 161
3DMESH command
  3D meshes and geometric generated surfaces, 145-147
  alternative 3D mesh applications, 160
3DORBIT command
  perspective views, 88
  rendering 3D models, 339
  UCS Per Viewport and 3D Orbit, 100-101
3point option, UCSs (User Coordinate Systems), 74
15-bit color, images, 357
? option, UCSs (User Coordinate Systems), 76
@ symbol, cylindrical coordinates and geometric modeling, 121

A

Add option, **SOLIDEDIT** command, 226
Adjust Planar Coordinates dialog box, 2D mapping of 3D models, 347
Adobe Premiere, animation, 386, 387
Algorithms
  choosing, 382
  defined, 380-381
  flat shading, 318, 381

  Gouraud shading, 220, 318, 382
  image-rendering, 380-383
  Phong shading, 220-221, 318, 382
ALIGN command, editing 3D models, 211-212
Aligned dimensions, 268
  DIMALIGNED command, 276-277
Aligned sections, section views, 249-250
Alpha channels, calculating color depth, 356-357
Alternative 3D mesh applications, 160-165.
  See also 3D meshes and geometric generated surfaces, Surface modeling.
  3DFACE command, 161
  3DMESH command, 160
  mesh generalizations, 161
  PFACE command, 161-165
Ambient light, 330-331. *See also* Lighting.
Ambiguity, geometric modeling, 116
Analysis of 3D computer models, 234-237
  MASSPROP command, 234-237
  overview, 234-235
Angle vertices, **DIMANGULAR** command, 280-281
Angular dimensions, **DIMANGULAR** command, 280-282
Animation, 383-392. *See also* Images.
  Adobe Premiere, 386, 387
  calculating frames, 387-388
  computer simulation, 383
  creating from single images, 386
  creating scripts and viewing slide files, 388-392
  defined, 383-384
  DELAY command, 390
  key frame, 385-386
  kinetic, 384-385
  MSLIDE command, 388
  overview, 383-384
  plan.dwg, 389
  preloading and showing slides via scripting, 390-392
  SCRIPT command, 388
  script writing for voice-overs, 386
  single path, 384
  sound and, 386
  types of, 384-386

voice-overs, 386

VSLIDE command, 388, 391-392

Annotation tab, Leader Settings dialog box, 289-290

ANSI dimension style sheet, 270-273

    Create New Dimension Style dialog box, 270, 271

    New Dimension Style dialog box, 271-273

Apply option, UCSs (User Coordinate Systems), 76

ARC command, **SOLIDEDIT** command, 223

arch-scale.dwg, printing multiple scales on same drawing sheet, 81-83

Arcs, **DIMANGULAR** command, 281

Assembly drawings, 3D graphics overview, 13-14

Assembly sections, section views, 248, 249

Associative dimensions, 302-305

    CENTER command, 303, 304

    definition points (grips), 304

    described, 208, 302-303

    LEADER command, 303, 304

    rules of, 304-305

Associative hatching, described, 208

Associative vs. nonassociative elements, editing 3D models, 205-208

Associativity

    3D faces and, 207-208

    3D meshes and, 206-207

    AutoCAD and, 208

    defined, 205

    parametric design and solid modeling, 199-201

    surface modeling and, 206

Attach button, Image Manager, 372

Attaching materials, 341-345

    by color, 342-344

    by layers, 344-345

    Materials dialog box, 342

    Materials Library dialog box, 342-343

    Modify Standard Material dialog box, 345

    overview, 341-342

    render-1.dwg, 341

    render-2.dwg, 345

Attachment tab, Leader Settings dialog box, 291

Attenuation, lighting, 334-335

AutoCAD 2000

    3D drawings, 33-56

    3D graphics overview, 3-31

    associativity, 208

    dimensions, 265-307

    editing 3D models, 203-238

    geometric modeling, 109-128

    images, 353-392

    perspective views, 87-105

    rendering 3D models, 311-351

    section views, 239-264

    solid modeling, 167-201

    surface modeling, 129-165

    UCSs (User Coordinate Systems), 57-85

Auxiliary sections, section views, 248, 249

B

B-Rep (boundary representation), solid modeling, 168, 169-172

B-splines and Bezier curves, surface modeling, 136-137

Background dialog box, Render dialog box, 324

Background illumination, rendering 3D models, 313

Baseline dimensions, **DIMBASELINE** command, 283-285

Basic primitive shapes, 3D graphics overview, 19-20

bezier2.dwg, editing smoothness for mesh surfaces, 219-221

Bezier curves and B-splines, surface modeling, 136-137

Bezier mesh surfaces, editing smoothness, 218-221

Bias property, editing splines and spline variables, 217

Bitmaps, 2D mapping of 3D models, 346-347

BMP files, described, 355

Body editing, **SOLIDEDIT** command, 227-228

Boolean operations, editing 3D models, 228-230

Borders, hiding viewport, 79

Boundaries, solid modeling, 177

BOUNDARY command

    geometric modeling, 125-127

    solid modeling, 176-179

Boundary representation (B-Rep), solid modeling, 168, 169-172

Bounding boxes, **MASSPROP** command, 236

BOX command
    solid modeling, 183-184
    SOLIDEDIT command, 222

Broken-out sections, section views, 244-245

Browse button, Image Manager, 373

Browsers, viewing DWF files with external, 378

Buildings, lighting, 362

C

CAD database, geometric modeling, 111-116

Calculating
    animation frames, 387-388
    color depth for images, 355-357

Camera (CA) option, **DVIEW** command, 95

CAMERA command
    dynamic viewing (perspective views), 93
    perspective views, 104-105

Cartesian and global coordinate systems, 58-59. *See also* UCSs (User Coordinate Systems).

CENTER command, associative dimensions, 303, 304

Center-mark and center-line dimensions, **DIMCENTER** command, 286-287

Centroids, **MASSPROP** command, 236

CHAMFER command, editing 3D models, 232-233

Check option, **SOLIDEDIT** command, 228

Circles, **DIMANGULAR** command, 281

clamp.dwg, creating 3D clamp via perspective views, 90-93

Clean option, **SOLIDEDIT** command, 227

Clip (CL) option, **DVIEW** command, 95

clip.dwg, solid modeling, 194, 195

Clipping, dynamic viewing (perspective views), 93

Color
    15-bit, 357
    attaching materials by, 342-344
    rendering 3D models, 313, 326-329

Color depth
    analyzing, 359-361
    calculating, 355-357

Color dialog box, rendering 3D models, 329

Color option, **SOLIDEDIT** command
    edges, 226
    faces, 225

Color palette, rendering 3D models, 314

Compare Dimension Styles dialog box, Dimension Style Manager, 270, 271

Compass and tripod, **VPOINT** command, 97-98

Compressing DWF (Drawing Web Format) files, 276-277

Computer animation. *See* Animation.

Computer simulation, 383

CONE command, solid modeling, 186-187, 196

conrod-sect.dwg, creating sections, 251

Construction lines, hiding in paper space with **MVIEW** command, 79

Construction planes, 62-71. *See also* UCSs (User Coordinate Systems).
    3D graphics overview, 12, 13
    creating 3D models with profiles, 66-71
    drawing in 3D, 24-30
    geometric modeling, 123-124
    INTERSECT command, 70-71
    overview, 62
    PLINE command, 67-69
    profiles, 63-71
    SHADEMODE command, 71
    UCS dialog box, 64, 69-70
    UCSMAN command, 64, 69-70
    work-plane.dwg, 63-66

Constructive solid geometry (CSG), solid modeling, 168, 169, 170

Continuing dimensions, **DIMCONTINUE** command, 285-286

Continuity property, editing splines and spline variables, 217

Control points, surface modeling, 135, 136

Coons surfaces, 3D meshes and geometric generated surfaces, 143

Coordinates. *See also* ECS (Entity Coordinate System), OCS (Object Coordinate System), UCSs (User Coordinate Systems), WCS (World Coordinate System).
    3D graphics overview, 7-8
    Cartesian and global systems, 58-59
    drawing in 3D, 25-26
    geometric modeling, 120-124

Copy option, **SOLIDEDIT** command
    edges, 226
    faces, 225

Corner option, **WEDGE** command, 187-188

corner-plate model, drawing in 3D, 22, 23

Create New Dimension Style dialog box
    ANSI dimension style sheet, 270, 271
    Dimension Style Manager, 269-270

cross-head.dwg, color depth analysis, 359-361

CSG (constructive solid geometry), solid modeling, 168, 169, 170

Cube option, **WEDGE** command, 187

Cubic B-spline curve, surface modeling, 138

Cubic mesh surfaces, editing smoothness, 218-221

Curve and surface parameters, surface modeling, 133-135

Curve types, surface modeling, 132, 133

Curve-fit spline curve, surface modeling, 138-139

Cutting planes, section views, 241

CYLINDER command
    perspective views (creating 3D clamp), 92
    solid modeling, 185-186, 196

Cylindrical coordinates, geometric modeling, 120-121

D

Datum dimensions, 287

DDEDIT command (editing dimensions), 296, 299-301
    Edit Text dialog box, 300
    Multiline Text Editor dialog box, 300-301

DDMODIFY command
    3D graphics overview, 16-19
    editing dimensions, 296
    SOLVIEW command, 53

DDVPOINT command
    perspective views, 88
    Viewpoint Presets dialog box, 96-97

Definition points (grips), associative dimensions, 304

Del option, UCSs (User Coordinate Systems), 76

DELAY command, creating and showing slides via scripting, 390

Delete option, **SOLIDEDIT** command, 225

Destination drop-down list, Render dialog box, 323

Destination section, Render dialog box, 326

Detach button, Image Manager, 372

Details button, Image Manager, 373

Diameter dimensions, **DIMDIAMETER** command, 278-280

Diffuse reflection, rendering 3D models, 313

dim3d.lsp, dimensions sample program, 305-307

DIMALIGNED command, aligned dimensions, 276-277

DIMANGULAR command, angular dimensions, 280-282

DIMBASELINE command, baseline dimensions, 283-285

DIMCENTER command, center-mark and center-line dimensions, 286-287

DIMCONTINUE command, continuing dimensions, 285-286

DIMDIAMETER command, diameter dimensions, 278-280

DIMEDIT command, editing dimensions, 296, 297-299

Dimension Style Manager, 268-273
    ANSI dimension style sheet, 270-273
    Compare Dimension Styles dialog box, 270, 271
    Create New Dimension Style dialog box, 269-270
    Modify Dimension Style dialog box, 270

Dimension toolbar, 274

Dimensions, 265-307
    aligned, 268, 276-277
    angular, 280-282
    ANSI style sheet, 270-273
    associative, 302-305
    baseline, 283-285
    center-mark and center-line, 286-287
    commands, 274-291
    commands quick reference, 275
    continuing, 285-286
    datum, 287
    DDEDIT command, 296, 299-301
    diameter, 278-280
    dim3d.lsp, 305-307
    DIMALIGNED command, 276-277

DIMANGULAR command, 280-282

DIMBASELINE command, 283-285

DIMCENTER command, 286-287

DIMCONTINUE command, 285-286

DIMDIAMETER command, 278-280

DIMEDIT command, 296, 297-299

Dimension Style Manager, 268-273

Dimension toolbar, 274

DIMLINEAR command, 274-276

DIMORDINATE command, 287-289

DIMOVERRIDE command and dimension variables, 301-302, 303

DIMRADIUS command, 277-278

DIMTEDIT command, 296, 299, 300

editing, 296-301

GD&T (geometric dimensioning and tolerancing), 287, 291-296

geometrics and, 266

leader lines (LEADER command), 287

Leader Settings dialog box, 289-291

linear, 274-276

ordinate, 287-289

OSNAP (Object Snap) tools, 274

overriding variables with DIMOVERRIDE command, 301-302, 303

overview, 266

QDIM command, 267, 282-283, 284

QLEADER command (quick leaders), 289

radius, 277-278

size and location of, 267

types of, 268

unidirectional, 268

DIMLINEAR command, linear dimensions, 274-276

DIMORDINATE command, ordinate dimensions, 287-289

DIMOVERRIDE command and dimension variables, 301-302, 303

DIMRADIUS command, radius dimensions, 277-278

DIMTEDIT command, editing dimensions, 296, 299, 300

Distance, dynamic viewing (perspective views), 93

Distance (D) option, DVIEW command, 95

Distant lights (directional lights), 313, 332, 333. See also Lighting, Rendering 3D models.

Lights dialog box, 335

Dithering images, 357

Drawing in 3D, 21-30. See also 3D drawings, 3D graphics overview.

coordinates, 25-26

corner-plate model, 22, 23

EXTRUDE command, 26, 28, 30

HIDE command, 29

LIST command, 29, 30

PLINE command, 23-24, 27-28

REGEN command, 29, 30

solid modeling, 21-24

startfile.dwg, 22

SUBTRACT command, 30

UCSs (User Coordinate Systems), 24-30

UNION command, 28

work plane (construction plane) of UCS, 24-30

Drawings, lining up in viewports, 83-85

DVIEW command

dynamic viewing (perspective views), 94-96

perspective views, 88

DVIEWBLOCK command, dynamic viewing (perspective views), 94-96

DWF (Drawing Web Format) files, 374-380

compressing, 276-277

DWF Properties dialog box, 376-377

HYPERLINK command, 374

hyperlinks, 378-380

Insert Hyperlink dialog box, 379

Plot dialog box, 374, 375-376

Plotter Configuration Editor dialog box, 376-377

Resolution And Color Depths section, 376, 377

viewing with external browsers, 378

WHIP driver plug-in, 374

DXFIN command, importing images, 368

DXFOUT command, exporting images, 366-368

Dynamic viewing (perspective views), 93-97

CAMERA command, 93, 104-105

clipping, 93

DDVPOINT command, 96-97

distance, 93

DVIEW command, 94-96

DVIEWBLOCK command, 94-96

field of vision, 93

lens focal length, 93

line of sight, 94

targets, 94

terminology, 93-94

E

ECS (Entity Coordinate System). *See also* Coordinates, OCS (Object Coordinate System), UCSs (User Coordinate Systems), WCS (World Coordinate System).

> 3D graphics overview, 11-12

EDGE command, 3D meshes and geometric generated surfaces, 144-145

Edge editing, **SOLIDEDIT** command, 226

EDGESURF command

> 3D meshes and geometric generated surfaces, 153-156
>
> surface system variables, 159

Edit Text dialog box, **DDEDIT** command (editing dimensions), 300

Editing 3D models, 203-238

> **3DARRAY** command, 209-210
>
> **ALIGN** command, 211-212
>
> analysis of 3D computer models, 234-237
>
> associative vs. nonassociative elements, 205-208
>
> Boolean operations, 228-230
>
> **CHAMFER** command, 232-233
>
> **EXTRUDE** command, 204-205
>
> **FILLET** command, 231-232
>
> general commands, 228-234
>
> **INTERFERE** command, 231
>
> **INTERSECT** command, 230
>
> **MIRROR3D** command, 210-211
>
> modifier commands, 208-212
>
> overview, 204-205
>
> profiles, 212-215
>
> **ROTATE3D** command, 211
>
> rotation, 208-209
>
> **SECTION** command, 233-234
>
> **SLICE** command, 233-234
>
> smoothness for 3D meshes, 218-221
>
> solids, 221-228
>
> splines, 215-218
>
> **SUBTRACT** command, 229-230
>
> **SWEEP** command, 205

translation, 208, 209

> **UNION** command, 229

Editing dimensions, 296-301

> **DDEDIT** command, 296, 299-301
>
> **DDMODIFY** command, 296
>
> **DIMEDIT** command, 296, 297-299
>
> **DIMTEDIT** command, 296, 299, 300
>
> overview, 296
>
> **PROPERTIES** command, 296

Editing smoothness for 3D meshes, 218-221

Editing solids. *See* **SOLIDEDIT** command.

Editing splines and spline variables, 215-218

> bias property, 217
>
> continuity property, 217
>
> overview, 215-216
>
> position property, 216
>
> **SPLINEDIT** command, 216-217, 218
>
> tension property, 216-217

Elements, associative vs. nonassociative, 205-208

ELEVATION command, 3D graphics overview, 9

Elevation vs. Front view (Frontal plane), 3D graphics overview, 9-10

ELLIPSE command, creating swept curves from profiles, 214

Engineering, 3D graphics overview, 4-6

Euler's formula, solid modeling, 171-172

EXPLODE command, geometric modeling, 125

EXPORT command, importing and exporting images, 366

Export Data dialog box, exporting images, 366, 367

Exporting images. *See* Importing and exporting images.

EXTRUDE command

> creating swept curves from profiles, 214-215
>
> drawing in 3D, 26, 28, 30
>
> editing 3D models, 204-205
>
> geometric modeling, 116, 117, 127
>
> solid modeling, 178-179, 190-191

Extrude option, **SOLIDEDIT** command, 222, 224

Extruding 2D objects, 3D graphics overview, 18-19

EXTRUSION command, 3D graphics overview, 11

Extrusion vs. thickness, 3D graphics overview, 10-11

F

Face editing, **SOLIDEDIT** command, 224-226

Face normals
> rendering speed and, 313-314
> solid modeling, 171

Face option, UCSs (User Coordinate Systems), 75

FACETRES variable, solid modeling, 174, 175

Feature size, GD&T (geometric dimensioning and tolerancing), 296

Field of vision, dynamic viewing (perspective views), 93

File Output Configuration dialog box, Render dialog box, 323

File types, image, 354-357

FILLET command
> creating swept curves from profiles, 214
> editing 3D models, 231-232

Fit tab, New Dimension Style dialog box, 272, 273

Flat Shaded, Edges On option, UCS Per Viewport and 3D Orbit, 103, 104

Flat Shaded option, UCS Per Viewport and 3D Orbit, 102, 103

Flat shading algorithm
> rendering 3D models, 318
> rendering algorithms for images, 381

Fog, lighting, 336

Fog/Depth dialog box, Render dialog box, 324-325

Form tolerance, GD&T (geometric dimensioning and tolerancing), 293

Frames, calculating animation, 387-388

Front view (Frontal plane) vs. elevation, 3D graphics overview, 9-10

Full sections, section views, 242-243

G

GD&T (geometric dimensioning and tolerancing), 287, 291-296. *See also* Dimensions.
> commands, 293
> feature size, 296
> form tolerance, 293
> Geometric Tolerance dialog box, 294-295
> Material Condition dialog box, 295
> overview, 291-293
> position tolerance, 293, 295
> rules of geometric tolerancing, 295-296
> Symbol dialog box, 294
> tolerance characteristic symbols, 292
> **TOLERANCE** command, 294-295
> tolerance zones, 293
> types of symbols, 293

Geographic Location dialog box, sunlight, 338-339

Geometric generated surfaces and 3D meshes, surface modeling, 141-156

Geometric modeling, 109-128
> 3D wireframe modeling from 2D geometry, 116-120
> @ symbol, 121
> ambiguity, 116
> **BOUNDARY** command, 125-127
> CAD database, 111-116
> construction planes, 123-124
> coordinate systems, 120-124
> cylindrical coordinates, 120-121
> **EXPLODE** command, 125
> **EXTRUDE** command, 116, 117, 127
> helixes, 122-123
> integrity and rules, 115-116
> **LINE** command, 126
> overview, 110-111
> primitive shapes, 124-128
> ray casting, 126
> **REGION** command, 125
> **REVOLVE** command, 116, 117
> revolving closed profiles, 114-115
> rules and integrity, 115-116
> solid modeling, 114
> spherical coordinates, 122
> **SUBTRACT** command, 127
> surface modeling, 113-114
> **Thickness** option, 116-120
> types of models, 110-111
> **UCS** command, 125
> wireframe modeling, 110, 111, 113, 116-120
> wireframes as primitive shapes, 124-128
> **ZOOM** command, 126

Geometric progression, rules of, 140

Geometric Tolerance dialog box, GD&T, 294-295

Geometric tolerancing, rules of, 295-296

Geometrics. *See also* Dimensions, GD&T.
defined, 266

Ghost sections (phantom sections), section views, 250

GIF files, described, 355

Global and Cartesian coordinate systems, 58-59. *See also* UCSs (User Coordinate Systems).

Gouraud Shaded, Edges On option, UCS Per Viewport and 3D Orbit, 103, 104

Gouraud shading algorithm
editing smoothness for mesh surfaces, 220
rendering 3D models, 318
rendering algorithms for images, 382

Graphics. *See* Images.

Graphics cards, images and, 354-355

Grips, associative dimensions, 304

H

Half sections, section views, 243-244

Hardware requirements, image processing, 354-355

Helixes, geometric modeling, 122-123

Hidden option, UCS Per Viewport and 3D Orbit, 102

HIDE command
drawing in 3D, 29
rendering 3D models, 315-317, 340

Hide (H) option, **DVIEW** command, 95

Hiding construction lines in paper space, **MVIEW** command, 79

Hiding viewport borders, 79

History of CAD, Sutherland, Ivan, 111

HLS color, rendering 3D models, 327-328, 329

Horizontal plane vs. Top view or Plan view, 3D graphics overview, 8-9

Hot grips, surface modeling, 135

Hue, rendering 3D models, 327

HYPERLINK command, DWF (Drawing Web Format) files, 374

Hyperlinks, DWF (Drawing Web Format) files, 378-380

I

Icons, UCSs (User Coordinate Systems), 60, 78

Ideation
3D drawings, 34
3D graphics overview, 12-13

Image Manager, 371-374
Attach button, 372
Browse button, 373
Detach button, 372
Details button, 373
Image File Details dialog box, 373
Image Found At field, 373
Image Manager dialog box, 371-372
List View button, 372
overview, 371
Reload button, 372
Save Path button, 373
shaded-image.dwg, 373-374
Tree View button, 372
Unload button, 372-373

Images, 353-392
15-bit color, 357
Alpha channels, 356-357
animation, 383-392
color depth analysis, 359-361
color depth calculations, 355-357
dithering, 357
DWF (Drawing Web Format) files, 374-380
exporting. *See* Importing and exporting images.
file types, 354-357
graphics cards and, 354-355
hardware requirements, 354-355
Image Adjust dialog box, 361, 362
Image Manager, 371-374
IMAGEADJUST command, 361
IMAGEATTACH command, 361
importing and exporting, 365-371
Insert Object dialog box, 363
Internet and. *See* DWF files.
lighting buildings, 362
lighting interiors, 362-363
lighting objects, 362

OLE (Object Linking and Embedding), 363-365

overview, 354

placing in presentation documents, 363-365

quality of, 354-357, 362-363

raster vs. vector files, 357-358

rendering algorithms, 380-383

screen resolution, 358-359

tips for improving quality of, 362-363

vector vs. raster files, 357-358

Importing and exporting images, 365-371

   DXFIN command, 368

   DXFOUT command, 366-368

   EXPORT command, 366

   Export Data dialog box, 366, 367

   IMPORT command, 365

   Import File dialog box, 365, 366

   Insert toolbar, 365

   PostScript Out Options dialog box, 369-370

   PSIN command, 370-371

   PSOUT command, 368-369

   WMF In Options dialog box, 365, 366

Importing materials, 2D mapping of 3D models, 347-348

Imprint option, **SOLIDEDIT** command, 227

INSERT command, **MVIEW** command, 51

Insert Hyperlink dialog box, DWF (Drawing Web Format) files, 379

Insert Object dialog box

   OLE (Object Linking and Embedding), 364

   placing images, 363

Insert toolbar, importing and exporting images, 365

Integrity and rules, geometric modeling, 115-116

INTERFERE command

   editing 3D models, 231

   solid modeling, 193-194

Interiors, lighting, 362-363

Internet, DWF (Drawing Web Format) files, 374-378

Interpolated spline curves, surface modeling, 135

INTERSECT command

   construction planes, 70-71

   editing 3D models, 230

ISOLINES variable, solid modeling, 174-175, 181-182, 197

J

JPEG files, described, 355

K

Key frame animation, 385-386

keyplate.dwg, **SOLVIEW** command, 53-55

Kinetic animation, 384-385

L

Landscape materials, 348-351. *See also* Materials, Rendering 3D models.

   LSEDIT command, 348-349

   LSLIB command, 348

   LSNEW command, 348

   Statistics dialog box, 351

   steps to creating and placing, 349-351

Layers

   attaching materials by, 344-345

   created by **SOLVIEW**, **SOLDRAW**, **SOLDPROF** commands, 255

LAYOUT command, viewports, 47-48

Layout tabs

   model space, 37

   VPORTS command and, 42-46

Leader lines (**LEADER** command)

   associative dimensions, 303, 304

   dimensions, 287

   Leader Settings dialog box, 289-291. *See also* Dimensions, **QLEADER** command (quick leaders).

   Annotation tab, 289-290

   Attachment tab, 291

   Leader Line & Arrow tab, 290-291

Length option, **WEDGE** command, 188

Lens focal length, dynamic viewing (perspective views), 93

Light color vs. pigment color, rendering 3D models, 326-327

Light sources, rendering 3D models, 313

Lighting, 330-339. *See also* Rendering 3D models.

   ambient light, 330-331

   attenuation, 334-335

   buildings, 362

   distant lights (directional lights), 313, 332, 333

fog, 336
interiors, 362-363
LIGHT command, 330
New Distant Light dialog box, 333, 334
New Point Light dialog box, 331, 332, 334-335
New Spotlight dialog box, 333, 334-335
objects, 362
omni light, 331
point light, 313, 331, 332
setting up with Lights dialog box, 335
shadow mapping, 336-337
shadows, 336
spotlights, 333, 334
sunlight, 336, 337-339
Lightness, rendering 3D models, 327
LINE command, geometric modeling, 126
Line of sight, dynamic viewing (perspective views), 94
Linear dimensions, **DIMLINEAR** command, 274-276
Lines, **DIMANGULAR** command, 282
Lining up drawings in viewports, **ZOOM** command, 83-85
LIST command
  drawing in 3D, 29, 30
  solid modeling, 176
List View button, Image Manager, 372
Local vs. world coordinate systems, 3D graphics overview, 11-12
Loops, solid modeling, 176
LSEDIT command, landscape materials, 348-349
LSLIB command, landscape materials, 348
LSNEW command, landscape materials, 348

M

Mapping
  3D models. *See* 2D mapping of 3D models.
  shadow, 336-337
Mapping dialog box, 2D mapping of 3D models, 346
mass.dwg, **MASSPROP** command, 235
MASSPROP command
  3D graphics overview, 15
  analysis of 3D computer models, 234-237
    bounding boxes, 236
    centroids, 236
    moments of inertia, 237
    principal moments, 237
    products of inertia, 237
    radii of gyration, 237
    surface area of products, 236
    volume of products, 235-236
Material Condition dialog box, GD&T (geometric dimensioning and tolerancing), 295
Materials
  attaching. *See* Attaching materials.
  defined, 341
  importing 2D into of 3D models, 347-348
  landscape, 348-351
  parametric, 347
Materials Library dialog box, attaching materials, 342-343
Meshes. *See* 3D meshes and geometric generated surfaces, Alternative 3D mesh applications.
metric-scale.dwg, printing multiple scales on same drawing sheet, 81
MIRROR3D command, editing 3D models, 210-211
Model space, 36-39. *See also* 3D drawings, Paper space.
  Layout tabs, 37
  MSPACE and **MS** commands to switch from paper space to, 38, 45
  overview, 36-37
  PSPACE and **PS** commands to switch to paper space from, 37-38, 46
  viewport characteristics, 38-39
  VPORTS command, 36, 37, 38
Model types, 3D graphics overview, 14-16
Modeling
  3D. *See* 3D models.
  geometric. *See* Geometric modeling.
  solid. *See* Solid modeling.
  surface. *See* Surface modeling.
  wireframe. *See* Wireframe modeling.
Modeling for closure, surface modeling, 140, 141
Modifier commands, editing 3D models, 208-212
Modify Dimension Style dialog box, Dimension Style Manager, 270
Modify Standard Material dialog box, attaching materials, 345

Moments of inertia, **MASSPROP** command, 237

Monge, Gaspard, orthographic projections, 34

Move option, **SOLIDEDIT** command, 224

Move option, UCSs (User Coordinate Systems), 76

Move UCS option, UCSs (User Coordinate Systems), 73

MSLIDE command, animation, 388

MSPACE and **MS** commands, switching to model space from paper space, 38, 45

Multiline Text Editor dialog box, **DDEDIT** command (editing dimensions), 300-301

Multiple scales, printing on same drawing sheet, 80-83

Multiview drawings
  3D views and, 34-35
  restoring into viewports with **MVIEW** command, 49-51

MVIEW command, 48-51
  alternative viewports, 48-51
  hiding construction lines in paper space, 79
  INSERT command, 51
  orthographic projections, 41
  paper space, 41, 79
  Polygonal feature, 49-50
  restoring multiviews into viewports, 49-51
  turning viewports on and off, 41

MVSETUP command
  solid modeling, 198, 199
  ZOOM command and, 84

N

Named UCS option, UCSs (User Coordinate Systems), 72-73

New Dimension Style dialog box, 271-273
  Fit tab, 272, 273
  Primary Units tab, 273
  Text tab, 272

New Distant Light dialog box, 333, 334
  sunlight, 338

New features, 3D graphics overview, 7

New Origin option, UCSs (User Coordinate Systems), 74

New Point Light dialog box, 331, 332
  attenuation, 334-335

New Scene dialog box, rendering 3D models, 340

New Spotlight dialog box, 333
  attenuation, 334-335

New UCS option, UCSs (User Coordinate Systems), 73

Nonassociative vs. associative elements, editing 3D models, 205-208

NURBS mathematics, surface modeling, 136-137

O

Object Linking and Embedding. *See* OLE.

Object option, UCSs (User Coordinate Systems), 74

Object Snap (OSNAP) tools, presetting, 274

Objects, lighting, 362

OCS (Object Coordinate System), 76-78. *See also* Coordinates, UCSs (User Coordinate Systems), WCS (World Coordinate System), ECS (Entity Coordinate System).
  3D graphics overview, 11-12

OFF (Off) option, **DVIEW** command, 96

Offset option, **SOLIDEDIT** command, 224

Offset sections, section views, 247-248

OLE (Object Linking and Embedding)
  Insert Object dialog box, 364
  placing images, 363-365

Omni light, 331

Ordinate dimensions, **DIMORDINATE** command, 287-289

Origins, UCSs (User Coordinate Systems), 59

OrthoGraphic option, UCSs (User Coordinate Systems), 76

Orthographic projections, 41-42
  3D drawings, 34, 41-42
  3D graphics overview, 13-14
  Monge, Gaspard, 34
  MVIEW command, 41
  third-angle projections, 41-42
  tiled viewports, 41-42
  views. *See* Viewports.
  VPORTS command, 41

Orthographic UCS option, UCSs (User Coordinate Systems), 73

Orthographic views, creating with **SOLVIEW** command, 257-262

OSMODE system variable, dim3d.lsp, 306-307

OSNAP (Object Snap) tools, presetting, 274

P

Page Setup dialog box, **SOLVIEW** command, 52

Pan (PA) option, **DVIEW** command, 95

Paper space, 36-41. *See also* 3D drawings, Model space.

    hiding construction lines with **MVIEW** command, 79

    MSPACE and **MS** commands to switch to model space from, 38, 45

    MVIEW command, 41, 79

    overview, 36

    PSPACE and **PS** commands to switch from model space to, 37-38, 46

    scaling (**ZOOM** command), 79-85

    SOLVIEW command, 36

    summary, 55

    viewport characteristics, 39-41

    VPORTS command, 37

Parallel and perspective projection, perspective views, 89-90

Parametric design and associativity, solid modeling, 199-201

Parametric materials, 2D mapping of 3D models, 347

PCX files, described, 355

PEDIT command

    creating swept curves from profiles, 214

    editing smoothness for mesh surfaces, 218-219

    surface modeling, 135, 137-138

    surface system variables, 159

Perspective views, 87-105

    3D viewing, 88, 97-99

    3DORBIT command, 88

    CAMERA command, 93, 104-105

    clamp.dwg (creating a 3D clamp), 90-93

    CYLINDER command, 92

    DDVPOINT command, 88, 96-97

    DVIEW command, 88, 94-96

    DVIEWBLOCK command, 94-96

    dynamic viewing, 93-97

    parallel and perspective projection, 89-90

    UCS Per Viewport and 3D Orbit, 99-104

    Viewpoint Presets dialog box, 96-97

    VPOINT command, 97-99

    VPORTS command, 90-91

    ZOOM command, 93

PFACE command, 161-165. *See also* Alternative 3D mesh applications.

    creating polyface meshes, 162-165

Phantom sections (ghost sections), section views, 250

Phong shading algorithm

    editing smoothness for mesh surfaces, 220-221

    rendering 3D models, 318

    rendering algorithms for images, 382

Photo Raytrace option, Render dialog box, 322

Photo Real option, Render dialog box, 322-323

Photo Real Render Options dialog box, rendering algorithms for images, 283

PICT files, described, 355

Pictures. *See* Images.

Pigment color vs. light color, rendering 3D models, 326-327

Plan view or Top view vs. Horizontal plane, 3D graphics overview, 8-9

Planar coordinates, Adjust Planar Coordinates dialog box, 347

plan.dwg, creating and showing slides via scripting, 389

Plants. *See* Landscape materials.

plate-1.dwg, **DIMORDINATE** command, 287-289

PLINE command

    construction planes, 67-69

    creating swept curves from profiles, 213

    drawing in 3D, 23-24, 27-28

    surface modeling, 134-135

Plot dialog box, DWF (Drawing Web Format) files, 374, 375-376

Plotter Configuration Editor dialog box, DWF (Drawing Web Format) files, 376-377

Point light, 313, 331, 332. *See also* Lighting, Rendering 3D models.

    Lights dialog box, 335

Points (PO) option, **DVIEW** command, 95

Polar option, **3DARRAY** command, 209

Polygonal feature, **MVIEW** command, 49-50

Polygonal shading, rendering 3D models, 313

POLYLINE command. *See* **PLINE** command.

Polyline spline curves
    surface modeling, 138
    true spline curves comparison, 137-141
Position property, editing splines and spline variables, 216
Position tolerance, GD&T (geometric dimensioning and tolerancing), 293, 295
PostScript files, described, 355
PostScript Out Options dialog box, exporting images, 369-370
Prev option, UCSs (User Coordinate Systems), 76
Primary Units tab, New Dimension Style dialog box, 273
Primitive shapes
    3D meshes and geometric generated surfaces, 144
    basic, 19-20
    solid modeling, 168, 181-194
    as wireframes in geometric modeling, 124-128
Principal moments, **MASSPROP** command, 237
Printing multiple scales on same drawing sheet, **ZOOM** command, 80-83
Printing and scaling, realtime, 83
Products of inertia, **MASSPROP** command, 237
Profile plane (Right Side view) vs. side elevation, 3D graphics overview, 10
Profiles
    construction planes and, 63-71
    creating swept curves from, 213-215
    editing 3D models, 212-215
PROPERTIES command
    3D graphics overview, 10-11, 16-19
    editing dimensions, 296
PSIN command, importing images, 370-371
PSOUT command, exporting images, 368-369
PSPACE and **PS** commands, switching model space to paper space, 37-38, 46

Q

QDIM command, size and location of dimensions, 267, 282-283, 284
QLEADER command (quick leaders). *See also* Leader Settings dialog box.
    dimensions, 289
Quadratic B-spline curves, surface modeling, 138
Quadratic mesh surfaces, editing smoothness, 218-221

R

Radii of gyration, **MASSPROP** command, 237
Radius dimensions, **DIMRADIUS** command, 277-278
radius.dwg, changing profiles in AutoCAD, 212-215
Raster vs. vector files, images, 357-358
Ray casting, geometric modeling, 126
Raytracing algorithm, rendering algorithms for images, 322, 382
Realtime scaling and printing, **ZOOM** command, 83
REGEN command, drawing in 3D, 29, 30
REGION command
    geometric modeling, 125
    solid modeling, 176-181
Reload button, Image Manager, 372
Remove option, **SOLIDEDIT** command, 226
Removed sections, section views, 246-247
RENDER command
    rendering 3D models, 315-316, 320-321
    SHADE command comparison, 321
Render dialog box, 322-326
    Background dialog box, 324
    Destination drop-down list, 323
    Destination section, 326
    File Output Configuration dialog box, 323
    Fog/Depth dialog box, 324-325
    options, 325
    Photo Raytrace option, 322
    Photo Real option, 322-323
    Rendering Procedure field, 324-325, 326
    rendering speed, 324
Render toolbar, 315
render-1.dwg, attaching materials, 341
render-2.dwg, attaching materials, 345
Rendering 3D models, 311-351
    2D mapping of 3D models, 346-348
    3DORBIT command, 339
    attaching materials, 341-345
    background illumination, 313
    color, 313, 326-329
    Color dialog box, 329
    color palette, 314
    commands, 315-321

diffuse reflection, 313
distant light, 313
face normals and rendering speed, 313-314
flat shading algorithm, 318, 381
Gouraud shading algorithm, 220, 318, 382
HIDE command, 315-317, 340
HLS color, 327-328, 329
hue, 327
landscape materials, 348-351
light color vs. pigment color, 326-327
light sources, 313
lighting, 330-339
lightness, 327
New Scene dialog box, 340
overview, 312
Phong shading algorithm, 220-221, 318, 382
pigment color vs. light color, 326-327
point light, 313, 331, 332
polygonal shading, 313
RENDER command, 315-316, 320-321
RENDER command vs. **SHADE**
   command, 321
Render dialog box, 322-326
Render toolbar, 315
rendering speed, 313-314
requirements, 312
RGB color, 327, 328-329
saturation, 328
scenes, 314, 340-341
screen color palette, 314
setting up for, 339-340
setting up scenes and views, 340-341
SHADE command, 315-316, 317-320, 339
SHADE command vs. **RENDER**
   command, 321
shading algorithms, 318
specular reflection, 314-315
spotlight, 315
terminology, 313-315
views, 314, 340-341
Rendering algorithms for images, 380-383
   flat shading algorithm, 318, 381
   Gouraud algorithm, 220, 318, 382
   Phong algorithm, 220-221, 318, 382

Photo Real Render Options dialog box, 283
   raytracing algorithm, 322, 382
   wireframe algorithm, 381
   Z-buffer algorithm, 381
Rendering Procedure field, Render dialog box,
   324-325, 326
Rendering speed, 313-314
   Render dialog box, 324
Resolution. *See also* Images.
   DWF (Drawing Web Format) files, 376-377
   screen, 358-359
Resolution And Color Depths section, DWF
   (Drawing Web Format) files, 376, 377
Restore option, UCSs (User Coordinate
   Systems), 76
Restoring multiviews into viewports, **MVIEW**
   command, 49-51
REVOLVE command
   geometric modeling, 116, 117
   section views, 262-264
   solid modeling, 191-193
Revolved sections, section views, 245-246
Revolving closed profiles, geometric modeling,
   114-115
Revolving objects about cylindrical axes, 3D
   graphics overview, 19
REVSURF command
   3D meshes and geometric generated surfaces,
      147-148
   surface system variables, 159
RGB color, rendering 3D models, 327, 328-329
RGB files, described, 355
Right Side view (Profile plane) vs. side elevation,
   3D graphics overview, 10
Right-hand rule
   3D graphics overview, 8
   UCSs (User Coordinate Systems), 61-62
ROTATE3D command, editing 3D models, 211
Rotate option, **SOLIDEDIT** command, 224
Rotate option, **VPOINT** command, 99
Rotation, editing 3D models, 208-209
Rules of associative dimensions, 304-305
Rules of geometric progression, surface
   modeling, 140
Rules of geometric tolerancing, GD&T, 295-296
Rules and integrity, geometric modeling, 115-116

RULESURF command
> 3D meshes and geometric generated surfaces, 150-153
>
> surface system variables, 159

S

Saturation, rendering 3D models, 328

Save option, UCSs (User Coordinate Systems), 76

Save Path button, Image Manager, 373

Scaling, paper space (**ZOOM** command), 79-83

Scaling and printing, realtime, 83

Scenes
> rendering 3D models, 314
>
> setting up, 340-341

Screen color palette, rendering 3D models, 314

Screen resolution, images, 358-359

SCRIPT command, animation, 388

Scripting
> creating animation and viewing slide files, 388-392
>
> preloading and showing slides via, 390-392
>
> voice-overs and animation, 386

Sculpted surfaces, 3D graphics overview, 14

SECTION command, 251-252
> editing 3D models, 233-234

Section views, 239-264
> aligned sections, 249-250
>
> assembly sections, 248, 249
>
> auxiliary sections, 248, 249
>
> broken-out sections, 244-245
>
> conrod-sect.dwg, 251
>
> creating sections, 250-251
>
> cutting planes, 241
>
> defined, 241
>
> full sections, 242-243
>
> ghost sections (phantom sections), 250
>
> half sections, 243-244
>
> offset sections, 247-248
>
> overview, 240
>
> phantom sections (ghost sections), 250
>
> removed sections, 246-247
>
> **REVOLVE** command, 262-264
>
> revolved sections, 245-246
>
> rules of, 240

SECTION command, 251-252

SLICE command, 252-253

SOLDRAW command, 254, 256

SOLPROF command, 254, 256-257

SOLVIEW command, 254, 255, 257-262

types of, 241-250

SHADE command
> **RENDER** command comparison, 321
>
> rendering 3D models, 315-316, 317-320, 339

shaded-image.dwg, Image Manager, 373-374

SHADEMODE command
> construction planes, 71
>
> UCS Per Viewport and 3D Orbit, 101-104

Shading, editing smoothness for mesh surfaces, 220-221

Shading algorithms, rendering 3D models, 318

Shadow mapping, lighting, 336-337

Shadows, lighting, 336

Shell option, **SOLIDEDIT** command, 227

Shrubbery. *See* Landscape materials.

Side elevation vs. Profile plane (Right Side view), 3D graphics overview, 10

Simulation, computer, 383

Single path animation, 384

Sketching, 2D. *See* Ideation.

SLICE command
> editing 3D models, 233-234
>
> section views, 252-253

Slide files, creating animation scripts and viewing, 388-392

Smooth Shade option, editing smoothness for mesh surfaces, 220-221

Smooth surfaces, described, 208

Smoothness, editing for 3D meshes, 218-221

SOLDRAW command
> layers created by, 255
>
> section views, 254, 256
>
> solid modeling, 173

SOLID command, 3D meshes and geometric generated surfaces, 141-143

Solid modeling, 167-201
> 3D graphics overview, 15-16, 18-20
>
> **3DARRAY** command, 197
>
> B-Rep (boundary representation), 168, 169-172

boundaries, 177
BOUNDARY command, 176-179
BOX command, 183-184
clip.dwg, 194, 195
CONE command, 186-187, 196
creating objects, 194-199
creating solids, 176
CSG (constructive solid geometry), 168, 169, 170
CYLINDER command, 185-186, 196
drawing in 3D, 21-24
Euler's formula, 171-172
EXTRUDE command, 178-179, 190-191
face normals, 171
FACETRES variable, 174, 175
geometric modeling, 114
INTERFERE command, 193-194
ISOLINES variable, 174-175, 181-182, 197
LIST command, 176
loops, 176
MVSETUP command, 198, 199
parametric design and associativity, 199-201
primitive shapes, 168, 181-194
REGION command, 176-181
REVOLVE command, 191-193
SOLDRAW command, 173
SOLIDEDIT command, 182
SOLVIEW command, 173
SPHERE command, 184-185
SUBTRACT command, 177-178, 197
tessellation lines, 174
TORUS command, 188-189, 196
types of modelers, 168-172
VIEWRES variable, 174, 175-176
visualization accuracy, 173-176
visualization process, 172-176
WEDGE command, 187-188, 195-196
SOLIDEDIT command, 221-228
 Add option, 226
 ARC command, 223
 body editing, 227-228
 BOX command, 222
 Check option, 228
 Clean option, 227

Color option
 edges, 226
 faces, 225
Copy option
 edges, 226
 faces, 225
Delete option, 225
edge editing, 226
editing functions, 221
Extrude option, 222, 224
face editing, 224-226
Imprint option, 227
Move option, 224
Offset option, 224
overview, 221
Remove option, 226
Rotate option, 224
Shell option, 227
solid modeling, 182
solidedit-2.dwg, 225-226
Solids Editing Toolbar, 221
Taper option, 224
Undo option,
 edges, 226
 faces, 225
SOLPROF command
 layers created by, 255
 section views, 254, 256-257
SOLVIEW command, 51-55
 3D graphics overview, 20
 creating orthographic views, 257-262
 DDMODIFY command, 53
 keyplate.dwg, 53-55
 layers created by, 255
 Page Setup dialog box, 52
 paper space, 36
 section views, 254, 255, 257-262
 solid modeling, 173
 tailstock.dwg, 258-262
 VPOINT command, 53
Sound, animation and, 386
Specular reflection, rendering 3D models, 314-315
SPHERE command, solid modeling, 184-185
Spherical coordinates, geometric modeling, 122

SPLFRAME, surface system variables, 156, 157

Spline curves

   editing, 215-218

   surface modeling, 133-141

SPLINEDIT command

   editing splines and spline variables,
      216-217, 218

   surface modeling, 138-139

   surface system variables, 160

SPLINESEGS, surface system variables, 156

SPLINETYPE, surface system variables, 156

Spotlights, 333, 334. *See also* Lighting.

   Lights dialog box, 335

   rendering 3D models, 315

startfile.dwg, drawing in 3D, 22

Statistics dialog box, landscape materials, 351

Style sheets, ANSI dimension, 270-273

SUBTRACT command

   drawing in 3D, 30

   editing 3D models, 229-230

   geometric modeling, 127

   solid modeling, 177-178, 197

Sunlight, 336, 337-339. *See also* Lighting.

   Geographic Location dialog box, 338-339

   New Distant Light dialog box, 338

Surface area of products, **MASSPROP**
   command, 236

Surface modeling, 129-165

   3D graphics overview, 14-15

   3D meshes and geometric generated
      surfaces, 141-156

   alternative 3D mesh applications, 160-165

   associativity, 206

   Bezier curves and B-splines, 136-137

   control points, 135, 136

   cubic B-spline curves, 138

   curve and surface parameters, 133-135

   curve types, 132, 133

   curve-fit spline curves, 138-139

   geometric generated surfaces and 3D
      meshes, 141-156

   geometric modeling, 113-114

   hot grips, 135

   interpolated spline curves, 135

   modeling for closure, 140, 141

   NURBS mathematics, 136-137

overview, 130-131

PEDIT command, 135, 137-138

PLINE command, 134-135

POLYLINE command, 134

polyline with spline curves, 138

quadratic B-spline curves, 138

rules of geometric progression, 140

spline curves, 133-141

SPLINEDIT command, 138-139

surface system variables, 156-160

surface types, 133

through points, 136

true spline curves, 139

true spline curves vs. polyline spline curves,
   137-141

types of curves and surfaces, 131-133

weighted control points, 135, 136, 137

Surface system variables, 156-160. *See also*
Surface modeling.

   adjusting surface smoothness, 158-160

   EDGESURF command, 159

   PEDIT command, 159

   REVSURF command, 159

   RULESURF command, 159

   SPLFRAME, 156, *157*

   SPLINEDIT command, 160

   SPLINESEGS, 156

   SPLINETYPE, 156

   SURFTAB1, 156

   SURFTAB2, 156

   SURFTYPE, 157-158, 159

   SURFU, 159

   SURFV, 159

   TABSURF command, 159

SURFTYPE command, editing smoothness for
mesh surfaces, 219

SURFU command, editing smoothness for mesh
surfaces, 219

SURFV command, editing smoothness for mesh
surfaces, 219

Sutherland, Ivan, history of CAD, 111

SWEEP command, editing 3D models, 205

Swept curves, creating from profiles, 213-215

Symbol dialog box, GD&T (geometric
dimensioning and tolerancing), 294

System variables, surface, 156-160

T

TABSURF command
>3D meshes and geometric generated surfaces, 149-150

>surface system variables, 159

tailstock.dwg, creating orthographic views with **SOLVIEW** command, 258-262

Taper option, **SOLIDEDIT** command, 224

TARGA files, described, 355

Target (TA) option, **DVIEW** command, 95

Targets, dynamic viewing (perspective views), 94

Tension property, editing splines and spline variables, 216-217

Terminology
>3D graphics overview, 8-12

>dynamic viewing (perspective views), 93-94

>rendering 3D models, 313-315

Tessellation lines, solid modeling, 174

Text tab, New Dimension Style dialog box, 272

Thickness option
>3D graphics overview, 11

>geometric modeling, 116-120

Thickness vs. extrusion, 3D graphics overview, 10-11

Third-angle projections, orthographic projections, 41-42

Through points, surface modeling, 136

TIFF files, described, 355

Tiled viewports, orthographic projections, 41-42

Tolerance characteristic symbols, GD&T (geometric dimensioning and tolerancing), 292

TOLERANCE command, GD&T (geometric dimensioning and tolerancing), 294-295

Tolerance zones, GD&T (geometric dimensioning and tolerancing), 293

Top view or Plan view vs. Horizontal plane, 3D graphics overview, 8-9

TORUS command, solid modeling, 188-189, 196

Translation, editing 3D models, 208, 209

Tree View button, Image Manager, 372

Trees. *See* Landscape materials.

Tripod and compass, **VPOINT** command, 97-98

True spline curves
>polyline spline curves comparison, 137-141

>surface modeling, 139

Twist (TW) option, **DVIEW** command, 95

U

UCS command
>creating swept curves from profiles, 214, 215

>geometric modeling, 125

>UCSs (User Coordinate Systems), 71-72

UCS dialog box, construction planes, 64, 69-70

UCS Per Viewport and 3D Orbit, 99-104. *See also* Perspective views.
>3d-orbit.dwg, 99-100

>**3DORBIT** command, 100-101

>Flat Shaded, Edges On option, 103, 104

>Flat Shaded option, 102, 103

>Gouraud Shaded, Edges On option, 103, 104

>Hidden option, 102

>**SHADEMODE** command, 101-104

>Wireframe option, 102

UCSICON command, UCSs (User Coordinate Systems), 78

UCSMAN command, construction planes, 64, 69-70

UCSs (User Coordinate Systems), 57-85. *See also* Coordinates, ECS (Entity Coordinate System), OCS (Object Coordinate System), WCS (World Coordinate System).
>3D graphics overview, 8-12

>3point option, 74

>? option, 76

>Apply option, 76

>Cartesian and global coordinate systems, 58-59

>construction planes, 62-71

>Del option, 76

>described, 24-25

>drawing in 3D, 24-30

>Face option, 75

>hiding viewport borders, 79

>icons, 60, 78

>lining up drawings in viewports, 83-85

>Move option, 76

>Move UCS option, 73

>**MVIEW** command, 79

>Named UCS option, 72-73

>New Origin option, 74

>New UCS option, 73

>Object option, 74

>OCS (Object Coordinate System) and, 76-78

options, 71-79
origins, 59
OrthoGraphic option, 76
Orthographic UCS option, 73
overview, 59-61
paper space scaling, 79-83
Prev option, 76
Restore option, 76
right-hand rule, 61-62
Save option, 76
UCS command, 71-72
UCSICON command, 78
View option, 75
WCS comparison, 24-25
WCS (World Coordinate System), 59
work plane (construction plane) of, 12, 13
World option, 76
X/Y/Z option, 75
Zaxis option, 74
Undo option, **SOLIDEDIT** command, 226
edges, 226
faces, 225
Undo (U) option, **DVIEW** command, 96
Unidirectional dimensions, 268
UNION command
3DARRAY command, 210
drawing in 3D, 28
editing 3D models, 229
Unload button, Image Manager, 372-373
User Coordinate System. *See* UCS.

V

Variables
DIMOVERRIDE command and dimension,
301-302, 303
editing spline, 215-218
surface system, 156-160
Vector option, **VPOINT** command, 99
Vector vs. raster files, images, 357-358
View option, UCSs (User Coordinate Systems), 75
Viewing DWF files with external browsers, 378
Viewing slide files, creating animation scripts
and, 388-392
Viewpoint Presets dialog box, **DDVPOINT**
command and, 96-97

Viewport characteristics
model space, 38-39
paper space, 39-41
Viewports, 46-55. *See also* **VPORTS** command.
3D graphics overview, 20
hiding borders, 79
LAYOUT command, 47-48
lining up drawings in, 83-85
MVIEW command, 48-51
overview, 46
restoring multiviews with **MVIEW**
command, 49-51
SOLVIEW command, 51-55
tiled, 41-42
turning on and off with **MVIEW**
command, 41
Viewports dialog box, **VPORTS** command, 43,
44
VIEWRES variable, solid modeling, 174, 175-176
Views
3D and perspective, 88, 97-99
creating orthographic with **SOLVIEW**
command, 257-262
dynamic viewing (perspective views), 93-97
perspective. *See* Perspective views.
rendering 3D models, 314
section. *See* Section views.
setting up, 340-341
Visualization accuracy, solid modeling, 173-176
Visualization process, solid modeling, 172-176
Voice-overs, animation and, 386
Volume of products, **MASSPROP** command,
235-236
VPOINT command, 97-98
3D and perspective views, 97-99
compass and tripod, 97-98
Rotate option, 99
SOLVIEW command, 53
Vector option, 99
VPORTS command, 42-46. *See also* Viewports.
3d-model.dwg, 42-43
layout tabs and, 42-46
model space, 36, 37, 38
orthographic projections, 41
paper space, 37

perspective views (creating 3D clamp), 90-91

Viewports dialog box, 43, 44

VPORTS layer, realtime printing and scaling, 83

VSLIDE command, animation, 388, 391-392

W

WCS (World Coordinate System). *See also* Coordinates, ECS (Entity Coordinate System), OCS (Object Coordinate System), UCSs (User Coordinate Systems).

    3D graphics overview, 8, 9, 11-12

    UCS comparison, 24-25

    UCSs (User Coordinate Systems), 59

Web, DWF (Drawing Web Format) files, 374-378

WEDGE command

    Corner option, 187-188

    solid modeling, 187-188, 195-196

Weighted control points, surface modeling, 135, 136, 137

WHIP driver plug-in, DWF (Drawing Web Format) files, 374

Wireframe algorithm, rendering algorithms for images, 381

Wireframe modeling

    3D graphics overview, 14, 15

    geometric modeling, 110, 111, 113, 116-120

Wireframe option, UCS Per Viewport and 3D Orbit, 102

Wireframes as primitive shapes, geometric modeling, 124-128

WMF In Options dialog box, importing and exporting images, 365, 366

Work planes. *See* Construction planes.

work-plane.dwg, construction planes, 63-66

World Coordinate System. *See* WCS.

World option, UCSs (User Coordinate Systems), 76

World vs. local coordinate systems, 3D graphics overview, 11-12

World Wide Web, DWF (Drawing Web Format) files, 374-378

X

X, Y, and Z coordinates. *See* Coordinates.

X/Y/Z option, UCSs (User Coordinate Systems), 75

XP option, **ZOOM** command, 80-85

Z

Z-buffer algorithm, rendering algorithms for images, 381

Zaxis option, UCSs (User Coordinate Systems), 74

ZOOM command

    geometric modeling, 126

    perspective views (creating 3D clamp), 93

ZOOM command (paper space scaling), 79-85

    lining up drawings in viewports, 83-85

    MVSETUP command, 84

    printing multiple scales on same drawing sheet, 80-83

    realtime scaling and printing, 83

    XP option, 80-83

Zoom (Z) option, **DVIEW** command, 95

COLOPHON

From start to finish, The Coriolis Group designed *AutoCAD 2000 3D f/x and design* with the creative professional in mind.

The cover was produced on a Power Macintosh using QuarkXPress 3.3 for layout compositing. Text imported from Microsoft Word was restyled using the Futura and Trajan font families from the Adobe font library. It was printed using four-color process, spot UV coating.

Select images from the Color Studio were combined to form the color montage art strip, unique for each Creative Professionals book.

The Color Studio was assembled using Adobe PageMaker 6.5 on a G3 Macintosh system. Images in TIFF format were color corrected and sized in Adobe Photoshop 5. It was printed using four-color process on gloss text paper.

The interior layout was built in Adobe PageMaker 6.5 on a Power Macintosh. Adobe fonts used include Stone Informal for body text, Avenir Black for heads, and Copperplate 31ab for chapter titles. Text originated in Microsoft Word. Adobe Photoshop was used to process grayscale images.

Imagesetting and manufacturing were completed by Courier, Stoughton, Massachusetts.

If you like this book, you'll love these...

ILLUSTRATOR 8 F/X AND DESIGN
Sherry London and T. Michael Clark
ISBN: 1-57610-408-7 • $49.99
500 pages with CD-ROM

Take an exciting journey into the world of Illustrator graphics. Harness the power of Adobe Illustrator 8's new features: Brushes, Gradient Mesh objects, the Pencil tool, and the Photo Crosshatch filter. And then practice these techniques while completing real-world projects such as creating packaging, ads, brochures, and more.

3D STUDIO MAX R3 F/X AND DESIGN
Jon Bell
ISBN: 1-57610-423-0 • $49.99
500 pages with CD-ROM

Get the newest and hottest techniques used in the movie industry firsthand from the pros. Learn how to produce cutting-edge effects, such as building a human face and modeling creatures. Hundreds of illustrations and examples from professional Hollywood artists teach you how to use 3D Studio MAX to get the effects you want.

3D STUDIO MAX R3 IN DEPTH
Rob Polevoi
ISBN: 1-57610-432-X • $49.99
700 pages with CD-ROM

Build your special effects skills while becoming familiar with the many features of 3D Studio MAX. By following along with the book's visual examples, you will receive quick answers to common MAX questions in an easy to use and easy to understand manner.

ADOBE PAGEMILL 3 F/X AND DESIGN
Daniel Gray
ISBN: 1-57610-214-9 • $39.99
250 pages with CD-ROM

Adobe PageMill 3 f/x and design puts you in the driver's seat by providing all the tools you'll need to create beautiful, functional Web sites. Hands-on tutorials quickly get you behind the wheel and on your way to Web success. Best-selling author, Daniel Gray, tears off the shrinkwrap and goes beyond the box—delivering information in an easy-to-read and informative manner.

The Coriolis Group, LLC   Telephone: 1.800.410.0192 • www.coriolis.com
Coriolis books are also available at bookstores and computer stores nationwide.

WHAT'S ON THE CD-ROM

AutoCAD 2000 3D f/x and design's companion CD-ROM contains elements specifically selected to enhance the usefulness of this book, including:

- More than 100 project drawings, image files, and sound files. Load the files and see firsthand how the techniques work.

- *Paint Shop Pro*—One of the most popular and highly acclaimed image-editing programs ever available, Paint Shop Pro 5 delivers professional-quality graphics and photo-editing tools with unrivaled ease of use, speed, and affordable functionality.

- *Mech-Q Professional Pack from ASVIC*—Offers mechanical, structural steel, piping, and HVAC engineering and drafting solutions for AutoCAD 12 to 2000.

System Requirements

PC Software

- Windows 95, 98, NT 4, or higher.
- AutoCAD 2000
- Web browser

Hardware

- An Intel (or equivalent) Pentium 266MHz processor is the minimum platform required; an Intel (or equivalent) Pentium 450MHz processor is recommended.
- 64MB of RAM is the minimum requirement.
- The project drawings for *AutoCAD 2000 3D f/x and design* require approximately 40MB of disk storage space.
- A true color monitor is recommended.